T0345085

Women Working Longer

**A National Bureau
of Economic Research
Conference Report**

Women Working Longer
Increased Employment
at Older Ages

Edited by **Claudia Goldin and Lawrence F. Katz**

The University of Chicago Press

Chicago and London

The University of Chicago Press, Chicago 60637
The University of Chicago Press, Ltd., London
© 2018 by the National Bureau of Economic Research
Published 2018
Printed in the United States of America

33 32 31 30 29 28 27 26 25   2 3 4 5 6

ISBN-13: 978-0-226-53250-9 (cloth)
ISBN-13: 978-0-226-53264-6 (e-book)
DOI: https://doi.org/10.7208/chicago/9780226532646.001.0001

Library of Congress Cataloging-in-Publication Data

Names: Goldin, Claudia Dale, editor. | Katz, Lawrence F., editor.
Title: Women working longer : increased employment at older ages /
    edited by Claudia Goldin and Lawrence F. Katz.
Other titles: National Bureau of Economic Research conference report.
Description: Chicago : The University of Chicago Press, 2018. | Series:
    National Bureau of Economic Research conference report
Identifiers: LCCN 2017025191 | ISBN 9780226532509 (cloth : alk.
    paper) | ISBN 9780226532646 (e-book)
Subjects: LCSH: Older women—Employment—United States. | Age
    and employment—United States.
Classification: LCC HD6056.2.U6 W67 2018 | DDC 331.4084/60973—
    dc23
LC record available at https://lccn.loc.gov/2017025191

Relation of the Directors to the
Work and Publications of the
National Bureau of Economic Research

1. The object of the NBER is to ascertain and present to the economics profession, and to the public more generally, important economic facts and their interpretation in a scientific manner without policy recommendations. The Board of Directors is charged with the responsibility of ensuring that the work of the NBER is carried on in strict conformity with this object.

2. The President shall establish an internal review process to ensure that book manuscripts proposed for publication DO NOT contain policy recommendations. This shall apply both to the proceedings of conferences and to manuscripts by a single author or by one or more co-authors but shall not apply to authors of comments at NBER conferences who are not NBER affiliates.

3. No book manuscript reporting research shall be published by the NBER until the President has sent to each member of the Board a notice that a manuscript is recommended for publication and that in the President's opinion it is suitable for publication in accordance with the above principles of the NBER. Such notification will include a table of contents and an abstract or summary of the manuscript's content, a list of contributors if applicable, and a response form for use by Directors who desire a copy of the manuscript for review. Each manuscript shall contain a summary drawing attention to the nature and treatment of the problem studied and the main conclusions reached.

4. No volume shall be published until forty-five days have elapsed from the above notification of intention to publish it. During this period a copy shall be sent to any Director requesting it, and if any Director objects to publication on the grounds that the manuscript contains policy recommendations, the objection will be presented to the author(s) or editor(s). In case of dispute, all members of the Board shall be notified, and the President shall appoint an ad hoc committee of the Board to decide the matter; thirty days additional shall be granted for this purpose.

5. The President shall present annually to the Board a report describing the internal manuscript review process, any objections made by Directors before publication or by anyone after publication, any disputes about such matters, and how they were handled.

6. Publications of the NBER issued for informational purposes concerning the work of the Bureau, or issued to inform the public of the activities at the Bureau, including but not limited to the NBER Digest and Reporter, shall be consistent with the object stated in paragraph 1. They shall contain a specific disclaimer noting that they have not passed through the review procedures required in this resolution. The Executive Committee of the Board is charged with the review of all such publications from time to time.

7. NBER working papers and manuscripts distributed on the Bureau's web site are not deemed to be publications for the purpose of this resolution, but they shall be consistent with the object stated in paragraph 1. Working papers shall contain a specific disclaimer noting that they have not passed through the review procedures required in this resolution. The NBER's web site shall contain a similar disclaimer. The President shall establish an internal review process to ensure that the working papers and the web site do not contain policy recommendations, and shall report annually to the Board on this process and any concerns raised in connection with it.

8. Unless otherwise determined by the Board or exempted by the terms of paragraphs 6 and 7, a copy of this resolution shall be printed in each NBER publication as described in paragraph 2 above.

Contents

Acknowledgments

Thanks go, first and foremost, to Kathleen Christensen of the Sloan Foundation's Working Longer program for having the wisdom to encourage the editors to pursue the subject regarding women. Because so little had been written on the topic, we decided to commission a set of papers. That process began with a working group meeting on December 6, 2014, the purpose of which was to encourage an impressive group of researchers to turn their attention to the issue of women's extended work lives. Each of the researchers had been working in a related area, and the idea of the meeting was to have the group join forces to understand the important trend of increased work of older women in the United States. The working group meeting led to the initial papers that were presented at a preconference on September 19, 2015. The final conference was held May 21–22, 2016. We gratefully acknowledge financial support from the Alfred P. Sloan Foundation's Working Longer program under grant 2013-6-16, "Women Working Longer," and grant G-2015-13937, which funded the preconference. The NBER conference staff was instrumental in each of these events.

The chapters benefited from comments at the conference provided by the following (in order of volume listing):

Katharine Abraham (University of Maryland) commented on Goldin and Katz
Claudia Olivetti (Boston College) commented on Maestas
Lawrence Katz (Harvard University) commented on Lahey
Alessandra Voena (University of Chicago) commented on Olivetti and Rotz
Mark Shepard (Harvard University) commented on Fahle and McGarry
Julie Agnew (College of William and Mary) commented on Lusardi and Mitchell

Melinda Morrill (North Carolina State University) commented on Fitz-patrick

Erzo Luttmer (Dartmouth College) commented on Gelber, Isen, and Song

Courtney Coile (Wellesley College) commented on Bee and Mitchell

Janice Compton (University of Manitoba) and Robert Pollak (Washington University in St. Louis) presented a preliminary paper at the conference that was commented on by Itzik Fadlon (University of California at San Diego). All authors and commentators contributed to the volume's chapters and to its coherence, and we are grateful to all of them. The volume editors and authors are also grateful to the reviewers for their suggestions and insights.

Introduction

Claudia Goldin and Lawrence F. Katz

American women from their fifties to their seventies are working more now than ever. Their increased participation at older ages started in the late 1980s, before the turnaround in older men's labor force participation and prior to the economic downturns of the first decade of the twenty-first century. Their participation rates when fifty-five to sixty-four years old differ from men's by less than 10 percentage points, whereas around 1970 they differed by about 40 percentage points (figure I.1). The higher labor force participation of older women is a real trend that has persisted for almost thirty years. It is, moreover, consequential and consists disproportionately of women who are working at full-time, not part-time, jobs. The nine chapters in this volume address the reasons for the increase in the United States and what the future will bring for women working longer.

Many other Organisation for Economic Co-operation and Development (OECD) nations have also experienced growth in the participation of older women. But few have had as large an increase and from as high a level as has the United States for both the sixty- to sixty-four- and the sixty-five- to sixty-nine-year-old groups.

From 1990 to 2015 participation rates for women sixty to sixty-four years old in the United States increased from 36 to 50 percent. Sweden, the only OECD nation with a higher participation rate in 2015 (and considerable

Claudia Goldin is the Henry Lee Professor of Economics at Harvard University and a research associate of the National Bureau of Economic Research. Lawrence F. Katz is the Elisabeth Allison Professor of Economics at Harvard University and a research associate of the National Bureau of Economic Research.

For acknowledgments, sources of research support, and disclosure of the authors' material financial relationships, if any, please see http://www.nber.org/chapters/c13797.ack.

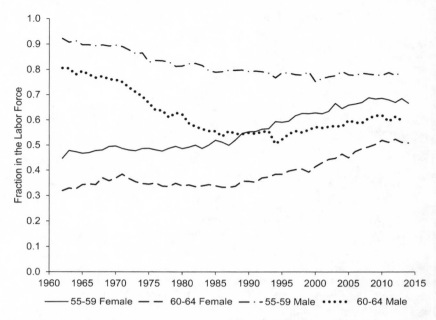

Fig. I.1 Labor force participation rates for males and females ages fifty-five to fifty-nine and sixty to sixty-four (1962 to 2014)
Source: CPS March.

full-time employment), increased from 53 to 67 percent. Older Japanese women also have significant participation, but they have experienced less change and have a far greater fraction working part time. Most important is that all seven nations in figure I.2, panel A, show significant increases in the participation rate of women sixty to sixty-four years old during the 1990 to 2015 period. For women sixty-five to sixty-nine years old levels are lower, as seen in figure I.2, panel B, but increases for the seven nations have also been large.[1]

Changes in national retirement rules can have large effects on women's participation at older ages. For example, Germany passed legislation in 1992 stipulating that by 2004 both men and women would reach their normal retirement ages at sixty-five, rather than earlier for women. German women sixty to sixty-four years old greatly increased their participation around that time, eventually catching up to US participation rates by 2015, as can be

1. Social security regulations in most countries incentivize the retirement age, particularly when replacement rates are high. For country rules concerning normal and early retirement ages and differential treatment of men and women, see Gruber and Wise (1999, 2007) and the US Social Security Administration, "Social Security Programs throughout the World," https://www.ssa.gov/policy/docs/progdesc/ssptw/, published in collaboration with the International Social Security Association.

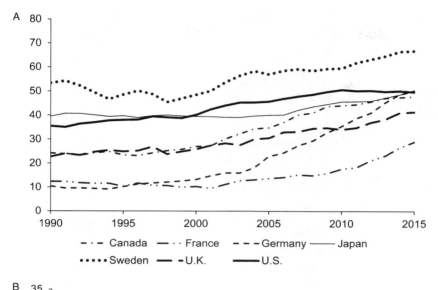

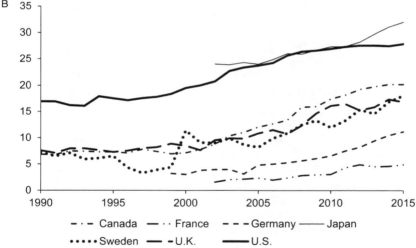

**Fig. I.2 Female labor force participation rates for seven nations (1990 to 2015).
(A) Women ages sixty to sixty-four. (B) Women ages sixty-five to sixty-nine.**

Source: OECD Stat Extracts, table LFS, Sex and Age Indicators (http://stats.oecd.org/Index
.aspx?DataSetCode=LFS_SEXAGE_I_R).

Notes: The female labor force participation rate is given. Hours of work and the fraction
considered part time varies by country and by year. Using the OECD "common definition" of
part-time employment, the fraction working part time among sixty- to sixty-four-year-olds in
2015 was as follows: Canada 0.31, France 0.33, Germany 0.45, Japan 0.48, Sweden 0.18, and
the United Kingdom 0.52. The United States is not included in the common definition, but
using national definitions it is below the lowest using the common definition, Sweden, for the
fifty-five- to sixty-four-year-old group (0.226 for the United States and 0.307 for Sweden
using the national definitions).

seen in figure I.2, panel A. In contrast, the labor force participation rate for German women sixty-five to sixty-nine, that is at or above normal retirement age, remains far below the US level, as seen in figure I.2, panel B. In other nations, increased women's participation at older ages is not as obviously related to a change in retirement regulations or to a decrease in the generosity of social security. What then are the factors mainly responsible for the change?

According to the analysis in the chapter by Claudia Goldin and Lawrence F. Katz, increased labor force participation of women in their older ages (they use fifty-nine to sixty-three years) is part of the general rising trend of cohort labor force participation throughout the life cycle. Women have worked a greater fraction of their years from twenty-five to fifty-four by birth cohort, at least up to the early 1950s cohorts.

Each birth cohort had a higher labor force participation rate than the previous cohorts at fifty-nine to sixty-three years old and the estimated cohort effects are due mainly to increased college graduation and greater accumulated lifetime work experience. Those who remain working at older ages have had a history of more rewarding jobs. In fact, those who continue to be employed, perhaps not surprisingly, reported six to eight years prior that they liked their jobs far more than those who did not persist in the labor force to their early sixties. But will these trends continue?

Job experience between ages twenty-five and fifty-four years rose from around fifteen to twenty-two years between cohorts born in the mid-1930s to those born in the late 1950s. But accumulated job experience has stopped rising among the most recent cohorts and that could mean that working longer at older ages will slow down. College graduation trends have continued to rise. In addition, participation at older ages for college-graduate women has recently increased beyond what would be predicted by the impact of life cycle experience. Thus, even though accumulated work experience by the most recent cohorts has reached a possibly temporary plateau, more educated women will probably be working even longer in the future. And there will be more of them.

The story told in the Goldin and Katz chapter is a useful overarching statement about the reasons why women are working longer, but it is not a complete one. Other factors can also help explain the rise of women working longer and they supplement the predictions of its future. Many are taken up in the next eight chapters.

The partners of a couple have in the past tended to retire around the same time. But because women are often married to older men, the members of the couple retire at different ages and, in consequence, many married women retire at younger ages than their spouse. That fact is at odds with their separate pecuniary interests. Because women have longer life expectancies, and often have had shorter careers, the opportunity cost of retirement in terms of the forgone potential earnings and accruals to Social Security wealth may be larger for married women. Nicole Maestas finds that the economic returns to additional work beyond midlife are greater for married women than for married men. The potential gain in Social Security wealth alone is enough to place married women on nearly equal footing with married men in terms of Social Security wealth at age seventy. Working longer makes sense for women, particularly in cohorts where education gains have been great and the pecuniary returns to employment are high.

Although most women have been working much longer into their fifties and sixties relative to earlier cohorts, black women have not. At ages fifty to seventy-two black women, recently, have had lower employment rates than similar white women. The fact holds even though these same black women had higher employment rates when they were middle-aged and younger. Furthermore, earlier cohorts of black women did work more than their white counterparts when they were older, although they no longer do so. The chapter by Joanna N. Lahey discusses factors that have contributed to these differential changes by race. She finds that changes in occupation, industry, and health outcomes can explain some of the differences. Black women enter their older years in worse health than white women. Their occupations when younger were more physically taxing and some of these employments have suffered serious declines.

Women's current marital status and past marital history greatly influence their later-life labor force participation. Claudia Olivetti and Dana Rotz explore the role of marriage by exploiting variation in laws governing divorce across states and over time. They quasi-experimentally identify how the timing of an exogenous increase in divorce risk, caused by the introduction of unilateral divorce, has impacted employment and retirement for older women. The spread of unilateral divorce, they find, was associated with cross-cohort differences in the probability of divorce over the life cycle. For women with an ex ante low risk of divorce (using their estimate of "risk"), later exposure to unilateral divorce significantly increased the probability of older age full-time employment and significantly decreased retirement wealth. Thus, these ever-divorced women are working longer remedially. For women with an ex ante high risk of divorce, later exposure to increased divorce risk does not impact full-time employment after age fifty, but is positively associated with investment in education after marriage. Those who had previously faced a high risk of divorce acted earlier to safeguard their futures.

At older ages, women face new competing demands on their time in the form of care for elderly family members. Due to increasing life expectancy, women who are now in their fifties and early sixties are more likely than ever before to have a living parent and are thus more likely to be at risk of providing care. Sean Fahle and Kathleen McGarry analyze the prevalence of the provision of long-term care for women in their preretirement years to see how caregiving affects their employment. They find a significant positive trend across cohorts in the need to provide care and a significant negative effect of caregiving on work. Caregiving is estimated to reduce the probability of work by more than 8 percent and the number of hours worked by 4 percent. These research findings imply that increased demands from aging parents and the lack of affordable long-term care options may have a substantial future negative impact on the employment rates of older women. Women have been working longer, but demands from their increasingly older surviving parents may provide a competing claim on their time.

Various factors such as more lifetime work experience, greater education, more unexpected marital disruption, and fewer children have been found in previous chapters to be of importance in the working longer phenomenon. But surely household finances are also of great importance. Annamaria Lusardi and Olivia S. Mitchell show how retirement wealth plays a key role.

Older women today have more debt than previous cohorts and they have lower savings and wealth. Lusardi and Mitchell show how financial fragility affects employment at older ages. A one standard deviation increase in the ratio of mortgage debt to home value is associated with a 3.4 to 5.5 percent rise in women's anticipated probability of working at age sixty-five. Women who were more financially literate were more likely to plan for retirement, were less likely to have excessive debt, and were less prone to be financially fragile. Income shocks play a key role in older women's debt status, but it is not enough to have resources. Women also need the financial literacy and capacity to manage their resources if they are to stay out of debt as they head into retirement.

The college educated are a distinctive group regarding working longer. One reason is that a large fraction of college-graduate women in the past were teachers, but that is no longer the case. About 45 percent of college-graduate women born in the 1930s were teachers at some point in their lives, but just 15 percent have been for women born in the late 1950s. Teachers, for various reasons, retired earlier than those in other employments. Therefore, the decrease in the fraction who are teachers should increase employment at older ages among college-graduate women.

Maria D. Fitzpatrick provides evidence supporting the hypothesis and she shows that older college-educated women who worked as teachers experienced lower increases in labor force participation than their counterparts who never taught. Goldin and Katz also estimate similar effects for women who were "ever a teacher." A main reason explored by Fitzpatrick is that teachers are generally covered by defined-benefit pensions, even more so in the past, and these pensions usually allow workers to retire earlier than Social Security. In addition, the collection of a defined-benefit pension generally requires the individual to leave her current employment. Although such individuals can take up employment elsewhere, particularly in a related line of work, they have generally not done so.

A key question in understanding trends in elderly women's work decisions is the extent to which changes in Social Security generosity have played a role. Alexander Gelber, Adam Isen, and Jae Song estimate the impact of changes in Social Security benefits on women's employment rates. They can examine the large and sudden end of an inadvertent increase in Social Security benefits that occurred when Congress, in 1972, double indexed benefits to both the Consumer Price Index (CPI) and wages. Ending the double indexation in 1977 cut women's (and men's) average Old-Age and Survivors Insurance (OASI) benefits substantially in the 1917 birth cohort relative to that of 1916. A "notch" in benefits was then produced by the 1977 Social Security Act amendments and led to sharply different benefits for similar women born just one day apart. Using Social Security Administration microdata on earnings in the full US population by day of birth, Gelber, Isen, and Song find substantial effects of the policy change on older women's employment rates. The slowdown in the growth of Social Security benefits in the mid-1980s can account for more than one-quarter of the increased growth of older women's employment in the subsequent period.

Some of the reasons that have been offered in the preceding chapters for women working longer have emphasized the increase in the positive aspects of employment in one's older years: better working conditions, rising incomes, and promotions in later years. Other chapters have stressed the constraints on women's wealth, particularly during the large economic downturn that began in 2008 and the fate of women whose divorces were unanticipated. C. Adam Bee and Joshua Mitchell show that our usual measures of retirement income are understated and that many women who are working longer could retire as previous cohorts had done but choose not to do so.

Despite women's increased labor force attachment over the life cycle, household surveys such as the Current Population Survey Annual Social and Economic Supplement (CPS-ASEC) do not show increases in retirement income such as pensions, 401(k)s, and individual retirement accounts (IRAs) for women at older ages. Using linked survey-administrative data, Bee and Mitchell demonstrate that retirement incomes are considerably underreported in the CPS-ASEC and that women's potential retirement income at older ages has been substantially understated. Specifically, the CPS-ASEC shows that median household income for women sixty-five to sixty-nine years old rose 21 percent since the late 1980s, whereas the administrative records show an increase of 58 percent.

In contrast to previous work, the authors find that most women do not experience noticeable drops in income up to five years after claiming Social Security and that retirement income plays an important role in maintaining their overall standard of living. The results of this compelling chapter suggest that total income replacement rates for recent female retirees are high.

The fact that so many women have continued to work despite having resources to retire reinforces the notion that work in one's older years has taken on a different meaning for women. Women have become about as attached to their métier, calling, and profession as men. Among women fifty-nine to sixty-three years old and currently married to employed husbands, 68 percent are working, up from 52 percent for cohorts born in the 1930s. Among those whose husbands are not working, 45 percent continue to work, up from 35 percent for cohorts born in the 1930s. Some of the chapters point to the possibility that these trends will not continue, but other essays suggest that they will. Only time will tell.

References

Gruber, Jonathan, and David A. Wise, eds. 1999. *Social Security and Retirement around the World.* Chicago: University of Chicago Press.
———. 2007. *Social Security Programs and Retirement around the World: Fiscal Implications of Reform.* Chicago: University of Chicago Press.
OECD Stat Extracts, Table LFS, Sex and Age Indicators, http://stats.oecd.org/Index .aspx?DataSetCode=LFS_SEXAGE_I_R.
US Social Security Administration. "Social Security Programs throughout the World." Published in collaboration with the International Social Security Association. https://www.ssa.gov/policy/docs/progdesc/ssptw/.

I

Transitions over the Life Cycle

1

Women Working Longer
Facts and Some Explanations

Claudia Goldin and Lawrence F. Katz

Women have been working longer for a long time in US history. Their labor market participation increased decade after decade during the twentieth century, as more women were drawn into the labor force. But that is an old story. The new story is that a large portion of women are working a lot longer into their sixties and even their seventies. Their increased participation at older ages started in the late 1980s before the turnaround in older men's labor force participation and before the economic downturns of the first decade of the twenty-first century.[1]

Claudia Goldin is the Henry Lee Professor of Economics at Harvard University and a research associate of the National Bureau of Economic Research. Lawrence F. Katz is the Elisabeth Allison Professor of Economics at Harvard University and a research associate of the National Bureau of Economic Research.

We are indebted to the University of Michigan, David Wise, and the staff at the NBER, especially Mohan Ramanujan, for enabling use of the restricted-access version of the HRS. We thank our research assistants who labored over the CPS, HRS, and the Social Security earnings files: Amira Abulafi, Natalia Emanuel, Celena (Yuezhou) Huo, and Jonathan Roth. We thank our discussant Katharine Abraham and others at the conference for providing valuable comments and to Maria Fitzpatrick for the "ever a teacher" variable code. We gratefully acknowledge the financial support of the Alfred P. Sloan Foundation's Working Longer program under grant no. 2013-6-16, "Women Working Longer." For acknowledgments, sources of research support, and disclosure of the author's or authors' material financial relationships, if any, please see http://www.nber.org/chapters/c13798.ack.

1. According to OECD data, most nations from around 2000 have had increased labor force participation of women in their sixties. These countries include Canada, France, Germany, Sweden, and the United Kingdom. Increases have also been experienced among women sixty-five to sixty-nine years old. In terms of levels for sixty- to sixty-four-year-olds, the United States and Japan had been the highest but most are now at about the 50 percent level. Levels are much lower for sixty-five- to sixty-nine-year-olds and considerably lower than that for the United States. Other than the United States and possibly Sweden, part-time work is reasonably high for older women in the nations mentioned. In only a few cases are changes in social security regulations obviously related to these increases. (For the data, see the introduction to

Women's increased participation beyond their fifties is a change of real consequence. Rather than being an increase in marginal part-time workers, the higher labor force participation of older women disproportionately consists of those working at full-time jobs. Women are remaining on their jobs as they age rather than scaling down or leaving for positions with shorter hours and fewer days.[2]

Why have women as a group increased their participation at older ages? Increased labor force participation of women in their older ages, we will emphasize, is part of the general increase in cohort labor force participation rates. Successive cohorts, for various reasons, increased their participation at all ages, resulting in an upward shift of participation by birth cohort. As more women graduated from college, held jobs with greater advancement potential, enjoyed their jobs more, were not currently married or were married to men who also extended employment into their senior years, more remained active in the labor force into their sixties and beyond.

Rising cohort effects in labor force participation across successive birth cohorts of US women are clearly visible in the microdata from the Current Population Survey (CPS) Annual Social and Economic Supplement (ASEC) and the Health and Retirement Survey (HRS). But these cohort effects are considerably dampened when education is considered. Higher participation at all ages has been due to greater levels of education, particularly college graduation. The increase in cohort effects in labor force participation for women in their late fifties and early sixties is also lessened by including work experience at younger ages and by adding information on the main prior occupation. We find some (negative) impact on employment at older ages from having been a teacher and discuss why that is the case.

Most important is that we find that those who "enjoyed" their jobs earlier in life remained employed for much longer later in life independent of their hours and earnings on the job six to eight years earlier. The difference between those who agree with the statement about enjoying their job versus those who disagree with the statement is 10 percentage points (on a base of 70) and the effect is twice that between those who strongly disagree with the statement and those who agree. Women who work more hours when fifty-nine to sixty-three years old are far more likely to have worked more hours six years before. But that is in addition to their greater satisfaction in the job earlier and their greater fulfillment contemporaneously. That is clearly not the case for all older workers, but it is the case for most.

Many of the cohorts we consider were those that also experienced greater divorce. Therefore, current marital status is related to employment at older

---

this volume and OECD.STAT, LFS by Sex and Age, Indicators http://stats.oecd.org/Index.aspx?DataSetCode=LFS_SEXAGE_I_R.)

2. Maestas (2010) discusses the emergence of nontraditional retirement paths, including the increasing role for planned transitions out of retirement and the greater fraction of those who state they are retired but who have positive and often substantial hours of work.

ages. Because couples often coordinate their work and leisure, current employment of the spouse is an additional correlate of whether a woman is working longer.

Most of the factors just mentioned, particularly educational attainment and earlier employment continuity, were determined prior to the employment decision under question. The addition of these factors almost nullifies the cohort effects, except in one important case. For the most recent cohorts of college-graduate women we can study to their sixties (those born from 1949 to 1955), the predetermined, observable factors do not eliminate the cohort effect. Something else, yet undetermined, is keeping them in the labor force at older ages.

Labor force participation rates of women in their early sixties can be observed today for cohorts born up to the mid-1950s. Participation rates of forty- and fifty-year-old women born in the late 1950s and early 1960s have not increased relative to those of prior cohorts. Life cycle cohort labor force functions are no longer the humped functions they once were. They have become flat lines, more like those of men than they had been. These flat lines, moreover, have intersected the humped life cycle participation functions of prior cohorts, showing the decrease in participation relative to previous cohorts. But these new and flatter participation functions appear not to be decreasing at older ages relative to prior cohorts. That may indicate that women will continue to work longer even though their participation rates at middle age had stagnated relative to prior cohorts.[3]

Several factors may operate to offset the stagnation or dip in the participation of US women in middle age. One of the reasons for the dip in women's participation in their late thirties and early forties is that women in these cohorts have had their children later. Therefore, the dip had been accompanied by an increase in their participation in their twenties relative to previous cohorts.

We find in our exploration of the correlates of participation that college-graduate women currently in their early sixties have positive cohort effects that remain substantial even after controlling for their earlier life cycle participation rates. Today's younger women will likely retire later than one would have predicted based on their educational attainment and life cycle participation rates. The finding is particularly noteworthy since female college-graduation rates are continuing to increase by birth cohort.[4]

3. See Goldin and Mitchell (2017) on changes in life cycle labor force participation. Hurd and Rohwedder (2014) use questions in the HRS on subjective probabilities of employment to predict future labor force participation rates. See also Maestas and Zissimopoulos (2010) for participation forecasts at older ages to 2030 and for an excellent summary of the issues.

4. The college graduation rate (the share with a bachelor's degree) for women age twenty-five to twenty-nine years increased from 30 percent in 2000 (for the 1971 to 1975 birth cohorts) to 39 percent in 2015 (for the 1986 to 1990 birth cohorts). (See US Department of Education 2015, table 104.20.)

1.1   Labor Force Participation Rates

1.1.1   By Age, Sex, and Education Level

The central facts concerning the labor force participation of women by age are shown in figure 1.1, which uses the March CPS-ASEC microdata samples and gives contemporaneous labor force participation rates during the survey reference week for women by five-year age groups since 1962. Throughout much of the period shown, participation rates increased for women in the thirty-five- to fifty-four-year-old group. The thirty-five- to forty-nine-year-old group flattens out in the early 1990s. In contrast, rates for women fifty-five years and older were flat until the 1980s, when an almost continuous increase ensued, even for the seventy- to seventy-four-year-old group.

The labor force participation data are also given in figure 1.2 for college-graduate women, since school attainment increases by birth cohort. The series is restricted to currently married women because a large fraction of the earlier cohorts of college-graduate women—those born from the 1890s to the 1910s—never married or married late. In consequence, a large fraction of college-graduate women, even those who eventually married, never had children and had higher labor force participation rates (Goldin 1997).

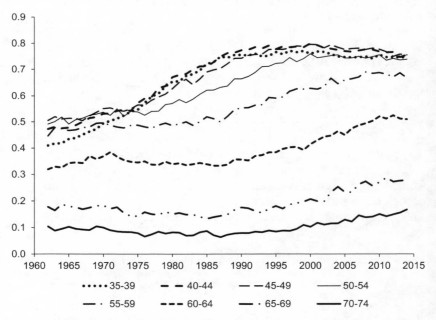

Fig. 1.1   Female labor force participation by five-year age groups, 1962 to 2014
Source: CPS-ASEC microdata, March 1962 to 2014.

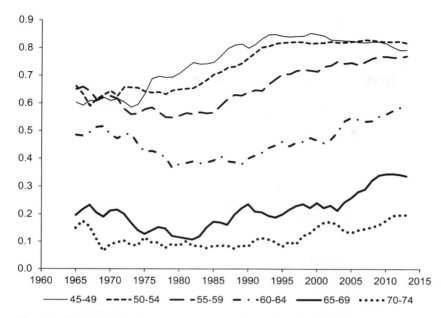

Fig. 1.2   Female labor force participation by five-year age groups for currently married college graduates, 1965 to 2013 (three-year centered moving averages)
Source: CPS-ASEC microdata, March 1962 to 2013.

Considering only the group who were currently married dampens the selection problem but does not eliminate it because of later marriage ages. Participation rates for college-graduate women, therefore, decline somewhat over time as their marriage and childbearing rates become more like others in their cohort.

If one ignores cohorts born before around 1920, the series for all women and that for college-graduate women fifty-five years or older are first relatively constant and then increase, particularly after the mid- to late 1980s.[5] The percentage point increase during the past twenty-five years, shown in table 1.1, is not much different between the aggregate group of women and the college graduates. But because college-graduate women have had considerably higher participation rates than less educated women, the shift toward college has increased participation rates for older women and the growth of women's employment at older ages.

Also clear in table 1.1 is that the increased participation of older women exceeds that of older men in the last twenty-five years, both absolutely and relative to the base levels. Among sixty- to sixty-four-year-old women, for

5. For the sixty- to sixty-four-year-old group, participation rates after 1980 are for individuals born after 1920.

Table 1.1   **Labor force participation rates for males and females, ages fifty-five to seventy-four: CPS**

Age group	Educational group	Labor force participation rate in 1987–89	Labor force participation rate in 2012–14	Percentage point change c. 1988 to c. 2013
Women				
55–59	All	0.522	0.673	15.1
	College graduates	0.685	0.779	9.4
	Not college grad.	0.499	0.627	12.8
60–64	All	0.341	0.514	17.3
	College graduates	0.454	0.612	15.8
	Not college grad.	0.330	0.472	14.3
65–69	All	0.153	0.276	12.3
	College graduates	0.240	0.367	12.7
	Not college grad.	0.145	0.244	9.9
70–74	All	0.072	0.157	8.6
	College graduates	0.130	0.214	8.3
	Not college grad.	0.066	0.142	7.5
Men				
55–59	All	0.796	0.779	−1.8
	College graduates	0.886	0.896	1.0
	Not college grad.	0.773	0.728	−4.6
60–64	All	0.548	0.607	5.9
	College graduates	0.682	0.727	4.5
	Not college grad.	0.516	0.543	2.8
65–69	All	0.258	0.380	12.2
	College graduates	0.402	0.491	8.9
	Not college grad.	0.231	0.321	9.0
70–74	All	0.155	0.232	7.7
	College graduates	0.254	0.324	7.0
	Not college grad.	0.141	0.191	5.0

Sources: CPS-ASEC microdata March 1987, 1988, 1989, 2012, 2013, and 2014.

example, participation increased by 17 percentage points on a base of 34 percent, but for males the increase is just 6 percentage points on a base of 55 percent. The percentage point increase for sixty-five- to sixty-nine-year-old males and females is similar in absolute magnitude, but the initial base for women is far lower (15 versus 26 percent).

The relative increase for older women has meant that the gender gap in participation at older ages has greatly decreased, as can be seen in figure 1.3. Differences in participation by sex have, of course, decreased more generally. But the absolute percentage point difference at some of the older ages is now smaller than for the younger age groups. For sixty- to sixty-four-year-olds, for example, the difference in participation rates between men and women was about 50 percentage points in 1962. In 2014, the difference was just 9 percentage points, when that for males and females in their thirties to mid-forties was around 16 percentage points.

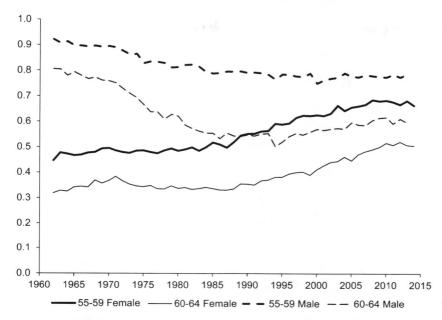

Fig. 1.3   Gender gap in labor force participation at older ages, 1962 to 2014: CPS
Source: CPS-ASEC microdata, March 1962 to 2014.

Men and women are doing more of the same things throughout their lives, and this is even truer at older ages. But is that also true within couples? The answer is that, for women fifty-nine to sixty-three years old and presently married, far more of these couples are both currently working than currently retired.[6] In addition, in 2014 about as many of these couples had a wife who was working and a husband who was not than the reverse. More women are working into their sixties and more are coupled with men who are also working. But there are also substantial numbers of women who are working into their sixties even though their husbands are retired. We return to the issue of joint employment and leisure below.

1.1.2   Full-Time versus Part-Time Employment of Women at Older Ages

The labor force participation rate for older women increased largely because of an increase in those working full time and full year. The expansion of full-time employment among participants has been especially evident for the sixty-five years and older group.

As seen in figure 1.4, the fraction of sixty-five- to sixty-nine-year-old women in the labor force who worked full time and full year increased from

---

6. This statement is true for HRS couples in which the wife is between fifty-nine and sixty-three years old. For couples in which the woman is sixty-two or sixty-three years old, the statement holds beginning in 2008.

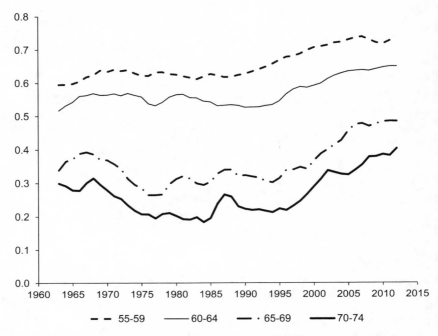

Fig. 1.4   Women employed full time, full year among labor force participants during the year, 1963 to 2013: CPS

Source: CPS-ASEC microdata, March 1962 to 2013.

Notes: Both numerator and denominator refer to the calendar year. A "labor force participant during the year" is anyone who worked during the year. Three-year centered moving averages are shown. Full-time, full-year workers are those who worked forty or more weeks and thirty-five or more hours per week.

around 30 percent to almost 50 percent, with much of the increase occurring after 2000.[7] The fraction of seventy- to seventy-four-year-old labor force participants working full time and full year increased from 20 percent to almost 40 percent. We emphasize that figure 1.4 gives the fraction working full time, full year among those in the labor force rather than among the population in that age group. Although the timing could indicate the impact of changes in the Social Security earnings test, the increase began before 2000 for both younger and older age groups of women.[8]

7. The pre-1970 data also show somewhat high fractions working full time among participants and it is not clear why there was a subsequent decrease.
8. The retirement earnings test was changed in 2000 to apply only to individuals below normal retirement age (NRA). The NRA had been sixty-five, but has been gradually increased to sixty-seven years for those born after 1959. Earnings taxed above the exempt amounts are repaid after NRA. From 1975 to 1982 the upper age was seventy-one and it was decreased to 69 until 2000. See Gelber, Jones, and Sacks (2016) on the retirement earnings test, its history,

1.1.3   Cohort Trends

Increased employment among older women would appear to be related to their increased participation earlier in their lives. The conclusion can be deduced from the fact that all cohorts in figure 1.5, panel A, that have had increased participation in their sixties, relative to earlier cohorts, also had increased participation relative to the same cohorts when they were younger. That is, the cohorts that have begun to "work longer" had higher participation rates throughout their life cycles than did previous cohorts.

Figure 1.5 begins with the cohort born in 1930, but the pattern just mentioned is evident as well for some of the earlier birth cohorts not shown. However, cohorts born in the early 1920s show no discernible increase in participation among women in their sixties despite modest increases earlier in their lives.[9] The data for college graduates given in figure 1.5, panel B, reveal similar findings, but participation levels are higher.

As will be emphasized later, regressions of the labor force rate at older ages on birth cohort dummies indicate that cohort effects are greatly muted by the addition of various predetermined factors such as education, earlier employment continuity, and women's past occupations. That is, cohort differences in labor force participation later in life are largely, but not entirely, a function of earlier changes in human capital accumulation. These human capital advances occurred because women perceived that their investments would pay off in the labor market and that their employment would be higher and more continuous than for previous cohorts.

We noted before that the function tracing out life cycle labor force participation was transformed from being hump-shaped to being almost a flat line after the mid-1950s birth cohorts. Participation rates around age twenty-five to the early thirties greatly increased from the 1930s to the 1950s birth cohorts because women with infants had much higher labor force participation and because the birth rate decreased.

The new flatter cohort life cycle functions have begun to cross each other. The crossing creates an interesting "twist" in participation for the most recent cohorts in figure 1.5, panel A, and more so for college-graduate women in figure 1.5, panel B. The twist is the cohort analog of the oft-mentioned decrease in the participation of women in their thirties and forties.[10] One clear way to see the change is to observe that slicing the cohort graphs at ages

---

and impact. Changes for men may, however, be related to the change in the retirement earnings test (see Gustman and Steinmeier 2009; Mastrobuoni 2009). Gelber, Isen, and Song (chapter 8, this volume) show that a slowdown in the rate of growth of Social Security benefits starting in the mid-1980s altered women's retirement.

9. These general trends are also apparent in figure 1.1. For example, the participation line for those sixty-five to sixty-nine years begins to increase around 1987, therefore for women born in the early 1920s.

10. See Goldin and Mitchell (2017) for a discussion of the "new life cycle of women's employment."

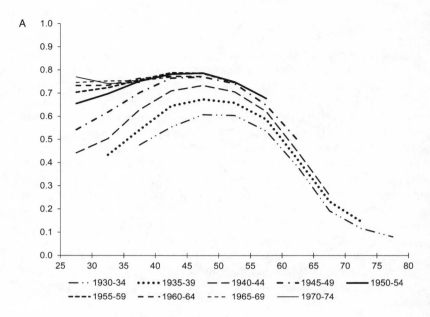

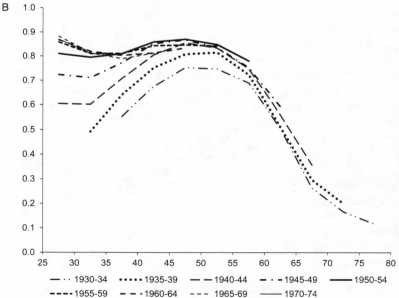

Fig. 1.5   Labor force participation rates for women by five-year birth cohorts (1930–34 to 1970–74) and five-year age groups (ages twenty-five to twenty-nine to seventy-four to seventy-nine): CPS. (A) All education groups. (B) College graduates.

Source: CPS-ASEC microdata, March 1962 to 2013.

Note: Every data point in each graph contains twenty-five birth years and ages.

thirty and fifty yields the usual cohort progression. Younger cohorts have higher participation rates than older cohorts. But slicing the cohort graphs in between, say at age forty, does not yield higher rates for the most recent cohorts, such as those born from 1959 to 1973. The cohort lines appear to have twisted.

Does this mean that participation rates for these women in their fifties, sixties, and beyond will also be lower? Their increased education and labor force participation in their younger years would argue the opposite. Why they have decreased participation is still an ongoing research question, although some of the answers concern the delay of births, on the one hand, and an absence of mandated leave policy of more than twelve weeks, on the other. The decrease in participation is not large, but the disruption of the increasing trend is clear and could argue for a break in the increase of women working longer.[11]

The bottom line for cohort change is that increased participation at older ages has occurred for cohorts that had greater attachment to the labor force throughout their lives. The upshot is that greater attachment to the labor force earlier in the work life means longer employment at older ages. We now turn to using longitudinal information from the HRS matched to Social Security earnings records to understand the role of cohort effects.

Because we rely on the CPS for the general trends and the HRS for analysis, we provide evidence that the HRS reasonably tracks general trends in the CPS for these cohorts and age groups. Appendix tables and figures show the close relationship between CPS and HRS participation rates (figure 1A.1), marital status (table 1A.2), education (table 1A.3), and number of children (figure 1A.2). Labor force participation rates in the HRS and the CPS are almost identical for women in their fifties and sixties; however, the HRS has higher participation rates than the CPS for women in their seventies.[12]

1.2   Exploring the Role of Cohort Effects Using the HRS

Cohorts born later have higher labor force participation rates at older ages than do those born earlier. We explore whether these cohort effects are

---

11. Hurd and Rohwedder (2014) note that subjective probabilities of future work at ages sixty-two and sixty-five are reliable predictors of actual employment and that current HRS respondents in their early fifties have subjective probabilities of future work that exceed the actual participation rates of individuals in their sixties. Lusardi and Mitchell (chapter 6, this volume) also find using the HRS that the share of women in their early fifties who anticipate working at age sixty-five continues to rise in recent cohorts, even as women's labor force participation rates in their early fifties has flattened across cohorts. These findings indicate a further increase in the participation rates of older women.

12. The reason for the difference in participation at older ages is not clear since each survey is supposed to cover those in nursing homes and similar care units. The HRS, in addition, has a lower fraction of women who state they never had a first birth.

primarily due to changes in factors determined largely prior to the retirement option. These variables can include educational attainment, number and ages of children, and earlier life cycle labor force participation. We will also consider the degree to which the individual had relatively high earnings when employed, which we term the "career condition." These largely predetermined characteristics will be measured in our empirical work prior to around age fifty-five, whereas the retirement option is considered from ages fifty-nine to sixty-three.

The retirement decision may instead be determined primarily by factors that are contemporaneous, such as a set of shocks or transitory factors. These factors may have served to increase participation at older years in the post-1980s period and may include marital status change, fluctuations in the value of real estate or financial assets, pension losses, reductions in Social Security payments, and deteriorating health status.

The evidence points to a large impact of changes in the predetermined factors. Education reduces cohort differences in labor force participation from ages fifty-nine to sixty-three by about a half. Life cycle labor force participation from thirty-five to forty-four years produces an overshooting of the cohort effects. Our measure of high career earnings does not perform better than the simpler measure of life cycle participation.

Once these variables are considered, adding information on the number and birth years of children has no impact. Children serve to reduce participation in the twenty-five- to forty-four-year range, but have no separate effect in later life.[13] The many contemporaneous factors mentioned are related to the variance within cohorts, but do not do much to explain changes across cohorts.

The one interesting anomaly concerns the most recent of the cohorts of college-graduate women that can be followed to their sixties. Those born from 1949 to 1951 have higher participation at ages fifty-nine to sixty-three, even given measures of their life cycle participation prior to age fifty-five and their educational attainment. That is, the cohort effect for the 1949 to 1951 group remains significant even including the various predetermined factors, including life cycle participation.

The finding that later cohorts have higher participation given their earlier life cycle participation may be useful in forecasting what more recent cohorts will be doing when they reach their sixties. Recall that labor force participation rates across the life cycle have become relatively flat from ages twenty-five to forty-five, and that the most recent cohorts of women do not always have higher participation compared with previous cohorts. In fact,

---

13. Lumsdaine and Vermeer (2015) find that a grandchild's arrival increases the hazard of a woman's retirement independent of her opportunity cost. It is not clear that the partial or total grandchild effect has decreased with time, thus that it can help to explain the working longer phenomenon.

the most recent data indicate a backtracking of younger cohorts of women in their forties. That is, for the college-graduate group, as well as for others, participation rates have not increased relative to prior cohorts and have even decreased at various ages.

The finding about those born between 1949 and 1951 may indicate that participation rates for even younger cohorts may be higher still in their sixties and seventies than prior generations, at least for college-educated women.

To explore the role of cohort and predetermined variables, data from the Health and Retirement Study (HRS) are used together with information on the earnings history of the respondents from Social Security earnings data and W-2 forms (starting with 1980).[14] Each of the respondents to the HRS, beginning with the first cohorts in 1992, was asked whether her Social Security earnings history could be linked. If the individual agreed to the linkage, then all past records were linked.[15] If not, then the individual was asked again in the subsequent biennial survey. Therefore, the older cohorts had more chances to agree to a linkage than the younger cohorts and linkage rates are higher in consequence.

Across all cohorts about 80 percent of respondents agreed to the linkage with Social Security (and W-2) records. For birth cohorts from 1931 to 1945 the response rate ranges from 85 to 90 percent; the range is 71 to 79 percent for birth cohorts from 1946 to 1951. (Linkage rates are given in appendix table 1A.1 by birth cohort.) When we use information on life cycle labor force participation, we must restrict the sample to individuals who gave permission to have their Social Security earnings (and W-2 forms) linked. Otherwise the full HRS sample is used, given age and other restrictions that may apply.

We mainly explore labor force participation rates of women fifty-nine to sixty-three years old and always include three-year birth cohort dummies. We begin in table 1.2, columns (1) to (5) by including characteristics largely determined prior to age fifty-five, such as educational attainment and life cycle participation during various intervals.[16] We add in column (6) current marital status and a summary measure of current health status.

Table 1.3 divides the group into two education levels, college graduates and

14. The W-2 data are also provided for 1977–79, but are incomplete in the HRS-SSA linked data.

15. A curious aspect of the HRS is that until 2006 individuals were asked every year if they would continue the linkage to the Social Security earnings data. If at any point they decided not to, the prior data were allowed but the contemporaneous and future data were not. For most HRS respondents, the break in the linkage will not matter since the HRS itself collected information on labor supply and earnings. But the break will matter for a spouse who entered the HRS at a younger age and who was folded when the individual's birth cohort relevant HRS cohort was added. See the appendix, especially the section "Social Security Earnings Record Linkage in the HRS," for details.

16. The addition of variables for children ever born adds no explanatory power for older women's labor force participation after including controls for earlier life cycle participation. Thus, we do not report specifications adding controls for children.

Table 1.2   Female labor force participation at ages fifty-nine to sixty-three, all education groups: HRS

	Full sample			Linked sample		
	(1)	(2)	(3)	(4)	(5)	(6)
Year of birth						
1934–36	−0.00810	−0.0110	−0.0139	−0.0158	−0.0128	−0.0143
	(0.0192)	(0.0207)	(0.0203)	(0.0197)	(0.0201)	(0.0186)
1937–39	0.0141	0.00448	0.000715	−0.0146	−0.00357	−0.00521
	(0.0191)	(0.0206)	(0.0202)	(0.0199)	(0.0202)	(0.0186)
1940–42	0.0163	0.0137	−0.00832	−0.0354	−0.0178	−0.0312
	(0.0203)	(0.0218)	(0.0211)	(0.0206)	(0.0210)	(0.0195)
1943–45	0.0464**	0.0320	−0.00461	−0.0402	−0.0184	−0.0321
	(0.0229)	(0.0247)	(0.0239)	(0.0235)	(0.0237)	(0.0223)
1946–48	0.0635*	0.0529**	0.00327	−0.0389	−0.0141	−0.0257
	(0.0217)	(0.0240)	(0.0238)	(0.0235)	(0.0238)	(0.0220)
1949–51	0.0973***	0.0888***	0.0300	−0.0110	0.0120	0.000839
	(0.0217)	(0.0259)	(0.0250)	(0.0246)	(0.0249)	(0.0234)
High school grad.			0.161***	0.121***	0.141***	0.0583***
			(0.0180)	(0.0176)	(0.0180)	(0.0171)
Some college			0.251***	0.199***	0.217***	0.106***
			(0.0205)	(0.0202)	(0.0207)	(0.0195)
College graduate			0.295***	0.237***	0.251***	0.115***
			(0.0252)	(0.0252)	(0.0260)	(0.0250)
MA			0.348***	0.280***	0.292***	0.159***
			(0.0288)	(0.0286)	(0.0298)	(0.0276)
PhD, MD, JD, etc.			0.468***	0.364***	0.400***	0.227***
			(0.0458)	(0.0453)	(0.0458)	(0.0451)
Life cycle LFP 35–44				0.233***		0.216***
				(0.0174)		(0.0165)

	(1)	(2)	(3)	(4)	(5)	(6)
Career cond. 35–44					0.128***	
					(0.0195)	
Currently married						−0.157***
						(0.0309)
Divorced						0.0806**
						(0.0321)
Widow						0.0113
						(0.0324)
Spouse in LF						0.186***
						(0.0146)
Health status	No	No	No	No	No	Yes
Age dummies	Yes	Yes	Yes	Yes	Yes	Yes
Race dummies	Yes	Yes	Yes	Yes	Yes	Yes
Constant	0.456***	0.430***	0.326***	0.261***	0.323***	0.165***
	(0.0331)	(0.0394)	(0.0365)	(0.0367)	(0.0366)	(0.0426)
N	18,383	15,431	15,431	15,431	15,431	15,431
R-squared	0.028	0.029	0.073	0.104	0.082	0.183

Sources: Health and Retirement Study (HRS) 1992 to 2012, RAND version with added variables from original HRS files. Social Security Administration earnings (and W-2) data are used to calculate life cycle labor force participation (Life cycle LFP <ages>) and the career condition (Career cond. <ages>).

Notes: The dependent variable is 1 if the woman is in the labor force and 0 otherwise. The HRS asks respondents their labor force status and a woman is in the labor force if she reported being employed or unemployed and searching for work. Health status is self-reported and is coded as 1 if "good" or better and 0 otherwise. Marital status variables refer to current status. "Life cycle LFP <ages>" is the fraction of the interval the woman was in the labor force as determined by a combination of the data sources described in the appendix. The "linked sample" indicates that the individual gave permission for Social Security earnings data to be linked. Omitted base group variables are 1931–33 birth cohort, below high school graduate (overall or for the less-than-college-graduate group), BA only for the college-graduate group, never married, other race, and age fifty-nine. Omitted from the table are dummy variables for missing variables regarding spouse in labor force, career condition thirty-five to forty-four, and health status. The regressions are weighted by HRS person weights; the weights are adjusted for sample selection into the linked sample in columns (2) to (6). Standard errors in parentheses have been clustered at the individual level.

***Significant at the 1 percent level.

**Significant at the 5 percent level.

*Significant at the 10 percent level.

Table 1.3 Female labor force participation at ages fifty-nine to sixty-three, by education: HRS

	Not college graduate (1)	College graduate (2)	Not college graduate (3)	College graduate (4)	Not college graduate (5)	College graduate (6)
Year of birth						
1934–36	−0.0234	0.0308	−0.0263	0.0346	−0.0246	0.0390
	(0.0219)	(0.0522)	(0.0212)	(0.0506)	(0.0200)	(0.0472)
1937–39	−0.00195	0.0182	−0.0218	0.0234	−0.0102	0.0182
	(0.0217)	(0.0543)	(0.0212)	(0.0545)	(0.0197)	(0.0521)
1940–42	−0.0133	0.0357	−0.0441**	0.0188	−0.0388	0.0160
	(0.0231)	(0.0515)	(0.0223)	(0.0506)	(0.0212)	(0.0475)
1943–45	−0.0101	0.0509	−0.0468	0.0219	−0.0370	0.0212
	(0.0266)	(0.0537)	(0.0260)	(0.0542)	(0.0245)	(0.0526)
1946–48	−0.00304	0.0589	−0.0470	0.0235	−0.0345	0.0377
	(0.0268)	(0.0522)	(0.0262)	(0.0527)	(0.0247)	(0.0489)
1949–51	0.00557	0.126**	−0.0389	0.103**	−0.0210	0.0980**
	(0.0291)	(0.0498)	(0.0287)	(0.0504)	(0.0272)	(0.0486)
High school grad.	0.158***		0.115***		0.0520*	
	(0.0180)		(0.0176)		(0.0172)	
Some college	0.249***		0.193***		0.101***	
	(0.0205)		(0.0202)		(0.0197)	
MA		0.0502		0.0420		0.0370
		(0.0316)		(0.0313)		(0.0295)
PhD, MD, JD, etc.		0.167***		0.136*		0.111**
		(0.0483)		(0.0492)		(0.0489)
Life cycle LFP 35–44			0.208***	0.0739	0.192***	0.0709
			(0.0273)	(0.0573)	(0.0254)	(0.0589)
Never in LF 35–44			−0.0548**	−0.153**	−0.0522**	−0.150*
			(0.0254)	(0.0730)	(0.0238)	(0.0716)

	(1)	(2)	(3)	(4)	(5)	(6)
Currently married					−0.147***	−0.243***
					(0.0350)	(0.0649)
Divorced					0.0613	0.119
					(0.0368)	(0.0638)
Widow					0.00458	−0.00416
					(0.0364)	(0.0712)
Spouse in LF					0.177***	0.225***
					(0.0160)	(0.0357)
Health status	No	No	No	No	Yes	Yes
Age dummies	Yes	Yes	Yes	Yes	Yes	Yes
Race dummies	Yes	Yes	Yes	Yes	Yes	Yes
Constant	0.285***	0.859***	0.258***	0.841***	0.167*	0.638***
	(0.0385)	(0.0629)	(0.0434)	(0.0751)	(0.0508)	(0.0999)
N	12,789	2,642	12,789	2,642	12,789	2,642
R-squared	0.060	0.041	0.097	0.059	0.179	0.140

Sources: Health and Retirement Study (HRS) 1992 to 2012, RAND version with added variables from original HRS files. Social Security Administration earnings (and W-2) data are used to calculate life cycle labor force participation (Life cycle LFP <ages>).

Notes: The dependent variable is 1 if the woman is in the labor force and 0 otherwise. The HRS asks respondents their labor force status and a woman is in the labor force if she reported being employed or unemployed and searching for work. Health status is self-reported and is coded as 1 if "good" or better and 0 otherwise. Marital status variables refer to current status. "Life cycle LFP <ages>" is the fraction of the interval the woman was in the labor force as determined by a combination of the data sources described in the appendix. "Never in LF" is 1 if the individual was recorded as having no years in the labor force during those years. All columns use the "linked sample." Omitted base group variables are 1931–33 birth cohort, below high school graduate (overall or for the less-than-college-graduate group), BA only for the college-graduate group, never married, other race, and age fifty-nine. Omitted from the table are dummy variables for missing variables regarding spouse in labor force and health status. Regressions are estimated separately for college graduates and those who did not graduate from college. College-graduate degrees beyond a bachelor's are added (MA, PhD, etc.), where MA includes all master's degrees, and PhD, MD, JD, and so forth includes all graduate and professional degrees. For those who did not graduate from college, dummy variables are added for those with a high school diploma and some college. The regressions are weighted by HRS person weights adjusted for sample selection into the linked sample. Standard errors in parentheses have been clustered at the individual level.

***Significant at the 1 percent level.

**Significant at the 5 percent level.

*Significant at the 10 percent level.

those who did not graduate college.[17] Columns (1) to (4) of table 1.3 include the predetermined characteristics and columns (5) and (6) add current marital status and health status. Table 1.4 includes only college-graduate women. In addition to the previous variables, we add information on whether the individual was ever a teacher. About 45 percent of college-graduate women in the 1930s cohorts were teachers for much of their working lifetimes, and teachers generally had defined-benefit pensions.

The use of the HRS linked to the Social Security earnings records (called the "linked" sample) reduces the number of observations, less so for the earlier than for the more recent cohorts as previously mentioned. When we use the data with Social Security earnings, we adjust the HRS person weights for selection into the linked sample.[18] In tables 1.2 and 1.4, we explore the sensitivity of the results to using the full HRS sample and the linked sample. Because the HRS is a longitudinal data set, many of the respondents are in the sample more than once between the ages of fifty-nine and sixty-three, and we cluster the standard errors at the individual level. We also include dummy variables for the single-year ages.

In table 1.2, column (1), the baseline regression is provided for the full sample and column (2) gives the baseline for the smaller linked sample. The variables of interest are those showing the effect of birth cohort in three-year bins from 1931 to 1951 (where 1931–33 is the omitted cohort group).[19]

The impacts of birth cohort on labor force participation from ages fifty-nine to sixty-three are highly similar between the two samples and both demonstrate the increase in participation at older ages for birth cohorts after 1943 and especially after 1949. The most recent cohort that can be analyzed for the fifty-nine- to sixty-three-year-old group, born from 1949 to 1951, has a participation rate that is around 10 percentage points higher in the full sample (9 for the linked sample) than for cohorts born in the 1930s. The only additional covariates included in the first two columns are single year of age and race dummies.

Educational attainment is added in column (3) and life cycle participation between ages thirty-five and forty-four is included in column (4). The life cycle labor force variables give the fraction of years in the interval that the woman was in the labor force. These have been computed mainly from the restricted-access Social Security earnings data (since 1951) and W-2 forms (when available). Additional information is used from the HRS to add labor force data for individuals exempt from Social Security taxes, gener-

17. Similar regressions to those in table 1.3 for women fifty-six to fifty-eight years old are in appendix table 1A.5.
18. The adjustment multiplies the person weight by the inverse of the predicted linkage rate, based on individual predetermined characteristics at the time of their birth cohort's entry into the HRS. Linkage rates are predicted using a logit model for whether the woman allowed the linkage on HRS cohort wave dummies and HRS measures of employment history, race, marital status, education, and financial wealth at HRS cohort entry.
19. The last year of the HRS available is 2012. The 1952–54 cohort is incomplete and thus is omitted.

ally because they were government employees, such as teachers. The HRS provides information concerning two periods prior to the start of the HRS interviews in which the respondent was a government employee. When HRS survey responses are available regarding participation, they are used in place of Social Security earnings and W-2 data. (For more details, see appendix: "Construction of Variables.") Various life cycle employment variables were created for each of the three decades from age twenty-five to fifty-four and for the entire period.

The addition of educational attainment eliminates the economic and statistical significance of the cohort coefficients for all but the most recent of the birth cohorts. Although only the linked sample coefficients are given, those for the full sample change in the same manner. The addition of the life cycle participation variable in column (4) further reduces the coefficient for the most recent of the birth cohorts to a slightly negative value. It also produces some modest reduction of the impact of educational attainment since the more educated have greater continuity in employment.

Instead of a variable that measures life cycle participation, one that measures the degree to which a woman reaches some career level may be more important in determining future participation. Since women with greater prior employment when first beginning their careers have greater attachment to the labor force later in the lives, those with higher earnings when employed should have even greater attachment.

To test whether employment per se or years of better earning performance matter, we create a variable giving the fraction of an age interval that a "career condition" was met. The condition used here is achieving an earnings level that is some fraction (50 percent in this case) of the median earnings of a full-time, year-round male worker for the ten-year age group considered during the relevant period.[20] That is, the career condition for a woman when she was in an age group is judged relative to the earnings of the median male in the same age group during the identical period. Women who were never in the labor force in the age interval are assigned a value of zero, as do those who never earned more than the condition but were in the labor force. We find that the variable giving the career condition (in column [5]) is related to later employment, but less strongly than the simpler variable giving the fraction of the interval a woman was employed.

Column (6) augments the column (4) specification by adding two contemporaneous variables: current marital status and current health status. The birth cohort coefficients were already extinguished with controls for

---

20. Earnings of the median male, in the same age group and year, are used. These data are available in published documents (US Census Bureau *P-60 Reports*) prior to the microdata for the CPS, which begins in 1962. The calculation of all the career conditions considered requires data from 1956 (1931 + twenty-five years). A fraction of the male median is used because the median is too high a bar for employed women during much of the period considered. Women in the exempt occupations are assumed to exceed the bar. See appendix: "Health and Retirement Survey: Construction of Variables."

education and earlier life cycle participation, and the added contemporaneous variables have little further impact on the cohort effects. The addition of health status reduces the impact of education and, in most instances, almost halves the schooling-level coefficients in column (4). The more highly educated are also the healthiest or, at least, they consider themselves to be so. The coefficient on earlier life cycle participation remains substantial and is only slightly reduced.

It is useful to explore the impact of current marital status even if it does little to change the birth cohort coefficients. Being currently married decreases participation for older women, but the effect is reduced if the woman's spouse is employed and the total impact is about equal to that of the omitted group (never married) and to widowed women.[21] Divorced women have participation rates about 8 percentage points higher than the base group of never married women.[22]

Disaggregating by education, as in table 1.3, reveals substantial differences between the higher (college graduate) and lower (below a college graduate) educated groups in the correlates of their later employment. Note that within the college-graduate group, dummy variables are added for degrees above the bachelor's (MA and the various graduate and professional degrees) and, within the noncollege group, dummy variables are added for high school diploma and having some college.

The regressions in columns (1) and (2) of table 1.3 include only cohort effects (plus age, race, and education dummies). Cohort effects for college graduates (relative to the 1931–33 cohorts) are modest, but the most recent of the cohorts has a participation rate about 12.6 percentage points higher. For the group that did not graduate from college, cohort effects are insubstantial. Because there was upgrading within each of the education groups as more attended college, participation rates for the entire group increased by birth cohort, even though within each of the groups there was no birth cohort trend.

In columns (3) and (4) we add life cycle participation variables, including whether the woman was never in the labor force during the interval. The addition of the life cycle measures has little impact on the cohort effect for the college-graduate women born most recently. Earlier labor force participation matters more for the less educated group than for the college educated. For college graduates, what matters most is whether the women did not work at all in the interval, even though that group is small. The much higher labor force participation for the 1949–51 cohort of college-graduate women remains unexplained, even with controls for current marital and health status, as seen in column (6).

Last, table 1.4 looks in more depth at college graduates in part because

21. We discuss, below, changes in the joint employment and retirement of couples.
22. Note that the mean labor force participation rate for a woman age fifty-nine, who is other race and in the 1931–33 birth cohort, is given by the constant term in column (2).

Table 1.4   **Labor force participation among college-graduate women at ages fifty-nine to sixty-three: HRS**

	Full sample	Linked sample			
	(1)	(2)	(3)	(4)	(5)
Year of birth					
1934–36	0.00774	0.0272	0.0308	0.0458	0.0294
	(0.0497)	(0.0524)	(0.0507)	(0.0470)	(0.0508)
1937–39	0.00217	0.0169	0.0221	0.0212	0.00996
	(0.0503)	(0.0543)	(0.0544)	(0.0508)	(0.0538)
1940–42	0.0389	0.0327	0.0154	0.0193	0.00204
	(0.0484)	(0.0518)	(0.0508)	(0.0473)	(0.0509)
1943–45	0.0370	0.0402	0.00983	0.0179	−0.0172
	(0.0503)	(0.0541)	(0.0543)	(0.0526)	(0.0550)
1946–48	0.0465	0.0482	0.0114	0.0110	−0.0256
	(0.0475)	(0.0525)	(0.0528)	(0.0503)	(0.0544)
1949–51	0.0957**	0.117**	0.0931	0.105**	0.0524
	(0.0452)	(0.0500)	(0.0505)	(0.0460)	(0.0510)
Ever a teacher	−0.0477	−0.0483	−0.0545	−0.0892*	−0.0591
	(0.0288)	(0.0315)	(0.0309)	(0.0294)	(0.0305)
MA	0.0538	0.0578	0.0504	0.0381	0.0405
	(0.0296)	(0.0326)	(0.0322)	(0.0306)	(0.0319)
PhD, MD, JD, etc.	0.160***	0.164***	0.133*	0.107*	0.111**
	(0.0447)	(0.0470)	(0.0479)	(0.0411)	(0.0461)
Life cycle LFP 35–44			0.0673		
			(0.0573)		
Never in LF 35–44			−0.164**		
			(0.0731)		
Life cycle LFP 45–54				0.379***	
				(0.0710)	
Never in LF 45–54				−0.178	
				(0.0973)	
Life cycle LFP 25–54					0.355***
					(0.0655)
Health status	No	No	No	No	No
Age dummies	Yes	Yes	Yes	Yes	Yes
Race dummies	Yes	Yes	Yes	Yes	Yes
Marital status dummies	Yes	Yes	Yes	Yes	Yes
Job status of husband	Yes	Yes	Yes	Yes	Yes
Constant	0.855***	0.876***	0.866***	0.580***	0.675***
	(0.0591)	(0.0629)	(0.0755)	(0.0857)	(0.0708)
N	3,137	2,642	2,642	2,642	2,642
R-squared	0.040	0.044	0.062	0.141	0.080

Sources: Health and Retirement Study (HRS) 1992 to 2012, RAND version with added variables from original HRS files. Social Security Administration earnings (and W-2) data are used to calculate life cycle labor force participation (Life cycle LFP <ages>) and the career condition (Career cond. <ages>).

(*continued*)

Table 1.4   (continued)

Notes: The dependent variable is 1 if the woman is in the labor force and 0 otherwise. The HRS asks respondents their labor force status and a woman is in the labor force if she reported being employed or unemployed and searching for work.

Health status is self-reported and is coded as 1 if "good" or better and 0 otherwise. Marital status variables refer to current status. "Life cycle LFP <ages>" is the fraction of the interval the woman was in the labor force as determined by a combination of the data sources described in the appendix. "Never in LF" is 1 if the individual was recorded as having no years in the labor force during those years. The "linked sample" indicates that the individual gave permission for Social Security earnings data to be linked. Omitted base group variables are 1931–33 birth cohort, BA only for the college-graduate group, never married, other race, and age fifty-nine. Omitted from the table are dummy variables for missing variables regarding spouse in labor force and health status. The regressions are weighted by the HRS person weights; the weights are adjusted for sample selection into the linked sample in columns (2) to (5). Standard errors in parentheses have been clustered at the individual level.

***Significant at the 1 percent level.
**Significant at the 5 percent level.
*Significant at the 10 percent level.

their participation rates are the highest at all ages, especially among those in their sixties. In addition, the fraction of older women who are college graduates has greatly expanded and will continue to do so given the increase of college graduates at younger ages. Both the increase of college graduation for future cohorts and their higher participation at older ages would imply an increase in the future employment of older women.

Table 1.4 includes the predetermined (life cycle participation and education) and contemporaneous (marital and health status) variables. In addition, we include whether the woman was ever employed as a teacher.

Cohort effects are large for the most recent in table 1.4, echoing the finding for college-graduate women in table 1.3. The coefficient remains large and statistically significant despite the inclusion of current marital status and life cycle participation variables. Only in column (5), with the inclusion of the fraction of years from twenty-five to fifty-four that the woman was in the labor force does the coefficient greatly decline.

Teaching was the single most important occupation for college-graduate women among many of the HRS cohorts. Around 45 percent of college-graduate women in the cohorts born from 1931 to 1941 were teachers at some point, as seen in figure 1.6. A much smaller fraction of women (around 30 percent) for the later cohorts considered here, 1945 to 1951, were teachers. And an even smaller fraction (around 20 percent) were teachers in the late 1950s birth cohort, a group still too young to be observed in their sixties.

Those who were ever a teacher had participation rates when they were fifty-nine to sixty-three years old that were about 5 percentage points lower than other college-graduate women. The impact of ever being a teacher increases when controlling for life cycle participation, showing that teachers work more than others earlier in their lives but are less likely to work later in their lives. Their earlier work would indicate they would be more likely

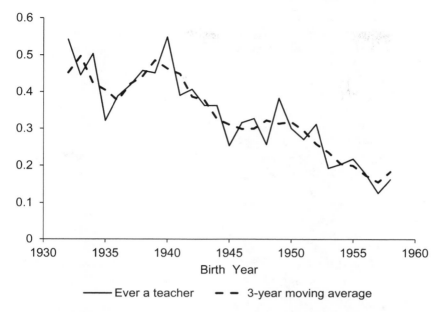

Fig. 1.6   Fraction of college-graduate women ever employed in teaching, for 1931 to 1959 birth cohorts: HRS

Source: HRS, restricted-access data.

Note: "Ever employed in teaching" is calculated with code provided by Maria Fitzpatrick (see chapter 7, this volume), which uses detailed occupations of respondents prior to their first HRS interview. The dashed line is the three-year centered moving average.

to work later, but they are less likely. Part of the reason why teachers have lower employment as they age is due to their defined-benefit pensions, and thus their long-term plans to retire after a fixed period. Other possibilities include "burnout" on the job and lack of advancement.[23]

The table 1.4 analysis reinforces the findings from table 1.3 that the cohort effect for the most recent birth group is not extinguished by the other covariates, even when the life cycle participation rate variable is included, as in columns (3), (4), and (5). The coefficient for the 1949–51 birth cohort is around 10 to 12 percentage points, a bit smaller than without the "ever a teacher" variable, but still large and significant.

Another important finding for forecasting women's future participation at older ages is that employment in the forty-five- to fifty-four-year-old range is the best predictor of whether an individual will remain employed into her early sixties. Therefore, even though participation rates have twisted, as noted in the discussion of figure 1.5, the fact that participation is still higher

---

23. Fitzpatrick (chapter 7, this volume) explores reasons for the decrease in employment at older ages among those who were ever a teacher.

for the most recent cohorts when they have reached their fifties suggests that recent cohorts of college-graduate women will remain in the labor force through their sixties and seventies even more than did their predecessors. The same does not appear true for the non-college-graduate group.

We have also run the same regressions as in tables 1.2, 1.3, and 1.4 where the outcome is working full time, rather than just being in the labor force. The results (given in appendix table 1A.4 for the table 1.3 comparison) for full-time work, for both college graduates and those below college-graduation level, reveal similar cohort trends.[24] Thus, the cross-cohort increases in labor force participation for older women are substantially driven by increases in full-time work. These findings are consistent with those from the CPS, given in figure 1.4, showing an increase in the fraction of female labor force participants employed full time among those fifty-five to seventy-four years old.

What about the role of job enjoyment? The HRS allows us to explore the answer for women fifty-nine to sixty-three years old for whom information exists on their attitude toward their job six years previously. Because of the restriction on having a job six years ago, we omit the earlier birth cohorts and include those born from 1937 to 1951. We ask how a woman's attitude about her job six years earlier impacts her contemporaneous employment. The attitude variable inquired in all years except 1992 whether an employed person enjoyed her job a lot or not at all in four gradations of strength.

We present the analysis in several ways. In table 1.5, columns (1) to (5), we include all who were employed six years before, and in column (6) we add those not employed six years previously and give them a separate dummy for the job-attitude response. Columns (1), (2), (4), and (6) contain the basic variables and columns (3) and (5) add the life cycle labor force variable, marital status, spousal work, and health status.

Column (1) provides baseline results excluding the attitude variable but using the same sample limited to those employed six years ago. Columns (4) and (5) explore the characteristics of the job held six years prior by adding the hours and earnings on that job.

Those who had expressed greater enjoyment about their jobs six years previously have a higher probability of being in the labor force from fifty-nine to sixty-three years old.[25] The differences, moreover, are large: 10 percentage points (on a base of around 70) between those who agree and disagree with

24. We also run the same labor force regressions as in tables 1.2, 1.3, and 1.4 for women fifty-six to fifty-eight years old and give the table 1.3 results in appendix table 1A.5. Using women fifty-six to fifty-eight years old allows us to include another birth cohort, 1952–54. Like the table 1.3 results, college-graduate women in cohorts born after 1948 show larger cohort effects than for earlier cohorts. Including the full set of preexisting characteristics lowers the cohort effect estimates for the more recent cohorts at age fifty-six to fifty-eight somewhat more than for the older group of women in table 1.3.

25. We have also done the same regressions for work eight years previously with similar results.

Table 1.5   Role of past work attitude for employment of women ages fifty-nine to sixty-three: HRS

	Labor force participation at ages fifty-nine to sixty-three					
	Worked six years ago					All
	(1)	(2)	(3)	(4)	(5)	(6)
Enjoy job 6 yrs. ago						
Strongly agree		0.223*	0.203*	0.235*	0.212*	0.229*
		(0.0720)	(0.0694)	(0.0723)	(0.0693)	(0.0718)
Agree		0.198*	0.189*	0.209*	0.198*	0.202*
		(0.0709)	(0.0680)	(0.0713)	(0.0680)	(0.0708)
Disagree		0.101	0.0932	0.105	0.0983	0.103
		(0.0710)	(0.0686)	(0.0715)	(0.0686)	(0.0709)
No job 6 yrs. ago						−0.322***
						(0.0708)
Year of birth						
1940–42	0.00466	−0.00237	−0.0113	−0.0000308	−0.00691	−0.00659
	(0.0253)	(0.0255)	(0.0243)	(0.0255)	(0.0243)	(0.0182)
1943–45	−0.000282	−0.00518	−0.00894	0.000100	−0.0000508	−0.00147
	(0.0281)	(0.0281)	(0.0271)	(0.0280)	(0.0270)	(0.0210)
1946–48	0.00712	0.00303	0.00475	0.00565	0.0116	0.000706
	(0.0285)	(0.0285)	(0.0270)	(0.0286)	(0.0271)	(0.0213)
1949–51	0.0153	0.00815	0.0102	0.0157	0.0210	0.00376
	(0.0290)	(0.0291)	(0.0282)	(0.0289)	(0.0280)	(0.0224)
High school grad.	0.0859*	0.0865*	0.0342	0.0799**	0.0304	0.0549*
	(0.0326)	(0.0325)	(0.0329)	(0.0325)	(0.0329)	(0.0199)
Some college	0.145***	0.138***	0.0682**	0.130***	0.0632	0.0972***
	(0.0335)	(0.0335)	(0.0340)	(0.0339)	(0.0341)	(0.0217)
BA	0.164***	0.153***	0.0594	0.143***	0.0550	0.119***
	(0.0377)	(0.0378)	(0.0385)	(0.0384)	(0.0389)	(0.0273)
MA	0.218***	0.210***	0.118*	0.198***	0.112*	0.171***
	(0.0384)	(0.0381)	(0.0390)	(0.0392)	(0.0397)	(0.0296)
Life cycle LFP 35–44			0.0456		0.0165	
			(0.0265)		(0.0271)	

(continued)

Table 1.5 (continued)

| | Labor force participation at ages fifty-nine to sixty-three | | | | | |
| | Worked six years ago | | | | | All |
	(1)	(2)	(3)	(4)	(5)	(6)
(ln) Earnings				−0.00252	−0.00558	
				(0.00966)	(0.00932)	
Health status	No	No	Yes	No	Yes	No
Age dummies	Yes	Yes	Yes	Yes	Yes	Yes
Race dummies	Yes	Yes	Yes	Yes	Yes	Yes
Marital status dummies	No	No	Yes	No	Yes	No
Job status of husband	No	No	Yes	No	Yes	No
Constant	0.560***	0.385***	0.293**	0.0942	0.0785	0.450***
	(0.0652)	(0.0936)	(0.0991)	(0.136)	(0.136)	(0.0794)
N	5,050	5,050	5,050	5,050	5,050	7,736
R-squared	0.032	0.041	0.104	0.051	0.112	0.288

Sources: Health and Retirement Study (HRS) 1992 to 2012, RAND version with added variables from original HRS files. Social Security Administration earnings (and W-2) data are used to calculate life cycle labor force participation (Life cycle LFP <ages>).

Notes: The dependent variable is 1 if the woman is in the labor force and 0 otherwise. In columns (1) through (5) only those with positive person weights and working six years ago (or who had a missing job-attitude question) are included; column (6) includes those not working. For variables that are identical to those in tables 1.2 to 1.4, see notes to those tables. All columns use the "linked sample." Omitted base group variables are "enjoy job 6 yrs. ago" strongly disagree, 1937–39 birth cohort, below high school graduate, other race, and age fifty-nine. Omitted from the table are the coefficients on dummy variables for various missing variables. These include missing (or zero) hours six years ago and missing earnings six years ago. In addition, the dummy variable for the "other" job attitude category (together with the small fraction of missing observations for that variable) is omitted in the table. "Enjoy job 6 yrs. ago" is from a question asked of respondents with a current job who are asked to express a level of agreement with the question "I really enjoy going to work." Columns (4) and (5) add (ln) hours (hours worked per week in main job) and (ln) annual earnings (sum of wage or salary income plus added pay and earnings from a second job as well as those from professional practice or trade income). Earnings are deflated to 1992 using the CPI. The regressions are weighted by HRS person weights adjusted for sample selection into the linked sample. Standard errors in parentheses have been clustered at the individual level.

***Significant at the 1 percent level.

**Significant at the 5 percent level.

*Significant at the 10 percent level.

the statement and 20 to 22 percentage points between those who strongly disagree and those who agree or strongly agree.[26]

The addition of the job-attitude question results in few changes in the other coefficients. Most important is that the impact of education is about the same, as can be seen by comparing the coefficients for education in columns (1) and (2). Therefore, the impact of job enjoyment adds to the influence on working longer of the type of jobs that more highly educated women have. Self-reported job enjoyment is not the mediating factor for why education matters in women working longer.

The results are not materially altered by the addition of various covariates including current health, marital status, and the fraction of years the woman worked from age thirty-five to forty-four. Also of interest is that the additions of the hours and earnings in the job six years prior have little impact on the attitudinal coefficients. Those who worked longer hours in the past are more likely to work now, and that is in addition to their enjoyment on that job.

The summary finding is that older women have had substantial increases in labor force participation. The inclusion of covariates, such as education and life cycle participation, reduces the pattern of rising cohort effects. But for the college-graduate group, the labor force increase for the most recent cohorts now in their sixties is not reduced by the inclusion of the additional covariates. The most recent cohorts with less than college completion, however, have had smaller increases and these do get extinguished with the expanded set of predetermined covariates (detailed education attainment and earlier labor force participation), although the increase in education within the non-college-graduate group served to increase participation rates.

Another finding of note is that job enjoyment six years earlier has a strong influence on women's later employment. As jobs become less onerous and more enjoyable and as occupations become part of one's identity, women work longer.

1.3   Life Cycle Labor Force Participation

Given the importance of life cycle labor force participation for later work, we now explore how lifetime employment changed across cohorts born from 1931 to 1954.[27] We divide lifetime employment into five quintiles—from 0 to 20 percent of the years under consideration to 80 to 100 percent. Figure 1.7, panel A, shows the percentage in the labor force in the five quintiles

---

26. The fraction agreeing with the statement about enjoying a current job is large, around 60 percent. An additional 25 to 30 percent strongly agreed with the statement. Only about 10 to 15 percent did not agree with the statement and college-graduate women had a somewhat larger fraction who greatly agreed with the statement.

27. For a detailed discussion of life cycle labor force participation, see Goldin and Mitchell (2017).

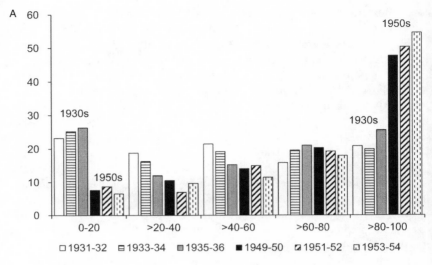

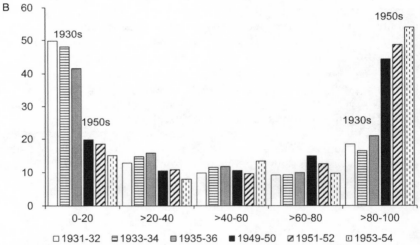

Fig. 1.7   Life cycle labor force participation in the HRS and Social Security earnings data for selected birth cohorts. (A) All women, ages twenty-five to fifty-four. (B) All women, ages twenty-five to thirty-four.

Sources: HRS and Social Security earnings data.

Notes: Figures give the distribution of years spent in the labor force by women in various cohorts and by age group. Labor force participation is defined as having at least one of the following: (a) having SS earnings above (ten hours × fifty-two weeks × minimum wage in that year) in the years prior to the HRS survey of the respondent; (b) responding in the HRS that the person was "in the labor force" when the person has a positive HRS weight; (c) having W-2 earnings above minimum yearly wage in that year; and (d) working for the state, federal, or municipal government in years prior to the HRS survey. The HRS person weights are use-adjusted for sample selection into the linked sample.

covering the thirty years from age twenty-five to fifty-four for all women. Panel B gives these figures for the group in the youngest ten-year grouping, twenty-five to thirty-four years old. To avoid complicating the figure, we show only the earliest and the most recent cohorts: 1931–1936 and 1949–1954 in two-year brackets.

The fraction of women in the labor force 80 to 100 percent of the time when they were twenty-five to fifty-four years old expanded from 20 percent to more than 50 percent across these cohorts (see figure 1.7, panel A). The flip side is the sharp decrease of those who spent fewer than 20 percent of the thirty-year period shown in the labor force. The middle three quintiles changed little in terms of the fraction of the total.

More extreme changes occurred for women in the twenty-five- to thirty-four-year-old group (see figure 1.7, panel B) than for the other ten-year age groups (not shown). Once again, the middle three quintiles show little change. All the change arises because of an increase in the highest and a decrease in the lowest quintiles.

The earliest cohorts shown had life cycle participation rates that were almost uniformly distributed across the quintiles. But by the 1949 to 1954 cohorts, about 50 percent were in the labor force for more than 80 percent of the thirty years and few were in the labor force for less than 20 percent of the interval.

To make sense of these life cycle trajectories, the concepts of heterogeneity and homogeneity will be useful.[28] When participation rates for a birth cohort increase with age, all women in the cohort could be working more weeks per year or more women could be entering the labor force. That is, change could be at the intensive or extensive margins (or a combination). The group that exhibits more of the former is termed "homogeneous," since all women are increasing their work level, and the group that exhibits more of the latter is termed "heterogeneous," because only some women increase their participation. The weight of the evidence historically is that most women are "heterogeneous" and that persistence is substantial.

Looking back at the constructed cohort lines in figure 1.5, the most recent cohorts display flat and even somewhat decreasing participation rates over their brief life cycles. That is, participation rates are higher at the lower ages than at the middle. But if most working women persist in the labor force, then the finding that early participation matters significantly implies that the reduction in participation, or the absence of an increase, for the most recent cohorts in their middle years will not matter much for their employment later in life. The key point is that for earlier cohorts, women who entered (or reentered) the labor force in midlife were probably the least persistent.

---

28. See Goldin (1989) and Heckman and Willis (1977) on the concepts of heterogeneity and homogeneity applied to labor force participation over the life cycle. Olivetti (2006) models an underlying reason for greater persistence in the returns to experience and demonstrates the increased returns from the 1970s to the 1990s.

1.4   Working Women, Working Couples

The regressions revealed a commonly known relationship that couples generally work together and enjoy leisure and consumption together. Currently married women are far more likely to be in the labor force in their older years if their husbands are also working. In the table 1.2, column (6) regression, married women with a working spouse are 20 percentage points more likely to be in the labor force than are other married women.

Figure 1.8 demonstrates two additional points. The data use three categories of women fifty-nine to sixty-three years old: those currently married with a husband working, those currently married with a nonworking husband, and those not currently married. Participation rates of all currently married women rose relative to the third group. In addition, the rates for currently married women with a working spouse increased the most.

A greater fraction of married couples today are both working rather than being retired together, whereas twenty years ago a greater percentage was retired together.[29] For married couples in which the wife was born from 1931 to 1936, 34 percent were both retired and 25 percent were both working when she was fifty-nine to sixty-three years old. Those fractions have changed to just 22 percent retired together for the most recent cohorts (1949 to 1951 birth years) and 41 percent both working. Furthermore, in the most recent cohorts an almost equal fraction had the wife working and the husband not working (18 percent) as had the husband working and the wife not working (19 percent).

1.5   Concluding Remarks

We have explored the increase in the labor force participation of older women. Our main findings and conclusions regarding "women working longer" are

- Increased participation of women from their late fifties and beyond began in the late 1980s, before the rise in older men's labor force participation and long before the economic downturns of the first decade of the twenty-first century, especially the Great Recession.
- The increases have been large. Among women sixty to sixty-four years old, participation increased from 34 to 51 percent during the last twenty-five years and from 45 to 61 percent for college graduates.
- Increased labor force participation of older women has been disproportionately for those working full time and full year.

---

29. These findings are consistent with the complementarity of the leisure time of older husbands and wives. Schirle (2008) demonstrates, for three countries, that the increase in women's labor force participation at older ages has led to increased men's participation (see also Blau 1998).

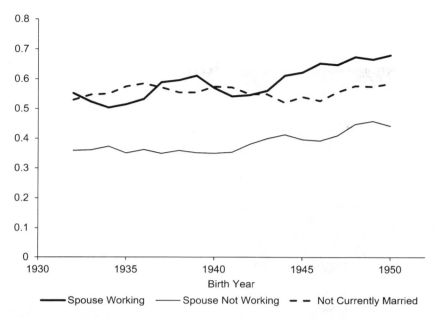

Fig. 1.8   Labor force participation by year of birth, current marital status, and husband's employment for women ages fifty-nine to sixty-three
Source: HRS
Notes: All women ages fifty-nine to sixty-three are included; HRS person weights applied.

- Women who worked more when young, work more when they are older.
- Women are working longer not mainly because of an insufficiency in retirement savings, although that is an important issue for many in recent years. Better health is a mediating factor; those with low wealth are far more often in worse physical condition.
- A greater fraction of married couples are now working together rather than being retired together, whereas twenty years ago a greater fraction of couples were both retired.
- Women who enjoyed their jobs six to eight years before their sixties are far more likely to remain employed.

What about the future of women working longer? The two-decade stagnation of participation rates for women in their thirties and forties could indicate that increases at later ages will not continue. But the stagnation may not impact working longer because there have been upticks for cohorts in their forties and there is an increased fraction of the population who are college graduates. The cohort effect for college graduates in the most recent birth cohort that can be explored, that from 1949 to 1951, remains large and statistically significant even after controlling for earlier labor force participation. The current challenge is to understand how the various factors included in our analysis are likely to impact the labor force participation of current cohorts as they age.

Appendix

Health and Retirement Study: General Comments

The Health and Retirement Study (known as the HRS and as the University of Michigan Health and Retirement Study) is a widely used data set. (More information can be found at http://hrsonline.isr.umich.edu/ and in the volume appendix on the HRS.)

Health and Retirement Study: Construction of Variables

Life Cycle Labor Force Participation

Life cycle labor force participation is intended to measure the fraction of a period during which the individual was in the labor force. The time period we consider is from twenty-five to fifty-four years, and we subdivide that into three decades. We primarily use the information from the Social Security earnings records (and the W-2 forms after 1977) to figure out whether an individual was employed during a year. We can do this only for individuals who gave permission to the HRS to link their survey to their Social Security earnings records. On average, 80 percent of the sample agree to this linkage.

In general, we define someone as a labor force participant if during a year their annual earnings were at least equal to the federal minimum wage in that year times ten hours times fifty-two weeks. Complications arise because some individuals were exempt from the Social Security earnings tax. These exempt employees were generally government workers and for our sample of women, teachers would have been an important exempt category. During the initial interview the HRS asked whether the individual had been employed by the government (including municipal, state, and federal government positions) and if that was the case, the person could list two periods of employment. We count the individual in the labor force if the person did not pay the Social Security earnings tax in some year but stated that their employment was in the government for that period. It should be noted that when the W-2 forms become available, there is no problem with exempt status since the forms include all W-2 income. In addition, some HRS respondents were surveyed when they were in their early fifties and we use the HRS survey data when it exists. Thus we determine labor force status on the basis of various pieces of information including the HRS survey, the Social Security earnings records, and the W-2 forms.

Career Condition Variable

Similar to the construction of the life cycle labor force variable, we create a "career condition" variable that assesses whether individuals who were in the labor force earned above some amount. The amount is given by some fraction (we have used both 0.5 and 0.75) of the median annual wage of a (full-time, full-year) male worker in the given year. Because the period we are considering predates the microdata for the CPS, we use the published surveys to obtain the male median annual wage. In our empirical work we define the career condition between ages thirty-five and forty-four years ("Career cond. 35–44") as the fraction of years in the age interval the individual exceeded 50 percent of the earnings of the median male full-time, full-year worker.

Earnings data for this calculation are obtained primarily from the Social Security earnings records, the W-2 forms when available, and the HRS earnings data when it exists for the individual. If the individual was in a tax-exempt employment (and did not have W-2 or HRS earnings data), we assume that the income was sufficient to exceed the given "career condition."

Social Security Earnings Record Linkage in the HRS

The fraction of female HRS respondents who agreed at some point to the linkage of their HRS study to their Social Security earnings record is high. Just around 11 percent are not linked from the 1931 to 1942 birth cohorts. The fraction increases to 15 percent for 1943 to 1945 and then to 21 percent for 1946 to 1948. The high rate of nonlinkage for the 1950s cohorts is probably because they have had fewer years to agree to have their records linked since respondents are asked during each wave. The fraction not linked will probably fall during the next waves of the HRS as more respondents agree to the linkage.

Individuals who did not agree to the linkage do not differ based on educational attainment and current marital status with those who did agree. The main determinant of linkage is the number of years the individual has been in the data set and, therefore, how many times the individual has been asked permission for the linkage.

Comparisons of the HRS and the CPS

Labor Force Participation Rates

The HRS closely tracks the labor force participation rates given by the CPS for the same age groups and birth cohorts. The only major differences occur for those sixty-five years and older. The HRS labor force data are always greater than the CPS data in every year from 1992 to 2010 for these age groups, but are not for the younger groupings. The precise reason is unclear. One possibility is that the CPS does a better job interviewing individuals in group quarters.

Marital Status and Education

Both the HRS marital status and education variables track the CPS well for individuals fifty-one to fifty-six years old. Cohorts born from 1935 to 1952 are given in appendix tables 1A.2 and 1A.3. The HRS samples are fairly small and are subject to considerable sampling error. It should be noted that the education distributions for fifty-one- to fifty-six-year-old women differ from those for younger women in the same birth cohorts due to a common phenomenon that individuals gain education, for real or fictitious reasons, as they age.

The HRS contains a potential complication because some people did not list a degree and their highest degree was inferred. According to the RAND HRS Codebook (Chien et al. 2015, 132–33): "The highest degree is assigned by looking at reports from Tracker and all waves of data. The first non-missing value is used." When the actual degree is missing, it is imputed and a bachelor's degree is given to those with RAEDYRS = 16 or 17. Interestingly, the HRS and the CPS data for the same age groups and birth cohorts is remarkably similar.

Children Ever Born

The information on children ever born in the HRS differs in various ways from that in the CPS June Fertility Supplements. But the mean number of children for the same cohorts in each of the two sources is not much different. It appears that the main difference is that the fraction of women who report no births in the HRS is lower than reported in the CPS. For example, for women with a college degree born from 1947 to 1951 the fraction with zero births in the HRS (all of the respondents are older than forty-four years) is 19 percent. But in the CPS the fraction with zero births at forty to forty-four years old is about 25 percent. For women with less than a college degree, the fraction with no births in the HRS for those born for 1947 to 1951 is 10 percent but is 13 percent in the CPS June Fertility Supplements.

Even though HRS respondents report a lower fraction with no birth, the mean number of children ever born, as given in appendix figure 1A.2, is similar to that given in the CPS June Fertility Supplements. The HRS number is almost always slightly higher, especially for cohorts from after 1945.

One possibility is that women in the HRS are also including adopted and stepchildren. That possibility has been explored and does not appear to be the source of the difference.

| Table 1A.1 | Fraction of female HRS respondents linked to Social Security earnings records by birth cohort |

Birth years	Fraction linked
1931–33	0.886
1934–36	0.888
1937–39	0.868
1940–42	0.893
1943–45	0.852
1946–48	0.790
1949–51	0.714
1952–54	0.682

Source: HRS, restricted-access data.

Note: Person weights used. Linkage uses HRS to 2012.

Table 1A.2   Comparing marital status for the HRS and CPS: Women ages fifty-one to fifty-six

	Fraction currently married			Fraction ever married but not currently married			Fraction never married		
Year of birth	HRS-SS	Full HRS	CPS	HRS-SS	Full HRS	CPS	HRS-SS	Full HRS	CPS
1931–32	—	—	0.730	—	—	0.230	—	—	0.040
1933–34	—	—	0.731	—	—	0.225	—	—	0.044
1935–36	0.737	0.730	0.716	0.236	0.246	0.237	0.026	0.024	0.047
1937–38	0.741	0.730	0.712	0.230	0.240	0.244	0.029	0.029	0.044
1939–40	0.739	0.734	0.704	0.214	0.222	0.244	0.047	0.043	0.051
1941–42	0.641	0.647	0.684	0.330	0.322	0.262	0.030	0.030	0.054
1943–44	0.552	0.537	0.678	0.378	0.387	0.273	0.070	0.075	0.049
1945–46	0.716	0.731	0.683	0.229	0.221	0.259	0.054	0.047	0.058
1947–48	0.647	0.643	0.669	0.302	0.305	0.269	0.052	0.052	0.063
1949–50	0.628	0.604	0.666	0.314	0.328	0.259	0.058	0.067	0.075
1951–52	0.676	0.684	0.661	0.266	0.266	0.261	0.058	0.049	0.078

Sources: HRS, restricted-access data for HRS-SS columns; CPS.

Notes: The HRS-SS columns refer to the sample linked to the Social Security Administration earnings data. The number of observations for the HRS sample is about 500 for the 1949–50 and 1951–52 birth cohorts and 1,000 for the 1937–38 and 1939–40 cohorts. Missing values (—) indicate lack of coverage using the particular HRS cohorts.

Table 1A.3   Comparing education for the HRS and CPS: Women ages fifty-one to fifty-six

Year of birth	Fraction college education and above			Fraction some college			Fraction high school diploma			Fraction less than a high school diploma		
	HRS-SS	Full HRS	CPS	HRS-SS	Full HRS	CPS	HRS-SS	Full HRS	CPS	HRS-SS	Full HRS	CPS
1931–32	—	—	0.121	—	—	0.146	—	—	0.450	—	—	0.282
1933–34	—	—	0.127	—	—	0.161	—	—	0.454	—	—	0.258
1935–36	0.150	0.145	0.143	0.183	0.191	0.174	0.453	0.435	0.432	0.214	0.229	0.251
1937–38	0.129	0.125	0.157	0.172	0.176	0.181	0.445	0.454	0.443	0.254	0.245	0.219
1939–40	0.176	0.171	0.172	0.225	0.224	0.206	0.376	0.379	0.431	0.222	0.226	0.191
1941–42	0.186	0.181	0.190	0.275	0.269	0.231	0.345	0.349	0.405	0.194	0.200	0.174
1943–44	0.254	0.251	0.211	0.214	0.217	0.245	0.369	0.378	0.395	0.163	0.155	0.148
1945–46	0.246	0.236	0.240	0.276	0.273	0.245	0.327	0.338	0.379	0.150	0.153	0.137
1947–48	0.197	0.227	0.265	0.334	0.304	0.272	0.360	0.371	0.358	0.109	0.098	0.105
1949–50	0.305	0.298	0.277	0.263	0.280	0.276	0.325	0.317	0.346	0.108	0.105	0.101
1951–52	0.295	0.288	0.296	0.275	0.282	0.288	0.339	0.333	0.315	0.091	0.097	0.102

Sources: HRS, restricted-access data for HRS-SS columns. CPS-ASEC microdata, March 1963 to 2014.

Note: The HRS-SS columns refer to the sample linked to the Social Security Administration earnings data.

Table 1A.4   Full-time participation for women at ages fifty-nine to sixty-three, by education: HRS

	Not college graduate (1)	College graduate (2)	Not college graduate (3)	College graduate (4)	Not college graduate (5)	College graduate (6)
Year of birth						
1934–36	−0.0340	0.0423	−0.0364**	0.0465	−0.0375**	0.0463
	(0.0192)	(0.0524)	(0.0183)	(0.0516)	(0.0177)	(0.0481)
1937–39	0.000660	0.0151	−0.0179	0.0205	−0.0102	0.0111
	(0.0196)	(0.0524)	(0.0190)	(0.0521)	(0.0184)	(0.0487)
1940–42	−0.00476	0.0349	−0.0343	0.0120	−0.0313	0.00402
	(0.0209)	(0.0523)	(0.0202)	(0.0518)	(0.0198)	(0.0481)
1943–45	−0.00972	0.0168	−0.0448	−0.0238	−0.0364	−0.0265
	(0.0242)	(0.0532)	(0.0235)	(0.0552)	(0.0232)	(0.0523)
1946–48	0.00969	0.0360	−0.0329	−0.0128	−0.0246	−0.00276
	(0.0250)	(0.0501)	(0.0240)	(0.0499)	(0.0233)	(0.0476)
1949–51	0.00881	0.120**	−0.0347	0.0860	−0.0231	0.0853
	(0.0285)	(0.0521)	(0.0279)	(0.0506)	(0.0273)	(0.0479)
High school grad.	0.107***		0.0659***		0.0276	
	(0.0151)		(0.0149)		(0.0149)	
Some college	0.177***		0.124***		0.0677***	
	(0.0187)		(0.0184)		(0.0183)	
MA		0.0810**		0.0706**		0.0612
		(0.0336)		(0.0332)		(0.0322)
PhD, MD, JD, etc.		0.190*		0.146**		0.118
		(0.0670)		(0.0677)		(0.0640)
Life cycle LFP 35–44			0.240***	0.139**	0.225***	0.127**
			(0.0247)	(0.0584)	(0.0240)	(0.0610)
Never in LF 35–44			−0.00226	−0.152**	−0.00113	−0.156**
			(0.0211)	(0.0660)	(0.0206)	(0.0639)

	(1)	(2)	(3)	(4)	(5)	(6)
Currently married					-0.110*	-0.258***
					(0.0397)	(0.0703)
Divorced					0.0322	0.0736
					(0.0414)	(0.0746)
Widow					-0.0118	-0.0473
					(0.0406)	(0.0784)
Spouse in LF					0.0688***	0.158***
					(0.0149)	(0.0357)
Health status	No	No	No	No	Yes	Yes
Age dummies	Yes	Yes	Yes	Yes	Yes	Yes
Race dummies	Yes	Yes	Yes	Yes	Yes	Yes
Constant	0.177***	0.653***	0.114*	0.593***	0.0776	0.505***
	(0.0326)	(0.0849)	(0.0373)	(0.0931)	(0.0477)	(0.120)
N	12,789	2,642	12,789	2,642	12,789	2,642
R-squared	0.043	0.052	0.084	0.079	0.125	0.134

Sources: Health and Retirement Study (HRS) 1992 to 2012, RAND version with added variables from original HRS files. Social Security Administration earnings (and W-2) data are used to calculate life cycle labor force participation (Life cycle LFP <ages>).

Notes: The dependent variable is 1 if the woman is in the labor force full time and 0 otherwise. A woman is in the labor force full time if she reported being employed for thirty-five or more hours per week. Health status is self-reported and is coded as 1 if "good" or better and 0 otherwise. Marital status variables refer to current status. "Life cycle LFP <ages>" is the fraction of the interval the woman was in the labor force as determined by a combination of the data sources described in the appendix. "Never in LF" is 1 if the individual was recorded as having no years in the labor force during those years. All columns use the "linked sample." Omitted base group variables are 1931–33 birth cohort, below high school graduate (overall or for the less-than-college-graduate group), BA only for the college-graduate group, never married, other race, and age fifty-nine. Omitted from the table are dummy variables for missing variables regarding spouse in labor force and health status. Regressions are estimated separately for college graduates and those who did not graduate from college. College-graduate degrees beyond a bachelor's are added (MA, PhD, etc.), where MA includes all master's degrees and PhD, MD, JD, and so forth includes all graduate and professional degrees. For those who did not graduate from college, dummy variables are added for those with a high school diploma and some college. The regressions are weighted by HRS person weights adjusted for sample selection into the linked sample. Standard errors in parentheses have been clustered at the individual level.

***Significant at the 1 percent level.

**Significant at the 5 percent level.

*Significant at the 10 percent level.

Table 1A.5   Female labor force participation at ages fifty-six to fifty-eight, by education: HRS

	Not college graduate (1)	College graduate (2)	Not college graduate (3)	College graduate (4)	Not college graduate (5)	College graduate (6)
Year of birth						
1937–39	0.00933	0.0128	−0.0184	0.0170	−0.0141	0.0120
	(0.0238)	(0.0552)	(0.0225)	(0.0531)	(0.0214)	(0.0509)
1940–42	0.0558**	−0.0112	0.0120	−0.0311	0.0257	−0.0248
	(0.0245)	(0.0519)	(0.0227)	(0.0491)	(0.0221)	(0.0454)
1943–45	0.0170	0.0504	−0.0419	0.00718	−0.0334	0.00633
	(0.0296)	(0.0529)	(0.0281)	(0.0516)	(0.0272)	(0.0505)
1946–48	0.00282	0.0269	−0.0607**	−0.0217	−0.0348	−0.0139
	(0.0283)	(0.0529)	(0.0267)	(0.0507)	(0.0259)	(0.0483)
1949–51	0.0357	0.0763	−0.0296	0.0324	0.00586	0.0309
	(0.0301)	(0.0486)	(0.0289)	(0.0482)	(0.0274)	(0.0460)
1952–54	0.00537	0.110**	−0.0599	0.0516	−0.0219	0.0484
	(0.0326)	(0.0510)	(0.0316)	(0.0500)	(0.0286)	(0.0498)
High school grad.	0.212***		0.144***		0.0719***	
	(0.0223)		(0.0220)		(0.0216)	
Some college	0.266***		0.188***		0.0999***	
	(0.0247)		(0.0249)		(0.0239)	
MA		0.0227		0.0137		0.0189
		(0.0310)		(0.0305)		(0.0287)
PhD, MD, JD, etc.		0.109**		0.0751		0.0517
		(0.0456)		(0.0454)		(0.0446)
Life cycle LFP 35–44			0.302***	0.0818	0.280***	0.0430
			(0.0315)	(0.0565)	(0.0297)	(0.0674)
Never in LF 35–44			−0.0711**	−0.258*	−0.0721**	−0.275***
			(0.0321)	(0.0802)	(0.0303)	(0.0820)
Currently married					−0.104**	−0.276***
					(0.0525)	(0.0696)

Divorced					0.0796	0.0120
					(0.0531)	(0.0457)
Widow					0.0313	−0.0132
					(0.0540)	(0.0592)
Spouse in LF					0.168***	0.200***
					(0.0207)	(0.0578)
Health status	No	No	No	Yes	Yes	Yes
Age dummies	Yes	Yes	Yes	Yes	Yes	Yes
Race dummies	Yes	Yes	Yes	Yes	Yes	Yes
Constant	0.341***	0.662***	0.302***	0.672***	0.149**	0.612***
	(0.0449)	(0.123)	(0.0484)	(0.124)	(0.0663)	(0.124)
N	7,354	1,649	7,354	1,649	7,354	1,649
R-squared	0.049	0.022	0.123	0.060	0.199	0.130

Sources: Health and Retirement Study (HRS) 1992 to 2012, RAND version with added variables from original HRS files. Social Security Administration earnings (and W-2) data are used to calculate life cycle labor force participation (Life cycle LFP <ages>).

Notes: The dependent variable is 1 if the woman is in the labor force and 0 otherwise. The HRS asks respondents their labor force status and a woman is in the labor force if she reported being employed or unemployed and searching for work. Health status is self-reported and is coded as 1 if "good" or better and 0 otherwise. Marital status variables refer to current status. "Life cycle LFP <ages>" is the fraction of the interval the woman was in the labor force as determined by a combination of the data sources described in the appendix. "Never in LF" is 1 if the individual was recorded as having no years in the labor force during those years. All columns use the "linked sample." Omitted base group variables are 1934–36 birth cohort, below high school graduate (overall or for the less-than-college-graduate group), BA only for the college-graduate group, never married, other race, and age fifty-six. Omitted from the table are dummy variables for missing variables regarding spouse in labor force and health status. Regressions are estimated separately for college graduates and those who did not graduate from college. College-graduate degrees beyond a bachelor's are added (MA, PhD, etc.), where MA includes all master's degrees and PhD, MD, JD, and so forth includes all graduate and professional degrees. For those who did not graduate from college, dummy variables are added for those with a high school diploma and some college. The regressions are weighted by the HRS person weights adjusted for sample selection into the linked sample. Standard errors in parentheses have been clustered at the individual level.

***Significant at the 1 percent level.

**Significant at the 5 percent level.

*Significant at the 10 percent level.

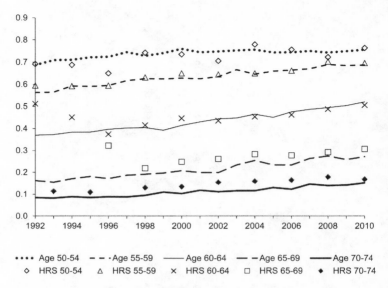

Fig. 1A.1 Comparing labor force participation for the HRS and the CPS: Women ages fifty to fifty-four and seventy to seventy-four

Sources: CPS-ASEC microdata, March 1963 to 2014; HRS.

Notes: The HRS is a biennial survey. Some age groups are not shown for the HRS because the group is incomplete and the participation rate would be biased since it would omit some of the older ages in the group.

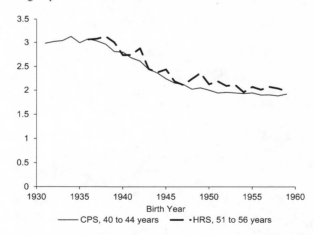

Fig. 1A.2 Children ever born for women ages fifty-one to fifty-six in HRS and forty to forty-four in CPS in birth cohorts 1936 to 1951

Sources: CPS June Fertility Supplements, microdata (1973 to 2014); HRS.

Notes: HRS person weights are used; no weights are used for the CPS. Children ever born is truncated below ten in both samples. In both data sets, the variable is supposed to give the number of children ever born to the respondent and not the number of live children or adopted or stepchildren.

References

Blau, David M. 1998. "Labor Force Dynamics of Older Married Couples." *Journal of Labor Economics* 16 (3): 595–629.

Chien, Sandy, Nancy Campbell, Chris Chan, Orla Hayden, Michael Hurd, Regan Main, Joshua Mallett, et al. 2015. *HRS Data Documentation, Version O.* Labor and Population Program. October. Santa Monica, CA: RAND. http://hrsonline.isr.umich.edu/modules/meta/rand/randhrso/randhrs_O.pdf.

Gelber, Alexander M., Damon Jones, and Daniel W. Sacks. 2016 "Earnings Adjustment Frictions: Evidence from the Social Security Earnings Test." Working Paper. August. https://dansacks.files.wordpress.com/2015/08/adjustment081716.pdf.

Goldin, Claudia. 1989. "Life-Cycle Labor-Force Participation of Married Women: Historical Evidence and Implications." *Journal of Labor Economics* 7 (1) January:20–47.

———. 1997. "Career and Family: College Women Look to the Past." In *Gender and Family Issues in the Workplace*, edited by F. Blau and R. Ehrenberg, 20–58. New York: Russell Sage Press.

Goldin, Claudia, and Joshua Mitchell. 2017. "The New Lifecycle of Women's Employment: Disappearing Humps, Sagging Middles, Expanding Tops." *Journal of Economic Perspectives* 31 (Winter): 161–82.

Gustman, Alan, and Thomas Steinmeier. 2009. "How Changes in Social Security Affect Recent Retirement Trends." *Research on Aging* 31 (2): 261–90.

Heckman, James J., and Robert J. Willis. 1977. "A Beta-Logistic Model for the Analysis of Sequential Labor Force Participation by Married Women." *Journal of Political Economy* 85 (February): 27–58.

Hurd, Michael, and Susann Rohwedder. 2014. "Predicting Labor Force Participation of the Older Population." Discussion Paper no. 14-011, Stanford Institute for Economic Policy Research.

Lumsdaine, Robin L., and Stephanie J. C. Vermeer. 2015. "Retirement Timing of Women and the Role of Care Responsibilities for Grandchildren." *Demography* 52 (2): 433–54.

Maestas, Nicole. 2010. "Back to Work: Expectations and Realizations of Work after Retirement." *Journal of Human Resources* 45 (3): 718–48.

Maestas, Nicole, and Julie Zissimopoulos. 2010. "How Longer Working Lives Ease the Crunch of Population Aging." *Journal of Economic Perspectives* 24 (1): 139–60.

Mastrobuoni, Giovanni. 2009. "Labor Supply Effects of the Recent Social Security Benefit Cuts: Empirical Estimates Using Cohort Discontinuities." *Journal of Public Economics* 93:1224–33.

Olivetti, Claudia. 2006. "Changes in Women's Hours of Market Work: The Role of Returns to Experience." *Review of Economic Dynamics* 9 (4): 557–87.

Schirle, Tammy. 2008. "Why Have the Labor Force Participation Rates of Older Men Increased since the Mid-1990s?" *Journal of Labor Economics* 26 (4): 249–94.

US Department of Education. 2015. *Digest of Education Statistics.* https://nces.ed.gov/programs/digest/d15/tables/dt15_104.20.asp.

2

The Return to Work and Women's Employment Decisions

Nicole Maestas

Husbands and wives tend to retire around the same time within couples. But because women tend to marry men older than they, the joint retirement of married couples means that married women retire at younger ages than their husbands do. This difference in age at retirement seems counterintuitive since women have longer life expectancies and have shorter careers due to delayed or interrupted labor force participation while raising children.[1] Thus, they should optimally retire at *older* ages than men.

The observation that husbands and wives tend to retire at the same time, even when they greatly differ in age, has been noted in several different data sets for the United States and across different cohorts (e.g., Blau 1998; Coile 2004; Gustman and Steinmeier 2000, 2004, 2014; Hurd 1990; Maestas 2001; Michaud and Vermeulen 2011; Schirle 2008). Evidence of coordinated retirement behavior has also been documented in Canada (Baker 2002; Schirle 2008), in England (Banks, Blundell, and Casanova Rivas 2010; Schirle 2008), and in continental Europe (Honoré and de Paula 2015).

Certainly, some degree of retirement coordination between married

Nicole Maestas is associate professor of health care policy at Harvard Medical School and a research associate of the National Bureau of Economic Research.

This chapter was presented at the NBER Women Working Longer Conference, May 21–22, 2016, Cambridge, MA. I thank my discussant Claudia Olivetti and the other conference participants for their valuable comments, and especially Claudia Goldin and Larry Katz for general guidance as well as detailed feedback. Cate Yoon and Kevin Friedman provided expert research. I gratefully acknowledge support from NIH/NIA grant no. R03AG023108 and the Alfred P. Sloan Foundation. For acknowledgments, sources of research support, and disclosure of the author's material financial relationships, if any, please see http://www.nber.org/chapters /c13799.ack.

1. The female-male difference in life expectancy conditional upon living to age sixty-five is about three years (Arias 2002), plus women are on average two to three years younger than their husbands, depending on birth cohort.

partners is expected, if for no other reason than because husbands and wives share a budget set. For example, married women with greater wealth might individually choose to consume more leisure by retiring earlier, and so might their husbands, who share the same assets. Married couples may also have similar, or even directly linked, pension incentives (e.g., Social Security spousal benefits) that make possible retirement around the same time. Nonetheless, the dominant explanation for joint retirement may not even arise through the budget set, but through common preferences for joint leisure (Gustman and Steinmeier 2000, 2004; Maestas 2001; Michaud and Vermeulen 2011). In other words, spouses value each other's company and leisure complementarity leads them to retire around the same time.

Despite the utility benefits of joint leisure, the relatively younger retirement of married women may be costly for at least two reasons. First, with delayed or discontinuous labor force participation, married women may experience their peak earnings years just as they retire. Their husbands, on the other hand, may be past their peak earnings years, both on account of being older and having had relatively continuous labor force participation. As such, married women may forgo earnings opportunities that could both increase their Social Security benefit entitlements[2] and increase private household net worth[3] through additional saving. Second, married women tend to retire before age sixty-five, when they would be eligible for Medicare, and they therefore face the additional cost of purchasing health insurance from the time they retire until they turn sixty-five. Even those with employer-subsidized retiree health benefits may face significantly greater costs for health insurance before age sixty-five than after. Unless married couples compensate by increasing other assets, women's younger retirement may result in lower resources during the couples' remaining life together, and during any subsequent divorce or widowhood.

We know significantly less about the retirement behavior of women than we do about men, and virtually no research attention has been devoted to considering the implications of the fact that women retire at younger ages than men do. Even if married men fully compensate for the relatively younger retirement of their wives by working longer than they otherwise would, or if the Social Security benefit formulas fully compensate women through spousal and survivor benefits, married women may nevertheless forgo the opportunity to accrue significant pension assets in their own names. Theories of household decision making posit that asset and income ownership determines control over household consumption (see, e.g., Browning and Chiappori 1998; Lundberg and Pollak 1993; Maestas 2001). It is thus

---

2. See Gelber, Isen, and Song (chapter 8, this volume) for an analysis of the reverse pathway—how Social Security income affects women's labor supply at older ages.
3. See Lusardi and Mitchell (chapter 6, this volume) for an analysis of household net worth and women's labor supply.

plausible that owning assets may give older women greater control over their allocation between the couple's joint lifetime and her expected years of survivorship.

I investigate the shape of the age-earnings profile for middle-aged and older married women to assess whether the return to continued work is larger for married women than for married men. Using the Health and Retirement Study (HRS), I document the changing patterns of employment at older ages among married women and married men, and establish the cross-spouse correlation in baseline work intentions and the likelihood of early retirement. I then estimate the shape of the age-earnings profile for married women, as compared to married men. Finally, I examine how continued work would affect the individual Social Security wealth of married women compared with married men, as well as the household-level Social Security wealth (which additionally accounts for the expected present value of spouse and survivor benefit entitlements).

Five key findings emerge from this study. First, preferences for joint leisure persist among married women and men in recent cohorts, suggesting that the trade-off between the potential return to continued work and preferences for joint leisure continues to be salient for couples. Second, married women in the boomer cohorts enter their fifties earning substantially more than their predecessors, and the growth across cohorts has been three times as great for married women than for married men. Third, estimates of the shapes of the age-earnings profiles indicate that the return to additional years of work is relatively larger for married women than for married men. Fourth, working until age seventy, that is, beyond the Social Security early and full retirement ages, would make a sizable increase in the magnitude of lifetime Social Security benefits to which married women are entitled. The gain in years worked at older ages would be sufficient to offset early gaps in their earnings records and would place women on par with men in terms of lifetime benefits. Finally, I find that individuals with the largest potential gains in Social Security wealth are just as likely to retire early as those with the least to gain. This suggests that individuals do not factor these potential gains into their employment decisions, and it raises the question of whether individuals are able to correctly assess the opportunity costs associated with reducing work effort before age seventy.

2.1   Data and Summary Statistics

2.1.1   Data

I use the 1992 to 2012 waves of the nationally representative Health and Retirement Study (HRS).[4] The cohort structure of the HRS allows one

---

4. For additional details, see the volume appendix on the HRS.

to compare cohorts at the same ages but across different years. I use the four birth cohort groups that enter the survey at ages fifty-one to fifty-six. The original HRS cohort (b. 1931 to 1941) entered the survey in 1992 at ages fifty-one to sixty-one, and has been observed in biennial interviews for twenty years. For age comparability with the other HRS cohorts, I use the younger members who were ages fifty-one to fifty-six in 1992 and label this group the HRS-Late cohort (b. 1936 to 1941). The War Babies cohort (b. 1942 to 1947) entered the survey in 1998 at ages fifty-one to fifty-six and has been observed for fourteen years. The Early Baby Boom (b. 1948 to 1953) entered at ages fifty-one to fifty-six in 2004 and has been observed for eight years, and the Mid-Baby Boom (b. 1954 to 1959) entered at ages fifty-one to fifty-six in 2010 and has been observed for two years. To increase statistical precision, I group the two "early cohorts" (HRS-Late and War Babies) and contrast them with the two "boomer cohorts" (Early Baby Boom and Mid-Baby Boom).

In the analyses that follow, I compare employment and earnings outcomes for married women and married men, by cohort. The HRS enrolls age-eligible respondents and their spouses. Some spouses are themselves age eligible for a cohort and are enrolled as primary respondents. As a result of this recruitment structure, in any contrast between married women and married men, most of the married women and men (though not all) are married to each other. I assign each respondent their marital status as of the baseline survey wave; that is, as of ages fifty-one to fifty-six. I use the RAND HRS Data, Version O (Chien et al. 2015).

2.1.2   Summary Statistics: Demographics and Labor Supply at Baseline

Table 2.1 presents cross-sectional summary statistics for married women and married men in the early cohorts compared to the boomer cohorts. As intended given the cohort structure of the analysis sample, the average age of respondents in each group is fifty-three years old. In line with national trends, the percent of married women with a college degree has risen substantially, from 19 percent in the early cohorts to 32 percent in the boomer cohorts. Among married men, the percent with a college degree has risen from 28 percent in the early cohorts to 35 percent in the boomer cohorts. Reflecting demographic trends in the US population, the boomer cohorts are more ethnically diverse than earlier cohorts. The boomer cohorts are slightly more likely to report "fair" or "poor" health than the earlier cohorts, particularly married men. Household wealth (measured as net worth) is substantially greater among the boomers compared to the early cohorts.

Table 2.1 also presents several measures of labor supply, all assessed at the baseline survey wave for each cohort (and therefore holding age constant). The employment rate of married women (at ages fifty-one to fifty-six) has risen from 64 percent in the early cohorts to 68 percent in the boomer cohorts. In contrast, the employment rate of married men (at the same ages)

Table 2.1   **Characteristics of analysis sample**

	Early cohorts		Boomer cohorts	
	Married women (1)	Married men (2)	Married women (3)	Married men (4)
Age at baseline	53.4	53.4	53.5	53.5
College (%)	19.1	28.0	32.0	34.9
White non-Hispanic (%)	84.3	82.9	78.6	76.3
Hispanic (%)	6.8	6.7	9.8	10.2
Black non-Hispanic (%)	6.7	7.3	7.1	8.3
Other race (%)	2.2	3.0	4.4	5.2
Fair/poor health (%)	17.2	16.5	18.6	19.4
Wealth ($)	477,807	415,877	517,085	509,055
Employed (%)	63.6	83.7	68.4	79.2
Lifetime number of years worked	23.25	33.30	24.03	27.79
Earnings at baseline ($)[a]	33,787	66,927	44,220	73,591
Wage at baseline ($/hour)[a]	20.37	30.74	25.75	36.14
Weekly wage at baseline ($)[a]	780	1,434	983	1,636
Hours worked per week[a]	38.2	46.7	38.4	45.8
Weeks worked per year[a]	49.4	50.6	48.8	50.3
Job tenure (years)[a]	11.4	15.1	11.4	13.9
Number of observations	3,385	3,169	2,793	2,677

Source: Health and Retirement Study (HRS) 1992 to 2012, RAND HRS Version O.

Notes: Analysis sample contains married men and women who are age-eligible members of early cohorts (HRS-Late and War Babies) and boomer cohorts (Early Baby Boom and Mid-Baby Boom). Data are structured in cross-sectional format such that units of observation are person-level. All variables measured as of the baseline wave for each cohort. All dollar values reported in 2012 dollars. HRS respondent weights used.

[a] Statistic is conditioned on employment at baseline.

has declined across cohorts, from 84 to 79 percent. The lifetime number of years worked by married women (as of their early fifties) has risen from a mean of twenty-three years in the early cohorts to twenty-four years in the boomer cohorts.[5] The lifetime number of years worked by married men is higher, but has declined by five years—from thirty-three years (early cohorts) to twenty-eight years (boomer cohorts). Baseline annual earnings (conditional on either full- or part-time employment and expressed in real 2012 dollars) are 31 percent higher among the boomer women ($44,220)

5. The lifetime number of years worked was constructed by the RAND HRS from a series of questions recording respondents' self-reported labor force history (Chien et al. 2015). The slight increase in mean years of work masks pronounced changes at the tails of the distribution. Goldin and Katz (chapter 1, this volume, figures 1.7 and 1.8) show that the share of women in the labor force 80 to 100 percent of the time when they were ages twenty-five to fifty-four rose from 20 percent to more than 50 percent across cohorts, while the fraction in the labor force only 20 percent of the time or less declined.

compared to married women in earlier cohorts ($33,787). This compares with cross-cohort growth in annual earnings of 10 percent among boomer men ($73,591) compared to married men in earlier cohorts ($66,927). The implied hourly wage grew by similar percentages across the cohort groups (26 percent for married women and 18 percent for married men), while hours worked per week and weeks worked per year were the same for both women and men. Thus, the earnings growth across cohorts appears to reflect a change in real wages for married women—perhaps as more of them have attained a college degree—and not simply growth in hours worked. Nor does it appear to reflect longer tenure in the job held at baseline. Mean job tenure for married women at baseline was 11.4 years in both the early and boomer cohorts. Mean job tenure among married men at the same ages fell by one year across cohorts—from fifteen years (early cohorts) to fourteen years (boomer cohorts).

2.2   Employment Patterns of Married Women and Married Men

2.2.1   Cohort Comparisons of Employment by Age

I next examine the full-time employment rate of married women by age and across cohorts, in comparison with married men. For this analysis, the underlying data are organized in longitudinal format, and the panel is unbalanced to create a semisynthetic age profile. A respondent first observed at age fifty-one contributes additional observations at fifty-three, fifty-five, and so forth. A respondent first observed at age fifty-two contributes additional observations at fifty-four, fifty-six, and so forth. The data for the Mid-Baby Boom cohort are largely cross-sectional since this cohort is only observed twice; the oldest member of the Mid-Baby Boom at baseline is only fifty-eight by their second interview in 2012.

Figure 2.1 shows that the full-time employment rate among married women in the boomer cohorts is higher than in the earlier cohorts at every age (from fifty-one to sixty-four).[6] The full-time employment rate for married men is higher than for women at all ages, but in contrast, the married men in the boomer cohorts are *less* likely to be employed full time than men in the early cohorts until about age fifty-eight—this pattern is driven by the Mid-Baby Boom cohort who experienced weaker employment conditions in the aftermath of the Great Recession than did earlier cohorts at those ages.

Figure 2.2 shows the age profiles in part-time employment. Among married women, the age profile in part-time employment is relatively flat with age (in the neighborhood of 20 percent) and perhaps somewhat higher among

---

6. Full-time work is defined as working at least thirty-five hours per week for at least thirty-six weeks per year. Part-time work is defined as working less than thirty-five hours per week or less than thirty-six weeks per year.

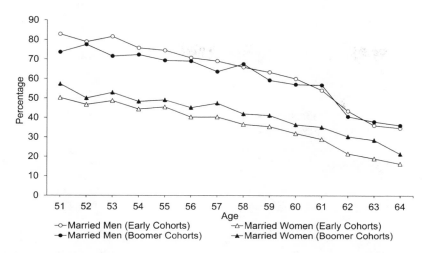

Fig. 2.1   Percent working full time by age

Source: Health and Retirement Study (HRS) 1992 to 2012, RAND HRS Version O.

Notes: Data are structured in (unbalanced) panel format such that units of observation are person-wave. Early cohorts are HRS-Late and War Babies. Boomer cohorts are Early Baby Boom and Mid-Baby Boom. Full-time work is defined as working at least thirty-five hours per week for at least thirty-six weeks per year. The hours and weeks from both the main and any second job are counted when determining whether the respondent is working full time.

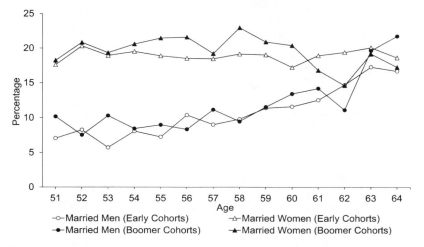

Fig. 2.2   Percent working part time by age

Source: Health and Retirement Study (HRS) 1992 to 2012, RAND HRS Version O.

Notes: Data are structured in (unbalanced) panel format such that units of observation are person-wave. Early cohorts are HRS-Late and War Babies. Boomer cohorts are Early Baby Boom and Mid-Baby Boom. Part-time work is defined as either working less than thirty-five hours per week or less than thirty-six weeks per year. The hours and weeks from both the main and any second job are counted when determining whether the respondent is working part time.

boomer women in their late fifties. In contrast, part-time employment among married men *rises* with age, so that by their midsixties, the part-time employment rate is similar for married men and women.

2.2.2   Labor Supply Correlations across Spouses

In table 2.2, I document the labor supply patterns of couples. As noted earlier, most respondents in the columns for married women are married to the men in the adjacent column for married men; however, the correspondence is not complete, which accounts for the modest differences in statistics measured at the couple level. Table 2.2 shows that in about one-half of couples, both spouses were employed at baseline. Perhaps surprisingly, this statistic is only slightly higher among the boomer cohorts (married women subsample). The husband-wife age difference has declined across cohorts, falling from 2.7 years among married women in the earlier cohorts to 2.0 years in the boomer cohorts. Correspondingly, while 69 percent of married women were married to older men in the early cohorts, somewhat fewer—63 percent—are married to older men in the boomer cohorts.

In the HRS, respondents are asked about their future employment expectations. Specifically, they are asked to state the chance they will work full time after age sixty-two and age sixty-five. Among married women, the mean stated chance of working full time after sixty-five has risen from 18 percent to 25 percent across cohorts. Men, too, increasingly expect to work full time after sixty-five, with the mean stated chance rising from 30 percent to 36 percent across cohorts.

I next use the longitudinal information in the HRS to measure observed transitions to early retirement, specifically the percent reducing work effort within eight years of their baseline interview (ages fifty-one to fifty-six). A reduction in work effort is defined as (a) a transition from full-time work to either part-time work or no work, or (b) a transition from part-time work to no work. Table 2.2 shows that 51 percent of married women in the early cohorts retired early compared with 47 percent among the boomer cohorts. Notably, married men are less likely to retire early than married women—43 percent in the early cohorts compared with 41 percent in the boomer cohorts. Rates of reentry, here defined as increasing work effort within two years of reducing effort, are similar for married women in the early and boomer cohorts (25 percent and 23 percent, respectively), but have fallen for married men across cohorts (from 28 percent to 21 percent).

Finally, table 2.2 shows that early retirement is somewhat more likely among women whose husbands themselves expressed (at baseline) a *below-average* chance of working full time after sixty-five.[7] Among these women, 52 percent in the early cohorts retired early compared with 48 percent of early cohort women whose husbands expressed an *above-average* chance of

---

7. A "below-average" stated probability of working full time after age sixty-five is a stated chance less than the married sample mean of 28 percent.

Table 2.2   **Reductions in work effort among couples**

	Early cohorts		Boomer cohorts	
	Married women (1)	Married men (2)	Married women (3)	Married men (4)
Both spouses employed at baseline (%)	45.7	52.9	48.5	51.5
Husband-wife age difference (years)	2.7	3.4	2.0	2.6
Husband older (%)	69.2	73.7	62.9	66.4
Stated chance of working FT after sixty-five (%)	17.8	29.6	25.2	36.1
Reduction in work effort w/in eight years (%)	51.0	42.9	46.7	41.0
Increase in work effort w/in two years of reduction (%)	25.0	27.7	22.9	20.9
Reduction in work effort w/in eight years | spouse does not plan to work longer (%)	52.3	44.1	47.7	41.6
Reduction in work effort w/in eight years | spouse plans to work longer (%)	47.6	37.1	44.5	39.0
Number of observations	3,385	3,169	2,793	2,677

Source: Health and Retirement Study (HRS) 1992 to 2012, RAND HRS Version O.

Notes: Analysis sample contains married men and women who are age-eligible members of early cohorts (HRS-Late and War Babies) and boomer cohorts (Early Baby Boom and Mid-Baby Boom). Data are structured in cross-sectional format such that units of observation are person-level. All variables measured as of the baseline wave for each cohort. Variable "spouse does not plan to work longer" is an indicator for stated chance of working full-time after age sixty-five being less than its mean value of 28 percent, while "spouse plans to work longer" is the complement. HRS respondent weights used.

working full time after sixty-five. This difference by husbands' expectation is smaller among boomer women, suggesting that women in later cohorts may be less influenced by their husbands' retirement expectations. Men, too, are more likely to retire early when their wives held a below-average baseline expectation of working full time after sixty-five than when their wives held an above-average expectation; that said, men in general appear somewhat less likely than women to be influenced by their spouse's retirement expectation.

2.3 The Return to Continued Work for Married Women

The relative rise in full-time employment among older married women compared with men in figures 2.1 and 2.2 indicates greater labor force attachment among more recent cohorts of older married women. One candidate explanation for this pattern is that the return to additional years of work has risen for married women relative to married men. The return to additional work has at least two key components: the additional earnings earned and the incremental gain in future Social Security benefit payments (also known as Social Security wealth).[8]

The first piece of evidence in support of the hypothesis of a rising return to additional work came from table 2.1, where we saw that boomer women enter their early fifties earning substantially more (31 percent) than women in earlier cohorts, and that this growth in earnings has outpaced cross-cohort growth in earnings for men (10 percent). In this section, I examine the subsequent trajectory of earnings from ages fifty-one to sixty-four for married women compared with married men to test if there are material differences in the slopes of the age-earnings profiles. I then turn to an analysis of Social Security wealth to investigate whether there are differential gains in Social Security wealth from additional years of earnings for married women relative to men.

2.3.1   Age-Earnings Profiles

The age-earnings profiles for married women and men in each cohort group are shown in figure 2.3. Earnings are in 2012 dollars, top coded at $250,000 to address extreme values, and exclude those with zero earnings. The age-earnings profile for married women is flat from age fifty-one until their early sixties, and is considerably higher for boomer women than for women in earlier cohorts. In contrast, the age-earnings profile for married men visibly declines with age in both cohort groups. This decline in real earnings for men—reflecting stagnant earnings growth as well as a rising incidence of part-time work—results in a marked narrowing of the male-female earnings gap by the early sixties.

To extract a clearer picture of the relative changes for married women and men, I next estimate the slopes of the female and male age-earnings profiles. Table 2.3 presents coefficients from ordinary least squares (OLS) regressions of real earnings (conditional on employment) on a quadratic function of age, estimated separately for married women and married men in each cohort group, and using the data in longitudinal format (person-wave) as described above. To account for selection into continued employment on the basis of labor force attachment and prior earnings, I include controls for baseline earnings, baseline hours worked per year, baseline weeks worked per year, tenure in the baseline job, lifetime number of years worked as of baseline, and a series of indicators for groups of three-digit

---

8. Another potential component is the incremental gain in lifetime pension benefits for those with an employer-sponsored pension plan, offset by the forgone value of the annual pension benefit if the individual could have collected pension benefits in the year in question (see Maestas [2001] for a model of the return to additional work).

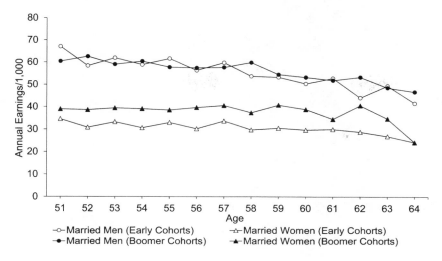

Fig. 2.3   Earnings of all workers by age

Source: Health and Retirement Study (HRS) 1992 to 2012, RAND HRS Version O.
Notes: Data are structured in (unbalanced) panel format such that units of observation are person-wave. Earnings are conditional on employment. All dollar values reported in 2012 dollars. Early cohorts are HRS-Late and War Babies. Boomer cohorts are Early Baby Boom and Mid-Baby Boom.

occupations.[9] Also included are indicators of college degree status, race and ethnicity, self-reported fair or poor health status (measured at baseline), household wealth quintile (measured at baseline), and HRS cohort designation. The coefficients on the quadratic age function indicate that each additional year of age is associated with a relative gain in real earnings for married women compared with married men. Since the shape of the age profile is difficult to infer from the coefficients alone, figure 2.4 plots predicted earnings by age relative to predicted earnings at age fifty-one, using the age coefficients from table 2.3. Panel A of figure 2.4 shows the age-earnings profile for married men and married women in the early cohorts, while panel B shows the profiles for the boomer cohorts. In both cohort groups, women's real earnings rise slightly until age fifty-five, stabilize, and then trend downward after age fifty-seven. In contrast, real earnings for

9. The groups of three-digit occupations are based on the 1980 census classification as follows: managerial specialty operation (003-037); professional specialty operation and technical support (043-235); sales (243-285); clerical, administrative support (303-389); service: private household, cleaning and building services (403-407); service: protection (413-427); service: food preparation (433-444); health services (445-447); personal services (448-469); farming, forestry, fishing (473-499); mechanics and repair (503-549); construction trade and extractors (553-617); precision production (633-699); operators: machine (703-799); operators: transport, etc. (803-859); operators: handlers, etc. (863-889); and member of armed forces (900).

Table 2.3 Estimates of the age-earnings profile for married women and men by cohort

	All		Early cohorts		Boomer cohorts	
	Married women (1)	Married men (2)	Married women (3)	Married men (4)	Married women (5)	Married men (6)
Age	11,047***	6,602**	10,538***	8,348**	13,623***	3,348
	(1,811)	(3,123)	(2,046)	(3,674)	(3,766)	(6,221)
Age squared	−99.5***	−71.1***	−94.5***	−85.9***	−123.9***	−43.9
	(15.8)	(27.2)	(17.8)	(31.9)	(33.4)	(54.9)
College educated	5,796***	15,166***	5,172***	12,151***	5,980***	17,551***
	(588)	(932)	(744)	(1,175)	(962)	(1,558)
Age at baseline	−590***	291	−611***	251	−397	603
	(127)	(221)	(144)	(260)	(249)	(426)
Earnings at baseline	0.529***	0.282***	0.603***	0.323***	0.482***	0.243***
	(0.007)	(0.004)	(0.010)	(0.006)	(0.010)	(0.006)
Hours worked per week at baseline	222.3***	169.1***	150.0**	57.8	324.8***	364.4***
	(18.8)	(30.2)	(22.1)	(37.3)	(33.7)	(51.6)
Weeks worked per year at baseline	269.8***	552.8***	236.6***	590.1***	269.8***	491.5***
	(32.8)	(61.9)	(39.8)	(81.2)	(56.5)	(97.0)
Job tenure at baseline	116.4***	171.0***	54.0*	110.9***	190.2***	282.3***
	(25.2)	(33.6)	(29.4)	(39.5)	(46.1)	(63.4)
Lifetime number of years worked at baseline	60.6**	13.4	2.1	−52.5	144.1**	3.4
	(23.8)	(54.2)	(27.0)	(75.9)	(45.9)	(81.8)
Black non-Hispanic	−312	−3,246***	555	−1,681	−1,625	−5,914***
	(661)	(1,143)	(771)	(1,412)	(1,213)	(1,949)
Hispanic	−2,124***	−8,054***	−1,651*	−5,296***	−2,586**	−11,806***
	(758)	(1,195)	(998)	(1,547)	(1,207)	(1,906)

Other race/ethnicities	4,319***	−5,480***	982	−3,671	6,864***	−9,378***
	(1,332)	(1,964)	(1,800)	(2,590)	(2,052)	(3,058)
Fair/poor health at baseline	−979	−4,925***	−28	−5,131***	−1,718	−3,609**
	(649)	(1,095)	(782)	(1,402)	(1,132)	(1,770)
Observations	16,701	18,714	10,393	12,283	6,308	6,431
R-squared	0.461	0.346	0.442	0.333	0.477	0.382

Source: Health and Retirement Study (HRS) 1992 to 2012, RAND HRS Version O.

Notes: Dependent variable in all columns is annual earnings conditional on employment. Models are OLS regressions and also include indicators for cohort and wealth quintile and indicators for missing values on job tenure at baseline, years in workforce at baseline, hours worked per week at baseline, weeks worked per year at baseline, and occupation at baseline. Analysis sample contains married men and women who are age-eligible members of early cohorts (HRS-Late and War Babies) and boomer cohorts (Early Baby Boom and Mid-Baby Boom). Data are structured in (unbalanced) panel format such that units of observation are person-wave. All dollar values reported in 2012 dollars. Standard errors in parentheses.

***Significant at the 1 percent level.

**Significant at the 5 percent level.

*Significant at the 10 percent level.

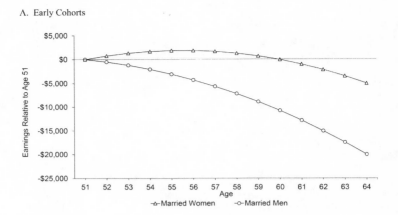

A. Early Cohorts

B. Boomer Cohorts

Fig. 2.4   Predicted annual earnings by age, relative to earnings at age fifty-one
Source: Health and Retirement Study (HRS) 1992 to 2012, RAND HRS Version O.
Notes: Data values are predicted earnings by age using the age and age squared coefficients from table 2.3. Data are structured in (unbalanced) panel format such that units of observation are person-wave. Earnings are conditional on employment. All dollar values reported in 2012 dollars. Early cohorts are HRS-Late and War Babies. Boomer cohorts are Early Baby Boom and Mid-Baby Boom.

men decline annually from ages fifty-one to sixty-one. As a result, at every age the return to continued work for women is greater than it is for men, and grows until at least age sixty-four.[10]

I next investigate whether the changes in annual earnings with age in figure 2.4 appear to correspond with changes in extensive margin labor supply, or changes in the real wage rate. Table 2.4 presents estimates from sepa-

10. The age-earnings profile for divorced and separated women (not shown) is similar to that of married women in both cohorts. See Olivetti and Rotz (chapter 4, this volume) for an analysis of divorce risk and labor supply.

Table 2.4   Estimates of the age profile in wage, hours, and weeks worked for married women and men by cohort

	All		Early cohorts		Boomer cohorts	
	Married women (1)	Married men (2)	Married women (3)	Married men (4)	Married women (5)	Married men (6)
	A. Age profile in wage					
Age	153.6***	198.2***	176.3***	255.4***	167.0**	184.7*
	(34.7)	(53.7)	(40.3)	(63.0)	(69.6)	(105.0)
Age squared	−1.399***	−1.858***	−1.579***	−2.335***	−1.566**	−1.836**
	(0.303)	(0.468)	(0.351)	(0.546)	(0.618)	(0.926)
Observations	14,628	16,287	9,055	10,749	5,573	5,538
R-squared	0.466	0.415	0.433	0.441	0.500	0.417
	B. Age profile in hours					
Age	3.344***	6.317***	4.330***	6.708***	0.105	5.825***
	(0.720)	(0.712)	(0.930)	(0.891)	(1.224)	(1.265)
Age squared	−0.033***	−0.061***	−0.042***	−0.064***	−0.004	−0.057***
	(0.006)	(0.006)	(0.008)	(0.008)	(0.011)	(0.011)
Observations	16,485	18,474	10,255	12,132	6,230	6,342
R-squared	0.397	0.366	0.342	0.333	0.495	0.442

(continued)

Table 2.4 (continued)

	All		Early cohorts		Boomer cohorts	
	Married women (1)	Married men (2)	Married women (3)	Married men (4)	Married women (5)	Married men (6)
			C. Age profile in weeks worked			
Age	1.016**	2.416***	1.603***	2.235***	−0.163	2.734***
	(0.476)	(0.414)	(0.616)	(0.515)	(0.809)	(0.746)
Age squared	−0.0100**	−0.0226***	−0.0150***	−0.0210***	0.0002	−0.0254***
	(0.0042)	(0.0036)	(0.0054)	(0.0045)	(0.0072)	(0.0066)
Observations	16,353	18,404	10,203	12,107	6,150	6,297
R-squared	0.317	0.231	0.269	0.185	0.409	0.33

Source: Health and Retirement Study (HRS) 1992 to 2012, RAND HRS Version O.

Notes: Dependent variables in all columns are conditional on employment. Models are OLS regressions and also include indicators for cohort and wealth quintile and indicators for missing values on job tenure at baseline, years in workforce at baseline, hours worked per week at baseline, weeks worked per year at baseline, and occupation at baseline. Number of observations for these models are slightly lower than in table 2.3 because of missing values in the dependent variables. Analysis sample contains married men and women who are age-eligible members of early cohorts (HRS-Late and War Babies) and boomer cohorts (Early Baby Boom and Mid-Baby Boom). Data are structured in (unbalanced) panel format such that units of observation are person-wave. All dollar values reported in 2012 dollars. Standard errors in parentheses.

***Significant at the 1 percent level.

**Significant at the 5 percent level.

*Significant at the 10 percent level.

A. Early Cohorts

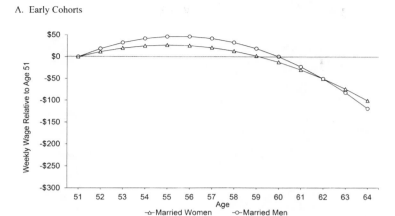

B. Boomer Cohorts

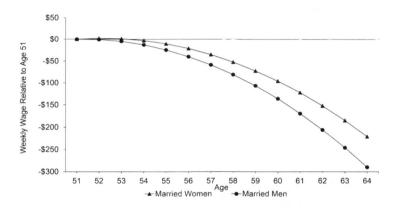

Fig. 2.5   Predicted weekly wage by age, relative to wage at age fifty-one

Source: Health and Retirement Study (HRS) 1992 to 2012, RAND HRS Version O.

Notes: Data values are predicted weekly wage by age using the age and age squared coefficients from table 2.4. Data are structured in (unbalanced) panel format such that units of observation are person-wave. Weekly wage is conditional on employment. All dollar values reported in 2012 dollars. Early cohorts are HRS-Late and War Babies. Boomer cohorts are Early Baby Boom and Mid-Baby Boom.

rate models of the age-wage (panel A), age-hours (panel B), and age-weeks (panel C) profiles, each estimated using the specification in table 2.3. Figure 2.5 plots the predicted weekly wage by age (relative to the weekly wage at age fifty-one). For married women in both cohorts, the age profile in the weekly wage largely tracks the age profile in earnings (although it is somewhat flatter for boomer women in their early fifties). The pattern for married men is more nuanced. Among men in the early cohorts, the weekly wage rises modestly

A. Early Cohorts

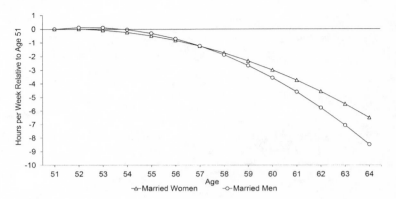

B. Boomer Cohorts

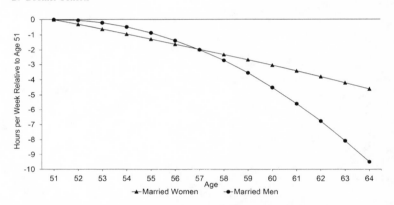

Fig. 2.6   Predicted hours per week by age, relative to hours at age fifty-one

Source: Health and Retirement Study (HRS) 1992 to 2012, RAND HRS Version O.

Notes: Data values are predicted hours per week by age using the age and age squared coeffi-cients from table 2.4. Data are structured in (unbalanced) panel format such that units of observation are person-wave. Hours per week are conditional on employment. All dollar values reported in 2012 dollars. Early cohorts are HRS-Late and War Babies. Boomer cohorts are Early Baby Boom and Mid-Baby Boom.

until their midfifties, when it begins to decline. The declining age-earnings profile for early cohort men in their early fifties, it appears, may have been driven by changes in extensive margin labor supply. Among boomer men, the weekly wage declines in tandem with earnings.

Figures 2.6 and 2.7 show the measures of extensive margin labor supply, predicted hours worked per week and predicted weeks worked per year, respectively. These figures indicate that among men in both cohorts, the

A. Early Cohorts

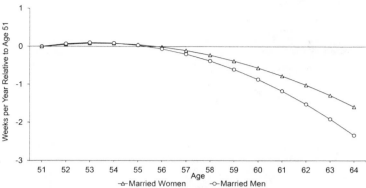

B. Boomer Cohorts

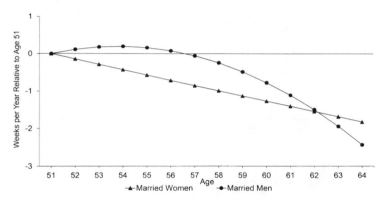

Fig. 2.7   Predicted weeks worked per year by age, relative to weeks worked at age fifty-one

Source: Health and Retirement Study (HRS) 1992 to 2012, RAND HRS Version O.

Notes: Data values are predicted weeks worked per year by age using the age and age squared coefficients from table 2.4. Data are structured in (unbalanced) panel format such that units of observation are person-wave. Weeks worked is conditional on employment. All dollar values reported in 2012 dollars. Early cohorts are HRS-Late and War Babies. Boomer cohorts are Early Baby Boom and Mid-Baby Boom.

decline in the earnings profile in their early fifties coincides with modest reductions in hours per week, while weeks worked are stable. For women, hours per week and weeks worked per year are either flat or trending downward beginning in their early fifties. Thus, it does not appear married women are achieving their stable earnings profile by compensating for real losses in earnings with increases in extensive margin labor supply.

2.3.2   Social Security Wealth

The earnings patterns documented thus far indicate that lifetime earnings for married women have risen across cohorts, both absolutely and relative to the earnings of men, thus resulting in a narrowing of the gender gap in earnings with age. The gain in lifetime earnings for married women has important implications for women's retirement security, particularly considering the risks of divorce and widowhood. In this section, I first examine the effects of continued work on individual Social Security wealth. I then turn to the relative contributions of continued work by women and men to the Social Security wealth of the household, accounting for the value of spouse and survivor benefits. Finally, I investigate whether it is the case that individuals with larger potential gains from delaying retirement and claiming are more likely to work longer.

Individual Social Security Wealth

Social Security retirement benefits are primarily determined by average earnings over a thirty-five-year period. As cultural norms once dictated married women should not engage in labor market activity while raising children, married women have typically accrued many more years of "zero" earnings than married men, resulting in low average lifetime earnings and, correspondingly low Social Security retirement benefits. But as married women in recent cohorts have accrued more years of work, along with higher annual earnings, their Social Security benefit entitlements should have also risen.

Figure 2.8 shows that this is indeed the case. The figure shows predicted Social Security wealth (SSW) for married women and married men in each cohort group, by potential claiming age. Social Security wealth is the expected present value of future Social Security retirement benefits based on the respondent's actual earnings history until their baseline survey wave, and assuming continued work at the same earnings until the target claiming age. Social Security wealth is computed by applying Social Security's benefit computation calculator (ANYPIA)[11] to the restricted Social Security earnings records of HRS respondents (Kapinos et al. 2016). The calculator applies all aspects of the benefit calculation formula, including adjustments for early and delayed retirement. Social Security wealth is included in the publicly available RAND HRS files. For each respondent, SSW is calculated for three potential claiming ages—the early retirement age (age sixty-two), the full retirement age (age sixty-five or sixty-six depending on birth cohort), and age seventy (the maximum benefit initiation age). For all three potential claiming ages, actual earnings are measured until the baseline survey wave,

11. The ANYPIA Social Security benefit calculator can be downloaded from https://www
.ssa.gov/oact/anypia/download.html.

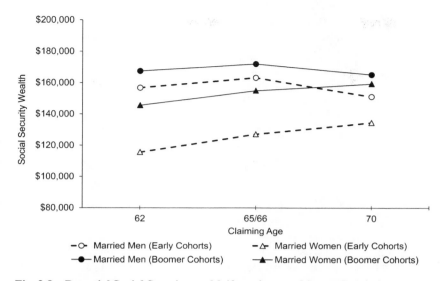

Fig. 2.8   Potential Social Security wealth if continue working until claiming age

Source: Health and Retirement Study (HRS) 1992 to 2012, RAND HRS Version O.

Notes: Data are structured in cross-sectional format such that units of observation are person-level. Social Security wealth (SSW) is the expected present discounted value of potential Social Security benefits earned on the respondent's own record if the respondent continued to work until the indicated claiming age. (For methodological details, see Kapinos et al. [2016] and Chien [2015].) Claiming age "65/66" pools respondents who have a full retirement age of either sixty-five or sixty-six. Early cohorts are HRS-Late and War Babies. Boomer cohorts are Early Baby Boom and Mid-Baby Boom. All dollar values reported in 2012 dollars. HRS respondent weights used.

and then projected forward to the indicated claiming age.[12] The projection uses a moving average of the last five years of earnings (unequally weighted), and effectively assumes a flat profile in real earnings beyond the baseline wave.

Figure 2.8 shows that at every claiming age, married women in the boomer cohorts (the solid line) have substantially greater individual SSW than women in the earlier cohorts (dotted line). For instance, mean SSW at age sixty-two among married women in the boomer cohorts is $145,644 compared with $115,609 in the early cohorts—an increase of 26 percent. Social Security wealth at age sixty-two is also higher among boomer men ($167,558) than early cohort men ($156,928), but by proportionately less (7 percent). Note that the underlying data are at the respondent level (as

12. This measure only includes own benefit entitlements based on the respondent's own earnings history. It does not include the present value of any spouse benefits that would be paid based on the respondent's earnings record to either a current, past, or surviving spouse. For methodological details, see Kapinos et al. (2016).

opposed to respondent-wave level in the age-earnings analyses), and since predicted SSW can be computed for all three potential claiming ages if it can be computed for one, the age profiles in SSW in figure 2.8 are a balanced panel.[13]

Figure 2.8 also reveals a related important finding: if married women continued working at the same annual earnings rate between ages sixty-two and seventy, their Social Security wealth would rise by a substantial amount—17 percent among early cohort women and 10 percent among boomer women (the *absolute* gain is larger for boomer women, but they have a higher base level at sixty-two, resulting in a smaller percent change). In striking contrast, mean predicted Social Security wealth declines slightly for men in both the early and boomer cohorts (by −3 percent and −1 percent, respectively).

Thus, whereas additional years of work after age sixty-two do not increase Social Security wealth for married men (even at constant real earnings), additional years of work make a measurable increase in the SSW of married women.[14] The reason is because the marginal earnings replace earlier years of lower (or zero) earnings in the benefit computation formula for women, but not for men. In fact, this is the only channel by which SSW can increase in figure 2.8. The increase in potential SSW is not due to the effect of delayed claiming, or to the more favorable survival probabilities for women.[15] Table 2.5 presents estimates of the relative gain for married women in an OLS regression with married women and men pooled, and including the same control variables as in table 2.3. The relative within-individual gain from ages sixty-two to seventy for married women compared to men is a statistically significant $22,547 in the early cohorts and $20,202 for the boomer cohorts.

Overall, the gender gap in individual SSW would narrow to such a degree across cohorts that continued work to age seventy would place married women on near equal footing with married men, at least in terms of SSW. The equivalence might seem surprising given married women earn less on

13. In instances where respondents did not consent to release their Social Security earnings records, HRS used imputation methods to construct the primary insurance amount (PIA) on which SSW is based. Some 19 to 27 percent of respondents, depending on their baseline wave, received some form of PIA imputation for this reason. A number of respondents did not consent at their first interview but did so at a later interview, which ultimately reduced the number of respondents with missing earnings records. See Kapinos et al. (2016) for details.

14. The same is also true for divorced and separated women.

15. Recall that the actuarial adjustments in the benefit amount for early (age sixty-two) and delayed (past full retirement age) claiming are designed to be actuarially fair. Thus *on average* in the US population, SSW is the same whether benefits are claimed at age sixty-two or seventy. Therefore, in the absence of growth in average lifetime earnings, the profile in SSW in figure 2.8 should be flat. The slight reduction in SSW between ages 65/66 and 70 for early cohort men arises because the actuarial adjustment for delayed claiming beyond the full retirement age (65/66) was *less than actuarially fair* until 2005, when the 1943 birth cohort turned sixty-two. Thus, for the early HRS cohorts, there was a small actuarial penalty associated with delayed claiming. The slight average reduction for boomer men is likely a consequence of sampling variation.

Table 2.5   Gain in Social Security wealth with continued work until age seventy for married women relative to married men

	Early cohorts (1)	Boomer cohorts (2)
Married women	22,547.0***	20,201.5***
	(471.5)	(652.2)
College educated	2,143.6***	1,035.80
	(502.0)	(708.7)
Age at baseline	−865.5***	556.2***
	(105.8)	(165.0)
Earnings at baseline/1,000	9.50***	0.14
	(2.96)	(2.72)
Hours worked per week at baseline	84.5***	92.5***
	(16.0)	(23.4)
Weeks worked per year at baseline	159.7***	37.7
	(36.2)	(45.3)
Job tenure at baseline	−3.41	−4.45
	(17.82)	(27.94)
Lifetime number of years worked at baseline	34.4	−168.1***
	(25.0)	(40.5)
Black non-Hispanic	−561.4	−537.1
	(734.8)	(1,077.3)
Hispanic	903.4	1,300
	(780.9)	(1,023.1)
Other race/ethnicities	2,144.2*	1,432.60
	(1,116.7)	(1,497.1)
Fair/poor health at baseline	−809.9	352.1
	(589.9)	(833.7)
Observations	4,591	1,692
R-squared	0.441	0.467

Source: Health and Retirement Study (HRS) 1992 to 2012, RAND HRS Version O.

Notes: Dependent variable in all columns is change in Social Security wealth if work until age seventy. Social Security wealth (SSW) is the expected present discounted value of potential Social Security benefits earned on the individual's own record if he or she continued to work until claiming at age seventy. Models are OLS regressions and also include indicators for cohort and wealth quintile. Analysis sample contains married men and women who are age-eligible members of early cohorts (HRS-Late and War Babies) and boomer cohorts (Early Baby Boom, excluding Mid-Baby Boom). Data are structured in cross-sectional format such that units of observation are person-level. HRS respondent weights used. Standard errors in parentheses.

***Significant at the 1 percent level.

**Significant at the 5 percent level.

*Significant at the 10 percent level.

average than married men. But the Social Security benefit formula features a progressive replacement rate structure, and thus married women, at their present position in the lifetime earnings distribution, benefit from this progressivity.

Overall, these patterns reveal the discordant individual incentives facing married women and married men for continued work as they progress through their fifties and early sixties. However, it is possible that this discordance is weakened by the role of spouse and survivor benefits. I turn to this issue next.

Household Social Security Wealth

Under Social Security rules, married individuals are entitled to the larger of (a) a retired worker benefit based on their own work history, or (b) a spouse benefit equal to 50 percent of their spouse's retired worker benefit. Historically, nearly all recipients of spouse benefits have been married women, whose own benefit entitlement was less than 50 percent of their husband's benefit (and included many women who did not have enough work history to qualify for any benefit on their own record). Social Security rules also contain survivorship provisions. Widowed spouses are entitled to the larger of their own retirement benefit or a survivor benefit equal to 100 percent of their spouse's retirement benefit. As with spouse benefits, nearly all recipients of survivor benefits have been women.[16]

I approximate the proportion of women who would likely receive spouse benefits at each potential claiming age with the percent whose predicted SSW is less than 50 percent of their husband's predicted SSW. By this approximation, 44 percent of early cohort women would have received spouse benefits had they and their husbands both claimed at age sixty-two. If, instead, both worked and delayed claiming until age seventy, some 34 percent would have received spouse benefits. However, among boomer women, only 15 percent would receive spouse benefits if they and their husbands claimed at age sixty-two, and this would fall to just 11 percent with continued work until age seventy.[17]

Similarly, I approximate the proportion of women who would receive survivor's benefits if they became widowed by the percent whose predicted SSW is less than 100 percent of their husband's predicted SSW. By this approximation, 77 percent of early cohort women would have received survivor benefits upon widowhood if both spouses had claimed at age sixty-two. In contrast, continued work to age seventy would reduce this number to 65 percent. Among boomer women, far fewer—30 percent—would receive

16. Spouse and survivor benefits are also available to divorced women if the marriage lasted at least ten years and they have not remarried.
17. These approximations give rise to similar estimates by cohort as reported by the Social Security Administration (Iams 2016).

survivor benefits in the event of widowhood if both spouses had claimed at age sixty-two, and continued work to age seventy would reduce the figure to 27 percent.

But do these gains in individual SSW have any effect on household-level SSW or do they simply crowd out SSW that was already held in the form of spouse and survivor entitlements? To assess this question I regress the gain in total household SSW—which as constructed by the HRS includes expected spouse and survivor benefit entitlements—on the potential change in individual SSW for the wife, and the potential change in individual SSW for the husband. Recall that any within-individual gain in SSW reflects the effect of added years of earnings, and so the marginal effect of an additional dollar of individual SSW indicates the degree to which this dollar matters for household SSW. Table 2.6 presents the coefficients from OLS regression models estimated separately by cohort group. Among the early cohorts, a one-dollar increase in the wife's individual SSW would have resulted in only ten cents additional household SSW—her SSW hardly matters. In contrast, a one-dollar increase in the husband's individual SSW would have yielded one dollar and thirty cents in additional household SSW, reflecting the incremental gains in spouse and survivor benefits based entirely on his earnings

Table 2.6   **Effect of change in individual Social Security wealth (SSW) on change in household SSW**

	Early cohorts (1)	Boomer cohorts (2)
Change in wife's individual SSW from 62 to 70	0.145***	0.357***
	(0.040)	(0.088)
Change in husband's individual SSW from 62 to 70	1.316***	0.867***
	(0.043)	(0.039)
Observations	1,547	590
R-squared	0.392	0.471

Source: Health and Retirement Study (HRS) 1992 to 2012, RAND HRS Version O.

Notes: Standard errors in parentheses. Dependent variable in all columns is change in household-level Social Security wealth (SSW) between ages sixty-two and seventy if both spouses continue to work until age seventy. Models are OLS regression models. Individual SSW is the expected present discounted value of potential Social Security benefits earned on the individual's own record if he or she continued to work until the claiming age of seventy. Analysis sample is households of married women in the early cohorts (HRS-Late and War Babies) and boomer cohorts (Early Baby Boom, excluding Mid-Baby Boom). Data are structured in cross-sectional format such that units of observation are household level. Household Social Security wealth is the sum of each spouse's individual SSW, any SSW attributable to spouse benefits, and SSW attributable to survivor benefits. HRS respondent weights used. (For methodological details, see Kapinos et al. [2016] and Chien [2015].)

***Significant at the 1 percent level.

**Significant at the 5 percent level.

*Significant at the 10 percent level.

Table 2.7   **Percent retiring early by quartile of potential change in SSW from continued work**

	Married women		Married men	
Gain quartile	Mean of gain quartile	Percent retiring early	Mean of gain quartile	Percent retiring early
1	1,315	49.7	−14,804	42.0
2	10,385	50.4	−6,898	43.9
3	19,848	46.0	−817	43.3
4	36,654	46.3	10,782	39.4
Observations	2,782		3,501	

Source: Health and Retirement Study (HRS) 1992 to 2012, RAND HRS Version O.
Notes: Percent retiring early is the percent who reduce work effort within eight years of their baseline wave. Social Security wealth (SSW) is the expected present discounted value of potential Social Security benefits earned on the individual's own record if he or she continued to work until claiming at age seventy. Analysis sample contains married men and women who are age-eligible members of early cohorts (HRS-Late and War Babies) and boomer cohorts (Early Baby Boom, excluding Mid-Baby Boom). Data are structured in cross-sectional format such that units of observation are person-level. HRS respondent weights used.

record for a large fraction of couples. However, the picture is quite different for the boomer cohorts: a one-dollar increase in the wife's individual SSW results in forty cents additional household SSW, while a one-dollar increase in the husband's individual SSW results in ninety cents additional household SSW. The earnings histories of married men continue to matter most, but by substantially less than before, as the earnings histories of married women begin to yield both individual and household-level benefits.

Potential Gains and Retirement Decisions

The potential gains in SSW from continued work are substantial, especially for married women, but an important question is whether women factor these potential gains into their employment decisions. To shed light on this question, I divide the potential gains in individual SSW from continued work to age seventy into quartiles. I then tabulate the percent of individuals in each quartile who are observed to "retire early"—that is, to reduce their work effort within eight years of baseline. This simple tabulation, presented in table 2.7, reveals very little correlation between the magnitude of the potential gain and the percent retiring early. For example, 49 percent of married women in the lowest potential gain quartile (with a mean gain in SSW of just $1,315) subsequently retired early, and 46 percent of married women in the top potential gain quartile (with a mean gain of $36,654) retired early. Interestingly, the pattern is similar for married men, although somewhat fewer married men retire early than married women: 42 percent of men in the bottom gain quartile (with a mean *loss* of $14,804) retired early, while 39 percent of men in the top gain quartile (with a mean gain of $10,782) retired early. These patterns suggest that potential gains in SSW do not factor into the retirement decisions of married women. This is also true for married men, whose earnings histories dominate the accrual of household SSW.

2.4 Discussion and Conclusion

This cross-cohort analysis of the employment patterns of married women has revealed several key findings. First, preferences for joint leisure persist among married women and men in recent cohorts, suggesting that the trade-off between the potential return to continued work and preferences for joint leisure continues to be salient for couples. Second, married women in the boomer cohorts enter their early fifties earning 31 percent more than their predecessors in earlier cohorts. Married men in the boomer cohorts also earn more than their predecessors, but the growth across cohorts was 10 percent, notably less. Third, estimates of the shape of the age-earnings profiles for married women and men in their fifties indicate that the return to additional work is stable for women, but declining for men. Fourth, additional years of work beyond age sixty-two (the early retirement age), would make a measurable increase in the Social Security wealth of married women. This is because the additional years of earnings at these ages replace earlier years of lower or zero earnings in the retirement benefit computation formula. The same is not true for men, who would see little, if any, increase in Social Security wealth if they worked beyond age sixty-two, presumably because the additional years of earnings do not replace earlier years of lower earnings. Among the boomer cohorts, continued work places married women and married men on equal footing in terms of Social Security wealth by age seventy. Finally, I find that individuals with the largest potential gains in Social Security wealth are just as likely to retire early as those with the least to gain. Individuals, it appears, do not factor these potential gains into their employment decisions, and this raises the question of whether individuals are able to accurately assess the opportunity costs associated with reducing work effort before age seventy.

In sum, these patterns provide evidence that married couples face discordant incentives for continued work as they progress through their fifties and early sixties. My analysis has quantified one component of the important trade-off faced by older women as they decide whether or not to work longer—the opportunity cost associated with reducing work effort in tandem with their husbands. On the other side of this trade-off is the utility value placed on joint leisure.

Among married boomer women in their fifties, the opportunity cost of leaving the labor force early has risen as their earnings have grown. This opportunity cost is substantial and consists of both forgone earnings as well as incremental gains in Social Security wealth. Additional work beyond age sixty-two makes up for lower labor supply earlier in life, and can place married women on par with married men in terms of the lifetime resources available to them in the latter part of life. Increasingly, these additional resources will matter for the financial well-being of not just women themselves, but their husbands as well.

References

Arias, Elizabeth. 2002. "United States Life Tables, 2000." *National Vital Statistics Reports* 51 (3), Washington, DC, National Center for Health Statistics. http://www.med.mcgill.ca/epidemiology/hanley/bios601/Lifetables/lifetb2000_01_06.pdf.
Baker, Michael. 2002. "The Retirement Behavior of Married Couples." *Journal of Human Resources* 37 (1): 1–34.
Banks, James, Richard Blundell, and Maria Casanova Rivas. 2010. "The Dynamics of Retirement Behavior in Couples: Reduced-Form Evidence from England and the US." Unpublished manuscript, University of California, Los Angeles.
Blau, David M. 1998. "Labor Force Dynamics of Older Married Couples." *Journal of Labor Economics* 16:595–629.
Browning, Martin, and Pierre-Andre Chiappori. 1998. "Efficient Intra-Household Allocations: A General Characterization and Empirical Tests." *Econometrica* 66 (6): 1241–278.
Chien, Sandy, Nancy Campbell, Chris Chan, Orla Hayden, Michael Hurd, Regan Main, Joshua Mallett, et al. 2015. "RAND HRS Data Documentation, Version O." Santa Monica, CA: RAND Labor & Population Program, RAND Center for the Study of Aging.
Coile, Courtney. 2004. "Retirement Incentives and Couples' Retirement Decisions." *B. E. Journal of Economic Analysis & Policy* 4 (1). Published online. DOI: https://doi.org/10.2202/1538-0653.1277.
Gustman, Alan L., and Thomas L. Steinmeier. 2000. "Retirement in Dual Career Families: A Structural Model." *Journal of Labor Economics* 18 (3): 503–45.
———. 2004. "Social Security, Pensions and Retirement Behaviour within the Family." *Journal of Applied Econometrics* 19 (6): 723–37.
———. 2014. "Integrating Retirement Models: Understanding Household Retirement Decisions." In *Factors Affecting Worker Well-Being: The Impact of Change in the Labor Market*, Research in Labor Economics, vol. 40, edited by Solomon W. Polachek and Konstantinos Tatsiramos, 79–112. Bingley, UK: Emerald Group Publishing Limited.
Honoré, Bo E., and Áureo de Paula. 2014. "Joint Retirement in Europe." Netspar Discussion Paper no. 10/2014-052, Network for Studies on Pension, Aging and Retirement. http://arno.uvt.nl/show.cgi?fid=135930.
Hurd, Michael D. 1990. "The Joint Retirement Decision of Husbands and Wives." In *Issues in the Economics of Aging*, edited by David A. Wise, 231–54. Chicago: University of Chicago Press.
Iams, Howard M. 2016. "Married Women's Projected Retirement Benefits: An Update." *Social Security Bulletin* 75 (2) 17–24.
Kapinos, Kandice, Charlie Brown, Michael Nolte, Helena Stolyarova, and David Weir. 2016. "Health and Retirement Study Prospective Social Security Wealth Measures of Pre-Retirees, Public Release Version 5.0: Data Description and Usage." Ann Arbor: Survey Research Center, Institute for Social Research, Uni-

versity of Michigan. http://hrsonline.isr.umich.edu/modules/meta/xyear/sswealth/desc/SSwealthP.pdf.

Lundberg, Shelly, and Robert A. Pollak. 1993. "Separate Spheres Bargaining and the Marriage Market." *Journal of Political Economy* 101 (6): 988–1010.

Maestas, Nicole. 2001. "Labor, Love & Leisure: Complementarity and the Timing of Retirement by Working Couples." PhD diss., Department of Economics, UC Berkeley.

Michaud, Pierre-Carl, and Frederic Vermeulen. 2011. "A Collective Labor Supply Model with Complementarities in Leisure: Identification and Estimation by Means of Panel Data." *Labour Economics* 18 (2): 159–67.

Schirle, Tammy. 2008. "Why Have the Labor Force Participation Rates of Older Men Increased since the Mid-1990s?" *Journal of Labor Economics* 26 (4): 549–94.

3

Understanding Why Black Women Are Not Working Longer

Joanna N. Lahey

3.1 Introduction

Black women once had labor force participation and employment rates that exceeded those of white women, even at older ages. But the pattern has eroded and, for most education groups, has reversed. Remarkably, older white women's participation has not just caught up with black women's. It has surpassed it. Although more women of both races are working at older ages, white women are working a lot more than are black women.

The change in relative employment by race is especially surprising given black women's greater attachment to the labor force throughout their life cycle, with longer work histories and a greater probability of full-time work. It is also surprising given older black women's greater potential need for income compared with white women. Older black women have fewer resources than do white women in terms of wealth and other household income and have more demand on these resources in the form of dependents.

Race differences in employment among older women are understudied in contrast to the extensive literature on men, or even compared with the smaller literature on younger women or all women (for an extensive literature review on race differences for male workers, see Lang and Lehmann [2012]). To provide some perspective on the group I am studying, the oldest cohorts

Joanna N. Lahey is an associate professor at the Bush School of Government and Public Service at Texas A&M University and a faculty research fellow of the National Bureau of Economic Research.

Particular thanks to Claudia Goldin, Larry Katz, and members of the Sloan Women Working Longer group for valuable feedback and to the SIEPR working group. Thanks also to Molly Beck, Meghan DeAmaral, Matthew Murphy, and Abby Mulcahy for research assistance. For acknowledgments, sources of research support, and disclosure of the author's material financial relationships, if any, please see http://www.nber.org/chapters/c13807.ack.

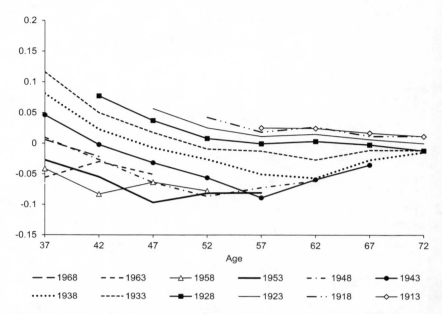

Fig. 3.1   Difference in employment rates for black women compared to white women
Source: Data from 1970–2000 census and 2004–2006 and 2009–2011 ACS.

in my sample were born in the 1910s during the Jim Crow era, while the youngest were born in the early 1960s after the landmark 1954 case *Brown v. Board of Education* overturning "separate but equal."[1] Older women today have lived through a number of society-wide changes. They have experienced narrowing racial inequality during the Great Society programs and the later effects of the erosion of many of those programs. They have seen large changes in (white) women's labor force participation (Goldin 1990, 2006), rapid advances in technology and in skill-biased technical change (e.g., Goldin and Katz 2008), and great strides in education.

Figure 3.1 shows the difference in the probability of being employed by age for birth cohorts from 1913 to 1968 for black women compared with white women. What is remarkable is the mostly steady decline in black women's employment in contrast to white women's at older ages and across cohorts. Figure 3.2 shows that black female employment initially increases across cohorts at younger ages and then flattens out at all ages, particularly for older groups in recent decades. In contrast, in figure 3.3 white women show stronger increases in employment at older ages across cohorts.[2] Given black

---

1. Brown v. Board of Education of Topeka, 347 U.S. 483 (1954).
2. The life cycle employment of women for cohorts born from the early 1930s to the late 1960s is explored by Goldin and Mitchell (2017). Goldin and Katz (chapter 1, this volume) show that labor force participation rates of the most recent cohorts in their forties are smaller

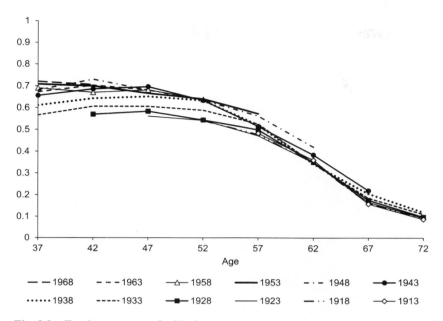

Fig. 3.2   Employment rates for black women
Source: Data from 1970–2000 census and 2004–2006 and 2009–2011 ACS.

women's rising educational attainment over this time period (for example, the average number of years of education for a black sixty-year-old woman rose from 7.5 in 1970 to 12.7 in 2010 [author's calculations from the census/ American Community Survey]), one might have expected a larger increase in employment for black women than what is shown in the cohort charts.

Although reasons for changes in black women's labor force participation are underexplored, and the age component of these changes is even more neglected, a somewhat larger literature looks at reasons for changes in the black-to-white female wage differential. The literature on changes in the racial wage gap in the 1970s and 1980s is sizable (e.g., Anderson and Shapiro 1996; Blau and Beller 1992; Bound and Dresser 1999; Cunningham and Zalokar 1992; Holzer 1998, among others). More recent papers update changes in wage differentials into the first decade of the twenty-first century (Browne and Askew 2005; Brown and Warner 2008; McHenry and McInerney 2014; Neal 2004; Pettit and Ewert 2009). In general, these papers find that black women's wages increased vis-à-vis white wages from the 1960s to 1980, but the wage gap widened between 1980 and 2000.[3] Wages and

than those of previous cohorts, but conclude that women are likely to continue to work even longer despite this decrease during midlife.

3. An interesting aspect of much of this earlier literature is that for some of these samples, black women's wages have been temporarily higher than white women's. Indeed, for the sample in this chapter, black women's earnings are briefly higher than those of white women in their late

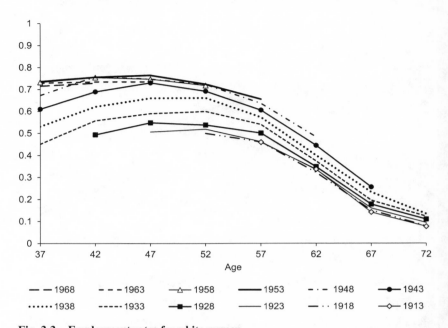

Fig. 3.3   Employment rates for white women
Source: Data from 1970–2000 census and 2004–2006 and 2009–2011 ACS.

employment capture different parts of the labor market experience and the relative status of black women compared with white women differs across these two outcomes.

Similar to some of the previous literature on wage differentials, I begin by making comparisons between black and white women as a whole. Cohort charts presenting employment outcomes by age show how employment outcomes have been changing by race over time.[4] I then explore potential reasons for the difference in racial employment rates over time using a regression framework that includes controls for education, marital status, children at home, home ownership, geography, and changes in welfare and Supplemental Security Income (SSI) using the census and the American Community Survey (ACS). None of the factors mentioned explains the racial difference and controlling for education exacerbates it.

I then focus on women with high school education to abstract from the effects of increased college going and find similar results. Finally, I use ordinary least squares (OLS) regressions on the full education sample in

---

thirties, early forties for cohorts born in the 1940s when limiting to the high school educated, but not when combining all education levels.

4. Employment was chosen as the outcome of interest, but patterns are nearly the same at these ages using "Not in the Labor Force" (NILF) as the outcome instead. The NILF results are not presented in the interest of brevity and are available from the author.

the Health and Retirement Survey (HRS) to explore the effects of wealth, occupation, industry, activities of daily living (ADL), gross motor skills, depression, and cognition on the racial difference in employment over time and find that changes in occupation, industry, ADL, and motor skills can help explain the change in participation by race.

3.2   Potential Reasons for Employment Changes by Race

3.2.1   Demographics

Lack of monetary resources and the need to provide for dependents may pull black women into the labor force (Bound, Schoenbaum, and Waidmann 1996). Differences in marital status and spousal income are important examples of differences in resources between black and white women, although historically unmarried black women have had stronger labor force attachment than have unmarried white women (Goldin 1977, 1990). In the 2011 ACS, 63 percent of white women ages fifty to seventy-two were married but only 36 percent of similar black women were married. The probability of being married decreases for both races by age and by cohort, but the decrease across cohorts is stronger for older black women than for older white women. For more information on the effect of marriage on women's work, see Maestas (chapter 2, this volume). Similarly, older black women are more likely to have dependents still in their households than are older white women. For example, in the 2011 ACS, 35 percent of black women ages fifty to seventy-two had any child at home in contrast with 26 percent of white women.[5]

Changes in educational status over time stand out as a determining factor of the black-white female wage gap in the wage literature (Anderson and Shapiro 1996; Conrad 2005; McElroy 2005; McHenry and McInerney 2014; Neal 2004).[6] From a theoretical standpoint, increasing education should increase labor force participation because education increases productivity and because investments in education are more likely to be made by those who can pay them off in the longer term (Goldin and Katz, chapter 1, this volume; Lusardi and Mitchell, chapter 6, this volume).

Geography is another demographic factor that may affect black and white employment differently over time. Several authors (e.g., see Cunningham and Zalokar [1992]; Kaplan, Ranjit, and Burgard [2008] for literature reviews) note that racial convergence in wages and health differs by geography, with the South converging later than other regions. It is not a priori clear how

5. Fahle and McGarry (chapter 5, this volume) also find that nonwhite women are more likely to provide care for their parents or in-laws, which leads to lower labor force attachment given their increased care responsibilities.

6. Cunningham and Zalokar (1992) is an exception; they find little effect of education on black women's increased relative wages between 1960 and 1980.

geographical differences will affect changes in employment outcomes for women by race.

3.2.2   Monetary Resources

Lack of retirement savings may encourage longer labor force participation (Lusardi and Mitchell, chapter 6, this volume). Using the 2010–2012 HRS, black women ages fifty to seventy-five have 21 percent of the total wealth of comparable white women, with $121,000 in assets compared with $558,000, and have 14 percent of the total nonhousing wealth of white women, with $54,000 in assets compared with $373,000. Home ownership is a form of forced retirement savings that may differ by race. Only 59 percent of black women ages fifty to seventy-two in the 2011 ACS own a home compared with 82 percent of white women.

Changes in government assistance can affect the opportunity cost of work (Neal 2004). Historically, lower wages for black women make employment less attractive, especially given higher wage replacement rates from Social Security. Biggs and Springstead (2008) find that the lowest quintile of earners has a greater than 100 percent replacement rate, whereas the second quintile is within the recommended 67 to 81 percent replacement rate (Munnell, Webb, and Delorme 2006). Indeed, looking at Social Security replacement rates by race, Bridges and Choudhury (2009) find higher replacement rates for blacks than for whites, and particularly for black women. Social Security generosity has been decreasing over time and across cohorts (Butrica, Iams, and Smith 2003/2004). In this volume (chapter 8), Gelber, Isen, and Song find that a reduction in Social Security benefits in the 1980s led to increases in labor force participation for older women. Moffitt (2015) notes that welfare spending has been increasing since a pause in the 1970s. The increase in spending has been shifting from poorer families to those with higher incomes and from single-parent families to married-parent families, both of which may increase white women's outside options compared to black women's. On the other hand, Moffitt (2015) finds a spending increase in favor of disability programs, which may favor older black women (who are more likely to be disabled) relative to older white women. Higher levels of government assistance mean that retirement can occur on a smaller nest egg.

3.2.3   Occupation and Industrial Changes

In addition to factors that lead to an increase in the supply of older black women in the labor force, the growth in the health care field may have increased the demand for older black women given the prevalence of these women in health care fields in previous years, particularly as nursing aides. Table 3.1 shows the most common occupations for middle-aged women in the 1990 census and for older women in the 2009–2011 ACS. In 1990, the most prevalent occupation for black middle-aged women was that of nursing aide, while white women were most likely to be employed in clerical posi-

Table 3.1   **Top ten occupations**

	Black		White	
Occupation title	No. obs.	Occupation title		No. obs.
Women ages fifty to seventy-five in the 2009–2011 ACS				
Nursing aides, orderlies, and attendants	330,297	Secretaries		1,707,987
Secretaries	137,083	Primary school teachers		1,070,439
Primary school teachers	115,771	Registered nurses		983,689
Housekeepers, maids, butlers, stewards	114,363	Nursing aides, orderlies, and attendants		713,891
Registered nurses	100,215	Bookkeepers and accounting and auditing		623,027
Cooks, variously defined	90,160	Other managers and administrators		619,669
Child care workers	86,327	Retail sales clerks		605,713
Other teachers	78,058	Other teachers		587,770
Janitors	71,989	Supervisors and proprietors of sales		540,277
Customer service reps, investigators	66,195	Cashiers		514,186
Women ages thirty-five to forty-nine in the 1990 census				
Nursing aides, orderlies, and attendant	196,485	Secretaries		1,486,971
Primary school teachers	133,880	Primary school teachers		1,195,672
Secretaries	116,600	Other managers and administrators		816,029
Janitors	74,716	Registered nurses		726,020
Registered nurses	74,306	Other salespersons		708,481
Cooks, variously defined	72,572	Bookkeepers and accounting and auditing		627,867
Housekeepers, maids, butlers, stewards	71,035	Supervisors and proprietors of sales		431,216
Assemblers of electrical equipment	68,543	Cashiers		414,459
Other managers and administrators	66,666	Nursing aides, orderlies, and attendants		403,098
General office clerks	63,327	General office clerks		355,867

Note: Occupation is coded using three-digit OCC 1990 coding from IPUMS. Number of women in each category is calculated using person weights. For 2009–2011, the number is averaged over the three years.

tions. Differential demand for these fields would suggest that black women would be more likely to be employed at older ages over time. On the other hand, the decline in manufacturing jobs has differentially hurt black women employed in those positions (Anderson and Shapiro 1996).

Related to occupational demand are occupational differences in the physical demands of jobs that can make women less able to do them as they age and potentially more prone to work-related health problems. Using O*NET data, Rho (2010) finds large differences by race in the physical demands for older women workers. In her paper, 38 percent of black women older than fifty-eight years are in physically demanding jobs in contrast to

30 percent of white women. Interestingly, she finds that the probability of being in a physically demanding job increases with age for black women older than fifty-eight years. The increase is consistent with a more general decrease in physically demanding jobs over time, noted in Johnson, Mermin, and Resseger (2007), although there is little information on changes in jobs with physical demands by cohort. Conversely, cognition and memory may be more important for desk jobs, which are more likely to be held by older white women.

3.2.4   Health

Poor health outcomes may lead to inability for women to work longer even if they need or desire to do so. On average black women have worse health than white women, leading to earlier retirement or disability. In the HRS, activities of daily living (ADL) provide a somewhat objective measure that signals poor health (Adams et al. 2004), and black women report more complications with ADL on a 1 to 5 scale. Using data from the 1992 HRS, Bound, Schoenbaum, and Waidmann (1996) find that black women in their forties and fifties would have greater attachment to the labor force than would white women if it were not for health conditions that limit their work ability. Similarly, higher mortality rates mean that less wealth is needed to finance retirement, all else being equal. Using the National Health Interview Survey Linked Mortality files from 1997 to 2004, Hummer and Chinn (2011) find that black women have 14 percent higher mortality than white women at age sixty-five. Although the racial gap in life expectancy at birth has been narrowing slowly but steadily (Masters et al. 2014), most literature has found the adult black-white mortality gap to be more constant (for the literature see Hummer and Chinn [2011]).

3.3   Data and Empirics

The primary data set used in this chapter is the US Census combined with the American Community Survey (ACS). Together, these provide basic labor market and demographic statistics from 1970 to 2011 to trace cohorts over time (Ruggles et al. 2015). The census and ACS were chosen as the main data sets because of their large sample size, the longevity of the repeated cross sections, and a wide array of variables that are consistent across years. Results that can be replicated in the Current Population Survey (CPS) are similar with the exception that the effect of adding marital status on the variable of interest is smaller.

The education variables used in these different data sets are not fully consistent and often change somewhat across years in the same data set. The variable for high school graduate used in this chapter includes those who have earned a high school diploma but have not earned a bachelor's degree (about 62 percent of the female black population ages fifty to seventy-five in the 2009–2011 ACS). The definition for "some college" changes across both census waves and the IPUMS ACS. Results are similar when those who are known to have earned an associate degree are excluded (about 7 percent of the black population ages fifty to seventy-five in the 2009–2011 ACS) and when results are limited to high school graduates known to have less than one year of college (about 38 percent of the same population), although this information is not available for all years. To get a measure of changing government income options specific to this group, average income variables for welfare income and Social Security income at the state × year level were created by collapsing the relevant income variables for the universe of women ages fifty to seventy-two.

To explore the effects of these different factors on the change in the black-to-white differential between the oldest and youngest cohorts, ordinary least squares regressions of the following form are used:[7]

$$(1) \quad \text{Employed}_{ist} = \beta_1 \text{Black}_{ist} + \text{Cohort}_{ist}\beta_2 + \text{Black}_{ist}\text{Cohort}_{ist}\beta_3 + X_{ist}\beta_4 + \delta_{st} + \gamma_a + \sigma_s + \alpha + \varepsilon.$$

Employed_{ist} is a dichotomous variable indicating whether or not the woman is employed; Black_{ist} is a dichotomous variable for whether a woman identifies as black; Cohort_{ist} is a vector of ten-year cohort dummies ranging from women born in the 1910s to those born in the 1940s. Similarly, $\text{Black}_{ist}\text{Cohort}_{ist}$ is the interaction of these latter two variables. When running the regressions, the omitted cohort will be women born in the 1910s and the variable of interest will be the comparison of black women born in the 1940s to those born in the 1910s.[8] In some regressions, X_{ist} is a vector of individual control variables including marital status, having a child at home, or owning a home. For some regressions, average dollars of welfare for black and white women ages fifty to seventy-two at the state × year level are included. Finally, γ_a age fixed effects are included in all regressions to account for different age distributions within cohorts and σ_s state fixed effects are included in some regressions to test for differences by geography that do not vary across time, and state × year fixed effects δ_{st} are included to test for differences in geography that do vary across time. Results are reported for ordinary least squares regression analysis for ease of interpretation and standard errors are clustered at the state level.

A second data set, the Health and Retirement Study (HRS) provides detailed wealth and health characteristics for women ages fifty to seventy-two

---

7. Probit analysis produces similar results.

8. For the census and ACS results, the universe was limited so that all cohorts include the full ages fifty to seventy-two year age band. In this case, consistency in ages was preferred over breadth given the large sample. The magnitude of the difference between the latest cohort and the earliest cohort is larger, but the patterns are the same when the 1900s cohort is used as the control and the 1950s cohort is included as the latest cohort.

from 1994 to 2012 (RAND 2016). This data set is discussed in more detail in the volume appendix.

Analysis for the HRS also uses equation (1), but uses a different universe because the HRS does not extend as far back as the census. $Cohort_{ist}$ is a vector of ten-year cohort dummies ranging from women born in the 1920s to those born in the 1950s with the 1920s cohort as the control.[9] Education dummies include no high school, high school graduate or some college, and bachelor's degree or more. The nonhousing wealth variable is inflated to 2014 dollars. The total wealth variable that also includes housing wealth provides nearly identical results to the nonhousing wealth variable despite losing more than 5,000 observations. The HRS includes information on the longest occupation and industry the individual was employed in prior to the start of the survey. I use the seventeen "longest occupation" dummies and the nineteen "longest industry dummies" included in the RAND HRS. Health and cognition measures include a 0 to 5 scale for ADLs, a 0 to 5 scale for gross motor skills, an indicator for feeling depressed, self-reported memory (1 to 5), immediate word recall (0 to 10), delayed word recall (0 to 10), and an indicator that the respondent could correctly count backward from twenty on the first try.[10] Other variables are defined as before. Results are weighted by person weight (the unweighted results are similar). Robust standard errors are presented.

3.4   Why Are Black Women, Relative to White, Not Working Longer?

3.4.1   Census and ACS

Table 3.2 provides results for equation (1) for the universe of all black and white women age fifty to seventy-two from cohorts born in the 1910s to those born in the 1940s. The variable of focus is the first row, black × 1940s cohort, and represents the change in the effect on employment of being black for women in the 1940s cohort in comparison with the 1910s cohort controlling for individual age dummies. A negative number means that the increase in employment between the earliest and latest cohorts in the sample is larger for white women than it is for black women. What is of more interest than the original magnitude of this difference is the effect of control variables on

9. The choice was made to provide the largest sample size possible and to make the results more comparable across ages and time with the ACS and census results. This choice creates a problem with consistency across years because the earliest cohort and the latest cohort include different ages. An alternative choice is to use consistent ages and fewer cohorts, which limits the age range to fifty-five to sixty-two and uses cohorts born from the 1930s to the 1950s. The magnitudes for these comparisons are different but the patterns are identical when making this choice, so it is omitted for brevity and is available from the author.

10. There are several other cognitive functioning measures in the HRS that provide nearly identical results. Counting backward from twenty was chosen because it provided the least loss of observations.

Table 3.2 Probability of employment for black women compared to white women ages fifty to seventy-two

	(1)	(2)	(3)	(4)	(5)	(6)	(7)	(8)
Black * 1940s cohort	-0.0798***	-0.0929***	-0.1041***	-0.1041***	-0.1039***	-0.1065***	-0.1040***	-0.0985***
	(0.0056)	(0.0054)	(0.0057)	(0.0057)	(0.0058)	(0.0054)	(0.0061)	(0.0049)
Black * 1930s cohort	-0.0411***	-0.0488***	-0.0577***	-0.0577***	-0.0580***	-0.0598***	-0.0578***	-0.0541***
	(0.0041)	(0.0042)	(0.0040)	(0.0041)	(0.0042)	(0.0036)	(0.0042)	(0.0035)
Black * 1920s cohort	-0.0169***	-0.0171***	-0.0235***	-0.0235***	-0.0235***	-0.0246***	-0.0235***	-0.0224***
	(0.0033)	(0.0035)	(0.0032)	(0.0033)	(0.0033)	(0.0031)	(0.0032)	(0.0032)
Black	0.0267***	0.0634***	0.0436***	0.0436***	0.0483***	0.0478***	0.0436***	0.0432***
	(0.0071)	(0.0069)	(0.0067)	(0.0066)	(0.0065)	(0.0064)	(0.0061)	(0.0067)
1940s cohort	0.1389***	0.0797***	0.0716***	0.0716***	0.0687***	0.0729***	0.0732***	-0.0171***
	(0.0049)	(0.0058)	(0.0053)	(0.0053)	(0.0056)	(0.0049)	(0.0213)	(0.0039)
1930s cohort	0.0719***	0.0349***	0.0325***	0.0325***	0.0298***	0.0330***	0.0342***	-0.0368***
	(0.0039)	(0.0048)	(0.0043)	(0.0043)	(0.0045)	(0.0039)	(0.0147)	(0.0035)
1920s cohort	0.0123***	-0.0068*	-0.0060*	-0.0060*	-0.0079**	-0.0065**	-0.0044	-0.0446***
	(0.0034)	(0.0035)	(0.0032)	(0.0032)	(0.0033)	(0.0028)	(0.0080)	(0.0027)
Observations	5,141,247	5,141,247	5,141,247	5,141,247	5,141,247	5,141,247	5,141,247	5,141,247
Age fixed effects	X	X	X	X	X	X	X	X
Education dummies		X	X	X	X	X	X	X
Marital status dummies			X	X	X	X	X	X
Any child at home				X				
Own home					X			
State fixed effects						X		
State * year welfare, SSI income for older women					X	X		
State * year fixed effects								X

Source: Data are from the 1970–2000 US Censuses and the 2004–2006 and 2009–2011 ACS.

Notes: Only black and white women ages fifty to seventy-two are included in the universe. Results are from an ordinary least squares regression using equation (1). Standard errors clustered on state are in parentheses. Omitted cohort is women born 1910–1919. The 1920s cohort includes women born 1920–1929, and so on. Education dummies include no high school, high school graduate and some college, bachelor's, and post-bachelor's degrees. Marital status dummies include never married, married, divorced, and widowed. Any child at home is any child at home. State * year welfare and SSI income variables are the average such income streams for older black and white women in the state of residence.

***Significant at the 1 percent level.

**Significant at the 5 percent level.

*Significant at the 10 percent level.

the coefficient of interest. First, note that in all of these regressions the black × cohort coefficients grow increasingly negative as the cohorts get younger, suggesting that this difference is increasing across cohorts.

Next, these telescoping regressions show the effect of adding controls to the regression on the variable of interest, the coefficient of black × 1940s cohort. When the coefficient becomes less negative (increases), that means the control helps to explain some of the difference between black and white employment outcomes in column (1). Conversely, when this coefficient becomes more negative (decreases) after a control is added, that means the control exacerbates the racial employment gap across cohorts.

The coefficient of black × 1940s cohort in column (1) provides the baseline black-white difference in employment across these two cohorts, in this case −0.080, suggesting that, controlling for age fixed effects, the change in employment for older black women from the 1910s cohort to the 1940s cohort is worse than the change for older white women across the same cohorts. Adding education controls to the regression, as in column (2), decreases the size of the black × 1940s cohort coefficient by 1.3 percentage points to −0.093. Including marital status controls decreases the size of the coefficient an additional 1.1 percentage points to −0.104 in column (3), which then becomes the new baseline for the remaining columns. The presence of a child at home, added in column (4), has no additional impact. Owning a home also has very little effect on the coefficient in column (5). Column (6) provides geographical controls at the state level and shows a slight decrease of 0.2 percentage points from column (3) to −0.1065. Controls for state × year income welfare and social security income in column (7) have little effect on the coefficient, which still rounds to −0.104. Finally, including state × year fixed effects decreases the coefficient of interest in column (8) to −0.099, indicating that although state-level differences may not affect the racial difference in employment over time, state-level differences on the aggregate that vary over time may explain a small part of the change.

Taking these results together, factors that might help explain the increased black-white employment gap include home ownership, changes in occupational and industrial demand broadly, government transfer payments, and unexplained state × year variation. None of these controls explains much of the gap. On the other hand, education, marital status, generalized state fixed effects, and controls for specific health and clerical occupations exacerbate the racial cohort employment gap. Overall, these results support the idea that, as with changes in wage differences, black-white educational differences between cohorts are especially important.

Although these educational differences are important, there are interesting changes even within educational groups. For example, figures 3.4 and 3.5 plot the black-white employment difference across cohorts for thirty-seven- to seventy-two-year-old non-high-school graduates and college graduates, respectively. Positive numbers mean that black women are more likely to be

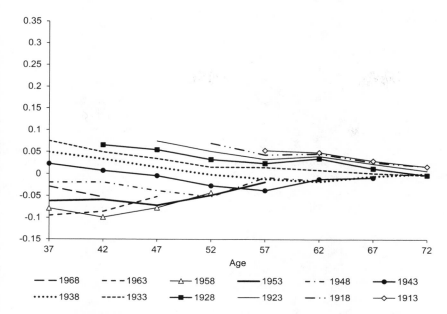

Fig. 3.4 Difference in employment rates for non-high-school-graduate black women compared to white women

Sources: Data from 1970–2000 census and 2004–2006 and 2009–2011 ACS.

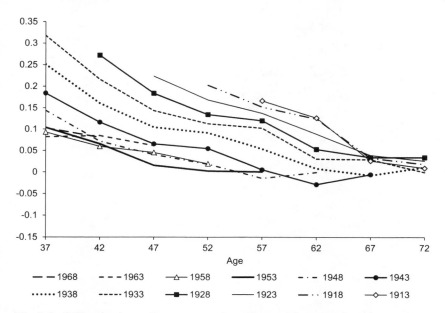

Fig. 3.5 Difference in employment rates for college-graduate black women compared to white women

Sources: Data from 1970–2000 census and 2004–2006 and 2009–2011 ACS.

employed than white women, and negative numbers mean that white women are more likely to be employed than black women. The patterns across the two groups are widely different. For the non-high-school-graduate group, black women work more than white women only in the oldest cohorts and predominately at younger ages. Black college graduates are still more likely to be employed than white college graduates at almost all ages. Though interesting, those without a high school diploma represent less than 20 percent of older black women in 2009–2011, and those with a college degree or more represent only 18 percent of these women.

To subtract out the effects of changes in educational attainment over the time period, the remainder of this section focuses on the largest educational group, high school graduates. Not only is this group relatively large, but it is also likely to have been negatively affected by skill-biased technical change (e.g., Goldin and Katz 2008), and increasing inequality (Autor 2014). The same group is likely to be on the margin of government program use (Irving and Loveless 2015). In this case, high school graduate is operationalized in this section as everyone with a high school degree but not a bachelor's degree. Results are similar looking at those with just a high school degree and no additional schooling, although additional schooling without further degrees is coded inconsistently across the census and ACS.

Figure 3.6 shows a version of the black-white employment differences

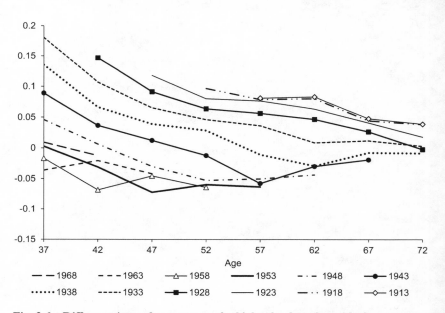

Fig. 3.6   Difference in employment rates for high-school-graduate black women compared to white women

Sources: Data from 1970–2000 census and 2004–2006 and 2009–2011 ACS.

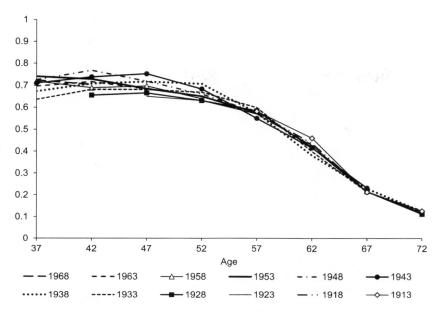

Fig. 3.7   Employment rates for black women with high school and some college
Sources: Data from 1970–2000 census and 2004–2006 and 2009–2011 ACS.

shown in figure 3.1, but for high school graduates only. The steady decline in black women's employment compared with white women's at older ages and across cohorts is larger for high school graduates than for all women. Figure 3.7 shows that, like in figure 3.2, black female employment initially increases across cohorts at younger ages and then flattens out at all ages, particularly for older groups in recent decades. The cohort lines are tighter, indicating less change across cohorts than for black women of all education levels. Limiting to only those with exactly a high school diploma (figures available from author) would show even closer lines. High-school-educated white women in figure 3.8, on the other hand, have more similar patterns to those for white women of all education levels, as in figure 3.3. Again, white women catch up to and then surpass black women's employment. In contrast, the employment of black women does not increase similarly.

As before with table 3.2, it is possible to explore how different controls affect the black × 1940s cohort coefficient using equation (1), this time limiting the universe to high school graduates in table 3.3. The difference in employment outcomes for this group in comparison with the 1910s cohort group is larger than it was for the entire sample, with a magnitude of −0.095 in column (1) compared with −0.080 for the all education sample.

Controlling for marital status again decreases the coefficient, this time by about 1.4 percentage points in column (2) to −0.109, which then becomes

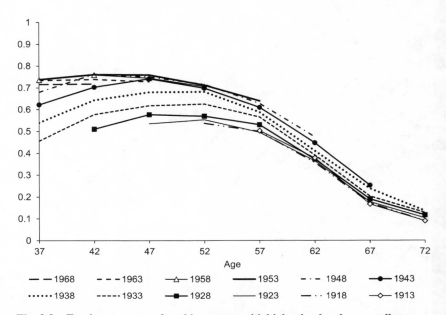

Fig. 3.8   Employment rates for white women with high school and some college
Sources: Data from 1970–2000 census and 2004–2006 and 2009–2011 ACS.

the base regression for the remainder of the columns. Any child at home again has little effect in column (3). Owning a home (column [4]) offers only a slight increase (0.1 percentage points) to −0.108 from the coefficient of black × 1940s cohort in column (2). State fixed effects slightly increase the coefficient by less than 0.1 percentage points to −0.108 in column (5). State × year controls for welfare and Social Security income increase the coefficient by less than 0.1 percentage points to −0.108 in column (6). State × year fixed effects have a smaller effect on the coefficient for this group, increasing the coefficient in column (2) by 0.8 percentage points to −0.100.

Taken as a whole, the results for the high school graduate and some college group are very similar to the results for all women, which should not be surprising given that this education group makes up the majority of the black women in recent samples.

3.4.2   Health and Retirement Study

Table 3.4 provides results for equation (1) for the universe of all black and white women age fifty to seventy-two from cohorts born in the 1920s to those born in the 1950s. The variable of focus is the first row, black × 1950s cohort, and represents the change in the effect on employment of being black for women in the 1950s cohort in comparison with the 1920s cohort controlling for individual age dummies. For none of the regressions in table

Table 3.3   Probability of employment for high-school-graduate black women compared to white women

	(1)	(2)	(3)	(4)	(5)	(6)	(7)
Black * 1940s cohort	-0.0951***	-0.1086***	-0.1089***	-0.1076***	-0.1080***	-0.1081***	-0.1002***
	(0.0067)	(0.0069)	(0.0068)	(0.0069)	(0.0061)	(0.0070)	(0.0061)
Black * 1930s cohort	-0.0492***	-0.0604***	-0.0608***	-0.0600***	-0.0596***	-0.0602***	-0.0540***
	(0.0058)	(0.0056)	(0.0057)	(0.0058)	(0.0047)	(0.0056)	(0.0049)
Black * 1920s cohort	-0.0089*	-0.0170***	-0.0172***	-0.0165***	-0.0161***	-0.0170***	-0.0135**
	(0.0052)	(0.0051)	(0.0052)	(0.0052)	(0.0050)	(0.0052)	(0.0052)
Black	0.0646***	0.0403***	0.0399***	0.0436***	0.0414***	0.0398***	0.0364***
	(0.0076)	(0.0071)	(0.0069)	(0.0072)	(0.0064)	(0.0064)	(0.0062)
1940s cohort	0.1078***	0.0999***	0.1001***	0.0968***	0.1008***	0.1065***	-0.003
	(0.0053)	(0.0048)	(0.0049)	(0.0051)	(0.0045)	(0.0229)	(0.0043)
1930s cohort	0.0588***	0.0575***	0.0574***	0.0545***	0.0573***	0.0622***	-0.0215***
	(0.0044)	(0.0039)	(0.0039)	(0.0041)	(0.0033)	(0.0157)	(0.0036)
1920s cohort	0.0059*	0.0080**	0.0078**	0.0059*	0.0071***	0.0106	-0.0359***
	(0.0034)	(0.0030)	(0.0029)	(0.0032)	(0.0026)	(0.0084)	(0.0028)
Observations	2,904,866	2,904,866	2,904,866	2,904,866	2,904,866	2,904,866	2,904,866
Age fixed effects	X	X	X	X	X	X	
Marital status dummies		X	X	X	X	X	
Any child at home			X	X			
Own home				X			
State fixed effects					X		
State * year welfare, SSI income for older women				X	X	X	
State * year fixed effects							X

Notes: Universe is limited to black and white women with high school degrees or some college, including associate degrees. Otherwise notes are the same as in table 3.2.

***Significant at the 1 percent level.

**Significant at the 5 percent level.

*Significant at the 10 percent level.

Table 3.4   Probability of employment for black women ages fifty to seventy-two compared to white women

	(1)	(2)	(3)	(4)	(5)	(6)	(7)	(8)	(9)
Black * 1950s cohort	-0.1057***	-0.1058***	-0.0762*	-0.0821**	-0.0978***	-0.0741**	-0.1170***	-0.1205***	-0.0406
	(0.0248)	(0.0248)	(0.0402)	(0.0398)	(0.0248)	(0.0298)	(0.0258)	(0.0311)	(0.0429)
Black * 1940s cohort	-0.1007***	-0.1014***	-0.0674*	-0.0623*	-0.0857***	-0.0628**	-0.1095***	-0.1109***	-0.019
	(0.0233)	(0.0233)	(0.0374)	(0.0370)	(0.0236)	(0.0289)	(0.0244)	(0.0300)	(0.0407)
Black * 1930s cohort	-0.026	-0.0275	-0.0339	-0.0373	-0.0195	-0.0013	-0.0344	-0.0326	0.0029
	(0.0228)	(0.0228)	(0.0370)	(0.0367)	(0.0231)	(0.0286)	(0.0240)	(0.0298)	(0.0405)
Black	0.0421**	0.0402*	0.0277	0.0202	0.0545**	0.0358	0.0591***	0.0819***	0.0085
	(0.0213)	(0.0213)	(0.0360)	(0.0356)	(0.0217)	(0.0275)	(0.0225)	(0.0285)	(0.0396)
1950s cohort	0.0588***	0.0584***	0.0351**	0.0367**	0.0717***	0.0723***	0.0542***	0.0757***	0.028
	(0.0124)	(0.0124)	(0.0162)	(0.0162)	(0.0123)	(0.0134)	(0.0125)	(0.0141)	(0.0173)
1940s cohort	0.0504***	0.0509***	0.0335**	0.0347**	0.0557***	0.0554***	0.0478***	0.0618***	0.019
	(0.0104)	(0.0104)	(0.0142)	(0.0142)	(0.0104)	(0.0118)	(0.0106)	(0.0121)	(0.0156)
1930s cohort	0.0222**	0.0234**	0.0306**	0.0328**	0.0210**	0.0173	0.0211**	0.0284**	0.0088
	(0.0095)	(0.0095)	(0.0135)	(0.0135)	(0.0096)	(0.0111)	(0.0098)	(0.0112)	(0.0150)
Observations	62,164	62,164	49,281	49,075	62,072	61,107	60,716	55,328	48,711
Age fixed effects	X	X	X	X	X	X	X	X	X
Marital status dummies	X	X	X	X	X	X	X	X	X
Education dummies	X	X	X	X	X	X	X	X	X
Nonhousing wealth		X							
Longest occupation dummies		X						X	
Longest industry dummies			X					X	
Activities of daily living (0–5)				X					

Gross motor scale (0–5)		X	X
Felt depressed		X	
Memory and counting backward		X	

Source: Data are from the 1994–2012 HRS.

Notes: Only black and white women ages fifty to seventy-two are included in the universe. Results are from an ordinary least squares regression using equation (1). Robust standard errors are in parentheses. Omitted cohort is women born 1922–1929 (1920–1921 are outside the age range). The 1930s cohort includes women born 1930–1939, and so on. Education dummies include no high school, high school graduate and some college, and bachelor's including post-bachelor's degrees. Marital status dummies include never married, partnered, married, divorced, and widowed. Memory controls include self-reported memory, immediate word recall (1–10), and delayed word recall. Counting backward indicates that the participant was able to correctly count backward from twenty on the first try.

***Significant at the 1 percent level.

**Significant at the 5 percent level.

*Significant at the 10 percent level.

3.4 is the change between the coefficient of black × 1930s cohort significantly different from that of the omitted 1920s cohort, but that may be because of the small sample size for the 1920s cohort in this set and because of the smaller sample size of the HRS. For the most part, the coefficients of the black × cohort interaction become more negative with increasing cohorts as they did with the census/ACS regressions.

The coefficient of black × 1950s cohort in column (1) provides the baseline black-white difference in employment across these two cohorts including controls for age, marital status, and education, in this case −0.106, suggesting that the increase in employment from the 1920s cohort to the 1950s cohort is larger for older white women than for older black women.[11] Controlling for nonhousing wealth in column (2) does not change the coefficient. Adding indicators for the longest occupation in column (3) decreases significance and increases magnitude to a marginal −0.076. Controls for longest industry in column (4) have a similar effect, increasing the magnitude to −0.082, though this result remains significant.[12]

Controlling for one measure of health, difficulty with ADL, in column (5) also increases the coefficient, but only to −0.098. Controlling specifically for difficulty with gross motor skills increases the coefficient to −0.074 in column (6). Controlling for depression decreases the coefficient of black × 1950s cohort in column (7) to −0.117, indicating that in the absence of differences in depression across the two groups, black employment would be higher in comparison with white employment. Similarly, including controls for memory and cognition also decreases the coefficient in column (8), indicating that absent these changes, black women's employment would also be higher.[13]

Column (9) includes all of the controls that increased the coefficient of black × 1950s cohort in the previous regressions. The coefficient drops to less than half of the original coefficient, at −0.041, and loses even marginal statistical significance. It should be noted that column (9) is only suggestive—the loss of significance and magnitude could also be caused by the drop in observations, from more than 62,000 in column (1) to fewer than 49,000, and a byproduct of having a large number of additional controls.[14]

---

11. Controlling for husband's income or for household income other than the respondent's income does not change the coefficient appreciably once marital status is controlled for.

12. Around 13,000 observations are dropped due to "missing," "not asked this wave," and "other census code." The results in column (1) are nearly identical when limited to the universe in column (3) and are slightly attenuated with a coefficient of −0.091 for black × 1950s cohort when limited to the universe in column (4), suggesting that sample selection is not a major cause of the decreased coefficients on black × 1950s cohort.

13. Nearly 7,000 observations are lost in column (8) to missing or proxy respondent. Limiting the regression in column (1) to the universe in column (8) produces a coefficient of −0.099, which is less negative than the full-sample coefficient, making the decrease to −0.12 by the addition of controls even more striking.

14. Note that the additional controls still retain their own significance and have the predicted sign for their direct effect on employment outcomes, suggesting that the regression results are not completely attenuated.

The HRS has a wealth of variables measuring different aspects of health and cognition that have been tested in addition to the ones presented here. The inclusion of self-reported health has no added effect on the coefficient of interest.[15] Debt may be of special interest given that Lusardi and Mitchell (chapter 6, this volume) find that debt is one reason for women's working longer in recent cohorts. There is no effect, however, on the coefficient of interest when debt is included as a control, suggesting that its effects are not differential by race over time.

Overall, factors that might help explain at least half of the increased black-white employment gap include changes in occupation, industries, ADL, and gross motor skills. On the other hand, controls for depression and cognition exacerbate the racial cohort employment gap.

3.5 Discussion and Conclusion

Why are black older women not working longer relative to white women? Older black women have worse employment outcomes, worse health, and fewer resources than comparable white women. Although increasing percentages of both black and white women across cohorts acquire bachelor's degrees or further education, black women's employment outcomes have stagnated whereas white women's have increased continually across cohorts, surpassing those of black women. The result is that each newer cohort sees a larger relative difference between the employment of blacks and whites across cohorts. The gap is even larger when the sample is limited to high-school-educated women, which is the largest educational subset of older black women, the most likely to be negatively affected by skill-biased technical change and increasing inequality, and the most likely to be on the margin of government program use.

The decrease in relative employment is surprising because middle-aged black women from these cohorts were more likely to work than similar white women, as were older black women from earlier cohorts. The relative picture for younger cohorts is not much better. Although the decline in outcomes such as relative employment or full-time wages seems to have stopped, it has mostly stagnated and stabilized at negative levels for black women compared with white women.

This chapter has investigated different factors that may affect black women's labor force participation differentially compared with white women's to explain changes over age and across cohorts for black women's

---

15. The inclusion of a variable for fine motor skills has no effect on the coefficient of interest. Other HRS variables that measure cognition have similar results to counting backward from twenty. Results are also similar in column (8) if the cognition and memory variables are included in separate regressions, though with these separate regressions the coefficient of interest is closer to -0.11. Self-reported health is not shown because, although the measure generally tracks with objective health measures such as mortality rates (Adams et al. 2004; Heiss et al. 2009), it may suffer reverse causality with employment.

lower employment compared with white. Differences in home ownership and government transfer payments account for at most a small part of the difference. Differences in occupation, industry, ADLs, and gross motor skills explain a larger amount of the difference. Other factors that could be expected to explain the gap such as education, marital status, depression, and cognition exacerbate the racial cohort employment gap.

Not all potential explanations for changes in the black-white employment gap could be tested in this framework. For example, even after controlling for levels of education, changes in education over time could still have additional impacts on employment outcomes. On the one hand, quality of schooling for black women in these cohorts has increased over time, potentially providing them with greater human capital (e.g., Carruthers and Wanamaker 2013; Conrad 2005; Margo 1990). On the other hand, removal of educational barriers allowed more high-ability black women to select into college and therefore out of the sample of high school graduates and into the sample of college graduates, which could affect the results for the high school graduate sample.

The national decline in unionization (Mishel 2012) also has ambiguous predictions for black women's labor force participation in comparison with white. Although union jobs are "better" jobs with higher wages and more benefits that render work more attractive, they also tend to have structures that encourage people to retire at earlier ages. For example, a 1999 study using the Employment Cost Index found that union workers were 22.5 percent more likely to receive pension benefits (Pierce 1999). The census does not have information on unionization and the CPS only has the variable easily available starting in 1990. Older black women in the 2014 CPS sample are about 2 percentage points more likely to be in a union than similar white women (14 percent versus 12 percent).

Discrimination is another factor that could change for black women by age and time. Although much research has documented and explored discrimination against younger black workers, we know very little about labor market discrimination against older black workers. Numerous empirical studies demonstrate race discrimination against younger entry-level workers, but much less work has been done exploring differential treatment of older workers and applicants by race. Indeed, there is no developed theory of discrimination specific to this age group. Statistical discrimination predictions could go in either direction based on whether positive or negative stereotypes of older black women or older white women dominate. For example, black women's strong previous labor force participation could lead to positive stereotypes about human capital and future labor force participation. In contrast, black women and white women are about equally likely to be working conditional on poor health, but the higher incidence of self-reported poor health among black women may increase negative employer stereotypes about the health of black workers. A recent laboratory study

(Lahey and Oxley 2016) suggests that hiring discrimination against black women compared with white women changes by the age of the worker, but much more work needs to be done in this area.

As this book should make clear, working longer is important for the economy, the solvency of government programs, and people's well-being. Black women have different histories and outcomes on average than white women. It is important to take these differences into consideration in policy analysis going forward.

References

Adams, Peter, Michael D. Hurd, Daniel L. McFadden, Angela Merrill, and Tiago Ribeiro. 2004. "Healthy, Wealthy, and Wise? Tests for Direct Causal Paths between Health and Socioeconomic Status." In *Perspectives on the Economics of Aging*, edited by David A. Wise, 415–526. Chicago: University of Chicago Press.

Anderson, Deborah, and David Shapiro. 1996. "Racial Differences in Access to High-Paying Jobs and the Wage Gap between Black and White Women." *Industrial & Labor Relations Review* 49:273–86.

Autor, David H. 2014. "Skills, Education, and the Rise of Earnings Inequality among the 'Other 99 Percent.'" *Science* 344:843–51.

Biggs, Andrew G., and Glenn R. Springstead. 2008. "Alternate Measures of Replacement Rates for Social Security Benefits and Retirement Income." *Social Security Bulletin* 68:1–19.

Blau, Francine D., and Andrea H. Beller. 1992. "Black-White Earnings over the 1970s and 1980s: Gender Differences in Trends." *Review of Economics and Statistics* 74:276–86.

Bound, John, and Laura Dresser. 1999. "Losing Ground: The Erosion of Relative Earnings of African American Women during the 1980s." In *Latinas and African American Women at Work: Race, Gender, and Economic Inequality*, edited by Irene Browne, 61–104. New York: Russell Sage.

Bound, John, Michael Schoenbaum, and Timothy Waidmann. 1996. "Race Differences in Labor Force Attachment and Disability Status." *Gerontologist* 36:311.

Bridges, Benjamin, and Sharmila Choudhury. 2009. "Examining Social Security Benefits as a Retirement Resource for Near-Retirees, by Race and Ethnicity, Nativity, and Disability Status." *Social Security Bulletin* 69:19–44.

Brown, Tyson H., and David F. Warner. 2008. "Divergent Pathways? Racial/Ethnic Differences in Older Women's Labor Force Withdrawal." *Journal of Gerontology: Social Sciences* 63B:S122–34.

Browne, Irene, and Rachel Askew. 2005. "Race, Ethnicity, and Wage Inequality among Women: What Happened in the 1990s and Early 21st Century?" *American Behavioral Scientist* 48:1275–92.

Butrica, Barbara A., Howard M. Iams, and Karen E. Smith. 2003/2004. "Changing Impact of Social Security on Retirement Income in the United States." *Social Security Bulletin* 65:1–13.

Carruthers, Celeste K., and Marianne H. Wanamaker. 2013. "Closing the Gap? The Effect of Private Philanthropy on the Provision of African-American Schooling in the US South." *Journal of Public Economics* 101:53–67.

Conrad, Cecilia. 2005. "Changes in the Labor Market Status of Black Women, 1960–2000." In *African Americans in the US Economy*, edited by Cecilia A. Conrad, John Whitehead, Patrick L. Mason, and James Stewart, 157–62. Lanham, MD: Rowman & Littlefield Publishers.

Cunningham, James S., and Nadja Zalokar. 1992. "The Economic Progress of Black Women, 1940–1980: Occupational Distribution and Relative Wages." *Industrial & Labor Relations Review* 45:540–55.

Goldin, Claudia. 1977. "Female Labor Force Participation: The Origin of Black and White Differences, 1870 and 1880." *Journal of Economic History* 37:87–108.

———. 1990. *Understanding the Gender Gap: An Economic History of American Women*. New York: Oxford University Press.

———. 2006. "The Quiet Revolution That Transformed Women's Employment, Education, and Family." *American Economic Review* 96:1–21.

Goldin, Claudia, and Lawrence F. Katz. 2008. *The Race between Education and Technology*. Cambridge, MA: Harvard University Press.

Goldin, Claudia, and Joshua Mitchell. 2017. "The New Life Cycle of Women's Employment: Disappearing Humps, Sagging Middles, Expanding Tops." *Journal of Economic Perspectives* 31:161–82.

Heiss, Florian, Axel Börsch-Supan, Michael Hurd, and David A. Wise. 2009. "Pathways to Disability: Predicting Health Trajectories." In *Health at Older Ages: The Causes and Consequences of Declining Disability among the Elderly*, edited by David M. Cutler and David A. Wise, 105–50. Chicago: University of Chicago Press.

Holzer, Harry J. 1998. "Employer Skill Demands and Labor Market Outcomes of Blacks and Women." *Industrial & Labor Relations Review* 52:82–98.

Hummer, Robert A., and Juanita J. Chinn. 2011. "Race/Ethnicity and US Adult Mortality: Progress, Prospects, and New Analyses." *Du Bois Review: Social Science Research on Race* 8:5–24.

Irving, Shelly K., and Tracy A. Loveless. 2015. "Dynamics of Economic Well-Being: Participation in Government Programs, 2009–2012: Who Gets Assistance?" Report no. P70-141, Household Economic Studies: US Department of Commerce, Economics and Statistics Administration, US Census Bureau. https://www.census.gov/library/publications/2015/demo/p70-141.html.

Johnson, Richard W., Gordon B. T. Mermin, and Matthew G. Resseger. 2007. "Employment at Older Ages and the Changing Nature of Work." Paper no. 2007-20, AARP Public Policy Institute and Urban Institute. http://www.urban.org/sites/default/files/publication/31146/1001154-Employment-at-Older-Ages-and-the-Changing-Nature-of-Work.PDF.

Kaplan, George A., Nalini Ranjit, and Sarah A. Burgard. 2008. "Lifting Gates, Lengthening Lives: Did Civil Rights Policies Improve the Health of African American Women in the 1960s and 1970s?" In *Making Americans Healthier: Social and Economic Policy as Health Policy*, edited by Robert F. Schoeni, James S. House, George A. Kaplan, and Harold Pollack, 145–69. New York: Russell Sage Foundation.

Lahey, Joanna, and Douglas Oxley. 2016. "Discrimination at the Intersection of Age, Race, and Gender: Evidence from a Lab-in-the-Field Experiment." Working Paper, Texas A&M University and University of Wyoming.

Lang, Kevin, and Jee-Yeon K. Lehmann. 2012. "Racial Discrimination in the Labor Market: Theory and Empirics." *Journal of Economic Literature* 50:959–1006.

Margo, Robert A. 1990. *Race and Schooling in the South, 1880–1950: An Economic History*. Chicago: University of Chicago Press.

Masters, Ryan K., Robert A. Hummer, Daniel A. Powers, Audrey Beck, Shih-Fan

Lin, and Brian Karl Finch. 2014. "Long-Term Trends in Adult Mortality for US Blacks and Whites: An Examination of Period- and Cohort-Based Changes." *Demography* 51:2047–73.

McElroy, Susan Williams. 2005. "Race and Gender Differences in the US Labor Market: The Impact of Educational Attainment." In *African Americans in the US Economy*, edited by Cecilia A. Conrad, John Whitehead, Patrick L. Mason, and James Stewart, 133–40. Lanham, MD: Rowman & Littlefield Publishers.

McHenry, Peter, and Melissa McInerney. 2014. "The Importance of Cost of Living and Education in Estimates of the Conditional Wage Gap between Black and White Women." *Journal of Human Resources* 49:695–722.

Mishel, Lawrence. 2012. "Unions, Inequality, and Faltering Middle-Class Wages." *Economic Policy Institute Issue Brief* 342:1–12.

Moffitt, Robert A. 2015. "The Deserving Poor, the Family, and the US Welfare System." *Demography* 52:729–49.

Munnell, Alicia, Anthony Webb, and Luke Delorme. 2006. "A New National Retirement Risk Index." Issue in Brief no. 48, Center for Retirement Research at Boston College. http://crr.bc.edu/wp-content/uploads/2006/06/ib_48.pdf.

Neal, Derek. 2004. "The Measured Black-White Wage Gap among Women is too Small." *Journal of Political Economy* 112 (S1): S1–28.

Pettit, Becky, and Stephanie Ewert. 2009. "Employment Gains and Wage Declines: The Erosion of Black Women's Relative Wages since 1980." *Demography* (pre-2011) 46:469–92.

Pierce, Brook. 1999. "Compensation Inequality." BLS Working Paper no. 323, US Department of Labor, Bureau of Labor Statistics. https://www.bls.gov/ore/pdf/ec990040.pdf.

RAND HRS Data, Version O. 2016. RAND Center for the Study of Aging with funding from the National Institute on Aging and the Social Security Administration, Santa Monica, CA, RAND.

Rho, Hye Jin. 2010. "Hard Work? Patterns in Physically Demanding Labor among Older Workers." CEPR Report, Center for Economic and Policy Research, Washington, DC. http://cepr.net/publications/reports/patterns-in-physically-demanding-labor-among-older-workers.

Ruggles, Steven, Katie Genadek, Ronald Goeken, Josiah Grover, and Matthew Sobek. 2015. "Integrated Public Use Microdata Series: Version 6.0 [Machine-Readable Database]." Minneapolis, University of Minnesota.

II

Family Matters: Caregiving, Marriage, and Divorce

Changes in Marriage and Divorce as Drivers of Employment and Retirement of Older Women

Claudia Olivetti and Dana Rotz

4.1 Introduction

Employment and marital history are both important determinants of labor force participation and financial security at later ages. But these outcomes and their relationships vary significantly by gender, education, and cohort. Understanding how employment and marital history impact later life outcomes is particularly relevant for today's older women who have substantially higher labor force participation rates than past cohorts (cf. Goldin and Katz, chapter 1, this volume, for evidence and discussion of determinants).

Marital status and marital history both shape employment behavior at later ages. Current marital status influences employment in the established way. But marital history is also important, as past marriages and divorces shape previous economic decisions and the processes of human and financial capital accumulation, and thus can have large impacts on a woman's

Claudia Olivetti is professor of economics at Boston College and a research associate of the National Bureau of Economic Research. Dana Rotz is a senior researcher at Mathematica Policy Research.

The views expressed in this chapter are those of the authors and do not necessarily represent the opinions of their respective institutions. This chapter was prepared for the Women Working Longer Conference hosted by the National Bureau of Economic Research in Cambridge, MA, on May 21–22, 2016. We thank Jesse Bruhn, Marco Ghiani, Elias Sanchez-Eppler, and James Ledoux who provided expert research assistance. We also thank Claudia Goldin, Larry Katz, Yue Li, Alessandra Voena, and participants in the "Women Working Longer" conference for valuable comments and suggestions. We gratefully acknowledge the financial support of the Alfred P. Sloan Foundation's Working Longer program under grant no. 2013-6-16, "Women Working Longer." For acknowledgments, sources of research support, and disclosure of the authors' material financial relationships, if any, please see http://www.nber.org/chapters/c13806 .ack.

budget set and choices at later ages. In a life cycle perspective, the age at which a woman experiences a divorce might matter because it could affect the probability of remarriage and her ability to invest in human and financial capital. Increased divorce risk (from, for example, changes in the legal environment) might also impact the work decisions of a married woman through changes in household bargaining power and economic incentives throughout married life. In the face of higher divorce risk, which increases the probability of being in a low consumption state in the future, married women have had an increased incentive to enhance their own earning potential through labor market experience, education, and/or occupational choice, as a kind of self-insurance (Greene and Quester 1982; Johnson and Skinner 1986). Moreover, if divorce is more likely, women can anticipate spending less of their adult life in marriage, thus reducing the returns from specializing in home production (Stevenson 2007). Increases in divorce risk might also affect married women's propensity to save and accumulate financial capital (Voena 2015).

The literature on retirement security has shown the importance of marital history in determining later-life economic outcomes, focusing mostly on women in the 1930 to 1949 birth cohorts (e.g., Couch et al. 2011; Holden and Fontes 2009; Munnell 2004; Tamborini and Whitman 2007; Tamborini, Iams, and Whitman 2009; Ulker 2009; Vespa and Painter 2011; Wilmoth and Koso 2002; Zagorsky 2005; Zissimopoulos, Karney, and Rauer 2008). The women in these cohorts had relatively low labor force attachment. Thus, their financial positions at later ages are intimately linked to their husbands' income and savings behaviors. We argue that these cohorts of women were also likely to have been greatly disadvantaged by the (probably unexpected) shift from consent to unilateral divorce that was associated with a large temporary increase in divorce rates (Friedberg 1998; Wolfers 2006).

Economists have previously used the shift to unilateral divorce to study the effects of divorce laws on the welfare of children (Gruber 2004), marital conflict (Stevenson and Wolfers 2006), and women's labor supply decisions (Fernández and Wong 2014b; Gray 1998; Peters 1986; Stevenson 2008). Unilateral divorce may also have important effects on household savings and investments. Stevenson (2007) evaluates the impact of divorce on marriage-specific investment such as the purchase of a house, showing that unilateral divorce tends to decrease such investments. Voena (2015) estimates the empirical relationship between divorce, married women's labor force participation, and household savings. Both papers show that property-division laws mediate the impact of unilateral divorce on the intertemporal behavior of married couples.

Changes in exposure to divorce risk across cohorts have also been shown to impact investments. In particular, Fernández and Wong (2014a) use a dynamic quantitative approach to understand the differences in labor supply and household savings between the 1935 and 1955 cohorts, demonstrating that increases in divorce risk explain a substantial component of the observed changes for both married and divorced women under the age of sixty.

This chapter contributes to our understanding of women's later-life labor force participation (and the impacts of unilateral divorce) by using the widespread changes in divorce laws occurring from the late 1960s to the 1980s as a quasi-experiment to assess the importance of marital history on women's outcomes between ages fifty and seventy-four. We first use data from the 1986 to 2008 waves of the Survey of Income and Program Participation (SIPP) to document the relationships between current marital status, past marital history, and current employment and retirement outcomes for women age fifty to seventy-four, born 1911 to 1958. We then exploit variation in laws governing divorce across states and over time (capturing changes in divorce risk) to identify the causal relationship between the age at divorce and employment and retirement outcomes for older women.

We find that the spread of unilateral divorce was associated with cross-cohort differences in the probability of divorce over the life cycle. We also show that past divorce has long-run consequences for older women's marital, work, and retirement decisions, above and beyond the impact of past divorce on current marital status. For ever-divorced women, age at divorce is also an important determinant of these outcomes. Finally, we show that women who were exposed to unilateral divorce at later ages tended to get divorced later in life (conditional on ever getting divorced).

In addition, women exposed to unilateral divorce laws at older ages exhibit patterns of labor force participation and retirement later in life that differ by their ex ante probability of divorce. We find that for women who were less likely to expect a divorce (based on birth cohort, age at first marriage, education, race, and urban status), exposure to unilateral divorce at a later age significantly increases the probability of full-time employment later in life and reduces the probability of having ever collected Social Security. For women with a low likelihood of divorce, age of exposure to unilateral divorce does not affect full-time employment, but is associated with an increased probability of having collected Social Security or retired. The pattern is stronger for white women and women with some college or less. For college-educated women, exposure to unilateral divorce at a later age increases the probability of full-time employment, irrespective of the divorce risk.

In exploring the mechanisms for the observed patterns of labor force participation, we find that, with the exception of women who were at low risk of divorce, later exposure to unilateral divorce is associated with increases in women's educational attainment after marriage. Furthermore, for all women, later exposure to unilateral divorce is associated with significantly lower levels of retirement wealth, but a significantly higher probability of having a 401(k) in one's own name. However, both effects are significantly larger for low-divorce-risk women than for high-divorce-risk women.

These findings are consistent with the literature suggesting that married women might invest more in their human capital (job experience, education) as a precaution against divorce when divorce risk increases. Women who were not likely to experience a divorce might have invested less in their own human capital as a hedge against future divorce. When this group was exposed to unilateral divorce later in life, and their divorce rate subsequently surged, they might have had to work more postdivorce and later in life to make up for lower earlier levels of human and financial capital accumulation.

4.2   Data

We used the Survey of Income and Program Participation (SIPP) to explore the relationship between marital status and later-life labor force participation, drawing data from the panels that began in 1986 to 1988, 1990 to 1993, 1996, 2001, 2004, and 2008. These data provide key demographic information; details on respondents' current employment situations and assets; and retrospective information about respondents' educational attainment (including the dates degrees were received), employment, and marriages (including the year of marriage and the date and way a marriage ended, if applicable).[1]

Although many possible measures of labor force participation are of interest and provided in the SIPP, we focus our analysis on a variable indicating whether a woman reported working full time at any point during her participation in the survey. We treat women employed full time and part time differently because part-time workers may be partially retired or could have only a slight attachment to the labor force. Differently, we chose a broader measure of full-time work (at any point in the SIPP panel, as opposed to a single point in time) to capture all women who at any recent point had strong attachment to the labor force. In any case, our results are largely robust to using different measures of employment.

In most of the analysis, we restrict the sample to ever-married women ages fifty to seventy-four. We further consider only women who provided information allowing us to identify their race, state of birth, age at marriage, marital status, employment status, urban location, and education at the time of their first SIPP interview. We drop all observations for which the status of a woman's first marriage could not be identified. The final sample contains 55,835 observations, including 38,313 never-divorced and 17,522 ever-divorced women.

Finally, while the sample sizes for all outcomes can vary due to item-specific nonresponse and nonresponse to one or more of the interviews throughout a SIPP panel, sample sizes also vary because of changes in

---

1. Kennedy and Ruggles (2014) argue that an increase in reporting errors in the retrospective marital history across SIPP surveys might lead to undercounting of divorces, thus overstating the decrease in divorce rates over the past few decades. That is, some of the women in our sample might be incorrectly classified as never divorced. This potential misclassification, if anything, might dampen the effect of marital history on current employment.

the content of the SIPP across waves. Summary statistics for the different samples are reported in appendix table 4A.1.

4.3   Changes in Divorce Rates by Age and Cohort

Divorce rates were particularly low in the 1950s and early 1960s. They then rose sharply, doubling between the mid-1960s and the mid-1970s and peaking in the early to mid-1980s. Starting in 2005, the crude divorce rate has lingered around 3.6 divorces per thousand people—the lowest divorce rate since 1970 (see figure 1 and related discussion in Stevenson and Wolfers [2007]). Although the issue has been somewhat contentious, a consensus has emerged in the economic literature that the shift from mutual consent divorce to unilateral divorce caused a short-run increase in the divorce rate (Friedberg 1998; Wolfers 2006).

Figure 4.1 shows how women in our different cohorts experienced increases in divorce rates at different points in the life cycle, as suggested by the relative timing of unilateral divorce legislation (to which we will return below). The figure describes the overall patterns in the share of women ever divorced by age and cohort. The shares are computed as a percentage of all women (panel A) and of ever-married women (panel B). The horizontal axis is age and different lines correspond to different cohorts. The patterns are similar for all women and ever-married women, with minor differences driven by the

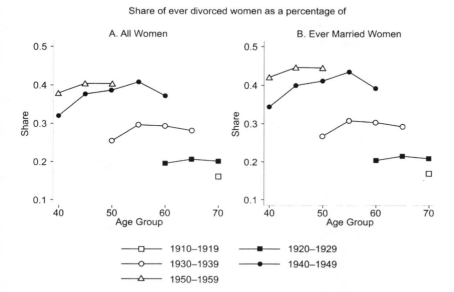

Fig. 4.1   Change in incidence of divorce, age profiles by cohort
Source: Women ages forty to seventy-four at first interview in the SIPP, 1986–2008 panels.

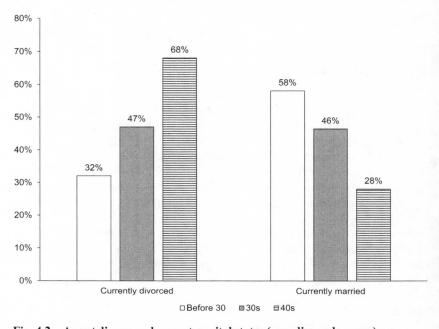

Fig. 4.2   Age at divorce and current marital status (ever-divorced women)
Source: Ever-divorced women ages fifty to seventy-four at first interview in the SIPP, 1986–2008 panels.

decline and postponement of marriage in the latest two cohorts. The graphs show that women in later cohorts are more likely to have ever divorced their spouses at any given age than women born in earlier cohorts.[2]

We also see that each cohort of interest exhibits a sharp increase in divorce at a different age. For the 1950 to 1959 cohort, this surge in divorce occurs prior to age forty and the share of women ever divorced is essentially unchanged thereafter. For the next earliest cohort (women born 1940 to 1949), we see a sharp increase in divorce between age forty and forty-five. A similar increase can be seen for women born between 1930 and 1939 around age fifty and a smaller, albeit notable, increase in divorce can be found for the 1920 to 1929 cohort around age sixty. Thus, the different cohorts exhibited similar increases in divorce in calendar time, but the increase in divorce occurred when the women were different ages.

Differences in age at divorce are notable for several reasons. Most prominently, such differences can affect women's marital status at later ages, as shown in figure 4.2. For example, when observed in the SIPP between age fifty and seventy-four, 58 percent of women who divorced before age thirty

2. By definition, the share of women ever divorced should not decrease by age, and any small downward changes in figure 4.1 are the result of sampling error.

were currently married and 32 percent were currently divorced. For women who divorced in their forties, these proportions are reversed: 68 percent of these women were currently divorced and only 28 percent were currently married. Differences in age at divorce could also lead to changes in later-life employment and retirement choices, either because of differences in current marital status or for other reasons. The next section explores this possibility.

4.4   The Influence of Current and Past Marital Status on Later-Life Outcomes

4.4.1   Descriptive Regressions

We use regression analysis to explore how both marital status and marital history relate to several employment outcomes for our sample of interest. Table 4.1 provides prima facie evidence that changes in patterns of marriage and divorce over time may explain a small but nontrivial share of the rise in later-life employment of women across birth cohorts.

The first column of table 4.1 contains coefficients from a regression predicting labor force participation for women age fifty to seventy-four by birth cohort, including only age, state of birth, and cohort fixed effects. Column (2) adds in controls for other demographic characteristics, including education and race; columns (3) to (5) add in controls for marital history, including current marital status, whether a woman was ever married, divorced, or widowed, and age at first marriage and divorce for women who ever marry or ever divorce, respectively. When marital history controls are added, the increasing trend in employment across cohorts flattens somewhat, with coefficients falling by about 10 percent. The effect of marital history on employment is stronger for the cohorts of women born between 1930 and 1939, especially when labor force participation is measured at ages fifty to fifty-nine or ages sixty to sixty-four (with coefficients dropping by about 20 percent and 15 percent, respectively, see results by age in appendix table 4A.2). As shown in figure 4.1, these are cohorts that experienced a surge in divorce around age fifty.

In the remainder of this chapter, we focus on the impact of marital history and current marital status on later life outcomes, conditional on having ever been married. Our main sample, therefore, is restricted to ever-married women. Our baseline specification controls for birth year, state of birth, and age fixed effects; age at marriage; and race, education, and urban location at the time of interview.

The results in table 4.2 indicate that ignoring current marital status (column [1]), ever-divorced women are 7 percentage points more likely to have been employed full time at some point during their participation in the SIPP, a difference equal to 22 percent of the mean employment rate. Results are similar if one instead focuses on whether a woman divorced prior to

Table 4.1   **Trends in employment for women ages fifty to seventy-four (all marital statuses)**

	Employed full time at any point in SIPP panel				
	(1)	(2)	(3)	(4)	(5)
Cohort (1920–1924 omitted)					
1925–1929	0.0176***	0.00573	0.00336	0.00228	0.00265
	(0.00511)	(0.00513)	(0.00514)	(0.00513)	(0.00516)
1930–1934	0.0400***	0.0209***	0.0174***	0.0144***	0.0148***
	(0.00536)	(0.00539)	(0.00540)	(0.00539)	(0.00542)
1935–1939	0.0990***	0.0589***	0.0499***	0.0457***	0.0466***
	(0.00575)	(0.00577)	(0.00579)	(0.00578)	(0.00581)
1940–1944	0.169***	0.112***	0.0975***	0.0926***	0.0935***
	(0.00655)	(0.00677)	(0.00682)	(0.00681)	(0.00683)
1945–1949	0.228***	0.159***	0.140***	0.134***	0.135***
	(0.00756)	(0.00793)	(0.00800)	(0.00799)	(0.00802)
1950–1954	0.268***	0.192***	0.170***	0.164***	0.164***
	(0.00865)	(0.00909)	(0.00917)	(0.00917)	(0.00920)
Ever married			−0.0787***	−0.0136	−0.0290
			(0.00895)	(0.0579)	(0.0599)
Ever divorced			0.0758***	0.0190***	−0.0313**
			(0.00420)	(0.00510)	(0.0128)
Ever widowed			0.0278***	−0.00890	0.000610
			(0.00447)	(0.00905)	(0.00983)
Currently married				−0.0717	−0.0878
				(0.0577)	(0.0592)
Currently divorced				0.0628	0.0338
				(0.0580)	(0.0595)
Currently separated				−0.0513	−0.0675
				(0.0596)	(0.0611)
Currently widowed				−0.00699	−0.0303
				(0.0583)	(0.0598)
Ever married × age at first marriage					0.00135***
					(0.000342)
Ever divorced × age at first divorce					0.00174***
					(0.000371)
Other demographic controls	No	Yes	Yes	Yes	Yes
Observations	56,866	54,160	53,673	53,673	53,236
R-squared	0.20	0.23	0.24	0.24	0.24

Source: Women ages fifty to seventy-four at first interview in the SIPP, 1986–2008 panels.

Notes: Ever married, ever divorced, and ever widowed are nonexclusive indicator variables. All currently married, divorced, separated, and widowed individuals are also classified as ever married, all currently divorced women are also classified as ever divorced, and all currently widowed women are also classified as ever widowed. All columns control for age fixed effects. Columns (2) to (5) additionally control for race (white, black, Hispanic, other race), education at interview (less than high school, high school, some college, college or more), and urban location at interview. Omitted categories: never married and cohort born 1920–1924. Robust standard errors in parentheses.

***Significant at the 1 percent level, two-tailed test.

**Significant at the 5 percent level, two-tailed test.

*Significant at the 10 percent level, two-tailed test.

Table 4.2   **Marital status and later-life employment—ever-married women**

	Employed full time at any point in panel			Employed at any point in panel	Employed full time in first panel month
	(1)	(2)	(3)	(4)	(5)
Ever divorced	0.0740*** (0.00406)	0.0202*** (0.00491)		0.0172*** (0.00502)	0.0159*** (0.00480)
Ever widowed	0.0277*** (0.00419)	−0.00590 (0.00835)		−0.00826 (0.00909)	−0.00479 (0.00806)
Currently divorced		0.126*** (0.00671)		0.0944*** (0.00653)	0.134*** (0.00674)
Currently widowed		0.0586*** (0.00893)		0.0586*** (0.00988)	0.0548*** (0.00858)
Currently separated		0.00793 (0.0166)		−0.0368** (0.0166)	0.0162 (0.0161)
Divorced by fifty			0.0762*** (0.00439)		
Widowed by fifty			0.0474*** (0.00701)		
Age at marriage	0.00194*** (0.000315)	0.00153*** (0.000315)	0.00213*** (0.000352)	0.000897*** (0.000328)	0.000788*** (0.000305)
Observations	55,835	55,835	49,242	55,835	55,835
R-squared	0.260	0.266	0.252	0.289	0.213

Source: Ever-married women ages fifty to seventy-four at first interview in the SIPP, 1986–2008 panels.

Notes: Ever divorced and ever widowed are nonexclusive indicator variables. All currently divorced women are also classified as ever divorced and all currently widowed women are also classified as ever widowed. Regressions also control for birth year, state of birth, age fixed effects, race (white, black, Hispanic, other race), education at interview (less than high school, high school, some college, college or more), and urban location at interview. Omitted category for marital status is currently married. Robust standard errors in parentheses.

***Significant at the 1 percent level, two-tailed test.
**Significant at the 5 percent level, two-tailed test.
*Significant at the 10 percent level, two-tailed test.

age fifty (column [3]). Including indicators for both current and past marital status in the regression (column [2]) reveals that both variables matter, though a woman's current marital status is a stronger predictor of current behavior. In particular, women who have ever divorced are 2 percentage points more likely than are other women to have worked during their SIPP panel, conditional on current marital status. Women who were divorced at the time they entered the SIPP panel were an additional 13 percentage points more likely to have worked (in total, these women are 15 percentage points, or 44 percent, more likely to have worked than a never-divorced, currently married woman). This relationship holds if we instead consider measures of any employment (both part time and full time, column [4]), or full-time employment at a given point in time during the SIPP panel (column [5]).

Table 4.3   Marital status and later-life employment by demographic group
             (ever-married women)

	Employed full time at any point in panel				
	White (1)	Nonwhite (2)	College + (3)	Some college or less (4)	60–69 (5)
Ever divorced	0.0206***	0.0129	0.0221	0.0202***	0.0172**
	(0.00567)	(0.00989)	(0.0135)	(0.00526)	(0.00739)
Ever widowed	0.00428	−0.0428**	−0.0138	−0.00616	0.00587
	(0.00940)	(0.0180)	(0.0278)	(0.00874)	(0.0115)
Currently divorced	0.141***	0.0903***	0.143***	0.121***	0.132***
	(0.00791)	(0.0128)	(0.0160)	(0.00745)	(0.0113)
Currently widowed	0.0621***	0.0584***	0.0902***	0.0539***	0.0432***
	(0.0102)	(0.0187)	(0.0305)	(0.00932)	(0.0125)
Currently separated	0.0204	0.000137	0.0854**	0.00173	0.0529*
	(0.0269)	(0.0212)	(0.0429)	(0.0178)	(0.0278)
Age at marriage	0.00161***	0.00147**	−0.000724	0.00202***	0.00215***
	(0.000376)	(0.000577)	(0.000781)	(0.000344)	(0.000484)
Observations	42,539	13,296	9,479	46,356	21,336
R-squared	0.267	0.272	0.275	0.248	0.124

Source: Ever-married women ages fifty to seventy-four at first interview in the SIPP, 1986–2008 panels.
Notes: Ever divorced and ever widowed are nonexclusive indicator variables. All currently divorced women are also classified as ever divorced and all currently widowed women are also classified as ever widowed. Regressions also control for birth year, state of birth, age fixed effects, race if applicable (white, black, Hispanic, other race), education at interview if applicable (less than high school, high school, some college, college or more), and urban location at interview. Omitted category for marital status is currently married. Robust standard errors in parentheses.
***Significant at the 1 percent level, two-tailed test.
**Significant at the 5 percent level, two-tailed test.
*Significant at the 10 percent level, two-tailed test.

We additionally explored whether the relationship between employment and marital status varied for women in different demographic groups. Focusing on full-time employment, we found the relationship was relatively stable (see table 4.3). Coefficients on both ever divorced and current marital status tend to be similar for both whites (column [1]) and nonwhites (column [2]), although the relationship between ever divorced and employment is statistically significant only among white women (see Lahey, chapter 3, this volume, for an analysis of differences in employment of older women by race). The relationships between the key independent variables and employment are also similar for women with a college education or more (column [3]) and women with some college or less education (column [4], see Goldin and Katz, chapter 1, this volume for details on overall differences by education level). The exception is the coefficient for being currently separated, which is 8 percentage points higher for women with college or more education than for women with some college or less education. We also see similar patterns in the sample of women ages sixty to sixty-nine (column [5]) and ever-married women of a broader age range (fifty to seventy-four; column [4], table 4.1).

We further examined whether marital status was associated with differences in two key outcomes closely related to employment: whether a woman classified herself as ever having retired from a job and whether a woman collected Social Security (measured at any point in the SIPP panel, see table 4.4).[3]

Overall, women who were ever divorced were about 2 percentage points more likely to have collected Social Security than never-divorced women (column [1]). Considering both ever having been through a divorce and current marital status further suggests that the former is more important than the latter (column [2]). The coefficient on the indicator for ever divorced is statistically significant, while that on the indicator for currently being divorced is not. This pattern could result because many women who were ever divorced can collect Social Security based on their ex-spouses earnings, making them more likely to collect Social Security overall.

A different pattern emerges when one focuses on the sample of women who were older than sixty-two years, and thus eligible to collect Social Security based on their own work history (column [3]). Within this group, the coefficient on ever divorced is halved and current marital status is significantly related to collection of Social Security. Specifically, conditional on past marital status, currently divorced women are 3 percentage points less likely to have collected Social Security than currently married women who had previously divorced. This suggests that the relationship between marital status and Social Security receipt may differ within populations with different Social Security eligibility.[4]

Past and present marital status appear to relate differently to the propensity to consider oneself as having ever retired (columns [4] and [5]), a status reported by 46 percent of all ever-married women. Ignoring the separate effect of current marital status (column [4]), women who have ever been through a divorce are about 1 percentage point less likely to have ever retired than women who have not done so. But currently divorced women drive this relationship. Indeed, conditional on past marital status, currently divorced women are 8 percentage points less likely to have ever retired than other women.

For ever-divorced women, the age at which a divorce occurred is also an important predictor of later-life outcomes, even conditional on contemporaneous marital status. Table 4.5 reports regression results for our three

---

3. We classify a woman as having ever retired if at any point in the SIPP panel she reports that she ever left a job for retirement. These women may have subsequently reentered the labor force.

4. See Maestas (chapter 2, this volume) for an analysis of Social Security eligibility on work and (joint) retirement of older women. See Iams and Tamborini (2012) for a study of the change in marital history and women's eligibility for Social Security marriage-based benefits at retirement across cohorts and its contribution to racial inequality at older ages.

Table 4.4 **Marital status, Social Security, and retirement (ever-married women)**

	Collected Social Security at any point in panel			Ever retired	
	All ever-married women		Age 62 +	All ever-married women	
	(1)	(2)	(3)	(4)	(5)
Ever divorced	0.0177***	0.0194***	0.00815*	−0.00767**	0.0267***
	(0.00304)	(0.00370)	(0.00419)	(0.00384)	(0.00476)
Ever widowed	0.0504***	0.0224***	−0.000693	0.00106	0.0195**
	(0.00349)	(0.00678)	(0.00697)	(0.00448)	(0.00871)
Currently divorced		−0.00152	−0.0255***		−0.0807***
		(0.00524)	(0.00650)		(0.00624)
Currently widowed		0.0359***	0.00218		−0.0346***
		(0.00735)	(0.00724)		(0.00950)
Currently separated		0.0365**	−0.0270		−0.0698***
		(0.0142)	(0.0179)		(0.0144)
Age at marriage	−0.000790***	−0.000830***	−0.00108***	0.000833***	0.00111***
	(0.000252)	(0.000253)	(0.000289)	(0.000313)	(0.000313)
Observations	55.835	55.835	24.958	55.835	55.835
R-squared	0.623	0.623	0.086	0.358	0.360

Source: Ever-married women ages fifty to seventy-four at first interview in the SIPP, 1986–2008 panels.

Notes: Ever divorced and ever widowed are nonexclusive indicator variables. All currently divorced women are also classified as ever divorced and all currently widowed women are also classified as ever widowed. Regressions also control for birth year, state of birth, age fixed effects, race if applicable (white, black, Hispanic, other races), education at interview if applicable (less than high school, high school, some college, college or more), and urban location at interview. Omitted category for marital status is currently married. Robust standard errors in parentheses.

***Significant at the 1 percent level, two-tailed test.

**Significant at the 5 percent level, two-tailed test.

*Significant at the 10 percent level, two-tailed test.

Table 4.5 Divorce timing and later-life outcomes—ever-divorced women

	Employed full time at any point in panel				Collected Social Security at any point in panel		Ever retired	
	(1)	(2)	(3)	(4)	(5)	(6)	(7)	(8)
Ever widowed	−0.0116	−0.0271	−0.0130	−0.0266	0.0354**	0.0356**	−0.0108	−0.0111
	(0.00977)	(0.0196)	(0.00977)	(0.0196)	(0.0162)	(0.0162)	(0.0194)	(0.0194)
Currently divorced		0.115***		0.116***	0.00745	0.00710	−0.0799***	−0.0798***
		(0.00768)		(0.00767)	(0.00598)	(0.00598)	(0.00708)	(0.00706)
Currently widowed		0.0746***		0.0738***	0.0428**	0.0428**	−0.0220	−0.0217
		(0.0211)		(0.0211)	(0.0176)	(0.0176)	(0.0214)	(0.0214)
Currently separated		0.0430		0.0434	0.0511**	0.0511**	−0.0628**	−0.0629**
		(0.0307)		(0.0307)	(0.0253)	(0.0253)	(0.0251)	(0.0251)
Age at divorce	0.00318***	0.00159***			−0.000723**		−0.000289	
	(0.000375)	(0.000388)			(0.000304)		(0.000372)	
Divorced in thirties			0.0407***	0.0306***		−0.00845		−0.00791
			(0.00828)	(0.00825)		(0.00642)		(0.00770)
Divorced in forties			0.0642***	0.0347***		−0.0108		−0.00142
			(0.00983)	(0.00995)		(0.00766)		(0.00923)
Divorced in fifties			0.0962***	0.0461***		−0.0300***		−0.0222
			(0.0148)	(0.0151)		(0.0115)		(0.0147)
Divorced at age sixty or older			0.0635**	0.00602		−0.00223		0.00246
			(0.0284)	(0.0288)		(0.0226)		(0.0309)
Age at marriage		0.00179**	0.00256***	0.00189**	−0.00102	−0.00111	0.00127	0.00132
		(0.000850)	(0.000843)	(0.000840)	(0.000681)	(0.000675)	(0.000815)	(0.000807)
Observations	17,054	17,054	17,054	17,054	17,054	17,054	17,054	17,054
R-squared	0.247	0.258	0.247	0.258	0.556	0.556	0.350	0.350

Source: Ever-divorced women ages fifty to seventy-four at first interview in the SIPP, 1986–2008 panels.

Notes: All currently widowed women are also classified as ever widowed. Regressions also control for birth year, state of birth, age fixed effects, race (white, black, Hispanic, other race), education at interview (less than high school, high school, some college, college or more), and urban location at interview. Omitted categories: currently married, divorced before age thirty. Robust standard errors in parentheses.

***Significant at the 1 percent level, two-tailed test.

**Significant at the 5 percent level, two-tailed test.

*Significant at the 10 percent level, two-tailed test.

outcomes within this sample. Women who divorced later are more likely to be employed full time. In particular, when we include in our regression a linear control for age at divorce, a ten-year increase in age at divorce is associated with a 3 percentage points increase in the propensity of a woman to work full time when observed between ages fifty and seventy-four (column [1]). However, about half of this effect can be explained by the impact of age at divorce on current marital status (column [2]).

Further, including controls for age at divorce in ten-year bins (column [3]), we find that, compared to women who divorced before age thirty, women who divorced in their thirties are 4 percentage points more likely to be employed full time and women who divorced in their forties are 6 percentage points more likely to be employed full time. Women who divorced in their fifties are the most likely to be working full time. These women are about 10 percentage points more likely than women who divorced before thirty to work full time when observed in the SIPP. Women who divorced after age fifty-nine are also about 6 percentage points more likely to work than those who divorced before age thirty (however, our sample contains relatively few women who divorced after age fifty-nine, so some caution should be taken in interpreting this result).

Current marital status is an important factor for explaining these results (column [4]). When controls for current status are added to the regression, the coefficients for divorcing in one's thirties, forties, or fifties decrease by about one-quarter or one-half. The coefficient on divorce at age sixty or older also decreases by an order of magnitude and becomes insignificant. Conditional on current marital status, age at divorce is also negatively associated with the probability a woman collects Social Security at any point in the panel, though the size of the effect is relatively small (columns [3] and [4]); however, once current marital status is accounted for, age at marriage is not significantly related to the probability a woman has ever retired from a job (column [5] and [6]).

Overall, these descriptive regressions demonstrate that both marital history and current marital status are important predictors of women's later-life employment behavior. Currently divorced women are about 38 percent more likely to be working full time at ages fifty to seventy-four than currently married women. But past marital status matters too. Women who have ever divorced, regardless of current marital status, are about 6 percent more likely than women who married but never divorced to be employed full time at later ages. In addition, among women who have ever divorced, divorcing ten years later is associated with a 5 percent increase in the probability of working full time at these ages. These factors are also important to understanding variation in receipt of Social Security and retirement.

4.4.2 Changes in Divorce Legislation

The associations laid out in the previous section, no matter how interesting, cannot be interpreted causally. To better understand how differences in marital history can cause differences in later-life labor force participation, we examine the relationship between divorce laws and our outcomes of interest. Changes in these laws over time and across states provide a quasi-experiment allowing us to measure plausibly exogenous variation in divorce risk across the life cycle.

Divorce laws indicate the conditions under which a couple can divorce, each spouse's property rights over household assets, and guidelines for alimony and child support. Prior to the 1960s, most states allowed divorce only under mutual consent. Fault-based divorce law implied that divorce could be granted only under specific circumstances (for example, adultery, cruelty, or mental illness) and only under the consent of the party proved innocent (Weitzman 1985). The late 1960s brought about the start of a shift in divorce laws from mutual consent to unilateral consent and from fault to no-fault grounds.[5] Under no-fault divorce, a couple can simply agree that they cannot stay married due to irreconcilable differences or "irretrievable breakdown." Though most states today have established no-fault, unilateral divorce laws, laws differ based on separation requirements (which may range from none to a one-year requirement) and on whether fault grounds shape the division of assets and spousal support. These variations have caused a small amount of variation in the definition of unilateral divorce in the literature.

We consider a state to have unilateral divorce if they allow no-fault marital dissolution and do not have a separation requirement. Spousal support and property division can still be at-fault under our definition. This classification is very similar to others used in the literature (e.g., Gruber 2004; Voena 2015; Wolfers 2006).[6] As a robustness check we use a second classification that relaxes the no-separation requirement (that is, a state has unilateral divorce if and only if no-fault divorce is allowed). Under the second definition, some states are classified as allowing unilateral divorce at an earlier date and an additional eleven states are classified as ever allowing unilateral divorce.[7] Our results are robust to using either of these definitions (but we only report findings based on our preferred definition).

5. The late 1970s and 1980s also saw a shift in divorce laws that establish each spouse's property rights over household assets. It would also be interesting to investigate whether the changing property division legislation had an independent impact on employment, but this is beyond the scope of this chapter.
6. In some cases, there is a one-year discrepancy between our definition and others in the literature. This is because we have chosen to classify a state as having unilateral divorce at the time the law becomes effective (for example, in Arizona the law passed May 1973 but went into effect on January 1974). (See our appendix for details.)
7. See appendix table 4A.3. We also include a third definition that classifies a state as unilateral if alimony/assets are also assigned on no-fault grounds. (See our appendix for details.)

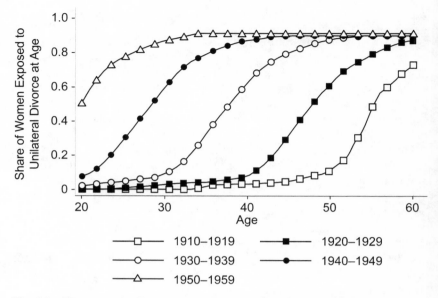

Fig. 4.3   Exposure to unilateral divorce over the life cycle by cohort (all women)
Source: Women ages fifty to seventy-four at first interview in the SIPP, 1986–2008 panels.

We use a woman's state of birth to determine access to unilateral divorce. Identification is thus necessarily limited to women born in states where there was a change of legislation prior to the women's SIPP interviews. Using our preferred definition of unilateral divorce, the resulting sample contains 30,321 women (including 10,420 ever-divorced and 19,901 never-divorced women).[8]

Our empirical strategy exploits cross-state, cross-cohort variation in access to unilateral divorce to identify the (pseudo) causal relationship between age at divorce and older women's outcome. Two stylized facts support this strategy.

First, as shown in figure 4.3, exposure to unilateral divorce increased at different times across cohorts. This figure plots the share of women in our sample who were exposed to unilateral divorce at a given age, showing how the legal changes affected different cohorts at different points over their life cycles and complementing the evidence on divorce rates in figure 4.1. Less than 10 percent of women born between 1910 and 1919 were exposed to unilateral divorce before age fifty. But by age sixty, over 70 percent had been exposed. Women in the 1920 to 1929 cohort experience minimal exposure until age forty. But by age sixty, over 80 percent of women in this cohort

---

8. Our alternative definition of unilateral divorce yields a sample of 49,806 women (16,174 ever divorced and 33,632 never divorced).

Fig. 4.4   Age at divorce and age unilateral divorce introduced (ever-divorced women)
Source: Ever-divorced women ages fifty to seventy-four at first interview in the SIPP, 1986–2008 panels.
Notes: Age when unilateral divorce became available is determined based on state of birth. Average age at divorce is computed conditional on having ever divorced. Women born in states where unilateral divorce was never available are omitted from this analysis.

would have had access to unilateral divorce in their birth state. Similarly, women in the 1930 to 1939 cohorts experience the shift in their thirties and early forties and those born from 1940 to 1949 did so in their midtwenties to midthirties. Of those in the most recent cohorts (born 1950 to 1959) 50 percent were exposed to unilateral divorce at age twenty.

Second, as shown in figure 4.4, there is a strong, positive correlation between the age at which divorce became unilateral and age at divorce among ever-divorced women. Thus, different cohorts exhibited similar increases in both divorce risk and divorce in calendar time, but this increase occurred when these women were at very different ages. We exploit this variation to study the relationship between the age divorce risk increased (that is, when unilateral divorce became available) and later outcomes.

4.4.3   A More Causal Empirical Specification

We use ordinary least squares (OLS) to explore the relationships of interest. The general version of the estimating equation is

$$(1) \qquad y_{isca} = \varphi_s + \eta_c + d_a + \alpha\, Z_i + \delta \text{Age at Unilateral}_{isc} + \varepsilon_{ics},$$

where y_{isca} is the outcome of interest (e.g., age at divorce, full-time employment, Social Security, or retirement) for person i, born in state s and in cohort c, and observed in the SIPP at age a; φ_s are state of birth dummies, η_c are year of birth dummies, d_a are current age dummies, and Z_i are individual-level covariates, including age at marriage or duration of marriage when unilateral divorce was introduced in a woman's birth state (depending on the specification), race (if applicable), education at interview (if applicable), and urban location at interview. Women born in states where unilateral divorce was never available are omitted from this analysis.[9]

The coefficient of greatest interest is that on the variable representing age when unilateral divorce became available determined based on state of birth, δ. This coefficient represents the (pseudo) causal effect of having one's risk of divorce increase one year later in life. An increase in divorce risk later in life could lead to changes in outcomes for a number of reasons. The change could affect age at divorce, current marital status, or choices during marriage. It could also impact the process of marriage formation by altering the reservation quality of matching; however, for 84 percent of women in our sample, marriage occurred before the law change, likely making this last mechanism less important.

The age at which unilateral divorce became available is associated with a marginally significant increase in the probability that a woman has ever been divorced, as shown in table 4.6.[10] For the entirety of our sample, we find that a ten-year increase in age at the legalization of unilateral divorce is associated with a 9 percentage point increase in the probability of ever divorcing.[11] As about 31 percent of our sample ever divorced, this is equivalent to a one-year increase in age at the legalization of unilateral divorce leading to a 2.8 percent increase in divorce. In column (2) we include controls for the age a woman gained access to unilateral divorce in ten-year bins, instead of a single, linear control. This reveals the relationship is highly nonlinear and likely driven by the very early legalization of unilateral divorce in a small number of states. People who were exposed to unilateral divorce in their thirties, forties, or fifties have a 3 percentage point higher probability of having ever been divorced relative to people who were exposed to unilateral divorce before age thirty, though only the difference including women exposed in their thirties is significant. Women who were only exposed to unilateral divorce after age fifty-nine have a significant, 5 percentage point higher probability of being ever divorced, compared to women exposed before age thirty.

9. We also omit nine women who were born in a state where unilateral divorce became available, but were interviewed for the SIPP prior to that law change. These women lived in the small number of states that allowed unilateral divorce starting in 1987.
10. The overall pattern of these results is similar when the outcome of interest is an indicator for having divorced by age fifty (see appendix table 4A.4).
11. The same results hold controlling for marriage duration, which is negatively correlated with the probability of having ever divorced.

Table 4.6   **Effect of age when unilateral divorce became available on divorce probability—ever-married women**

	Indicator for ever divorced						
	All women		White	Nonwhite	College or more	Some college or less	60–69
	(1)	(2)	(3)	(4)	(5)	(6)	(7)
Age when unilateral divorce introduced	0.00887*		0.00945*	-0.0130	0.0687***	-0.0156***	0.0141***
	(0.00452)		(0.00487)	(0.0163)	(0.00937)	(0.00502)	(0.000894)
Unilateral divorce introduced:							
Thirties		0.0254**					
		(0.0111)					
Forties		0.0307					
		(0.0185)					
Fifties		0.0249					
		(0.0220)					
Sixty and older		0.0500*					
		(0.0295)					
Age at marriage	-0.0141***	-0.0141***	-0.0147***	-0.0123***	-0.0144***	-0.0140***	-0.0121***
	(0.000456)	(0.000457)	(0.000475)	(0.000631)	(0.00153)	(0.000471)	(0.000673)
Observations	30,321	30,321	23,001	7,320	5,050	25,271	11,357
R-squared	0.086	0.086	0.093	0.081	0.084	0.091	0.076

Source: Ever-married women ages fifty to seventy-four at first interview in the SIPP, 1986–2008 panels.

Notes: The dependent variable is an indicator that equals one if ever divorced and zero otherwise. Age when unilateral divorce became available is determined based on state of birth. Regressions also control for state of birth year, state of birth, age fixed effects, race (if applicable; white, black, Hispanic, other race), education at interview (if applicable; less than high school, high school, some college, college or more), and urban location at interview. Omitted category for age when unilateral divorce was introduced is before age thirty. Women born in states where unilateral divorce was never available are omitted from this analysis. Standard errors clustered by state of birth are reported in parentheses.

***Significant at the 1 percent level, two-tailed test.

**Significant at the 5 percent level, two-tailed test.

*Significant at the 10 percent level, two-tailed test.

This finding may seem counterintuitive since people who were older when unilateral divorce was introduced are exposed to the increased divorce risk for fewer years. But this positive age effect is consistent with theoretical and empirical findings on the impact of unilateral divorce. As discussed in the literature, the passage of unilateral divorce was associated with a "pipeline" effect, causing marriages with the smallest surpluses to dissolve (Rasul 2006; Wolfers 2006). Our findings are consistent with older couples being more likely to have marriages characterized by very small surpluses because, for example, they are more likely to have older children and reduced gains from specialization. It is also possible that the shock introduced by the divorce revolution might have been larger or more salient for individuals who were socialized and lived most of their adult life in a conservative society where marriages should be saved at all costs and divorce was stigmatized.

A similar relationship between age at exposure to unilateral divorce and the probability of divorce holds for whites (column [3]) and women age sixty to sixty-nine (column [5]) as that seen in the sample as a whole. However, the relationship is not significant for nonwhites and is negative for women with some college or lower levels of educational attainment, which might be consistent with stricter or slower-moving societal norms for the less educated. Differently, for college-educated women, age when unilateral divorce became available is strongly associated with a higher probability of ever divorce.

Additionally, later exposure to unilateral divorce is associated with later age at divorce for ever-divorced women (see table 4.7). For all such women, a ten-year increase in age when unilateral divorce was first allowed is associated with a 2.8 year delay in age at divorce (2.6 years controlling for age at marriage). Looking at subgroups, we find a stronger association within samples of white women, women with some college or less education, and women age sixty to sixty-nine. For these samples, a ten-year increase in the age at which unilateral divorce was introduced is associated with a four- to five-year delay in age at divorce. Consistent with the results in the previous table, we also find that age when unilateral divorce was implemented does not correlate with age at divorce for nonwhite women.

Having established these associations, we investigate the impact of the age when unilateral divorce was introduced on full-time employment later in life in table 4.8. In addition to the entire population, we split the sample based on an indicator of divorce risk. Specifically, we estimated a (probit) regression predicting whether a woman ever divorced using birth cohort, age at first marriage, education, race, and urban status at interview. We then estimate each woman's probability of divorce. Low-divorce-risk women are defined as those in the lower quartile of the predicted probability distribution; high-divorce-risk women are defined as those in the upper quartile of the predicted probability distribution.

We find that the association between later-life employment and the age unilateral divorce was introduced varies substantially depending on the

Table 4.7   Effect of age when unilateral divorce became available on age at divorce—ever-divorced women

				Age at divorce				
	All ever-divorced women			White	Nonwhite	College +	Some college	60–69
	(1)	(2)	(3)	(4)	(5)	(6)	(7)	(8)
Age when unilateral divorce introduced	0.281**	0.258**	0.790***	0.443***	0.00457	0.174	0.484***	0.537***
	(0.122)	(0.111)	(0.134)	(0.144)	(0.337)	(0.208)	(0.141)	(0.0566)
Age at marriage		0.967***		0.987***	0.920***	0.847***	0.996***	0.991***
		(0.0215)		(0.0275)	(0.0235)	(0.0536)	(0.0237)	(0.0406)
Marriage duration when unilateral divorce introduced			0.694***					
			(0.00995)					
Observations	10,133	10,133	10,133	7,457	2,676	1,672	8,461	3,370
R-squared	0.074	0.228	0.560	0.229	0.264	0.296	0.210	0.215

Source: Ever-divorced women ages fifty to seventy-four at first interview in the SIPP, 1986–2008 panels.

Notes: Age when unilateral divorce became available is determined based on state of birth. Regressions also control for birth year, state of birth, age fixed effects, race (if applicable; white, black, Hispanic, other race), education at interview (if applicable; less than high school, high school, some college, college or more), and urban location at interview. Women born in states where unilateral divorce was never available are omitted from this analysis. Standard errors clustered by state of birth are reported in parentheses.

***Significant at the 1 percent level, two-tailed test.

**Significant at the 5 percent level, two-tailed test.

*Significant at the 10 percent level, two-tailed test.

Table 4.8   **Effect of age when unilateral divorce became available on later-life employment—ever-married women**

	Employed full time at any point in panel			
	(1)	(2)	(3)	(4)
All ever married				
Age when unilateral divorce introduced	−0.00226 (0.00428)	−0.00510 (0.00422)	−0.00110 (0.00412)	−0.00541 (0.00412)
Age at marriage	0.000492* (0.000268)	0.000953*** (0.000286)		
Marriage duration when unilateral divorce introduced			−0.000765*** (0.000153)	−0.000160 (0.000144)
Control for current marital status	No	Yes	No	Yes
Observations	30,370	30,370	30,370	30,370
R-squared	0.251	0.262	0.251	0.261
Low divorce risk				
Age when unilateral divorce introduced	0.106*** (0.0263)	0.107*** (0.0264)	0.108*** (0.0262)	0.107*** (0.0263)
Age at marriage	0.000172 (0.000679)	0.000493 (0.000653)		
Marriage duration when unilateral divorce introduced			−0.000767*** (0.000260)	−0.000217 (0.000242)
Control for current marital status	No	Yes	No	Yes
Observations	7,582	7,582	7,582	7,582
R-squared	0.246	0.256	0.247	0.256
High divorce risk				
Age when unilateral divorce introduced	0.00223 (0.00488)	−0.00142 (0.00470)	0.00177 (0.00506)	−0.00299 (0.00485)
Age at marriage	0.00943*** (0.00302)	0.0105*** (0.00289)		
Marriage duration when unilateral divorce introduced			−0.00118 (0.000732)	−0.000251 (0.000775)
Control for current marital status	No	Yes	No	Yes
Observations	7,586	7,586	7,586	7,586
R-squared	0.139	0.150	0.138	0.148

Source: Ever-married women ages fifty to seventy-four at first interview in the SIPP, 1986–2008 panels.

Notes: Age when unilateral divorce became available is determined based on state of birth. Regression also control for birth year, state of birth, age fixed effects, race (white, black, Hispanic, other race), education at interview (less than high school, high school, some college, college or more), and urban location at interview. Women born in states where unilateral divorce was never available are omitted from this analysis. Standard errors clustered by state of birth are reported in parentheses.

***Significant at the 1 percent level, two-tailed test.

**Significant at the 5 percent level, two-tailed test.

*Significant at the 10 percent level, two-tailed test.

sample considered. For all ever-married women together (the first panel of table 4.8) and high-divorce-risk women (third panel), full-time employment in later life is not significantly affected by the age when unilateral divorce became available. This pattern is consistent with a model in which women who face a higher divorce risk respond by remaining employed during marriage as a precaution, thus insuring themselves against a potential future loss of income due to divorce (Johnson and Skinner 1986) and allowing them to retire earlier. In this case, delays in the age of exposure to unilateral divorce should have only small (or no) impacts on later-life work decisions.

The age when unilateral divorce became available has very different implications for low-divorce-risk women (the second panel). For this group, later exposure to unilateral divorce is associated with higher full-time employment at age fifty to seventy-four. This is consistent with low-divorce-risk women having to work remedially postdivorce and later in life if they are exposed to an increase in divorce risk when they are older. In other words, women facing a low divorce risk are less likely to have engaged in "precautionary working."

The size and significance of the coefficient is relatively consistent across specifications and does not depend on whether we control for age at marriage or the duration of marriage when unilateral divorce became available or whether we control for current marital status. The estimates imply that a ten-year delay in unilateral divorce legislation would be associated with a decline in the probability of full-time employment by 10 percentage points. Given that the fraction of women in our sample who were employed full time increased from 28 to 49 percent between the 1930 to 1939 and 1940 to 1949 cohorts, this is a (possibly too) large effect.

Endogeneity bias may be responsible for some of the magnitude of the effect. Although the age unilateral divorce was introduced is plausibly exogenous, the variable also likely affects some of the (endogenous) control variables—age at marriage, current marital status, education at interview—that have been shown to be important in predicting divorce (Bac 2015; Rotz 2016). Moreover, other factors discussed in this volume and elsewhere (for example, for financial literacy see Lusardi and Mitchell [2008] and chapter 6 in this volume, and for changes in the normal retirement age and delay retirement credits, see Cribb, Emmerson, and Tetlow [2014] and Panis et al. [2002]) are obviously also important determinants and potentially correlated with both our key variables.

Looking at other outcomes of interest (table 4.9), we can see that for all ever-married women, being older when unilateral divorce was introduced is associated with a lower probability of being employed (either full time or part time) at ages fifty to seventy-four. Additionally, a later age when unilateral divorce was introduced is associated with an increase in both the probability of having collected Social Security at any point in the panel or having ever retired by the end of the panel. This relationship also holds for the high-divorce-risk group. The results for low-divorce-risk, ever-married

Table 4.9   Effect of age when unilateral divorce became available on later-life outcomes—
                    ever-married women

	Employed at any point in panel (1)	Collected Social Security at any point in panel (2)	Ever retired (3)
All			
Age when unilateral divorce introduced	−0.00877**	0.00820**	0.0487***
	(0.00335)	(0.00350)	(0.00332)
Marriage duration when unilateral divorce introduced	−0.000715***	−5.14e-05	−0.000670***
	(0.000205)	(0.000121)	(0.000170)
Observations	30,370	30,370	30,370
R-squared	0.281	0.621	0.356
Low divorce risk			
Age when unilateral divorce introduced	0.0617***	−0.0159***	−0.00851
	(0.0156)	(0.00514)	(0.0162)
Marriage duration when unilateral divorce introduced	−0.00110***	0.000114	−0.00148***
	(0.000366)	(0.000156)	(0.000385)
Observations	7,582	7,582	7,582
R-squared	0.255	0.641	0.303
High divorce risk			
Age when unilateral divorce introduced	−0.00242	0.00991**	0.0475***
	(0.00471)	(0.00464)	(0.00473)
Marriage duration when unilateral divorce introduced	−9.11e-05	0.000216	0.00133**
	(0.000846)	(0.000652)	(0.000610)
Observations	7,586	7,586	7,586
R-squared	0.160	0.427	0.264

Source: Ever-married women ages sixty to seventy-four at first interview in the SIPP, 1986–2008 panels.
Notes: Age when unilateral divorce became available is determined based on state of birth. Regressions also control for birth year, state of birth, age fixed effects, race (white, black, Hispanic, other race), education at interview (less than high school, high school, some college, and college or more), and urban location at interview. Women born in states where unilateral divorce was never available are omitted from this analysis. Standard errors clustered by state of birth are reported in parentheses.
***Significant at the 1 percent level, two-tailed test.
**Significant at the 5 percent level, two-tailed test.
*Significant at the 10 percent level, two-tailed test.

women (second panel) show that being older at the introduction of unilateral divorce is also associated with an increase in employment (full time or part time) and with a lower probability of having collected Social Security within this sample.

We further consider how our results for employment vary by education and race in table 4.10. The patterns for white women and women with some

Table 4.10   Effect of age when unilateral divorce became available on later-life employment—subsamples of ever-married women

	Employed full time during panel				
	White (1)	Nonwhite (2)	College + (3)	Some college or less (4)	60–69 (5)
All					
Age when unilateral divorce introduced	−0.0121** (0.00509)	0.0329*** (0.0103)	0.0577*** (0.00897)	−0.0276*** (0.00598)	−0.0138*** (0.000941)
Marriage duration when unilateral divorce introduced	−0.000812*** (0.000195)	−0.000439 (0.000277)	−0.00179** (0.000749)	−0.000683*** (0.000151)	−0.00117*** (0.000215)
Observations	23,047	7,323	5,053	25,317	11,380
R-squared	0.251	0.267	0.273	0.233	0.111
Low divorce risk					
Age when unilateral divorce introduced	0.0688** (0.0280)	−0.00197 (0.00614)	0.0572*** (0.0206)	0.0778** (0.0380)	−0.0200*** (0.00298)
Marriage duration when unilateral divorce introduced	−0.000806*** (0.000262)	−0.00104** (0.000507)	−0.00174 (0.00164)	−0.000654** (0.000265)	−0.000878* (0.000443)
Observations	5,747	1,830	1,262	6,317	2,841
R-squared	0.249	0.273	0.341	0.218	0.131
High divorce risk					
Age when unilateral divorce introduced	0.000621 (0.00485)	−0.0310* (0.0182)	0.0489** (0.0186)	−0.0128** (0.00501)	−0.0295*** (0.00249)
Marriage duration when unilateral divorce introduced	−0.00117 (0.00104)	−0.00187 (0.00164)	−0.00533* (0.00279)	−0.00115 (0.000728)	−0.00185** (0.000725)
Observations	5,757	1,830	1,264	6,326	2,841
R-squared	0.135	0.192	0.182	0.128	0.118

Source: Ever-married women ages sixty to seventy-four at first interview in the SIPP, 1986–2008 panels.

Notes: Age when unilateral divorce became available is determined based on state of birth. Regressions also control for birth year, state of birth, age fixed effects, race if applicable (white, black, other race), education at interview if applicable (less than high school, high school, some college), and urban location at interview. Omitted categories: Hispanic, college or more. Women born in states where unilateral divorce was never available are omitted from this analysis. Standard errors clustered by state of birth are reported in parentheses.

***Significant at the 1 percent level, two-tailed test.

**Significant at the 5 percent level, two-tailed test.

*Significant at the 10 percent level, two-tailed test.

Table 4.11   **Potential mechanisms—ever-married women**

	Obtained additional education after marriage (1)	Have IRA, Keogh, 401(k), 403(b), or thrift plan (2)	Total market value of all retirement accounts in own name (3)
	All ever-married women		
Age when unilateral divorce introduced	0.0284*** (0.00175)	0.0244*** (0.00409)	−3,125*** (459.5)
Observations	30,275	21,830	21,837
R-squared	0.608	0.230	0.063
	Low divorce risk		
Age when unilateral divorce introduced	0.00613 (0.00892)	0.103*** (0.0179)	−6,657** (2,774)
Observations	7,569	5,346	5,351
R-squared	0.785	0.353	0.098
	High divorce risk		
Age when unilateral divorce introduced	0.0279*** (0.00223)	0.0269*** (0.00699)	−4,354*** (662.3)
Observations	7,553	5,347	5,347
R-squared	0.454	0.128	0.048

Source: Ever-married women ages sixty to seventy-four at first interview in the SIPP, 1986–2008 panels.
Notes: Age when unilateral divorce became available is determined based on state of birth. Regressions also control for birth year, state of birth, age fixed effects, race (white, black, Hispanic, other race), education at interview (less than high school, high school, some college, and college or more), urban location at interview, and age at marriage. Women born in states where unilateral divorce was never available are omitted from this analysis. Standard errors clustered by state of birth are reported in parentheses.
***Significant at the 1 percent level, two-tailed test.
**Significant at the 5 percent level, two-tailed test.
*Significant at the 10 percent level, two-tailed test.

college or less educational attainment are similar to those in the overall sample of ever-married women with one exception. For less educated, high-divorce-risk women, older age when unilateral divorce was introduced also decreases the probability of being employed full time. For nonwhite and more educated women, a ten-year increase in the age when unilateral divorce was introduced is associated with increases in full-time employment of about 3 and 6 percentage points, respectively. For women ages sixty to sixty-nine, the coefficient on age when unilateral divorce was introduced is about 1 percentage point.

Finally, table 4.11 investigates some of the potential mechanisms for the relationship between age at exposure to unilateral divorce and labor force participation. In the sample of all ever-married women, older age at the introduction of unilateral divorce is associated with an increase in the probability of obtaining additional education after marriage and an increase in the probability of having one's own 401(k) or other retirement plan, but a decrease in the balance of reported retirement accounts.[12] The findings are roughly similar within the low- and high-divorce-risk subsamples with one exception. For women with low divorce risk, later exposure to the unilateral laws does not affect the probability of having obtained additional education after their first marriage started. This suggests that some of the observed effects on labor force participation may be explained by changes in education and savings; however, the pattern of results suggests that other forces must also be at play.

4.5 Conclusions

Overall, we demonstrate that the spread of unilateral divorce was associated with cross-cohort differences in the probability of divorce over the life cycle. We also show that past divorce has long-run consequences for older women's marital, work, and retirement decisions, above and beyond the impact of past divorce on current marital status. For ever-divorced women, the age at divorce is also an important determinant of these outcomes. Finally, we show that women who were exposed to unilateral divorce at later ages tended to get divorced later in life (conditional on ever getting divorced). They also exhibit different patterns of labor force participation and retirement at older ages.

For women with a low risk of divorce, an increase in divorce risk at a later age significantly increases the probability of full-time employment later in life (and reduces the probability of having ever collected Social Security). Additionally, later exposure to unilateral divorce is associated with a significantly lower level of retirement wealth. These findings suggest that ever-divorced women are working longer remedially. When they unexpectedly divorce at later ages, they are less likely to have engaged in precautionary human capital investment and have to work longer to increase their assets prior to retirement.

For all other women, a later exposure to divorce risk does not impact full-time employment after age fifty, but is associated with investment in education postmarriage. These women invest more in their own human capital within marriage, and seem to be insured against increasing exogenous divorce risk at later ages.

Our results suggest that changes in marital history and marital status,

---

12. However, see Bee and Mitchell (chapter 9, this volume) for a caution against drawing conclusions based on this data.

though not unilateral divorce law, can explain a nontrivial fraction of the increase in women's employment later in life. Controlling for age, race, education, and urban location, we estimate that women born in the early 1950s were about 19 percentage points more likely to be employed full time at ages fifty to seventy-four, compared to women born in the 1920s, a difference equal to more than half of the mean employment rate for women in this age range. Changes in the share of women ever married, ever divorced, or ever widowed explain about 11 percent of the difference. Likewise, changes in marital history can explain 12 percent of the 4 percentage point difference in later-life employment between cohorts born in the 1920s and 1930s and 16 percent of the 14 percentage point difference between cohorts born in the 1920s and 1940s. However, we find no evidence that the timing of the large-scale introduction of unilateral divorce, which represents a substantial, one-time increase in divorce risk, plays a major role in understanding the increase in women's employment for the population as a whole. There is no statistically significant relationship between the timing of unilateral divorce legislation and later-life employment, on average. This null effect, however, masks substantial heterogeneity across women. We find that women facing a relatively low risk of divorce, especially women with a college degree, were more likely to work later in life if they were older when unilateral divorce laws were passed. Conversely, women with less education were less likely to work at ages fifty to seventy-four if they gained access to unilateral divorce later in life.

Appendix
Timing of Divorce Law Reforms

Note that in the descriptions below, "fully unilateral" means meeting all criteria, including no-fault alimony and having no separation requirement. "Unilateral" means that the state was not no-fault for alimony and/or assets.

Alaska

Alaska became a no-fault state in 1935. Its first unilateral law was passed in 1962 and went into effect in 1963. The state became no-fault for alimony and asset division in 1974.

Alabama

Alabama became fully no-fault in 1971 (alimony and asset division included).

Arkansas

Became no-fault in 1937 with a three-year mutually agreed upon separation requirement, and unilateral divorce allowed in 1979. The unilateral law had an eighteen-month separation requirement, and was no-fault for alimony/asset division.

Arizona

Arizona became fully no-fault (alimony included) with a law passed in 1973, which was implemented beginning in 1974.

California

California passed a fully unilateral law (alimony included) in 1969, which went into effect in 1970.

Colorado

Colorado introduced fully unilateral divorce with a law passed in 1971, effective starting 1972.

Connecticut

Unilateral law passed in 1973 with no separation requirement.

Delaware

Unilateral with six-month separation requirement in 1968, where couples also had to show that the marriage had been irretrievably broken for two years prior to the divorce. Became no-fault for alimony in 1979 (passed 1978) but still had a separation requirement.

District of Columbia

Unilateral law passed in 1977. There was a six-month separation requirement if mutually agreed upon or a twelve-month separation requirement if contested.

Florida

Introduced unilateral divorce with no separation requirement in 1971. Went no-fault for alimony in 1978.

Georgia

Introduced unilateral divorce with no separation requirement in 1973.

Hawaii

Introduced fully unilateral divorce in 1972.

Iowa

Iowa introduced unilateral divorce with no separation requirement in 1970, and without fault for alimony in 1972.

Idaho

Idaho introduced unilateral divorce with no separation requirement in 1971, and for alimony in 1990.

Illinois

Illinois became no-fault in 1984, with a law initially passed in 1983. The state had a two-year separation requirement and was no-fault for alimony.

Indiana

Indiana introduced fully unilateral divorce in 1973.

Kansas

Kansas introduced unilateral divorce in 1969 and no-fault for alimony in 1990.

Kentucky

Kentucky introduced unilateral divorce in 1972 and no-fault for alimony in 1987.

Louisiana

We are omitting Louisiana. There was little reliable and consistent information to be found on its historical divorce laws. This state allows covenant marriages, which only allow mutual consent or fault-based divorce. This is consistent with much of the literature.

Massachusetts

Massachusetts introduced unilateral divorce in 1975.

Maryland

Allowed divorce after a five-year separation in 1937, but was not unilateral. This was shortened to three years in 1969. The state introduced unilateral divorce with a two-year separation requirement in 1983.

Maine

Introduced unilateral divorce in 1973, and added no-fault alimony in 1985.

Michigan

Introduced unilateral divorce with no separation requirement in 1972.

Minnesota

Introduced fully unilateral divorce in 1974.

Missouri

Introduced unilateral divorce in 1973.

Mississippi

Mississippi added no-fault provisions to its grounds for divorce in 1976, but did not allow unilateral divorce. This was expanded upon in 1978 by adding no-fault alimony, but the state remains non-unilateral.

Montana

Montana added no-fault provisions to its allowed grounds for divorce in 1973. It introduced fully unilateral divorce, no-fault alimony included, in 1975.

North Carolina

We omit North Carolina. This state only allowed divorce on grounds of separation (originally ten years, shortened to one year in 1965) and adultery, and not on other traditional grounds such as cruelty, neglect to provide, and desertion.

North Dakota

North Dakota introduced fully unilateral divorce in 1971.

Nebraska

Nebraska introduced fully unilateral divorce in 1972.

New Hampshire

New Hampshire introduced unilateral divorce in 1971.

New Jersey

New Jersey introduced unilateral divorce in 1971 with an eighteen-month separation requirement.

New Mexico

New Mexico became no-fault in 1933, and unilateral in 1973. The state then became no-fault for alimony in 1976.

Nevada

Nevada had loose divorce laws preceding the no-fault revolution, but was not fully unilateral until 1973.

New York

New York is a fault state for divorce. Reforms in 1966 and 1967 only served to expand the list of allowed fault grounds for divorce.

Ohio

Ohio introduced unilateral divorce with a one-year separation requirement in 1974.

Oklahoma

Oklahoma was a unilateral state as early as 1953, and became no-fault for alimony in 1975.

Oregon

Oregon introduced fully unilateral divorce in 1973.

Pennsylvania

Pennsylvania introduced unilateral divorce with some noteworthy restrictions in 1980. There was a three-year separation requirement, and if the divorce was contested, the court had to rule the marriage was broken in order for the divorce to be completed immediately. If the court did not rule that the marriage was broken, the judge had the authority to assign counseling before effectively ending the marriage. In practice, this appears to have allowed unilateral divorce.

Rhode Island

Rhode Island introduced unilateral divorce in 1976.

South Carolina

South Carolina introduced unilateral divorce with a three-year separation requirement in 1969. This requirement was shortened to one year in 1979.

South Dakota

South Dakota introduced unilateral divorce in 1985.

Tennessee

Tennessee introduced unilateral divorce in 1977 with a separation requirement that varied upon whether the couple had children (minimum two years).

Texas

Texas introduced unilateral divorce in 1970.

Utah

Utah introduced unilateral divorce in 1987.

Virginia

Virginia introduced unilateral divorce in 1960 with a varying separation requirement (minimum six months).

Vermont

Vermont introduced unilateral divorce in 1969 with a six-month separation requirement.

Washington

Washington introduced fully unilateral divorce in 1973.

Wisconsin

Wisconsin introduced unilateral divorce with a one-year separation requirement in 1978.

West Virginia

West Virginia introduced unilateral divorce with a two-year separation requirement in 1977, which has since been reduced to one year.

Wyoming

Wyoming introduced unilateral divorce in 1977.

Table 4A.1   Summary statistics

	Ever-married women		Ever-divorced women		Women where unilateral divorce ever available		Ever-divorced women where unilateral divorce ever available	
	Mean (1)	Std. deviation (2)	Mean (3)	Std. deviation (4)	Mean (5)	Std. deviation (6)	Mean (7)	Std. deviation (8)
Age	60.76	7.11	59.34	6.77	60.72	7.08	59.35	6.76
Marital status at first SIPP interview								
Currently married	0.68	0.47	0.44	0.50	0.70	0.46	0.46	0.50
Currently divorced	0.14	0.35	0.44	0.50	0.13	0.34	0.43	0.49
Currently separated	0.01	0.12	0.02	0.13	0.01	0.11	0.02	0.12
Currently widowed	0.17	0.37	0.10	0.30	0.15	0.36	0.10	0.30
Ever divorced	0.32	0.47	1.00	0.00	0.31	0.46	1.00	0.00
Age at divorce (conditional on divorce)	33.61	9.97	33.61	9.97	33.41	9.93	33.41	9.93
Divorced by age fifty	0.29	0.46	0.98	0.15	0.29	0.45	0.98	0.16
Age at marriage	22.08	5.79	20.85	4.45	21.99	5.70	20.77	4.37
Education at first SIPP interview								
Less than HS	0.19	0.40	0.18	0.39	0.19	0.40	0.18	0.39
High school graduate	0.37	0.48	0.32	0.47	0.37	0.48	0.32	0.47
Some college	0.26	0.44	0.32	0.47	0.27	0.44	0.33	0.47
College or more	0.17	0.37	0.17	0.38	0.17	0.37	0.16	0.37
Education at marriage								
Less than HS	0.28	0.45	0.32	0.47	0.32	0.47	0.34	0.47
High school graduate	0.40	0.49	0.38	0.49	0.38	0.48	0.37	0.48
Some college	0.24	0.43	0.25	0.43	0.23	0.42	0.24	0.43
College or more	0.08	0.26	0.05	0.22	0.07	0.25	0.05	0.21

Obtained additional education after marriage	0.80	0.40	0.85	0.36	0.80	0.40	0.85	0.36
Obtained additional degree after marriage	0.28	0.45	0.39	0.49	0.28	0.45	0.39	0.49
Worked during first marriage	0.66	0.47	0.63	0.48	0.66	0.47	0.63	0.48
Employed full time at any point in panel	0.33	0.47	0.43	0.50	0.33	0.47	0.43	0.50
Employed at any point in panel	0.49	0.50	0.58	0.49	0.49	0.50	0.58	0.49
Employed full time in first panel month	0.28	0.45	0.36	0.48	0.27	0.45	0.36	0.48
Collected Social Security at any point in panel	0.53	0.50	0.48	0.50	0.52	0.50	0.48	0.50
Ever retired	0.46	0.50	0.44	0.50	0.45	0.50	0.43	0.50
Have IRA, Keogh, 401(k), 403(b), or thrift plan	0.48	0.50	0.44	0.50	0.49	0.50	0.45	0.50
Total market value all retirement accounts in own name	8,461	32,251	9,739	33,833	82,967	31,737	9,630	33,536
Observations	54,964		17,970		49,882		16,174	

Source: Ever-married women ages fifty to seventy-four in the SIPP 1986–2008 panels.

Table 4A.2A   Trends in women's employment by age—women ages fifty to fifty-nine

	Employed full time at any point in SIPP panel			
	(1)	(2)	(3)	(4)
Cohort (omit 1920–1924)				
1925–1929	0.0703*			
	(0.0416)			
1930–1934	0.104**	0.0258	0.0184	0.00537
	(0.0408)	(0.0178)	(0.0180)	(0.0181)
1935–1939	0.191***	0.0787***	0.0629***	0.0459**
	(0.0410)	(0.0178)	(0.0180)	(0.0181)
1940–1944	0.288***	0.149***	0.127***	0.109***
	(0.0408)	(0.0180)	(0.0183)	(0.0184)
1945–1949	0.328***	0.177***	0.149***	0.132***
	(0.0408)	(0.0177)	(0.0180)	(0.0180)
1950–1954	0.361***	0.201***	0.172***	0.155***
	(0.0410)	(0.0180)	(0.0183)	(0.0184)
Ever married			−0.0871***	0.0174
			(0.0128)	(0.0994)
Ever divorced			0.0895***	−0.0588***
			(0.00651)	(0.0202)
Ever widowed			0.0242**	−0.0108
			(0.0101)	(0.0188)
Currently married				−0.135
				(0.0981)
Currently divorced				−0.00849
				(0.0984)
Currently separated				−0.128
				(0.100)
Currently widowed				−0.0504
				(0.0995)
Ever married × age at first marriage				0.000974
				(0.000596)
Ever divorced × age at first divorce				0.00297***
				(0.000591)
Demographic controls	No	Yes	Yes	Yes
Observations	27,763	25,891	25,594	25,397
R-squared	0.054	0.077	0.084	0.092

Source: Women ages fifty to fifty-nine at first interview in the SIPP, 1986–2008 panels.

Notes: Ever married, ever divorced, and ever widowed are nonexclusive indicator variables. All currently married, divorced, separated, and widowed individuals are also classified as ever married, all currently divorced women are also classified as ever divorced, and all currently widowed women are also classified as ever widowed. All columns control for age fixed effects. Columns (2) to (4) additionally control for race (white, black, Hispanic, other race), education at interview (less than high school, high school, some college, college or more), and urban location at interview. Omitted categories: never married and cohort born 1920–1924. Robust standard errors in parentheses.

***Significant at the 1 percent level, two-tailed test.

**Significant at the 5 percent level, two-tailed test.

*Significant at the 10 percent level, two-tailed test.

Table 4A.2B   **Trends in women's employment by age—women ages sixty to sixty-four**

	Employed full time at any point in SIPP panel			
	(1)	(2)	(3)	(4)
Cohort (omit 1920–1924)				
1925–1929	0.0341***	0.0274*	0.0164	0.00210
	(0.0115)	(0.0140)	(0.0143)	(0.0144)
1930–1934	0.0938***	0.0717***	0.0605***	0.0424***
	(0.0131)	(0.0159)	(0.0162)	(0.0163)
1935–1939	0.145***	0.111***	0.0933***	0.0799***
	(0.0142)	(0.0170)	(0.0173)	(0.0174)
1940–1944	0.167***	0.128***	0.107***	0.0912***
	(0.0128)	(0.0155)	(0.0159)	(0.0160)
1945–1949	0.216***	0.166***	0.144***	0.128***
	(0.0149)	(0.0177)	(0.0180)	(0.0182)
1950–1954				
Ever married			−0.0877***	−0.0268
			(0.0217)	(0.147)
Ever divorced			0.0705***	−0.0715**
			(0.00942)	(0.0283)
Ever widowed			0.0261**	0.00439
			(0.0104)	(0.0205)
Currently married				−0.120
				(0.145)
Currently divorced				0.0251
				(0.146)
Currently separated				−0.0784
				(0.148)
Currently widowed				−0.0644
				(0.146)
Ever married × age at first marriage				0.00228***
				(0.000755)
Ever divorced × age at first divorce				0.00245***
				(0.000834)
Demographic controls	No	Yes	Yes	Yes
Observations	12,686	11,854	11,755	11,665
R-squared	0.052	0.070	0.076	0.087

Source: Women ages sixty to sixty-four at first interview in the SIPP, 1986–2008 panels.

Notes: Ever married, ever divorced, and ever widowed are nonexclusive indicator variables. All currently married, divorced, separated, and widowed individuals are also classified as ever married, all currently divorced women are also classified as ever divorced, and all currently widowed women are also classified as ever widowed. All columns control for age fixed effects. Columns (2) to (4) additionally control for race (white, black, Hispanic, other race), education at interview (less than high school, high school, some college, college or more), and urban location at interview. Omitted categories: never married and cohort born 1920–1924. Robust standard errors in parentheses.

***Significant at the 1 percent level, two-tailed test.
**Significant at the 5 percent level, two-tailed test.
*Significant at the 10 percent level, two-tailed test.

Table 4A.2C   **Trends in women's employment by age—women ages sixty-five to sixty-nine**

	Employed full time at any point in SIPP panel			
	(1)	(2)	(3)	(4)
Cohort (omit 1920–1924)				
1925–1929	0.0330***	0.0259***	0.0232***	0.0235***
	(0.00754)	(0.00767)	(0.00768)	(0.00769)
1930–1934	0.0620***	0.0494***	0.0455***	0.0447***
	(0.00905)	(0.00976)	(0.00974)	(0.00973)
1935–1939	0.0897***	0.0752***	0.0682***	0.0662***
	(0.00881)	(0.00892)	(0.00885)	(0.00889)
1940–1944	0.106***	0.0858***	0.0766***	0.0772***
	(0.0110)	(0.0113)	(0.0114)	(0.0114)
1945–1949				
1950–1954				
Ever married			−0.0676***	−0.124
			(0.0183)	(0.105)
Ever divorced			0.0688***	0.0258
			(0.00802)	(0.0250)
Ever widowed			0.0226***	0.0132
			(0.00675)	(0.0147)
Currently married				0.0179
				(0.104)
Currently divorced				0.118
				(0.105)
Currently separated				0.0733
				(0.111)
Currently widowed				0.0438
				(0.105)
Ever married × age at first marriage				0.00144**
				(0.000605)
Ever divorced × age at first divorce				0.000140
				(0.000741)
Demographic controls	No	Yes	Yes	Yes
Observations	10,057	10,055	9,978	9,895
R-squared	0.021	0.030	0.040	0.047

Source: Women ages sixty-five to sixty-nine at first interview in the SIPP, 1986–2008 panels.

Notes: Ever married, ever divorced, and ever widowed are nonexclusive indicator variables. All currently married, divorced, separated, and widowed individuals are also classified as ever married, all currently divorced women are also classified as ever divorced, and all currently widowed women are also classified as ever widowed. All columns control for age fixed effects. Columns (2) to (4) additionally control for race (white, black, Hispanic, other race), education at interview (less than high school, high school, some college, college or more), and urban location at interview. Omitted categories: never married and cohort born 1920–1924. Robust standard errors in parentheses.

***Significant at the 1 percent level, two-tailed test.
**Significant at the 5 percent level, two-tailed test.
*Significant at the 10 percent level, two-tailed test.

Table 4A.3　　　Unilateral divorce laws

	Definition 1: No-fault dissolution, no separation requirement	Definition 2: No-fault dissolution, allows for separation requirement	Definition 3: No-fault dissolution, no separation, no-fault property/alimony	Wolfers (2006)	Gruber (2004)	Friedberg (1998)	Voena (2015)
AK	1963	1963	1974	1935	1935	No	pre-1967
AL	1971	1971	1971	1971	1971	1971	1971
AR	No	1979	No	No	No	No	No
AZ	1974	1974	1974	1973	1973	1973	1973
CA	1970	1970	1970	1970	1970	1970	1970
CO	1972	1972	1972	1971	1972	1971	1972
CT	1973	1973	No	1973	1973	1973	1973
DC	No	1977	No	No	No	No	No
DE	1974	1968	No	No	1968	No	1968
FL	1971	1971	1978	1971	1971	1971	1971
GA	1973	1973	no	1973	1973	1973	1973
HI	1972	1972	1972	1973	1972	1973	1972
IA	1970	1970	1972	1970	1970	1970	1970
ID	1971	1971	1990	1971	1971	1971	1971
IL	No	1984	No	No	No	No	No
IN	1973	1973	1973	1973	1973	1973	1973
KS	1969	1969	1990	1969	1969	1969	1969
KY	1972	1972	1987	1972	1972	1972	1972
LA	No	No	No	No	No	No	No
MA	1975	1975	No	1975	1975	1975	1975
MD	No	1983	No	No	No	No	No
ME	1973	1973	1985	1973	1973	1973	1973
MI	1972	1972	No	1972	1972	1972	1972
MN	1974	1974	1974	1974	1974	1974	1974
MO	No	1973	No	No	No	No	No
MS	No	No	No	No	No	No	No
MT	1975	1975	1975	1975	1973	1975	1973

(continued)

Table 4A.3   (continued)

	Definition 1: No-fault dissolution, no separation requirement	Definition 2: No-fault dissolution, allows for separation requirement	Definition 3: No-fault dissolution, no separation, no-fault property/alimony	Wolfers (2006)	Gruber (2004)	Friedberg (1998)	Voena (2015)
NC	No	No	No	No	No	No	No
ND	1971	1971	1971	1971	1971	1971	1971
NE	1972	1972	1972	1972	1972	1972	1972
NH	1971	1971	1971	1971	1971	1971	1971
NJ	No	1971	No	No	No	No	No
NM	1973	1973	1976	1973	1933	1973	1973
NV	1973	1973	1973	1973	1967	1973	1967
NY	No	No	No	No	No	No	No
OH	No	1974	No	No	No	No	1992
OK	1953	1953	1975	1953	1953	No	pre-1967
OR	1971	1971	1971	1973	1971	1973	1971
PA	No	1980	No	No	No	No	No
RI	1976	1976	No	1976	1975	1976	1975
SC	No	1969	No	No	No	No	No
SD	1985	1985	No	1985	1985	1985	1985
TN	No	1977	No	No	No	No	No
TX	1970	1970	No	1974	1970	1974	1970
UT	1987	1987	No	No	1987		1987
VA	No	1960	No	No	No	No	No
VT	No	1969	No	No	No	No	No
WA	1973	1973	1973	1973	1973	1973	1973
WI	No	1978	No	No	1978	No	1978
WV	No	1977	No	No	No	No	1984
WY	1977	1977	No	1977	1977	1977	1977

Table 4A.4 **Effect of age when unilateral divorce became available on indicator for divorce by age fifty—ever-married women**

| | Indicator for divorced by fifty | | | | | |
	All women (1)	White (2)	Nonwhite (3)	College or more (4)	Some college or less (5)	60–69 (6)
Age when unilateral divorce became available	0.00828*	0.00943*	−0.0112	0.0568***	−0.0113**	0.0132***
	(0.00456)	(0.00489)	(0.0158)	(0.00858)	(0.00540)	(0.000919)
Age at marriage	−0.0152***	−0.0155***	−0.0139***	−0.0159***	−0.0150***	−0.0129***
	(0.000488)	(0.000526)	(0.000599)	(0.00137)	(0.000452)	(0.000671)
Observations	29,623	22,518	7,105	4,873	24,750	11,050
R-squared	0.096	0.103	0.094	0.097	0.100	0.081

Source: Ever-married women ages fifty to seventy-four at first interview in the SIPP, 1986–2008 panels.

Notes: The dependent variable is an indicator that equals one if divorced by fifty and zero otherwise. Age when unilateral divorce became available is determined based on state of birth. Regressions also control for birth year, state of birth, age fixed effects, race (if applicable; white, black, Hispanic, other race), education at interview (if applicable; less than high school, high school, some college, and college or more) and urban location at interview. Women born in states where unilateral divorce was never available are omitted from this analysis. Standard errors clustered by state of birth are reported in parentheses.

***Significant at the 1 percent level, two-tailed test.

**Significant at the 5 percent level, two-tailed test.

*Significant at the 10 percent level, two-tailed test.

References

Bac, Mehmet. 2015. "On the Selection Effects under Consent and Unilateral Divorce." *American Law and Economics Review* 17 (1): 43–86.

Couch, Kenneth A., Christopher R. Tamborini, Gayle L. Reznik, and John W. R. Phillips. 2011. "Impact of Divorce on Women's Earnings and Retirement over the Life Course." Paper presented at the Conference on Unexpected Lifecycle Events and Economic Well-Being: The Roles of Job Loss, Disability, and Changing Family Structure, Federal Reserve Bank of San Francisco, San Francisco, California, May.

Cribb, Jonathan, Carl Emmerson, and Gemma Tetlow. 2014. "How Does Increasing the Early Retirement Age for Women Affect the Labour Supply of Women and Their Husbands?" Netspar Discussion Paper no. 01/2014-003, Network for Studies on Pension, Aging and Retirement. http://arno.uvt.nl/show.cgi?fid=133592.

Fernández, Raquel, and Joyce C. Wong. 2014a. "Divorce Risk and Working Wives: A Quantitative Life-Cycle Analysis of Female Labor Force Participation." *Economic Journal* 124 (576): 319–58.

———. 2014b. "Unilateral Divorce, the Decreasing Gender Gap, and Married Women's Labor Force Participation." *American Economic Review* 104 (5): 342–47.

Friedberg, Leora. 1998. "Did Unilateral Divorce Raise Divorce Rates? Evidence from Panel Data." *American Economic Review* 88 (3): 608–27.

Gray, Jeffrey. 1998. "Divorce-Law Changes, Household Bargaining and Female Labor Supply." *American Economic Review* 88 (3): 628–42.

Greene, W. H., and A. O. Quester. 1982. "Divorce Risk and Wives' Labor Supply Behavior." *Social Science Quarterly* 63 (1): 16–27.

Gruber, Jonathan. 2004. "Is Making Divorce Easier Bad for Children? The Long-Run Implications of Unilateral Divorce." *Journal of Labor Economics* 22 (4): 799–833.

Holden, Karen, and Angela Fontes. 2009. "Economic Security in Retirement." *Journal of Women, Politics & Policy* 30 (2): 173–97.

Iams, Howard M., and Christopher R. Tamborini. 2012. "The Implications of Marital History Change on Women's Eligibility for Social Security Wife and Widow Benefits, 1990–2009." *Social Security Bulletin* 72 (2): 23–38.

Johnson W. R., and J. Skinner. 1986. "Labor Supply and Marital Separation." *American Economic Review* 76 (3): 455–69.

Kennedy, Sheela, and Steven Ruggles. 2014. "Breaking Up is Hard to Count: The Rise of Divorce in the United States, 1980–2010." *Demography* 51 (2): 587–98.

Lusardi, Annamaria, and Olivia S. Mitchell. 2008. "Planning and Financial Literacy: How Do Women Fare?" *American Economic Review* 98 (2): 413–17.

Munnell, Alicia. 2004. "Why Are So Many Older Women Poor?" JTF no. 10, Just the Facts on Retirement Issues Brief, April. Center for Retirement Research, Boston College. http://crr.bc.edu/briefs/why-are-so-many-older-women-poor/.

Panis, Constantijn, Michael Hurd, David Loughran, Julie Zissimopoulos, Steven Haider, and Patricia St. Clair. 2002. "The Effects of Changing Social Security Administration's Early Retirement Age and the Normal Retirement Age." This report was prepared for the Social Security Administration by RAND. https://www.ssa.gov/policy/docs/contractreports/agereport.pdf.

Peters, H. Elizabeth. 1986. "Marriage and Divorce: Informational Constraints and Private Contracting." *American Economic Review* 76 (3): 437–54.

Rasul, Imran. 2006. "Marriage Markets and Divorce Laws." *Journal of Law, Economics, and Organization* 22 (1): 30–69.

Rotz, Dana. 2016. "Why Have Divorce Rates Fallen? The Role of Women's Age at Marriage." *Journal of Human Resources* 51 (4): 961–1002.

Stevenson, Betsey. 2007. "The Impact of Divorce Laws on Marriage-Specific Capital." *Journal of Labor Economics* 25 (1): 75–94.

———. 2008. "Divorce Law and Women's Labor Supply." *Journal of Empirical Legal Studies* 5 (4): 853–73.

Stevenson, Betsey, and Justin Wolfers. 2006. "Bargaining in the Shadow of the Law: Divorce Laws and Family Distress." *Quarterly Journal of Economics* 121 (1): 267–88.

———. 2007. "Marriage and Divorce: Changes and Their Driving Forces." *Journal of Economic Perspectives* 21 (2): 27–52.

Tamborini, Christopher R., Howard M. Iams, and Kevin Whitman. 2009. "Marital Histories, Race, and Social Security Spouse and Widow Benefit Eligibility in the United States." *Research on Aging* 31 (5): 577–605.

Tamborini, Christopher R., and Kevin Whitman. 2007. "Women, Marriage, and Social Security Benefits: Revisited." *Social Security Bulletin* 67 (4): 1–20.

Ulker, Aydogan. 2009. "Wealth Holdings and Portfolio Allocation of the Elderly: The Role of Marital History." *Journal of Family and Economic Issues* 30 (1): 90–108.

Vespa, Jonathan, and Matthew A. Painter II. 2011. "Cohabitation History, Marriage, and Wealth Accumulation." *Demography* 48 (3): 983–1004.

Voena, Alessandra. 2015. "Your, Mine and Ours: Do Divorce Laws Affect the Inter-Temporal Behavior of Married Couples?" *American Economic Review* 105 (8): 2295–332.

Weitzman, Lenore. 1985. *The Divorce Revolution.* New York: Free Press, Collier Macmillan.

Wilmoth, Janet, and Gregor Koso. 2002. "Does Marital History Matter? Marital Status and Wealth Outcomes among Preretirement Adults." *Journal of Marriage and Family* 64 (1): 254–68.

Wolfers, Justin. 2006. "Did Unilateral Divorce Laws Raise Divorce Rates? A Reconciliation and New Results." *American Economic Review* 96 (5): 1802–20.

Zagorsky, Jay L. 2005. "Marriage and Divorce's Impact on Wealth." *Journal of Sociology* 41 (4): 406–24.

Zissimopoulos, Julie, Benjamin Karney, and Amy Rauer. 2008. "Marital Histories and Economic Well-Being." MRRC Working Paper no. WP 180, Michigan Retirement Research Center.

Women Working Longer
Labor Market Implications of Providing Family Care

Sean Fahle and Kathleen McGarry

5.1 Introduction

The aging of the US population brings with it a number of difficult issues for our economy. As the declining number of workers per retiree places increasing financial pressure on the Social Security and Medicare programs, the concurrent increase in longevity portends a growing risk that elderly individuals will exhaust their economic resources, further taxing the resources of the working age population. The growing number of retired elderly will also impose greater demands on our health care system, including the need to provide long-term care for those elderly with dementia and other disabilities.

As policymakers and economists have repeatedly noted, the impacts of population aging can be dampened to a large extent by increasing labor force participation among older workers and delaying the transition to retirement. And indeed, recent trends appear to be in this direction: the decades-long shift toward early retirement among men has reversed, and women are continuing to participate in the labor force in growing numbers and at older ages. Numerous factors, many addressed in this volume, can provide some explanation for these trends: changes in marriage and divorce rates, shifts in

Sean Fahle is assistant professor of economics at the State University of New York at Buffalo. Kathleen McGarry is department chair and professor of economics at the University of California, Los Angeles, and a research associate of the National Bureau of Economic Research.

Chapter prepared for the Women Working Longer Conference, May 21–22, 2016, Cambridge, MA. We wish to thank Claudia Goldin, Larry Katz, and Mark Shepard for their helpful suggestions, and the participants at the conference for comments. We gratefully acknowledge financial assistance from the Alfred P. Sloan Foundation through grant number G-2015-14131 and from the Social Security Administration grant R-UM-16-07 through the University of Michigan Retirement Research Center. For acknowledgments, sources of research support, and disclosure of the authors' material financial relationships, if any, please see http://www.nber.org/chapters/c13800.ack.

pension coverage, and improvements in health. In this chapter, we consider the role of competing demands on a woman's time, focusing in particular on the potential need to care for elderly family members. We examine how this caregiving role has evolved over time and how it might impact women's labor market behavior as they approach retirement age.

An extensive literature exists about the relationship between child care and labor force participation, but somewhat less is known about the effect of caregiving for parents and spouses on employment behavior. This caregiving can impose an enormous burden on the caregiver—a burden measured not just in terms of the emotional stress and physical tasks borne by the caregiver, but also in the opportunity cost of the caregiver's time. Time spent caregiving may come at the expense of time in the labor force, the ability to invest in a career and experience wage growth, and the risk of reduced or lost retirement benefits. These labor market outcomes may lead the caregivers themselves to be far less prepared to finance their own retirement, and more dependent on families and public support later in life, than they would have been absent such caregiving experience.

The burden on potential caregivers is also likely to increase as the population ages. The demand for long-term care in the United States is projected to increase sharply over the coming decades. Coming generations of retirees will likely have fewer children than those that were responsible for the baby boom, so the burden of care will need to be shared by fewer siblings. In addition, daughters, who traditionally provided much of the care, are increasingly likely to have strong attachments to the labor force, meaning that the opportunity cost of care is likely to be greater. Finally, divorce rose throughout the 1970s meaning that the current generation of elderly might be less likely to have a spouse present. Thus, even men, who traditionally relied on care from a spouse, may lack support in old age, and absent a spouse, children (daughters) may again be called on to provide assistance. Conversely, the increase in the fraction of the population that is unmarried may reduce the caregiving burden on women as fewer women will face the prospect of potentially caring for parents-in-law in addition to their own parents.

In this chapter, we use ten waves of data from the Health and Retirement Study (HRS), spanning nearly twenty years, to examine the labor force and caregiving behavior of women. We first document the extent of care for both elderly parents and parents-in-law and for spouses. Because our interest is in the relationship between caregiving and work, we will focus solely on parent and parent-in-law care for the majority of our analyses. Caregiving to elderly parents and in-laws peaks for women in their fifties. Few women at these ages are caring for their spouses, who are likely to be only a few years older and thus still in good health. Care for spouses does not become significant until somewhat older ages and so is less relevant for labor market behavior.

Our sample consists of women who are first observed during their prime working years, and we follow them for the duration of the survey period. We primarily use observations from three cohorts from the HRS, and depending on the specific cohort, follow women for anywhere from six to eighteen years. We find that approximately one-third of the women in our sample provided care for an elderly parent, parent-in-law, or spouse at some point during the window of observation, with the majority of this care being for parents. We also find that caregiving for parents and parents-in-law has a significant negative effect on employment, reducing the probability of working by 3.3 percentage points on a mean of 41 percent, or 8 percent when calculated across the whole of the sample period. Caregiving also results in a reduction of approximately 1.3 hours of work per week. We find a consistent trend across cohorts with more recent cohorts facing a greater risk of providing care and a significantly larger negative effect on employment.

Our chapter is organized as follows. The next section provides some background on the provision of informal care in the United States, and section 5.3 describes our data in detail. In section 5.4, we illustrate patterns of caregiving for our population of women, including the type of care provided and the amount of hours of care supplied. Section 5.5 provides an analysis of labor market behavior as a function of caregiving using ordinary least squares (OLS) and fixed effects analyses. A final section concludes and offers avenues for future work.

5.2   Background

Though the need for long-term care is already pervasive, the demand is expected to increase sharply with the aging of the population. It is estimated that 69 percent of individuals reaching age sixty-five will need help with the activities of daily living (ADLs) at some point in their lives.[1] Of these, one-fifth will require sustained assistance over a period of five or more years (Kemper, Komisar, and Alecxih 2006). For the vast majority of individuals, this care will come from family members, primarily from wives and daughters. Among those in the community receiving help with ADLs, 66 percent receive help exclusively from family members, 26 percent receive assistance from both family (informal) and paid (formal) care providers, and just 9 percent rely only on formal care (Doty 2010). This reliance on informal care means that family members shoulder much of the burden of caregiving.

The economic value of this care is immense. Feinberg et al. (2011) estimate that the value of informal care in 2009 exceeded $450 billion. This figure is more than twice the estimated value of formal care and is equivalent to approximately 19 percent of national health care expenditures (O'Shaughnessy

---

1. The activities of daily living (ADLs) include basic tasks such as bathing, eating, dressing, and toileting.

2014).[2] Thus, while there is great concern about the level and growth of health care expenditure in the United States, in ignoring the economic value of informal care, our official statistics are missing an important component of the true cost and significantly underestimating the economic impact of health care costs for the elderly. Furthermore, because these imputations are calculated by simply multiplying the hours of care provided by an hourly wage, we also likely underestimate the true economic cost borne by the caregivers if lost earnings or declines in earnings growth exceed the inferred wage.

The National Association of Insurance Commissioners (2016) reports that 10 percent of caregivers cut back on hours worked because of the demands of caregiving while an estimated 6 percent of caregivers leave paid work entirely. Seventeen percent of caregivers take a leave of absence, and 4 percent reportedly turn down promotions. The figures from a 2015 survey by Genworth (2016) are even starker: 11 percent of caregivers lost their jobs due to caregiving, and 52 percent had to reduce work hours by an average of seven hours per week. Twenty six percent of those surveyed reported missed career opportunities. The latter figure is suggestive of a broader phenomenon in which caregivers invest less intensively in a job because of other responsibilities. They may also do so in less obvious ways than turning down promotions, such as not volunteering for important, high visibility assignments, not putting in overtime to ensure that projects are done in a timely manner, or simply not accepting extra responsibility in the anticipation of greater wage increases in the future.

Complete departures from the labor force are relatively easily documented, and many researchers have examined labor market responses on this extensive margin (Bolin, Lindgren, and Lundborg 2008; Carmichael, Charles, and Hulme 2010; Ettner 1996; Heitmueller 2007; Johnson and Lo Sasso 2006; McGarry 2003; Van Houtven, Coe, and Skira 2013). It is more difficult to measure a reduction in hours and considerably harder to capture a reduction in effort on the job. For these reasons, fewer researchers have studied the impact of caregiving on the intensive margin of labor supply. Among those that have, results differ widely. Whereas Van Houtven et al. (2013) report that helping parents with errands and personal care has no impact on hours worked, Johnson and Lo Sasso (2006), when examining the intensive and extensive margins together, find that those women who provide care to an elderly parent reduce hours of work by approximately 40 percent. With such sizable reductions can come a loss of benefits on the job, such as health insurance or pension contributions, and a reduction in wage growth.

---

2. According to the National Health Policy Forum (O'Shaughnessy 2014), Americans spent $219 billion on paid long-term care for the elderly in 2012. In that year, this expenditure represented 9.3 percent of all US personal health care spending. Adding the value of informal care to this amount provides clear evidence that caring for the elderly is an enormously important economic activity.

Because the burden of care is borne primarily by women, these losses could help explain the much higher poverty rates for older women relative to men.[3]

5.3   Data

Our data are drawn from the first ten waves of the Health and Retirement Study (HRS), specifically 1992–2010.[4] The HRS is a panel survey that is approximately representative of the US population ages fifty-one or older and their spouses or partners (see the volume appendix on the HRS). Because we are interested in the relationship between caregiving and work, we focus our attention on three "cohorts" of the survey: members of the original HRS cohort who were ages fifty-one to sixty-one when first observed in 1992, those in the "War Babies" (WB) cohort, ages fifty-one to fifty-six in 1998, and the "Early Baby Boomer" (EBB) cohort, ages fifty-one to fifty-six in 2004.[5] The original HRS cohort covers a wider age range than the WB or EBB cohorts. In order to maintain a similar age span across cohorts, we therefore divide the original HRS sample into two groups: the "Early HRS" born between 1931 and 1935 (ages fifty-seven to sixty-one when first observed), and the "Late HRS" who were born between 1936 and 1941, and who, like our other cohorts, were approximately fifty-one to fifty-six when they entered the survey. We refer to these cohorts as EHRS and LHRS, respectively.

Because spouses and partners of HRS respondents are interviewed regardless of age, there are individuals younger than fifty-one in the survey. (For the same reason, there are also individuals older than sixty-one [or fifty-six] when first observed.) We include these individuals in our sample, but "reassign" them to the cohort in which they fall based on their own birth year. For example, a husband who was born in 1947 and who was interviewed as part of the War Babies cohort might well have a spouse who was born in 1950. We would consider her to be part of the Early Baby Boomers cohort based on her birth year. Likewise, we include women who are married to men in the older AHEAD (born 1923 or earlier) and CODA (born 1924 to 1930) samples who themselves are young enough so that their birth year places them in one of the more recent cohorts. However, because these

---

3. Although recent work (Bee and Mitchell, chapter 9, this volume) suggests that retirement income may be underreported, it is not clear if underreporting differentially affects the estimated poverty rates of men and women, or poverty rates overall.

4. While the RAND HRS data were available through 2012 at the time of this writing, the corresponding RAND Family Data File was only available through 2010.

5. Individuals in the two other cohorts, "Asset and Health Dynamics of the Oldest Old" (AHEAD) and "Children of the Depression Era" (CODA), were first observed when they were seventy years old or older and sixty-eight to seventy-four, respectively. Because our interest is in labor market behavior and most of the women in these cohorts had already exited from the labor market by the time they were first interviewed, we do not use them for our analyses. We also exclude from all analyses women from the 2010 Early Baby Boom Minority Over-Sample (EBB MOS), who were added to the EBB cohort in 2010.

women are not considered "sample persons" until their cohort is included in the HRS sampling frame, the HRS assigns them a zero person weight until they reach age fifty-one. Thus, because we use person weights to maintain a population representative sample, these women do not contribute to our analysis until they reach the appropriate age. With this sampling scheme, we have a total sample size of 9,498 women and 60,989 person-wave observations. This sample includes 2,305 women considered to be in the Early HRS (EHRS) cohort, 3,171 in the Late HRS (LHRS) cohort, 2,050 from the WB cohort, and 1,972 from the EBB cohort. Using observations from the different cohorts gives us an unbalanced sample with a varying number of observations per respondent and observations in different calendar years.

Our central variables of interest are derived from a question regarding whether the respondent provided care:

> Did you (or your husband/wife/partner) spend a total of 100 or more hours (since the previous wave/in the last two years) helping your (parents/mother/father) with basic personal activities like dressing, eating, and bathing?

The same information was collected regarding parents-in-law. The question asks about total care for the respondent couple, but follow-up questions allow us to identify the number of hours provided by each individual. We define a woman as a caregiver if the above question is answered affirmatively for care to either parents or parents-in-law and the woman contributes positive hours of care. The 1992 and 1994 interviews differed slightly in that they asked about assistance provided over the previous twelve months rather than the (approximately) two-year span between interviews.[6] Similarly, in all interview waves except 1994, respondents were asked to report caregiving only if it exceeded a total of 100 hours; in 1994, the threshold was fifty hours. We have not corrected the data for the difference in hours or the period of time covered by the question.

We also look (briefly) at care for a spouse. This information comes from a separate set of questions posed to the care recipient (i.e., the caregiver's husband or partner in our case—or a proxy if that person is unable to respond to the survey):

> Let's think for a moment about the help you receive that we just talked about. . . . During the last month, on about how many days did [HELPER] help you?

This information was not collected in 1992 or 1994, so in those years we are limited to examining only care for parents and parents-in-law. Note also that whereas caregiving to parents and parents-in-law is measured as the

---

6. The median time between interviews is two years, so the questions generally refer to caregiving over a period of approximately two years. We cannot impute a two-year total for the 1992 and 1994 interviews because we do not know if care was provided continuously over this period at the same rate.

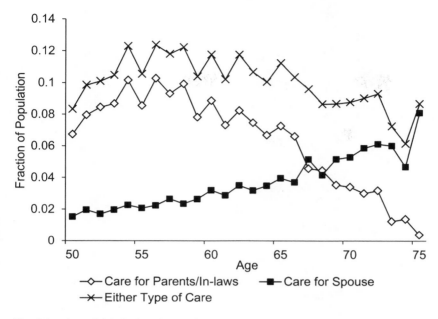

Fig. 5.1   Caregiving during the previous two years

Notes: Caregiving since the previous interview (approximately two years) for reinterviewees or during the past two years for new interviewees. The figure uses data for women from the HRS, WB, and EBB cohorts (see text and volume appendix for a discussion of HRS cohorts). All lines are weighted using person weights. Note that because respondents are not asked about care for a spouse/partner in the 1992 and 1994 interviews, we underestimate spouse/partner caregiving in those years.

total number of hours provided since the previous interview, care to spouses is measured as the number of hours of care provided in the *past month*. Thus, not only do we fail to capture the full extent of caregiving among those providing spousal care, but we also completely miss care that ceased a month or more prior to the interview date.

5.4   Descriptive Analysis

The relationship between caregiving and work, and the impact of any labor market effects on lifetime earnings, likely depends strongly on the age at which caregiving occurs. In figure 5.1, we stack observations from the four birth cohorts in our sample and show the fraction of women providing care at each age. Our focus for most of the chapter is on care for parents and parents-in-law. But, for comparison, we include care for spouses and partners as well as the fraction of women providing either of these types of care.[7]

7. The prevalence of parent-in-law care is low, reaching 2 percent at its peak, and follows the same path with respect to age as care to parents. While 22 percent of the women in our sample

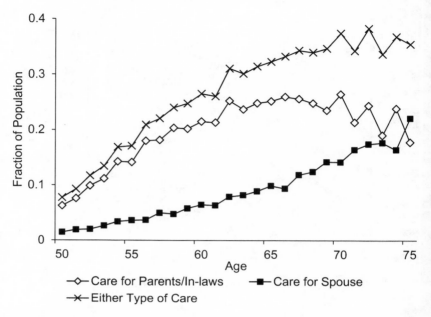

Fig. 5.2   Cumulative caregiving since first observed in sample
Notes: Series show caregiving since first observed in sample—that is, the fraction of women ever observed providing care since appearing in sample. These cumulative values decline for some series due to changes in the sample composition (see footnote 9). See notes for figure 5.1 for additional sample information.

As the figure illustrates, caregiving for parents peaks around age fifty-six and falls thereafter as fewer parents remain alive and those that do become sufficiently infirm that they require formal care. Conversely, caregiving for a spouse, while important, does not become a widespread phenomenon until the respondents are in their late sixties, by which time many of these women will have already left the labor force independent of the need to provide care.

Figure 5.2 illustrates the cumulative burden of care and gives the fraction of women *ever* providing care by a given age, again disaggregating by type of care recipient. If we consider sixty-five to be the normal retirement age for these cohorts, we see that 32 percent of our sample had provided care to a parent, parent-in-law, or spouse prior to this point in the life course.[8] One-

provide care to a parent at some point, just 7 percent ever care for a parent-in-law. For ease of exposition, we combine the two types of parental care. All analyses presented here were done with the types of parental care separated as well. We also make no distinction in this chapter between care given to mothers and care given to fathers. Because women tend to outlive their husbands, older men typically receive care from their spouses, and thus the majority of parental care is to women. In our sample, 23 percent of women provide care to a mother or mother-in-law at some point while only 8 percent ever care for a father or father-in-law.

8. The full retirement age for most women in our sample is older than sixty-five. Those born in 1937 or earlier have a full retirement age of sixty-five. For women born later, the full retirement age increases gradually, reaching sixty-six years for women in our EBB cohort.

quarter of women had been caregivers for parents or parents-in-law. Even these large numbers may understate the true extent of caregiving if some women provided care prior to entering the survey. In results not shown, if we restrict the sample to those women with a living parent or parent-in-law at some point during our window of observation, the fraction of women ever providing care rises to more than 50 percent.[9]

One can imagine that there might be differences across cohorts in the age at which care begins and in to whom this care is provided. As noted earlier, among these cohorts, sib-ships have increased over time (recall that the most recent cohort are members of the "baby boom"), thereby reducing the need for any one child to provide care for a parent. In addition, the labor force attachment of women has increased over time, likely increasing the opportunity cost of providing care and perhaps also decreasing the amount of care provided.[10] Conversely, on the demand side, more recent cohorts may be more likely to have parents alive than earlier cohorts making them *more* likely to provide care. Yet, if frailty is declining, the parents of the more recent cohorts may be less in need of help at a given age than parents of earlier cohorts.

In figure 5.3, we show caregiving by age and by cohort. Here, and for the remainder of the chapter, we focus solely on care to parents and parents-in-law, ignoring care for spouses. The most striking observation is that caregiving among the two HRS cohorts (early and late), particularly the "early" one, is substantially lower during the respondent's late fifties and early sixties than is the case for the more recent cohorts. We hypothesize that this difference is due, in part, to the shorter lifetimes of their parents born a generation before.[11] The two more recent cohorts show greater levels of caregiving across the span of ages we observe, reaching 10 to 11 percent at the peak. As expected, caregiving declines with age, as parents die and the women themselves become frailer. For both HRS cohorts and for the WB cohort, caregiving to parents and parents-in-law falls steeply as women enter their late sixties. For our earliest cohort, whom we follow for a longer period and to older ages, the fraction of women providing care approaches zero by age seventy-five.

Figure 5.4 reports the cumulative probabilities of providing care to parents and parents-in-law by cohort and age. The same patterns are evident as in figure 5.3: caregiving is substantially lower among the earlier HRS

9. Note that our sample is not a balanced panel; the decline in "ever caregiving" after age sixty-five is due to changes in the composition of the sample, as the cumulative value for any one woman obviously cannot decline over time.

10. Bee and Mitchell (chapter 9, this volume) report that among those born between 1921 and 1925 (in the oldest HRS cohort) labor force participation at age fifty-seven was 46 percent, compared to a 61 percent participation rate for the cohort born between 1944 and 1948.

11. As shown in appendix table 5A.1, the two HRS cohorts are significantly less likely to have parents alive than other groups: 47 percent of early HRS respondents had a living parent/parent-in-law in the first wave, compared to 70 percent of late HRS respondents and 74 percent of those belonging to the two more recent cohorts.

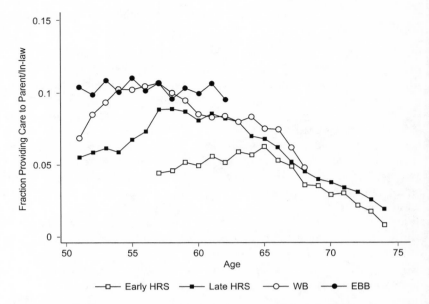

Fig. 5.3   Caregiving to parents and parents-in-law during the previous two years, by cohort

Notes: The series are three-year moving averages of reported values. The reported values are weighted by the number of observations in its cohort-age cell. See notes for figure 5.1 for additional information.

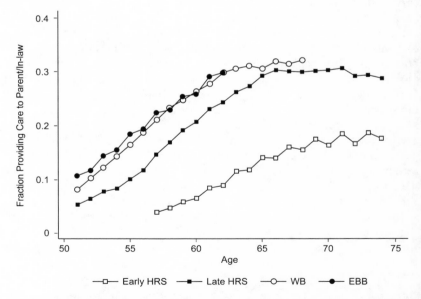

Fig. 5.4   Cumulative caregiving to parents and parents-in-law since first observed in sample, by cohorts

Notes: The series are three-year moving averages of reported values. The reported values are weighted by the number of observations in its cohort-age cell. See notes for figure 5.1 and figure 5.2 for additional information.

cohort and is highest for the two most recent cohorts. By the oldest ages, less than 20 percent of the early HRS cohort had provided care to a parent or parent-in-law, compared with 30 percent of the late HRS and even slightly more for the WB cohort. Even for the EBB cohort, which is observed just until age sixty-six (for its oldest members) and for which we have just four waves of data, 30 percent of women were already observed to have provided some care to parents or in-laws by the time they reached their early sixties.

A key factor determining the effect of caregiving on labor market behavior is the amount of time devoted to care. Figure 5.5 illustrates the distribution of combined hours of care to parents and parents-in-law over a two-year period, conditional on a nonzero amount. Whereas the lowest category (0, 100] is the most common, with 25 percent of the sample providing this level of care, a substantial fraction, 10 percent, provided more than 2,000 hours of care across the past two years, or approximately twenty hours per week if this care is uniformly distributed over the interval. An even larger fraction, 12 percent, provided 1,000 to 2,000 hours. If spread evenly over a full year, these amounts would be equivalent to a regular job, but because this care need not have taken place uniformly over the time period, the magnitudes

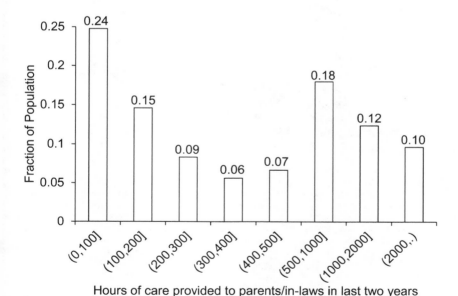

Hours of care provided to parents/in-laws in last two years
conditional on providing non-zero hours

Fig. 5.5   Distribution of care hours to parents/in-laws

Notes: Distribution of combined hours of care provided to parents and in-laws in the last two years for new interviewees or since the previous interview (approximately two years) for reinterviewees. The sample is limited to women who provided care in the last two years or since the prior interview. The height of each bar is the fraction of women who provided hours of care in the range listed on the x-axis. Bars were constructed using sample weights.

are difficult to interpret. Even so, it seems safe to conclude that, for many caregivers, the burden is substantial and is likely to impact the caregiver's labor supply and well-being.

Having demonstrated the extent and intensity of caregiving, another question relevant for our analysis of the relationship between caregiving and work is whether the women who select into caregiving differ from the overall population. To address this question, in table 5.1, we report the means and standard errors of a set of demographic and economic variables for our sample as a whole and separately by caregiving status.[12] We define four "types" of women: (a) those who are observed to be providing care to parents or parents-in-law on (or before) the first interview at which they appear with positive person weights,[13] (b) those who begin providing care at some later point during the survey window after the first appear with positive weight, (c) those who are never observed to provide care but who have living parents or parents-in-law and are thus "at risk" of needing to provide care, and (d) those who have neither living parents nor parents-in-law and therefore will not be "at risk" of providing care based on our measure.[14] An observation in table 5.1 is a woman, and unless otherwise indicated, the data are taken from the first interview in which the woman appears with a positive person weight.

The average age of our respondents is 54.3, and 68 percent are married. Among the women in our sample, 17 percent are nonwhite, and 8 percent are Hispanic. While 54 percent of the sample have a high school education or less, 25 percent attended some college, and 21 percent have college degrees. With respect to the potential need to provide care, 56 percent have living parents, and 34 percent have living parents-in-law (69 percent have either parents or parents-in-law or both). The majority of these women (67 percent) are working when first observed (49 percent are working full time), and the average annual earnings of workers conditional on being nonzero

12. We weight using the person-specific weights provided by the HRS. For a woman who enters the sample as the spouse of an age-eligible husband but who is not age eligible, the HRS assigns a zero person weight until the woman's birth-year cohort is added to the sample. We adhere to this weighting scheme.

13. In table 5.1, we define a woman's "first interview" as the interview in which she first has a positive person weight. As was mentioned above, some women are first interviewed as part of a cohort that is not their birth cohort, and when this occurs, they are assigned zero person weights until their birth cohort is first interviewed. When defining these women's caregiver statuses in table 5.1, we still make use of the information from the period before they first had positive sample weights. It is in this sense that we observe a woman "before" her "first interview."

14. In appendix table 5A.1, we present the means of the variables in table 5.1 by cohort. Age varies by cohort as expected, but there are also significant differences in schooling, with the most recent cohort twice as likely to have graduated from college. There is a monotonic decline in the number of children across cohorts, a rise in financial resources, and a significant rise in employment probabilities. Important for our study, the probability of having a living parent/parent-in-law at the respondent's first interview increases from 0.47 for the earliest cohort to 0.74 percent for the most recent cohort, suggesting a greater "risk" of needing to provide care among more recent groups.

Table 5.1 **Means of selected variables by caregiver status**

	Care at later interview	Care on/ before first interview	Never at risk	Never caregiver but at risk	All
Age	53.6	53.8	55.8	53.8	54.3
	[0.068]	[0.089]	[0.069]	[0.042]	[0.032]
Nonwhite	0.16	0.15	0.21	0.15	0.17
	[0.0090]	[0.013]	[0.0075]	[0.0056]	[0.0038]
Hispanic	0.071	0.068	0.078	0.080	0.077
	[0.0064]	[0.0091]	[0.0049]	[0.0042]	[0.0027]
High school education	0.37	0.35	0.40	0.36	0.37
	[0.012]	[0.017]	[0.0090]	[0.0075]	[0.0050]
Some college	0.28	0.27	0.21	0.25	0.25
	[0.011]	[0.016]	[0.0075]	[0.0068]	[0.0044]
College +	0.22	0.24	0.15	0.24	0.21
	[0.010]	[0.015]	[0.0066]	[0.0066]	[0.0042]
Married	0.70	0.72	0.53	0.75	0.68
	[0.011]	[0.016]	[0.0091]	[0.0067]	[0.0048]
Number of children	2.95	2.91	3.08	2.95	2.98
	[0.047]	[0.067]	[0.039]	[0.030]	[0.020]
Household income	91.2	104.5	63.8	100.9	89.4
	[2.86]	[6.96]	[1.62]	[1.94]	[1.27]
Assets	389.3	482.5	291.2	423.4	386.9
	[17.9]	[31.0]	[12.5]	[13.4]	[8.14]
Work 0/1	0.70	0.68	0.61	0.70	0.67
	[0.011]	[0.017]	[0.0089]	[0.0072]	[0.0048]
Hours worked	38.5	37.9	36.7	38.1	37.8
	[0.37]	[0.60]	[0.31]	[0.25]	[0.17]
Earnings (conditional on > 0)	40.6	37.9	31.9	40.1	37.9
	[1.21]	[1.44]	[0.63]	[0.70]	[0.44]
Spouse/partner works 0/1	0.79	0.75	0.62	0.78	0.75
(conditional on spouse/	[0.012]	[0.018]	[0.012]	[0.0074]	[0.0054]
partner)					
Spouse/partner earnings	70.1	81.5	53.8	71.8	68.9
(conditional on > 0)	[3.46]	[10.9]	[1.94]	[1.69]	[1.49]
Work experience (years)	24.7	25.6	23.7	23.8	24.1
	[0.29]	[0.41]	[0.24]	[0.19]	[0.13]
Tenure current job (years,	11.4	10.5	11.1	10.9	11.0
conditional on working)	[0.29]	[0.46]	[0.24]	[0.18]	[0.13]
Any parents	0.91	0.72	0	0.72	0.56
	[0.0072]	[0.016]	[0]	[0.0070]	[0.0051]
Any parents-in-law	0.46	0.36	0	0.49	0.34
	[0.012]	[0.018]	[0]	[0.0080]	[0.0050]
Number of siblings	2.86	2.95	3.16	3.10	3.06
	[0.055]	[0.082]	[0.050]	[0.039]	[0.025]
Number of sisters	1.45	1.48	1.67	1.63	1.60
	[0.036]	[0.054]	[0.032]	[0.025]	[0.017]
Parent/in-law care at first	0	0.73	0	0	0.075
interview	[0]	[0.016]	[0]	[0]	[0.0029]

(continued)

Table 5.1   (continued)

	Care at later interview	Care on/ before first interview	Never at risk	Never caregiver but at risk	All
Ever give parent/in-law care	1	1	0	0	0.28
	[0]	[0]	[0]	[0]	[0.0046]
Parent/in-law care mean hours	751.6	752.3	.	.	751.8
	[27.6]	[31.7]	[.]	[.]	[21.2]
Observations	1,638	779	2,981	4,100	9,498

Notes: Statistics are means. Standard errors in brackets. Each woman in our sample contributes one observation. Unless otherwise indicated, the data are taken from the first interview in which a woman enters our sample. The columns are defined as follows. "Care on/before first interview" includes women who reported providing care to parents or parents-in-law at or before their first interview, "care at later interview" refers to women who did not provide care to parents or parents-in-law at or before their first interview but who were observed providing such care at a later interview, "never at risk" refers to women who did not have living parents or parents-in-law during the period of observation, and "never caregiver but at risk" includes women who had living parents or parents-in-law but who were never observed providing care to those individuals.

is $37,900. (All dollar-denominated values in this chapter are measured in 2010 dollars.) For 75 percent of those with a spouse, the spouse is working, and the average earnings of these spouses is $68,900 (conditional on being nonzero), far greater than the earnings of their working wives. Among the entire sample, 28 percent provide care to parents or parents-in-law at some point in the survey period, and 7.5 are observed providing care at their first interview. Among the caregivers, the average amount of time spent caring for parents and in-laws over the previous two-year period is 752 hours.[15]

When looking across groups, those not "at risk" of caring for parents are older, are more likely to be nonwhite or Hispanic, and have lower schooling levels.[16] All of these differences are consistent with a shorter life expectancy and thus a lower probability of having parents still alive. Focusing on just those with parents or parents-in-law, the differences in these demographic variables by caregiving status are small and seldom significantly different from zero. Whereas one might have expected caregivers to have a lower opportunity cost of time, the differences between either group of caregivers and those who do not provide care (but are "at risk") in the probability of working are not significantly different from zero, nor are the differences in

15. For comparison, we find that 13 percent of our full sample ever provided care for a spouse or partner during the survey period. Despite the lower prevalence of this type of care, there are indications that providing care to a spouse or partner is more intensive, averaging 126 hours *in the past month*. However, without knowing for how many months care was provided, it is not possible to compare the intensities of the two types of care.

16. See Lahey (chapter 3, this volume) for a comparison of participation rates for black and white women.

the number of hours worked or earnings. Those who eventually provide care do have significantly lower household income when first measured, though this may be partly due to the fact that fewer of these women are married.

The strongest difference is in the number of siblings, and particularly the number of sisters, with both groups of caregivers having significantly fewer sisters than the noncaregivers. These descriptive results and the small differences between groups appear to belie the standard economic intuition that the women who choose to care for a parent or parent-in-law would be selected from those with weaker attachments to the labor force. Instead, the differences indicate the role of chance in that the women who are more likely to need to provide care are the ones that have fewer substitutes within the family.

5.5   Regression Analysis

With this information as background, we now turn to a multivariate analysis that allows us to examine changes in labor market behavior surrounding caregiving controlling for other factors that might also impact the decision. Again, because our focus is on labor market outcomes and because the majority of spousal care comes at older ages (and also because we have incomplete information on spousal care), we limit our regression analyses to the caregiving of parents and parents-in-law. In order to understand how caregiving can affect the likelihood of women working longer, and how this probability may be changing over time, we first analyze the relationship between individual characteristics and the decision to provide care before turning our attention to the relationship between caregiving and work.

In our analysis of caregiving behavior, we are interested in determining how much of the differences across cohorts in the observed propensity to provide care might be due to changes in demographic characteristics that themselves have changed over time—factors such as fertility, schooling, or marital status—and how much is due to unobserved factors, such as the pull of familial obligations, that may also vary across cohorts. Whereas in our graphical analysis we adhered to the categorical birth cohorts, in our regressions we employ year of birth in lieu of cohort dummy variables, which we recognize are arbitrarily defined. Later, in our analysis of labor market outcomes, we also include interactions between birth year and caregiving to assess the extent to which the effect of caregiving on work changes over time.

5.5.1   Determinants of Caregiving

Table 5.2 reports results from regressions that model the probability that a woman in our sample provides care to a parent or parent-in-law during a particular survey period. The three columns report the coefficient estimates from three linear probability models. The first column includes birth year (minus 1941) as the only regressor. The second column adds dummy

Table 5.2   **Probability of providing care to a parent or parent-in-law**

	Care 0/1	Care 0/1	Care 0/1
Birth year − 1941	0.0035***	0.0016***	0.00073**
	[0.00028]	[0.00035]	[0.00033]
Number living parents ($t - 1$)			0.039***
			[0.0055]
Number living in-laws ($t - 1$)			−0.011**
			[0.0055]
Age of eldest parent/in-law ($t - 1$)			0.0016***
			[0.000087]
Number of siblings			−0.0000027
			[0.0011]
Number of sisters			−0.0030*
			[0.0016]
High school			0.0093**
			[0.0038]
Some college			0.0027
			[0.0046]
College or more			0.0066
			[0.0053]
Nonwhite			0.011***
			[0.0038]
Hispanic			−0.000046
			[0.0053]
Number of children			−0.00047
			[0.00068]
Married			−0.0068**
			[0.0030]
Child under 18			−0.024***
			[0.0084]
Fair/poor health			0.0088***
			[0.0031]
Second wealth quartile ($t - 1$)			0.0071**
			[0.0035]
Third wealth quartile ($t - 1$)			0.002
			[0.0038]
Highest wealth quartile ($t - 1$)			0.0051
			[0.0043]
Experience ($t - 1$)			0.00034***
			[0.00011]
Current tenure ($t - 1$)			−0.00035**
			[0.00017]
N	46,005	46,005	46,005
R-squared	0.006	0.012	0.105
Mean of the dependent variable	0.064	0.064	0.064

Notes: Coefficients are OLS estimates. See section 5.3 of the text for a discussion of the sample. Models in the second and third columns include single-year age dummy variables. The notation "($t - 1$)" refers to data taken from the previous interview. Standard errors in brackets.
***Significant at the 1 percent level.
**Significant at the 5 percent level.
*Significant at the 10 percent level.

variables for single years of age, and the third column adds a variety of other covariates. The covariates in the third specification include the number of living parents and the number of living in-laws at the previous interview; the age of the eldest parent or in-law at the prior interview; the numbers of living siblings and sisters; a categorical measure of education; a count of the respondent's children; indicators for whether the respondent is nonwhite, Hispanic, married, in fair or poor health, or has any children under the age of eighteen; quartiles of lagged wealth; and measures from the previous interview of years of work experience and tenure on the current job (the latter of which is set to zero for those not previously working). These variables are intended to account for numerous differences between the different birth cohorts that could explain observed differences in caregiving behavior.

When we look at the simple correlation between birth year and caregiving, we see the same strong differences in caregiving behavior across cohorts that we documented earlier in our figures. In particular, women born more recently are much more likely to provide care to parents or parents-in-law than are women from earlier cohorts. As we progressively add more right-hand-side variables, it is apparent that much of the observed differences in caregiving patterns across cohorts may be attributed to other factors. Simply accounting for age reduces the magnitude of the coefficient estimate on year of birth by more than half. The coefficient is again cut in half with the addition of other controls in the third column. In each case, the change in the estimate is statistically significant and different from zero, yet birth year itself remains a significant factor in predicting caregiving.[17]

We find that many of our explanatory variables are important predictors of caregiving behavior. The most obvious predictor is having living parents at the previous interview, which positively predicts caregiving to parents or in-laws. The age of the eldest parent or in-law, likely a good proxy for need, is also positively related to care. Interestingly, although the dependent variable is caregiving to parents *and/or* parents-in-law, having living parents-in-law significantly reduces the likelihood of providing care.

The gendered nature of caregiving is readily apparent in these estimates: having additional siblings has no effect on the likelihood of providing care, but having additional sisters significantly decreases the probability of providing care, with each sister reducing the probability by approximately one-third of a percentage point. Married women and those with children under eighteen are considerably less likely to provide care, owing perhaps to the greater competition for their time. Nonwhite women are more likely to provide care as, surprisingly, are those in poor health.

Perhaps more related to the goal of this volume are the associations between caregiving and measures of labor force attachment. On the one

---

17. Estimating each pair of models jointly as a set of seemingly unrelated regressions and testing equality of the coefficients on birth year minus 1941 strongly rejects equality in each instance.

hand, years of experience, a measure of lifetime attachment, positively predicts caregiving. The result conforms with the results in our descriptive analysis where we found that caregivers do not appear to be negatively selected on characteristics associated with success in the labor market. On the other hand, we find that lagged tenure on the current job, a proxy for current market attachment, negatively predicts care.

Finally, we note the significantly positive coefficient on birth year despite the inclusion of numerous controls for observable differences across cohorts. Being born ten years later is associated with a statistically significant 0.73 percentage point increase in caregiving, which is an 11 percent increase relative to the estimation sample mean of 6.4 percent. This finding suggests the existence of additional omitted time-varying determinants of caregiving, with more recent cohorts more apt to provide care.

This "cohort effect" works in concert with other factors that vary across cohorts, leading toward the greater care among more recent cohorts seen so prominently in the figures. The more recent cohorts are significantly more likely to have living parents during their prime working years than the earlier cohorts, increasing the likelihood that they provide care. They are also less likely to be married, this too increasing caregiving. However, as members of the baby boom generation, the youngest in our sample are also more likely to have sisters who could function as alternative providers, suggesting lower rates of caregiving. They are also more likely to delay childbearing and therefore to have younger children when parents begin to need care, again suggesting lower rates of caregiving. Yet, the net effect of all of these factors is a significant trend toward increasing caregiving by more recent cohorts.

5.5.2   Determinants of Work

In table 5.3, we investigate the effect of caregiving on work, examining both the binary decision to work and the number of hours worked conditional on employment. Our primary right-hand-side variable of interest is the indicator variable "currently caring for parent/in-law," which is equal to one if the respondent reports providing care to a parent or parent-in-law during the survey period and zero otherwise. We also include a measure of prior caregiving ("previously cared for parent/in-law") that is equal to one if the respondent reports such caregiving at a previous interview but is *not* currently providing care, and is equal to zero otherwise.[18] This measure allows us to assess whether caregiving has an effect after the care ceases. We again include a measure of birth year as well as interactions between birth year and our caregiving measures, allowing us to assess whether the effect of caregiving on work differs across cohorts. In addition to these variables, we include many of the same demographic and socioeconomic characteristics as in the caregiving models.

---

18. We note that previous care is not perfectly measured in our data because we do not observe caregiving histories for women prior to their entry into the survey.

Table 5.3   Regressions of labor market outcomes

	Probability of working		Hours worked if > 0	
	OLS	FE	OLS	FE
Currently caring for parent/in-law	−0.034***	−0.033***	−0.38	−1.29**
	[0.0096]	[0.012]	[0.48]	[0.56]
Current care * (birth year − 1941)	−0.0033**	−0.0039*	−0.023	−0.11
	[0.0017]	[0.0022]	[0.084]	[0.100]
Previously cared but not currently	−0.019**	−0.017	0.37	−1.27*
	[0.0084]	[0.014]	[0.49]	[0.65]
Previously cared * (birth year − 1941)	−0.00022	−0.0051**	−0.065	−0.099
	[0.0014]	[0.0025]	[0.081]	[0.12]
Birth year − 1941	0.0035***		0.058*	
	[0.00068]		[0.033]	
High school	0.036***		0.19	
	[0.0084]		[0.58]	
Some college	0.056***		0.91	
	[0.010]		[0.61]	
College or more	0.070***		1.84***	
	[0.012]		[0.68]	
Nonwhite	−0.036***		−1.06***	
	[0.0079]		[0.40]	
Hispanic	0.014		0.041	
	[0.0099]		[0.66]	
Number of children	0.0091***		0.057	
	[0.0015]		[0.087]	
Married	−0.043***	−0.041***	−2.17***	−0.83
	[0.0067]	[0.011]	[0.34]	[0.55]
Child under 18 (0/1)	0.018	−0.026	−0.64	−0.94
	[0.016]	[0.017]	[0.64]	[0.71]
Fair/poor health	−0.17***	−0.068***	−0.67*	−0.27
	[0.0060]	[0.0062]	[0.40]	[0.37]
Second wealth quartile ($t − 1$)	0.0018	−0.00088	−0.35	0.17
	[0.0072]	[0.0075]	[0.36]	[0.35]
Third wealth quartile ($t − 1$)	−0.032***	−0.034***	−1.73***	−0.28
	[0.0086]	[0.0098]	[0.41]	[0.46]
Fourth wealth quartile ($t − 1$)	−0.069***	−0.062***	−3.32***	−1.16**
	[0.0095]	[0.012]	[0.52]	[0.57]
Experience ($t − 1$)	0.0068***		0.11***	
	[0.00023]		[0.018]	
Current tenure ($t − 1$)	0.018***		0.18***	
	[0.00033]		[0.016]	
Number of observations	46,748	46,748	18,918	18,918
R-squared	0.364	0.172	0.119	0.109
Mean of dependent variable	0.413	0.413	34.02	34.02

Notes: Coefficients are OLS estimates. See section 5.3 of the text for discussion of the sample. All models include single-year age dummy variables. The notation "($t − 1$)" refers to data taken from the previous interview. Standard errors in brackets.

***Significant at the 1 percent level.
**Significant at the 5 percent level.
*Significant at the 10 percent level.

In analyzing the relationship between work and caregiving, it is likely that unobservable factors affect both outcomes. Consider industriousness or conscientiousness, for example. Individuals who are less industrious may be less likely to work or work fewer hours and may similarly be unlikely to take on the burden of care.[19] Because we have multiple observations per respondent, we include individual fixed effects to control for these unobserved characteristics. The first column in each pair reports results from a linear probability model, and the second displays the results from a specification with individual fixed effects.

In our OLS estimates from column (1), we see that both measures of caregiving are significantly negatively related to work. Those providing care are 3.4 percentage points less likely to work on a mean of 41.3 percent, or approximately 8 percent. Those who previously provided care but are not currently doing so are 1.9 percentage points less likely to be working, more than a 4 percent decrease relative to the mean. These estimates are significant at the 1 and 5 percent levels, respectively. The latter finding suggests that caregiving does appear to have a long-term effect.

We also find that the labor supply of more recent cohorts is more likely to be impacted by the decision to provide care than is true for earlier cohorts. A woman born ten years later is an additional 3.3 percentage points less likely to be working if she is providing care to a parent or in-law. In contrast, the negative impact on work of having previously been a caregiver does not appear to vary with year of birth.

The other explanatory variables operate as expected: nonwhites are significantly less likely to work, as are those in poor health and those who are married.[20] Work increases with education and decreases with wealth. Women with more lifetime work experience and those with longer tenure on their current job (both measured at the previous interview) are more likely to be working. Even accounting for differences in these observables, cohort differences in work behavior remain visible: ceteris paribus, a woman born ten years later is 3.5 percentage points, or 8.5 percent, more likely to be working.

Looking at the fixed effects results in the second column, the estimated effect of caregiving on work is similar to the OLS specification. Contemporaneous caregiving is associated with a reduction in the probability of working of 3.3 percentage points. The effect remains significant at the 1 percent level. The effect of having previously provided care is also similar in magnitude to the OLS estimate, although here it is not significantly different from zero. Both previous and current caregiving have significantly larger negative

---

19. This possibility is related to the work of Freeman (1997), who finds that individuals who volunteer their labor are highly skilled and have a high opportunity cost of time.

20. See Olivetti and Rotz (chapter 4, this volume) for a discussion of the relationship between work at older ages and marital status.

impacts on more recent cohorts, though the estimate underlying the latter claim is significant at only the 10 percent level.

The third and fourth columns repeat the analysis with hours worked conditional on employment as the dependent variable. While there does not appear to be a significant effect of caregiving on hours worked in the OLS specification, the fixed effects regression results indicate that women who are currently providing care, or who previously did so, work approximately 1.3 fewer hours per week than noncaregivers.[21] These results are significant at the 5 and 10 percent levels, respectively. Relative to a mean of thirty-four hours worked per week, these effects represent 4 percent decreases in hours. The impact does not appear to differ by birth year. Other effects are as expected: more educated individuals work longer hours; nonwhites, married women, those in poor health, and those with greater wealth work fewer hours. Conditional on working, those with more lifetime work experience and more tenure on the current job work longer hours. We find small differences by birth year suggesting that more recent cohorts work slightly longer hours, but the result is just marginally significant.

5.6 Conclusion

The retirement of the baby boom and the aging of the population more generally present a number of challenges. Two of the most pressing are the need to care for the elderly and the need to retain a large and productive workforce when this large cohort reaches retirement age. These two issues are interrelated in that workers, particularly women, may reduce their labor force participation in order to care for an elderly parent. In this chapter, we examined the relationship between work and caregiving.

We find that caregiving is quite prevalent, with approximately one-third of our sample of women in their fifties and early sixties providing care at some point during our window of observation. Because we are focusing on prime age working women, the majority of care provided is for elderly parents. Were we to extend our window of observation, we would see even more care, with much of this later care provided to spouses. However, it is unlikely that such care would affect labor market behavior to a significant extent given the age the women in our sample would be at that point.

We also observe different caregiving patterns across the HRS birth cohorts, with younger cohorts providing significantly more care in their fifties and early sixties than women born a decade or so earlier. We find that these differences are explained to some extent by observables correlated with birth year. Perhaps the most dominant and obvious explanation is that, because of increases in longevity, more recent cohorts are more likely

---

21. We note that previous research has shown that workers often do not have the flexibility to vary hours on a current job (Hurd and McGarry 1993).

to have living parents during the prime age working years, and thus experience a greater likelihood of providing care. Yet, even after accounting for differences in this "risk" of needing to provide care, and controlling for other factors such as schooling and labor force attachment, we still find that later cohorts provide more care to parents, possibly suggesting a change in attitudes toward family care.

We find a relationship between caregiving and work similar to what has been documented in previous studies. Using both ordinary least squares and fixed effects specifications, we find a significant effect of caregiving on the probability of work, with the OLS estimate implying a reduction of 3.4 percentage points and the fixed effects estimate a nearly identical 3.3 percentage point reduction. Notably, the effect of caregiving on work also appears to be persistent. In our OLS specification, we find that women who previously provided care but are not currently doing so are 1.9 percentage points less likely to be working. The fixed effects estimate is similar in magnitude but not significantly different from zero. In contrast to some previous work (e.g., Van Houtven et al. 2013), when we control for individual fixed effects, we find a small but significant reduction in hours worked for those currently or previously caregiving.

Taken together, the results in our chapter indicate that changes in family caregiving responsibilities are unlikely to explain why women are working longer than in the past. Instead, if anything, caregiving responsibilities may have dampened the trend toward longer work lives.

Appendix

Table 5A.1   **Means of selected variables, by cohort**

	HRS early	HRS late	WB cohort	EBB cohort	All
Age	59.1	53.6	53.3	53.2	54.3
	[0.05]	[0.05]	[0.05]	[0.04]	[0.03]
Nonwhite	0.15	0.15	0.16	0.19	0.17
	[0.01]	[0.01]	[0.01]	[0.01]	[0.00]
Hispanic	0.058	0.075	0.078	0.086	0.077
	[0.00]	[0.00]	[0.01]	[0.01]	[0.00]
High school education	0.42	0.41	0.36	0.34	0.37
	[0.01]	[0.01]	[0.01]	[0.01]	[0.00]
Some college	0.19	0.21	0.27	0.28	0.25
	[0.01]	[0.01]	[0.01]	[0.01]	[0.00]
College +	0.14	0.15	0.22	0.28	0.21
	[0.01]	[0.01]	[0.01]	[0.01]	[0.00]
Married	0.69	0.71	0.67	0.67	0.68
	[0.01]	[0.01]	[0.01]	[0.01]	[0.00]
Number of children	3.44	3.28	2.90	2.62	2.98
	[0.05]	[0.04]	[0.04]	[0.04]	[0.02]
Household income	65.9	78.5	92.9	105.2	89.4
	[1.55]	[2.40]	[2.47]	[3.18]	[1.27]
Assets	361.9	350.4	391.8	419.1	386.9
	[12.74]	[14.61]	[16.58]	[19.86]	[8.14]
Work 0/1	0.54	0.64	0.71	0.73	0.67
	[0.01]	[0.01]	[0.01]	[0.01]	[0.00]
Hours worked	35.4	37.3	38.2	38.7	37.8
	[0.39]	[0.29]	[0.33]	[0.34]	[0.17]
Earnings (conditional on earnings > 0)	29.5	32.2	38.0	44.6	37.9
	[0.77]	[0.56]	[0.91]	[1.11]	[0.44]
Spouse/partner works 0/1 (conditional on spouse/partner)	0.57	0.72	0.79	0.81	0.75
	[0.01]	[0.01]	[0.01]	[0.01]	[0.01]
Spouse/partner earnings (conditional on earnings > 0)	53.2	62.9	67.5	81.1	68.9
	[2.35]	[3.26]	[1.90]	[3.62]	[1.49]
Work experience (years)	23.7	21.9	24.9	25.2	24.1
	[0.30]	[0.22]	[0.25]	[0.25]	[0.13]
Tenure current job (years) (conditional on working)	12.0	10.7	11.3	10.5	11.0
	[0.31]	[0.21]	[0.26]	[0.26]	[0.13]
Any parents	0.34	0.58	0.60	0.62	0.56
	[0.01]	[0.01]	[0.01]	[0.01]	[0.01]
Any parents-in-law	0.20	0.35	0.36	0.39	0.34
	[0.01]	[0.01]	[0.01]	[0.01]	[0.01]
Number of siblings	2.77	2.96	2.98	3.33	3.06
	[0.05]	[0.04]	[0.05]	[0.06]	[0.03]
Number of sisters	1.47	1.55	1.53	1.74	1.60
	[0.03]	[0.03]	[0.03]	[0.04]	[0.02]
Parent/in-law care at first interview	0.037	0.052	0.084	0.097	0.075
	[0.00]	[0.00]	[0.01]	[0.01]	[0.00]

(continued)

Table 5A.1   (continued)

	HRS early	HRS late	WB cohort	EBB cohort	All
Ever give parent/in-law care	0.16	0.28	0.33	0.28	0.28
	[0.01]	[0.01]	[0.01]	[0.01]	[0.00]
Parent/in-law care mean hours	766.0	610.3	862.9	738.1	751.8
	[57.42]	[28.17]	[47.01]	[42.68]	[21.17]
Observations	2,305	3,171	2,050	1,972	9,498

Notes: Statistics are means. Standard errors in brackets. An observation in the table is a woman. Unless otherwise indicated, the data are taken from the first interview in which the woman is assigned a positive person weight. See text for a description of the HRS cohorts.

References

Bolin, Kristian, Bjorn Lindgren, and Petter Lundborg. 2008. "Your Next of Kin or Your Own Career? Caring and Working among the 50+ of Europe." *Journal of Health Economics* 27 (3): 718–38.

Carmichael, Fiona, S. Charles, and Claire Hulme. 2010. "Who Will Care? Employment Participation and Willingness to Supply Informal Care." *Journal of Health Economics* 29 (1): 182–90.

Doty, Pamela. 2010. "The Evolving Balance of Formal and Informal, Institutional and Non-Institutional Long-Term Care for Older Americans: A Thirty-Year Perspective." *Public Policy & Aging Report* 20 (1): 3–9.

Ettner, Susan. 1996. "The Opportunity Costs of Elder Care." *Journal of Human Resources* 31 (1): 189–205.

Feinberg, Lynn, Susan Reinhard, Ari Houser, and Rita Choula. 2011. *Valuing the Invaluable: 2011 Update: The Growing Contributions and Costs of Family Caregiving.* Washington, DC: AARP Public Policy Institute.

Freeman, Richard. 1997. "Working for Nothing: The Supply of Volunteer Labor." *Journal of Labor Economics* 15 (1): S140–66.

Genworth. 2016. *The Expanding Circle of Care: Beyond Dollars 2015.* Richmond, VA: Genworth Financial Inc.

Heitmueller, Alex. 2007. "The Chicken or the Egg? Endogeneity in Labour Market Participation of Informal Careers in England." *Journal of Health Economics* 26 (3): 536–59.

Hurd, Michael, and Kathleen McGarry. 1993. "The Relationship between Job Characteristics and Retirement." NBER Working Paper no. 4558, Cambridge, MA.

Johnson, Richard, and Anthony T. Lo Sasso. 2006. "The Impact of Elder Care on Women's Labor Supply." *Inquiry: The Journal of Health Care Organization, Provision, and Financing* 43 (3): 195–210.

Kemper, Peter, Harriet Komisar, and Lisa Alecxih. 2006. "Long Term Care over an Uncertain Future: What Can Current Retirees Expect?" *Inquiry: The Journal of Health Care Organization, Provision, and Financing* 42 (4): 335–50.

McGarry, Kathleen. 2003. "Does Caregiving Affect Work? Evidence Based on Prior Labor Force Experience." In *Health Care Issues in the United States and Japan,* edited by David A. Wise and Naohiro Yashiro, 209–28. Chicago: University of Chicago Press.

National Association of Insurance Commissioners. 2016. *The State of Long-Term Care Insurance: The Market, Challenges, and Future Innovations.* Kansas City, MO: National Association of Insurance Commissioners.

O'Shaughnessy, Carol. 2014. "National Spending for Long-Term Services and Supports (LTSS), 2012." *National Health Policy Forum, The Basics.* Washington, DC: National Health Policy Forum, George Washington University.

Van Houtven, Courtney Harold, Norma B. Coe, and Meghan M. Skira. 2013. "The Effect of Informal Care on Work and Wages." *Journal of Health Economics* 32 (1): 240–52.

III

Financial Considerations: Resources, Pensions, and Social Security

6

Older Women's Labor Market Attachment, Retirement Planning, and Household Debt

Annamaria Lusardi and Olivia S. Mitchell

Economic research has shown convincingly that young and middle-aged women's attachment to the paid labor force has risen substantially over time in America.[1] To examine whether this pattern might also characterize older women, we examine several cohorts of older women in the Health and Retirement Study (HRS) to document the size of possible future changes and to pinpoint which groups might be most likely to extend their work lives. In addition, we investigate what role debt might play in older women's continued work. For this, we examine the 2012 National Financial Capability Study (NFCS), which provides detailed information on how older women appear to be managing their debt and their retirement planning efforts. Our focus throughout is on descriptive analysis rather than proving causal links between retirement and debt.

Our findings from the HRS show that recent cohorts of older women were

Annamaria Lusardi is the Denit Trust Chair of Economics and Accountancy at the George Washington University School of Business and a research associate of the National Bureau of Economic Research. Olivia S. Mitchell is the International Foundation of Employee Benefit Plans Professor, as well as Professor of Insurance/Risk Management and Business Economics/Policy, Executive Director of the Pension Research Council, and Director of the Boettner Center on Pensions and Retirement Research, all at the Wharton School of the University of Pennsylvania and a research associate of the National Bureau of Economic Research.

The authors thank Julie Agnew, Claudia Goldin, Larry Katz, and participants at the Women Working Longer conference for comments, and Noemi Oggero and Yong Yu for expert programming and research assistance. Research support was provided by the TIAA Institute and the Pension Research Council/Boettner Center at the Wharton School of the University of Pennsylvania. Opinions and conclusions expressed herein are solely those of the authors and do not represent the opinions or policy of the funders or any other institutions with which the authors are affiliated. For acknowledgments, sources of research support, and disclosure of the authors' material financial relationships, if any, please see http://www.nber.org/chapters/c13801.ack.

1. See, for instance, Goldin (2006, 2014) and the citations included therein.

more likely to be working at both ages fifty-one to fifty-six and fifty-seven to sixty-one than the earliest cohort of the same age, first surveyed in 1992.[2] Effects differ significantly over time, in that the mean probability of being at work for the baseline HRS sample ages fifty-one to fifty-six when surveyed was 64.9 percent, and 54.8 percent for ages fifty-seven to sixty-one. All subsequent cohorts displayed higher rates of work, particularly for the fifty-one- to fifty-six-year-old group, controlling on other factors. Thus, there is a rising probability of working among older women across cohorts.

We also find that recent cohorts of women drawing near to retirement have more debt than before, and their increased debt is positively associated with these women being more likely to work currently, as well as to plan to continue to work in the future. Somewhat surprisingly, total debt more than doubled in constant dollars and, in recent waves, older women were increasingly likely to hold mortgage debt in excess of half their residential value. Additionally, the percentage of women having less than $25,000 in savings for recent cohorts is roughly double that of the earlier cohorts.

We also draw on data from the 2012 NFCS to explore the factors associated with retirement planning, debt and debt management, and an indicator of financial fragility. As shown in previous work, planning for retirement is associated with better retirement security (Lusardi and Mitchell 2007a, 2011a, 2014). Moreover, many people are found to pay high interest and fees on the debt they carry, and debt is part of household balance sheets throughout the lifetime and even close to retirement (Lusardi and Mitchell 2013; Lusardi and Tufano 2015). Correlates of retirement planning include having higher income, more education, and greater financial literacy, for both age groups we evaluate (ages fifty-one to fifty-six and fifty-seven to sixty-one). Factors associated with overindebtedness and financial fragility include lower financial literacy, having more financially dependent children, and experiencing unexpected large income declines. Accordingly, shocks do play a role in the accumulation of debt close to retirement. Nevertheless, it is not enough to have resources: people also need the capacity to manage those resources, if they are to stay out of debt and find retirement security at older ages.

6.1   Prior Studies

Many prior studies have explored American women's labor supply patterns over time (see, e.g., Attanasio, Low, and Sánchez-Marcos 2008; Goldin 2006; Michaud and Rohwedder 2015). Yet there has been relatively little

2. The fifty-one to fifty-six age groups of women were surveyed in 1992 (the HRS baseline group, born 1936 to 1941), the 1998 War Babies (WB) group (born 1942 to 1947), the 2004 Early Baby Boomers (EBB) cohort (born 1948–1953), and the 2010 Middle Baby Boomer (MBB) group (born 1954 to 1959). The three fifty-seven to sixty-one age cohorts of women were surveyed in 1992 for the baseline HRS cohort, in 2004 for the WB, and in 2010 for the EBB.

work focusing on cohort changes in older women's participation patterns and debt, as well as financial literacy. In this section, we review relevant literature on these issues.

Several authors have evaluated the links between debt management and financial literacy, and they have concluded that the least financially literate incurred high fees and used high-cost borrowing. The least financially knowledgeable also report that their debt loads were excessive and they were often unable to judge their debt positions (Lusardi and Tufano [2015], and the references therein). This group was also more likely to borrow from their 401(k) and pension accounts (Lu et al. 2017; Utkus and Young 2011) and to use high-cost methods of borrowing such as payday loans (Lusardi and de Bassa Scheresberg 2013).

Some research has linked the quality of financial decision making and age, and the findings offer little reason for complacency. For instance, one influential study (Agarwal et al. 2009) found that the quality of financial decision making fell at older ages in ten financial areas, including credit card balance transfers, home equity loans and lines of credit, auto loans, credit card interest rates, mortgages, small-business credit cards, credit card late-payment fees, credit card over-the-limit fees, and credit card cash-advance fees. Older persons pay higher financial service fees and interest.

In the wake of the financial crisis, these age-linked patterns are now translating into awareness that older Americans are nearing retirement with levels of debt that are of increasing concern.[3] For instance, debt held by borrowers between ages fifty to eighty rose roughly 60 percent between 2003 and 2015, while aggregate debt balances held by younger borrowers declined modestly (Brown et al. 2016). Much of this rise consisted of home mortgages, held by over half (55 percent) of the American population ages fifty-five to sixty-four, and about the same fraction (50 percent) had credit card debt (Bucks et al. 2009). Moreover, among people ages sixty-five to seventy-four, two-thirds held some form of debt, almost half had mortgages or other loans on their primary residences, over one-third held credit card debt, and a quarter had installment loans. In recent years, on average, older borrowers held substantially more debt than did borrowers of the same age in the 1990s: for instance Lusardi and Mitchell (2013) showed that the percentage of people ages fifty-six to sixty-one having debt swelled to 71 percent in 2008, up from 64 percent in 1992. Additionally, the value of their debt rose sharply over time. Median household debt in 1992 was about $6,200, but by 2002 it had more than tripled. By 2008, it was $28,300—more than quadruple the 1992 level.

Accompanying this trend has been an increase over time in the proportion of older Americans filing for bankruptcy: people sixty-five years and

---

3. For a few recent examples, see AARP (2013), Cho (2012), Copeland (2013), Pham (2011), Securian (2013), Lusardi and Mitchell (2013), and the references therein.

older are the fastest-growing group in terms of bankruptcy filings, which stood at 2 percent in 1991 and rose to over three times that rate by 2007 (Pottow 2012). Credit card interest and fees was the most cited reason for bankruptcy filings by older people, with two-thirds of them providing this reason.[4] Moreover, there is also a continuing tendency of women filing for bankruptcy more often than men, and women report being overextended on credit as the key reason for filing (Institute for Financial Literacy 2011).

Another key factor spurring the increase in debt over time has been the much higher prices paid by recent cohorts for housing, and their resulting larger residential mortgages. For example, the median amount older homeowners owed on mortgages increased 82 percent, from approximately $43,400 in 2001 to $79,000 in 2011. Further, data show older consumers owe more on their mortgages in relation to the value of their home than their peers did a decade ago. The outstanding balance on their mortgages relative to the value of their homes (debt-to-value ratio) increased from 30 to 46 percent between 2001 and 2011 (CFPB 2014). Until 2009, single women—the fastest growing segments of the housing market—purchased more homes than single men. Since, on average, women pay more for their mortgages than do men, it is unsurprising that mortgage debt is reported to be especially high among older women (Cheng, Lin, and Liu 2011; Clark 2015; Drew 2006).

A related point is that subprime mortgage lenders targeted minority, elderly, and female buyers in the years leading up to the financial crisis. Prior to the financial crisis, female homebuyers were 32 percent more likely to have subprime mortgage loans, despite having higher credit scores on average (US Congress Joint Economic Committee 2008). These mortgages, which made up only 13 percent of all home loans but accounted for 55 percent of foreclosure starts, left older Americans vulnerable, and when housing prices sharply declined many turned to delinquency (Leland 2008). This led to a fivefold rise in the serious delinquency rate between 2001 and 2011 for older mortgage holders ages sixty-five to seventy-four (CFPB 2014), underscoring the risk of holding such high levels of debt at older ages.

There is also evidence that rapid changes in housing prices altered older Americans' labor market attachment. For example, Begley and Chan (2015)

---

4. Other data sources confirm these findings. People fifty-five years and older hold widespread credit card debt and pay considerable fees for late payment and exceeding credit limits, when they should be at the peak of their wealth accumulation (Lusardi 2011; Lusardi and Tufano 2015). Data from the 2012 National Financial Capability Study highlighted that 60 percent of preretirees had at least one source of long-term debt, and 26 percent had at least two. Nearly 40 percent of preretirees used credit cards expensively, and the same percentage felt heavily indebted (Lusardi and de Bassa Scheresberg 2014). Other surveys suggest similar conclusions. The 2013 Survey of Consumer Finances showed that family net worth—the difference between families' gross assets and their liabilities—generally increases with age, with a plateau or modest decreases for the oldest age groups relative to the near-retirement age groups (Bricker et al. 2014). The median net wealth of near retirees (households headed by someone between the ages of fifty-five and sixty-four) was lower in 2013 than in 1989 (Rosnick and Baker 2014).

explored the relationship between unanticipated changes in housing wealth, such as those experienced during the Great Recession, and retirement behavior by examining how the variation in the timing of housing price influenced work effort. They showed that women experiencing large negative housing price shocks were 25 percent less likely to retire, relative to those experiencing positive shocks. Moreover, homeowners having mortgages were less likely to retire (if not yet retired) or more likely to reverse retirement (if already retired). Farnham and Sevak (2016) found that people responded to rising home prices by revising down their expected retirement ages. Specifically, they estimated that a 10 percent real increase in home value reduced expected retirement ages by about four months. One might anticipate that the mechanism worked in reverse when housing prices fell during the financial crisis and thereafter.

The trend in debt is beginning to attract attention from the media, with recent articles exhorting people to cut their debt as they near retirement (e.g., Derousseau 2016). Additionally, the high and rising levels of household debt are increasingly troubling older persons (FINRA 2006, 2007; United States Government Accountability Office 2015). For instance, just 9 percent of workers in 2016 who described their debt as a major problem said they were very confident of having enough money to live comfortably throughout retirement. Yet retirement saving efforts are still lagging, according to the 2016 Retirement Confidence Survey (RCS) (Blakely, VanDerhei, and Copeland 2016). Instead, people who admitted they were undersaving indicated that they would likely cope with the shortfall by either saving more or working longer.[5]

Our contribution here examines cohort changes in older women's work plans and debt burdens using the HRS, as well as the links between financial literacy and debt stresses in the NFCS. Our results point to the need for boosting older women's retirement security and the important role of managing debt later in life.

6.2   Cohort Trends in Continued Work and the Role of Debt in the HRS

In this section we analyze cohorts of women observed in the HRS, a nationally representative survey of respondents older than fifty years. Specifically, we focus on four birth cohorts of women first surveyed when ages fifty-one to fifty-six and three cohorts of women surveyed when ages fifty-seven to sixty-one, to evaluate each of them on the verge of retirement. We utilize extensive information gathered by the HRS about these women's current employment status and future work plans, along with their sociodemographic characteristics including marital and family histories. In so

---

5. A worrisome point is that some retirees indicate that they could not work longer because they were forced to leave the workforce earlier than planned (for reasons such as health problems or disability) (Banerjee 2014).

doing, we evaluate whether there are statistically significant differences across the cohorts after controlling on other factors.[6] We also evaluate whether debt is correlated with anticipated future work. Finally, we assess the extent to which birth cohorts of older women differ with regard to how much debt they held as they entered their fifties, permitting us to judge whether rising levels of debt are associated with plans to work longer.

6.2.1   Cohort Differences

For the cohort analysis, we examine four groups of women initially surveyed when they were ages fifty-one to fifty-six, and three groups surveyed between ages fifty-seven to sixty-one. This analysis is facilitated by the structure of the HRS (see volume appendix, figure VA.1), which periodically enrolls refresher cohorts over time. For the age fifty-one to fifty-six group, we include those first surveyed in 1992 (the HRS baseline group, born 1936 to 1941), the 1998 War Babies (WB) group (born 1942 to 1947), the 2004 Early Baby Boomers (EBB) cohort (born 1948 to 1953), and the 2010 Middle Baby Boomer (MBB) group (born 1954 to 1959). The three cohorts of fifty-seven- to sixty-one-year-old women were surveyed in 1992 for the baseline HRS cohort, in 2004 for the War Babies, and in 2010 for the Early Baby Boomers.[7]

Our empirical modeling involves multivariate analysis of each respective outcome variable (y) on a vector of cohort dummies, where the HRS baseline is the reference category. The main outcomes analyzed are an indicator of the respondents' current employment status, and their estimated chances of working at age sixty-five. In both cases, the estimated coefficients on the cohort dummies refer to the differential behavior of subsequent cohorts versus the HRS baseline 1992 cohort. In all cases, we control for the respondent's age, race (white versus other), and ethnicity (Hispanic versus other). These factors are, of course, most likely to be exogenous to past work patterns. We also control on the respondent's level of education, whether she had experienced marital disruption (ever divorced or widowed), whether she was in fair or poor (subjective) health, her number of children, and ratios of her household primary residence and other debt to, respectively, housing value and liquid assets. These factors permit us to ascertain whether what might appear to be cohort differences could instead be associated with differences in socioeconomic and demographic factors over time, including changes in financial markets and the increased opportunities to borrow and take on debt. The entire sample includes slightly more than 6,700 women ages fifty-one to fifty-six, and around 4,200 women ages fifty-seven to sixty-one.

Our first set of results examines whether women reported working for pay at the time of their interview, and table 6.1 reports coefficient estimates of the linear probability analysis. Panel A provides results for current work

---

6. See also Goldin and Katz (chapter 1, this volume).
7. Descriptive statistics for our sample appear in appendix table 6A.1.

Table 6.1 **Factors associated with older women's current employment in the Health and Retirement Study (HRS)**

	A. Women ages 51–56		B. Women ages 57–61	
WB	0.069***	0.067***	0.029	0.018
	(0.017)	(0.017)	(0.023)	(0.024)
EBB	0.051***	0.047***	0.061***	0.045*
	(0.018)	(0.018)	(0.023)	(0.024)
MBB	0.041**	0.034*		
	(0.018)	(0.018)		
Age	−0.001	−0.001	−0.028***	−0.026***
	(0.004)	(0.004)	(0.007)	(0.007)
White	0.005	0.005	0.039	0.038
	(0.016)	(0.016)	(0.025)	(0.025)
Hispanic	0.003	0.003	−0.050	−0.046
	(0.024)	(0.024)	(0.037)	(0.037)
Education, HS	0.101***	0.096***	0.112***	0.106***
	(0.019)	(0.019)	(0.027)	(0.027)
Education, come college	0.153***	0.146***	0.172***	0.172***
	(0.019)	(0.019)	(0.028)	(0.028)
Education, college +	0.195***	0.188***	0.223***	0.219***
	(0.019)	(0.020)	(0.029)	(0.029)
Marital disruption	0.083***	0.088***	0.064***	0.067***
	(0.015)	(0.015)	(0.022)	(0.022)
Fair/poor health self-reported	−0.300***	−0.300***	−0.291***	−0.287***
	(0.019)	(0.019)	(0.024)	(0.024)
Number of children	−0.008**	−0.009**	−0.004	−0.006
	(0.004)	(0.004)	(0.005)	(0.005)
All primary res. loans/primary res. value		0.062***		0.090**
		(0.022)		(0.035)
Other debt/liquid assets		0.001*		−0.001
		(0.000)		(0.001)
N	6,677	6,677	4,160	4,160
R-squared	0.107	0.112	0.100	0.104
Mean of dep. var.	0.709	0.709	0.607	0.607
St. dev. of dep. var.	0.454	0.454	0.488	0.488
Mean of dep. var., HRS only	0.649	0.649	0.548	0.548
St. dev. of dep. var., HRS only	0.477	0.477	0.498	0.498

Note: Coefficient estimates from linear probability analysis, standard errors in parentheses. Controls for missing values included where relevant. Four cohorts of women ages fifty-one to fifty-six were surveyed: in 1992 the HRS baseline group (born 1936–1941); the 1998 War Babies (WB) group (born 1942–1947); the 2004 Early Baby Boomers (EBB) cohort (born 1948–1953); and the 2010 Middle Baby Boomer (MBB) group (born 1954–1959). Three cohorts of women ages fifty-seven to sixty-one were surveyed: in 1992 for the baseline HRS cohort, in 2004 for the WB, and in 2010 for the EBB. Marital disruption defined as divorced/separated or widowed, all primary res. loans/primary res. value is defined as the value of all primary residence loans divided by the value of the primary residence, and other debt/liquid assets is defined as the ratio of other debt to liquid assets (excluding the home). (See also appendix table 6A.1.)

***Significant at the 1 percent level.
**Significant at the 5 percent level.
*Significant at the 10 percent level.

among the women ages fifty-one to fifty-six when surveyed, while panel B looks at the same outcomes for the older ages fifty-seven to sixty-one. For both age groups, the first column excludes debt-to-asset ratio variables, while the second includes them to allow comparison of results.

Looking across the first three rows of coefficient estimates, it is clear that, compared with the first HRS baseline group, recent cohorts of women were increasingly likely to be working in their fifties. The mean probability of being at work for the baseline HRS sample age fifty-one to fifty-six when surveyed was 64.9 percent, and 54.8 percent for those age fifty-seven to sixty-one. All subsequent cohorts displayed higher rates of work, particularly for the age fifty-one to fifty-six cohort. For instance, younger War Babies women ages fifty-one to fifty-six had about a 7 percentage point greater labor force attachment, or around 11 percent higher, than the HRS reference cohort. Early Boomer women ages fifty-one to fifty-six were 4.7–5.1 percentage points more attached to the labor force, or about 8 percent more than the HRS, while the older group (ages fifty-seven to sixty-one) had participation rates of 4.5 to 6.1 percentage points higher, or 8 to 11 percent more than the HRS reference group. The younger Middle Boomers (MBB) also were working more than the reference group, with 3.4 to 4.1 percentage point greater employment rates, or about 6 percent over the HRS reference cohort.

The measured effects are robust to the inclusion or exclusion of the financial variables, as are virtually all of the other coefficient estimates.[8] In other words, these estimates confirm that the probability of working rose across the cohorts compared with the HRS baseline. Nevertheless, the magnitudes were somewhat larger for the younger War Babies group, a bit less for the Early Boomers, and smallest (though still statistically significantly different from zero) for the Middle Baby Boomer group. Among the older women, the Early Boomers were substantially more likely to be working compared with the baseline HRS.

In table 6.2 we focus on intentions to keep working, where among the baseline HRS cohort, 22.5 percent of the younger group (ages fifty-one to fifty-six) and 23.4 of the older group (ages fifty-six to sixty-one) reported they would still be working at age sixty-five. Interestingly, there is no significant difference between the baseline HRS cohort and the War Babies in terms of women's plans to continue working, but both Boomer cohorts were significantly more likely to say they intended to work at age sixty-five, compared with the original HRS cohort.[9] Moreover, intentions to work at age sixty-five rose over time. That is, the age fifty-one to fifty-six Early Boomers were about 3.3 to 3.6 percentage points (or 16 percent) more likely to work at

8. In results not detailed here, we have explored additional models where we interacted the debt variables with marital disruption to test whether including these terms alters the estimated cohort effects. Doing so does not change conclusions reported in the text.

9. The reader is reminded that the question about chances of working at age sixty-five was asked only of those working when surveyed at a younger age.

Table 6.2 **Factors associated with older women's anticipated future work (HRS)**

	A. Women ages 51–56		B. Women ages 57–61	
WB	−0.590	−0.603	1.777	1.456
	(1.517)	(1.517)	(1.852)	(1.852)
EBB	3.451**	3.332**	4.894***	4.455***
	(1.430)	(1.428)	(1.705)	(1.702)
MBB	7.643***	7.422***		
	(1.427)	(1.427)		
Age	−0.628*	−0.592*	−1.033*	−0.988*
	(0.350)	(0.349)	(0.562)	(0.560)
White	3.550***	3.536***	4.436***	4.616***
	(1.209)	(1.210)	(1.671)	(1.671)
Hispanic	2.442	2.406	−2.005	−1.768
	(1.937)	(1.941)	(2.328)	(2.328)
Education, HS	4.398***	4.133**	1.485	1.304
	(1.691)	(1.691)	(2.155)	(2.149)
Education, some college	6.972***	6.519***	6.283***	6.264***
	(1.807)	(1.814)	(2.422)	(2.417)
Education, college +	9.043***	8.597***	5.694**	5.581**
	(1.904)	(1.911)	(2.598)	(2.593)
Marital disruption	9.602***	9.731***	8.390***	8.473***
	(1.309)	(1.310)	(1.693)	(1.694)
Fair/poor health self-reported	−10.860***	−10.870***	−14.460***	−14.215***
	(1.385)	(1.384)	(1.772)	(1.769)
Number of children	−0.371	−0.399	−0.141	−0.201
	(0.322)	(0.322)	(0.394)	(0.396)
All primary res. loans/primary res. value		2.635**		2.364**
		(1.034)		(1.001)
Other debt/liquid assets		0.014*		0.052
		(0.008)		(0.059)
Intercept	47.610**	45.271**	77.168**	74.089**
	(18.750)	(18.734)	(32.996)	(32.885)
N	5,152	5,152	2,976	2,976
R-squared	0.060	0.063	0.064	0.066
Mean of dep. var.	26.289	26.289	25.737	25.737
St. dev. of dep. var.	32.484	32.484	33.338	33.338
Mean of dep. var., HRS only	22.537	22.537	23.379	23.379
St. dev. of dep. var., HRS only	31.617	31.617	32.773	32.773

Note: Question about the probability of working at age sixty-five asked only of those working at survey date. (See also notes to table 6.1.)

***Significant at the 1 percent level.

**Significant at the 5 percent level.

*Significant at the 10 percent level.

age sixty-five, where the Middle Boomers were 7.4 to 7.6 percentage points (or about 35 percent) more likely to plan to work longer, compared to the benchmark. For the older group (ages fifty-seven to sixty-one) the increase was similar in percentage points (4.5 to 4.9), but as it was measured on a slightly higher base, the 20 percent increase was slightly lower. In any case, the most recent cohorts for which we have data appear to be notably more attached to the labor force into their midsixties. As before, comparing panels A in tables 6.1 and 6.2, we again see that the magnitudes of the cohort effects are relatively invariant to including additional controls.[10] Therefore little of what we have attributed to cohort differences is associated with more recent waves of older women having more education, higher rates of marital disruption, and fewer children.

6.2.2   Impacts of Other Factors

We also seek to analyze the impact of other factors on women's current and future work patterns. Looking across tables 6.1 and 6.2, we see that age has a generally negative effect when it is statistically significant, indicating that even within these narrow age bands, older women's labor market attachment does decline. Nevertheless, the estimated age coefficients are only weakly significant in table 6.2 across the board, and not significant for the younger women in table 6.1. Thus, older women's workforce attachment does not decline in lockstep with age, by any means. Another factor consistently significant and positively associated with work is additional educational attainment. For instance, having a college degree raised labor force participation by around 20 percentage points for both age groups in table 6.1, compared to being a high school dropout, and raised the probability of working at age sixty-five by 6–9 percentage points (table 6.2). Interestingly, widowed/divorced women were 6 to 8 percentage points more likely to be working currently, and they have an 8 to 9 percentage point greater expectation of working at age sixty-five.[11] Women in poor health are much less likely to be employed: thus, those in fair or poor health were 29 to 30 percentage points less likely to be working than those reporting being healthier. Among workers, those in fair/poor health were 11 to 15 percentage points less likely to project that they would still be working at age sixty-five, compared to their healthier counterparts. Finally, the number of children has a significant negative effect on older women's current employment, but only for the fifty-one to fifty-six age group and the impact is small (−0.9 percentage points).

10. In results not detailed here we have also explored models where we interacted the debt variables with marital disruption, to test whether including these terms alters the estimated cohort effects. Doing so does not change conclusions reported in the text.

11. Consistent with our results, Olivetti and Rotz (chapter 5, this volume) found that changes in marital history and marital status can explain a fraction of the increase in women's employment later in life.

6.2.3   What Role for Debt?

The last two rows of tables 6.1 and 6.2 speak to the question of how debt is associated with older women's work patterns, a topic of substantial current interest (Lusardi, Mitchell, and Oggero 2016). Our findings show that having mortgage debt, in particular, is associated with a higher probability of women working for pay and expecting to be working at age sixty-five. For instance, an increase of a standard deviation in the ratio of mortgage debt to home value in table 6.2 is associated with a large increase in women's anticipated probability of working at age sixty-five for both age groups.[12] This finding is in line with Fortin (1995), who suggested that liquidity constraints related to home down payments prompted many women to work more. The effect we discern here is complementary, suggesting that women may defer retirement due to the need to help repay their mortgage debt. The second debt variable we included in the model, the ratio of nonmortgage debt to liquid assets, is generally small and not statistically significant across tables 6.1 and 6.2.

To further examine the role of debt, we note that previous research has reported that people are reaching retirement age today holding more debt than in the past.[13] Accordingly, we devote some additional attention to various measures of older women's debt and financial fragility across cohorts in table 6.3.

Results show that Baby Boomer cohorts are more likely to have debt later in life for both age groups (fifty-one to fifty-six and fifty-seven to sixty-one), compared with the baseline HRS cohort (panel 1). Moreover, recent cohorts have higher levels of total debt late in life (panel 2). It is also striking that cohort mean and medial debt levels have been steadily rising over time. For example, while the median ($p50$) debt of the HRS baseline was a little more than $15,000 for women ages fifty-one to fifty-six, this level almost tripled for the Middle Baby Boomers ($43,200; all values are in $2015). Increases in debt are even more striking for the older group of women ages fifty-seven to sixty-one: the Early Baby Boomer cohort had almost eight times as much debt as the baseline HRS cohort ($31,320 versus $4,175).

One reason for the huge expansion in debt is that households have taken on larger mortgages in recent years. This is the pattern we observe for both of the age groups we examine (panel 3 of table 6.3). Mortgages along with loans related to the primary residence not only grew in absolute value, but they also rose as a percentage of the value of the primary residence. These ratios more than doubled for the older respondents. The older HRS baseline

---

12. We note that 80 percent of the sample owns a home.
13. See, for instance, AARP (2013), Bucks et al. (2009), Butrica and Karamcheva (2013), Copeland (2013), Lusardi and Mitchell (2013), Lusardi, Mitchell, and Oggero (2016), and Pottow (2012).

Table 6.3   Differences in older women's debt by type, by cohort and age group (HRS)

		p50	Mean	N
1. Have debt (0/1)				
Age group 51–56	HRS	0	0.42	2,806
	WB	0	0.41	847
	EBB	0	0.44	1,207
	MBB	1	0.51	1,872
Age group 57–61	HRS	0	0.37	2,056
	WB	0	0.39	699
	EBB	0	0.44	1,424
2. Total debt ($2015)				
Age group 51–56	HRS	15,030	59,003	2,806
	WB	27,360	62,990	847
	EBB	37,386	91,398	1,207
	MBB	43,200	98,210	1,872
Age group 57–61	HRS	4,175	32,976	2,056
	WB	23,560	68,066	699
	EBB	31,320	96,701	1,424

		p50	Mean	N
3. All primary res. loans/primary res. value > 0.5 (0/1)				
Age group 51–56	HRS	0	0.18	2,788
	WB	0	0.24	839
	EBB	0	0.26	1,195
	MBB	0	0.32	1,860
Age group 57–61	HRS	0	0.11	2,052
	WB	0	0.22	690
	EBB	0	0.28	1,414
4. Have less than $25,000 in savings (0/1)				
Age group 51–56	HRS	0	0.18	2,806
	WB	0	0.20	847
	EBB	0	0.23	1,207
	MBB	0	0.33	1,872
Age group 57–61	HRS	0	0.16	2,056
	WB	0	0.18	699
	EBB	0	0.26	1,424

Note: Total debt includes the value of mortgages and other loans on the household's primary residence, other mortgages, and other debt (including credit card debt, medical debt, etc.). Savings is defined as total net worth or total assets minus total debt. All dollar values in $2015. (See also notes to table 6.1.)

cohort (age fifty-seven to sixty-one) neared retirement with a ratio of mortgages and loans to the value of the primary residence of 0.11, but the ratio grew to 0.28 for the Early Boomers. Moreover, older women are more likely to be in households where the ratio of mortgage debt to residential value has doubled, from 18 to 32 percent, comparing the Middle Boomers to the HRS baseline cohort. Many older women will need to manage mortgage debt well into their older years, consistent with the findings reported by Lusardi, Mitchell, and Oggero (2016). In other words, during retirement Boomer cohorts will have to use their income and assets to repay debt, in contrast to the earlier cohort.

Even more striking is the fact that higher proportions of older women are in financially fragile circumstances, compared to two decades ago. Only 18 percent of the younger HRS cohorts had less than $25,000 in savings,[14] whereas one-third of the Middle Baby Boomer group reported having so little savings (panel 4). We conclude that higher debt levels in later life could well be contributing to rising labor force attachment among older women.

We provide four panels in table 6.4 to identify the key factors associated with financial fragility, using the measures introduced in table 6.3. Panel A provides a multivariate probit analysis for the probability that women had any debt (marginal effects reported). Here we see that the Middle Boomers are significantly more likely to have debt than previous cohorts. Being in fair/poor health is also statistically significantly associated with having debt, and for the younger age group, owning a home plays a role. Panel B summarizes the correlates of total debt (in $10,000, for 2015 dollars), and again we confirm that debt is higher for the more recent cohorts versus the HRS baseline, particularly among homeowners. Panel C focuses on which groups have the highest ratio of residential mortgage relative to the value of their primary residence. Here we see that relative to the HRS baseline, all subsequent cohorts prove to be more indebted. And once again, homeowners are particularly likely to have relatively higher mortgages, compared to their home values. Finally, panel D summarizes the key factors associated with financial fragility, which we measure as someone reporting that she had less than $25,000 in savings. The recent cohorts are once again far more likely to be financially fragile by this measure, with the Middle Boomers being two to three times as likely to be in poor financial shape compared to their earlier counterparts. Interestingly, in this table, homeowners appear to be less vulnerable, as they are less likely to report being cash-poor. Overall, the impact of poor health is uneven, reducing the chance of having any debt but raising the probability of not having savings worth $25,000.

---

14. Savings is defined as total net worth or total assets minus total debt.

Table 6.4   **Factors associated with debt among HRS women**

	A. Women ages 51–56	B. Women ages 57–61
A. Having any debt (marginal effects reported from probit models)		
WB	−0.020	0.020
	(0.021)	(0.024)
EBB	0.013	0.077***
	(0.020)	(0.023)
MBB	0.091***	
	(0.020)	
Age	−0.014***	−0.002
	(0.005)	(0.007)
White	−0.020	−0.058**
	(0.018)	(0.024)
Hispanic	−0.024	−0.145***
	(0.026)	(0.032)
Education, HS	0.097***	0.109***
	(0.024)	(0.029)
Education, some college	0.110***	0.042
	(0.025)	(0.032)
Education, college +	0.076***	0.036
	(0.027)	(0.035)
Marital disruption	0.035*	0.041*
	(0.018)	(0.022)
Fair/poor health self-reported	0.053***	0.063**
	(0.019)	(0.024)
Number of children	0.006	0.010**
	(0.004)	(0.005)
Own home	0.040*	−0.018
	(0.020)	(0.027)
N	6,732	4,179
R-squared	0.013	0.021
Mean of dep. var.	0.453	0.401
St. dev. of dep. var.	0.498	0.490
Mean of dep. var., HRS only	0.417	0.368
St. dev. of dep. var., HRS only	0.493	0.482
B. Total household debt (OLS)		
WB	−0.322	3.011***
	(0.515)	(0.467)
EBB	2.240***	5.658***
	(0.544)	(0.583)
MBB	3.163***	
	(0.594)	
Age	−0.317***	−0.646***
	(0.108)	(0.199)
White	−0.131	0.570
	(0.437)	(0.417)

Table 6.4   (continued)

	A. Women ages 51–56	B. Women ages 57–61
Hispanic	1.088	−1.295***
	(0.780)	(0.474)
Education, HS	1.245***	0.788**
	(0.481)	(0.400)
Education, some college	3.514***	1.250**
	(0.511)	(0.490)
Education, college +	7.573***	6.938***
	(0.760)	(0.831)
Marital disruption	−1.739***	−2.045***
	(0.380)	(0.416)
Fair/poor health self-reported	−0.933**	−0.805**
	(0.412)	(0.394)
Number of children	0.257**	0.311***
	(0.118)	(0.102)
Own home	7.552***	5.344***
	(0.328)	(0.358)
Intercept	14.123**	34.750***
	(5.691)	(11.774)
N	6,732	4,179
R-squared	0.129	0.169
Mean of dep. var.	8.007	6.895
St. dev. of dep. var.	14.176	12.373
Mean of dep. var., HRS only	5.900	3.298
St. dev. of dep. var., HRS only	17.315	6.801

C. Having housing loan > half of primary residence value
(marginal effects from probit models)

	A. Women ages 51–56	B. Women ages 57–61
WB	0.022***	0.019***
	(0.008)	(0.005)
EBB	0.030***	0.034***
	(0.008)	(0.007)
MBB	0.069***	
	(0.010)	
Age	−0.004**	−0.003***
	(0.002)	(0.001)
White	−0.023***	−0.003
	(0.007)	(0.003)
Hispanic	0.006	−0.008***
	(0.010)	(0.003)
Education, HS	0.024**	0.006*
	(0.010)	(0.004)
Education, some college	0.049***	0.003
	(0.012)	(0.004)
Education, college +	0.044***	0.006
	(0.012)	(0.004)

(*continued*)

Table 6.4 (continued)

	A. Women ages 51–56	B. Women ages 57–61
Marital disruption	0.003	0.004
	(0.006)	(0.003)
Fair/poor health self-reported	0.002	0.002
	(0.007)	(0.003)
Number of children	0.003*	0.002***
	(0.001)	(0.001)
Own home	0.321***	0.245***
	(0.008)	(0.010)
N	6,682	4,156
R-squared	0.159	0.158
Mean of dep. var.	0.257	0.209
St. dev. of dep. var.	0.437	0.406
Mean of dep. var., HRS only	0.178	0.106
St. dev. of dep. var., HRS only	0.383	0.308
D. Having < $25,000 in savings (OLS)		
WB	0.051**	0.043**
	(0.022)	(0.021)
EBB	0.078***	0.135***
	(0.021)	(0.021)
MBB	0.183***	
	(0.023)	
Age	−0.007	−0.012**
	(0.004)	(0.005)
White	−0.105***	−0.087***
	(0.017)	(0.019)
Hispanic	−0.015	0.027
	(0.020)	(0.024)
Education, HS	−0.074***	−0.029
	(0.018)	(0.019)
Education, some college	−0.112***	−0.069***
	(0.017)	(0.018)
Education, college +	−0.155***	−0.123***
	(0.017)	(0.017)
Marital disruption	0.126***	0.086***
	(0.018)	(0.018)
Fair/poor health self-reported	0.161***	0.120***
	(0.021)	(0.020)
Number of children	0.005	0.011***
	(0.004)	(0.004)
Own home	−0.592***	−0.602***
	(0.020)	(0.025)
N	6,732	4,179
R-squared	0.412	0.483

Table 6.4   (continued)

	A. Women ages 51–56	B. Women ages 57–61
Mean of dep. var.	0.244	0.202
St. dev. of dep. var.	0.430	0.402
Mean of dep. var., HRS only	0.184	0.161
St. dev. of dep. var., HRS only	0.388	0.367

Note: See also notes to tables 6.1–6.3.
***Significant at the 1 percent level.
**Significant at the 5 percent level.
*Significant at the 10 percent level.

6.3   Financial Frailty at Older Ages: Findings from the NFCS

To further explore how older women are managing their debt and retirement planning, we draw on the 2012 wave of the National Financial Capability Study (NFCS).[15] The overarching research objectives of the NFCS are to benchmark key indicators of financial capability and evaluate how these indicators vary with underlying demographic, behavioral, attitudinal, and financial literacy characteristics.[16] The 2012 NFCS is a state-by-state online survey of approximately 25,000 American adults (roughly 500 per state, plus the District of Columbia) that is representative of the US population.[17] In order to thoroughly explore the financial capability of Americans, the NFCS covers several aspects of behavior including how people manage their resources, how they make financial decisions, what skill sets they use in making these decisions, and how they search for information when making these decisions (Lusardi 2011).

Consistent with the HRS analysis above, we again focus on two separate age groups of women in the NFCS: those ages fifty-one to fifty-six, and fifty-seven to sixty-one. There are over 1,800 observations for the first age group, and around 1,300 women for the second. The empirical analysis evaluates whether older women tried to figure out how much they need to

15. The data are publicly available at http://www.usfinancialcapability.org/. The first survey was fielded in 2009, and it is slated to be repeated triennially.
16. FINRA Investor Education Foundation commissioned the NFCS in 2009 in consultation with the US Department of the Treasury and the President's Advisory Council on Financial Literacy. The 2012 study—similarly developed in consultation with the US Department of the Treasury, other federal agencies, and President Obama's Advisory Council on Financial Capability—updated key measures from the 2009 study and deepened the exploration of topics that are highly relevant for research and policy. Lusardi serves as academic advisor to the study.
17. In our analysis, data are weighted to be representative of the national population in terms of age, gender, ethnicity, and education based on the Census Bureau's American Community Survey. However, breakdowns of subpopulations may not necessarily be representative.

save for retirement, their perceived level of indebtedness, and their financial fragility, which relies on respondent answers to whether they could come up with $2,000 in thirty days if an unexpected need arose.[18]

Descriptive statistics for older women in the NFCS data set appear in appendix table 6A.2. The sample is mostly married, white, working, and has at least some college education. Women of ages fifty-seven to sixty-one indicated they were more likely to plan for retirement (or to have planned, if they had retired), but fewer than half (45 percent) had tried to figure out how much they needed to put aside for retirement. Moreover, many of them (39–43 percent) indicate they are carrying too much debt, and that they are financially fragile (39–43 percent). This is consistent with the HRS evidence showing high levels of debt on the verge of retirement.

Other indicators of financial distress are reported in table 6.5. Results show that about a third of women (ages fifty-one to fifty-six) are able to cover easily their expenses in a typical month, or have set aside emergency or rainy day funds that would cover expenses for three months. The NFCS data confirm that mortgage debt and other debts turn out to be problematic for a relatively large subset of women. Twenty percent of the female home-owners in the younger age group, and 15 percent in the older age group, report being underwater, owing more on their homes than they thought they could sell them for. As far as nonmortgage debt is concerned, many women said they did not pay off credit card balances in full (if they had them), and they engaged in many costly credit card behaviors such as paying only the minimum due, using the card for cash advances, being charged fees for late payment or exceeding the limits. These findings underscore the point that many older women are exposed to illiquidity and/or problems in debt management. Turning to other indicators, many older women reported having unpaid medical bills, and having engaged in high-cost borrowing using alternative financial services, such as rent-to-own stores, pawn shops, payday loans, auto title loans, and tax refund loans.

The NFCS also included a set of questions to assess respondents' levels of financial literacy. Five questions were asked to test fundamental concepts regarding numeracy and the capacity to do calculations related to interest rates, knowledge of inflation, risk diversification, understanding of interest

---

18. The precise wordings of the questions are (1) retirement planning: "Have you ever tried to figure out how much you need to save for retirement?" Or, if already retired: "Before you retired, did you try to figure out how much you needed to save for retirement?" Possible answers: yes, no, don't know, prefer not to say; (2) debt: "How strongly do you agree or disagree with the following statement: I have too much debt right now. Please give your answer from a scale from 1 to 7, where 1 = strongly disagree, 7 = strongly agree and 4 = neither agree nor disagree." Possible answers: 1–7; don't know, prefer not to say; (3) financial fragility: "How confident are you that you could come up with $2,000 if an unexpected need arose within the next month?" Possible answers: I am certain I could come up with the full $2,000, I could probably come up with $2,000, I could probably not come up with $2,000, I am certain I could not come up with $2,000, don't know, prefer not to say.

Table 6.5   **Indicators of financial distress in the NFCS**

Variables	N	Mean	Median	Min.	Max.	SD
		A. Women ages 51–56				
Making ends meet	1,844	.34	0	0	1	.47
Rainy day savings	1,844	.34	0	0	1	.47
Underwater with home value	886	.20	0	0	1	.40
Credit card fees	1,303	.41	0	0	1	.49
Loan on retirement accounts	908	.08	0	0	1	.27
Withdrawal from retirement accounts	908	.05	0	0	1	.22
Unpaid medical bills	1,844	.28	0	0	1	.45
High-cost borrowing	1,800	.25	0	0	1	.43
		B. Women ages 57–61				
Making ends meet	1,332	.38	0	0	1	.49
Rainy day savings	1,332	.41	0	0	1	.49
Underwater with home value	606	.15	0	0	1	.35
Credit card fees	1,004	.38	0	0	1	.48
Loan on retirement accounts	713	.07	0	0	1	.26
Withdrawal from retirement accounts	713	.05	0	0	1	.23
Unpaid medical bills	1,332	.25	0	0	1	.43
High-cost borrowing	1,309	.22	0	0	1	.41

Note: The sample includes all age-eligible women ages fifty-one to fifty-six and fifty-seven to sixty-one in the 2012 NFCS. Making ends meet refers to the ability to balance monthly income and expenses. Statistics related to underwater with home value and credit card fees are conditional on holding the asset or debt. Statistics related to loan on retirement accounts and hardship withdrawal from retirement accounts are conditional to having a retirement account. High-cost methods of borrowing refer to auto title loans, payday loans, pawn shops, rent-to-own stores, and tax refund loans. All statistics are weighted using survey weights. (See also appendix table 6A.2.)

payments on a mortgage, and understanding of basic asset pricing (Lusardi 2011). Table 6.6 reports the proportion of correct and incorrect answers and the "do not know" responses to each of these questions. Overall, we find that financial literacy is rather low. A large fraction of women does not know simple financial concepts, and many indicate that they do not know the answer to the questions. The proportion of "do not know" responses was particularly high on the risk diversification question; as many as 52 percent of women ages fifty-one to fifty-six and 51 percent of women ages fifty-seven to sixty-one indicated that they did not know whether a single company stock is riskier than a stock mutual fund. There is also a high proportion of "do not know" responses for the question on asset pricing. These two questions will help us differentiate among different degrees of financial literacy among older women.

Next we present multivariate linear probability analyses of indicators of financial planning, debt, and financial fragility. For the first dependent

Table 6.6   Financial literacy in the NFCS

Questions	Correct (%)	Incorrect (%)	Don't know (%)	N
A. Women ages 51–56				
Interest rate question	72	15	12	1,844
Inflation question	63	13	22	1,844
Risk diversification question	42	5	52	1,844
Mortgage question	74	10	16	1,844
Basic asset pricing question	24	29	46	1,844
B. Women ages 57–61				
Interest rate question	71	17	11	1,332
Inflation question	66	14	18	1,332
Risk diversification question	41	6	51	1,332
Mortgage question	76	7	15	1,332
Basic asset pricing question	24	29	45	1,332

Note: The sample includes all age-eligible women ages fifty-one to fifty-six and fifty-seven to sixty-one in the 2012 NFCS. All statistics are weighted using survey weights.

variable, we use the NFCS question about whether respondents ever tried to figure out how much they need to save for retirement. The question is important in light of prior research showing that planners accumulate far more retirement wealth than nonplanners (Lusardi 1999; Lusardi and Beeler 2007; Lusardi and Mitchell 2007a, 2007b; Lusardi and Mitchell 2011a, 2011b). In the regressions, we control for the same factors as in the HRS analysis, namely age and ethnicity, marital status, education, and number of children. In addition, the richness of the NFCS allows us to control for whether respondents experienced a large and unexpected drop in income the previous year, and also the respondent's level of financial literacy (defined as the number of correct answers to the five financial literacy questions). Results are reported in the first column of table 6.7.

Both panels A and B in table 6.7 confirm that higher education and income are strongly positively correlated with women having tried to figure out how much to save for retirement. The number of dependent children is negatively associated with the probability of having tried to plan for women ages fifty-one to fifty-six but not the older group, suggesting some potential for a "catch-up" after children leave home. Interestingly, financial literacy is also an important determinant of financial planning: being able to answer one additional financial literacy question correctly is associated with a 4 to 6 percentage point higher probability of figuring out how much to put aside for retirement. Because only 39 to 45 percent of the respondents indicated

Table 6.7 Determinants of having tried to figure out how much to save for retirement, having too much debt, and not being able to come up with $2,000 (NFCS)

Variables	Retirement planning (1)	Having too much debt (2)	Financial fragility (3)
	A. Women ages 51–56		
Age	0.004	−0.008	−0.006
	(0.006)	(0.030)	(0.006)
Black	−0.021	0.453***	0.099***
	(0.033)	(0.159)	(0.030)
Hispanic	−0.068**	−0.456***	−0.010
	(0.034)	(0.164)	(0.032)
Asian	−0.050	−0.397	−0.070
	(0.058)	(0.284)	(0.054)
Others	−0.063	−0.193	−0.039
	(0.068)	(0.328)	(0.063)
Single	0.079**	−0.197	−0.063*
	(0.035)	(0.174)	(0.033)
Separated or divorced	0.011	−0.237*	0.005
	(0.029)	(0.140)	(0.027)
Widow	0.029	0.022	−0.126***
	(0.050)	(0.239)	(0.046)
Number of dependent children	−0.027**	0.121**	0.023**
	(0.012)	(0.056)	(0.011)
High school	0.046	−0.042	0.107***
	(0.042)	(0.212)	(0.039)
Some college	0.148***	0.169	0.034
	(0.044)	(0.221)	(0.041)
College +	0.191***	0.152	0.058
	(0.048)	(0.238)	(0.045)
$15–25K	0.098**	−0.038	−0.155***
	(0.040)	(0.197)	(0.037)
$25–35K	0.097**	−0.161	−0.195***
	(0.044)	(0.213)	(0.040)
$35–50K	0.130***	−0.179	−0.364***
	(0.041)	(0.200)	(0.038)
$50–75K	0.227***	−0.072	−0.485***
	(0.042)	(0.206)	(0.039)
$75–100K	0.264***	−0.319	−0.535***
	(0.046)	(0.226)	(0.043)
$100–150K	0.365***	−0.693***	−0.677***
	(0.048)	(0.236)	(0.044)
$150K +	0.440***	−1.293***	−0.724***
	(0.056)	(0.275)	(0.052)
Income shock	−0.025	0.779***	0.205***
	(0.022)	(0.109)	(0.021)
N correct answers fin. lit. questions	0.061***	−0.105**	−0.021***
	(0.008)	(0.042)	(0.008)

(*continued*)

Table 6.7 (continued)

Variables	Retirement planning (1)	Having too much debt (2)	Financial fragility (3)
Constant	−0.253	4.834***	1.041***
	(0.330)	(1.601)	(0.306)
Observations	1,844	1,813	1,844
R-squared	0.194	0.082	0.326
	B. Women ages 57–61		
Age	0.023**	−0.075*	0.002
	(0.009)	(0.042)	(0.008)
Black	0.001	0.080	0.116***
	(0.036)	(0.167)	(0.032)
Hispanic	0.009	0.086	0.160***
	(0.049)	(0.228)	(0.043)
Asian	−0.064	0.187	0.122**
	(0.070)	(0.332)	(0.062)
Others	−0.025	0.018	0.101
	(0.091)	(0.426)	(0.081)
Single	−0.052	0.513***	−0.013
	(0.043)	(0.198)	(0.038)
Separated or divorced	−0.032	0.304*	0.040
	(0.036)	(0.165)	(0.032)
Widow	0.049	0.675***	0.065
	(0.050)	(0.231)	(0.044)
Number of dependent children	−0.024	0.330***	0.034**
	(0.017)	(0.079)	(0.015)
High school	0.098*	−0.182	−0.159***
	(0.057)	(0.262)	(0.050)
Some college	0.151**	−0.269	−0.202***
	(0.059)	(0.274)	(0.053)
College +	0.225***	−0.370	−0.201***
	(0.064)	(0.295)	(0.057)
$15–25K	0.087*	0.250	−0.092**
	(0.053)	(0.242)	(0.047)
$25–35K	0.212***	−0.078	−0.224***
	(0.051)	(0.238)	(0.045)
$35–50K	0.204***	−0.116	−0.360***
	(0.052)	(0.242)	(0.047)
$50–75K	0.251***	−0.173	−0.443***
	(0.053)	(0.244)	(0.047)
$75–100K	0.259***	−0.356	−0.504***
	(0.062)	(0.290)	(0.055)
$100–150K	0.373***	0.017	−0.607***
	(0.064)	(0.299)	(0.057)

Table 6.7   (continued)

Variables	Retirement planning (1)	Having too much debt (2)	Financial fragility (3)
$150K+	0.469***	−0.845***	−0.590***
	(0.066)	(0.306)	(0.059)
Income shock	0.050*	0.685***	0.153***
	(0.028)	(0.131)	(0.025)
N correct answers fin. lit. questions	0.044***	−0.083*	−0.029***
	(0.010)	(0.049)	(0.009)
Constant	−1.398***	8.394***	0.760
	(0.541)	(2.494)	(0.480)
Observations	1,332	1,312	1,332
R-squared	0.153	0.087	0.307

Note: "Retirement planning" coded as 1 for those who tried to figure out how much they need to save for retirement. "Having too much debt" ranges from 1 to 7, where 1 means I strongly disagree and 7 means I strongly agree with the statement "I have too much debt right now." "Financial fragility" coded as 1 for those certain or probably could not come up with $2,000. Explanatory variables include age, race/ethnicity, marital status, number of financially dependent children, education, income, having experienced an income shock, and an indicator of financial literacy. Baseline categories: white, married, less than high school education, and income lower than $15,000. Standard errors in parentheses; weighted data.
***Significant at the 1 percent level.
**Significant at the 5 percent level.
*Significant at the 10 percent level.

they had tried to plan for retirement (table 6.4), the impact of the literacy question is large. The finding is consistent with data from the 2009 wave of the NFCS (Lusardi and Mitchell 2011b), where we use a similar empirical specification but all respondents and all age groups (Lusardi and Mitchell 2014).[19]

Next we turn to respondents' answers to the NFCS question about their degree of agreement with the statement: "I have too much debt right now." We use this variable to proxy for peoples' concerns about their debt, since debt levels (as reported in the HRS) are not available in the NFCS. Results are reported in column (2) of table 6.7 for both age groups (panels A and B).

Once again, we find that women reporting having too much debt are also those with more dependent children, with the effect among the older age group almost three times as large as for those ages fifty-one to fifty-six. Shocks also matter: those having had a large unexpected income drop in the prior year were 68 to 78 percentage points more likely to state that they

19. It is also consistent with data from a special module we designed for the HRS on retirement planning and financial literacy. In that work we showed that financial literacy is an important predictor of retirement planning for older women as well (Lusardi and Mitchell 2008).

were overindebted. Those with higher income (income greater than $100,000 for women ages fifty-one to fifty-six and income greater than $150,000 for women ages fifty-seven to sixty-one) are less likely to have too much debt. Once again, the more financially literate were less likely to report they had excessive debt (answering one more financial literacy question decreases the probability of "too much debt" by 8–10 percentage points), confirming findings in other surveys (Lusardi and Tufano 2015). In other words, shocks do contribute to debt concerns for women on the verge of retirement, but people who have the capacity to manage their resources are more likely to stay out of debt as they head into retirement.

The financial fragility measure available in the NFCS is a proxy for low savings. The HRS reports whether women have less than $25,000 in savings. The NFCS, however, asks if they could come up with $2,000 within a month (multiplying that figure by 12 would bring $24,000). Findings in column (3) of table 6.7 show that, for both age groups, having more dependent children and having experienced an income shock are positively and significantly associated with the probability of being financially fragile. Those with higher income are less likely to be financially fragile. Moreover, those who are more financially literate are associated with a lower probability of being financially fragile.

6.4   Conclusions

Our goal has been to ascertain whether older women's current and anticipated future labor force patterns have changed over time, and if so, to evaluate the factors associated with longer work lives and plans to continue work at older ages. We have also sought to evaluate debt and debt management as a factor spurring older women's continued work.

The analysis has yielded several findings. First, we show that each cohort of older women worked more currently, and intended to work more in the future, than our HRS baseline surveyed in 1992. The mean probability of being at work for the baseline HRS sample ages fifty-one to fifty-six when surveyed was 64.9 percent, and 54.8 percent for those ages fifty-seven to sixty-one. All subsequent cohorts displayed higher rates of work, particularly for the fifty-one- to fifty-six-year-old group. For instance, younger War Babies women ages fifty-one to fifty-six had about a 7 percentage point greater labor force attachment, or around 11 percent higher, than the HRS reference cohort. Early Boomer women ages fifty-one to fifty-six were 5.3 to 5.7 percentage points more attached to the labor force, or 8 percent more than the HRS, while the older Early Boomers had participation rates of 4.7 to 6.2 percentage points higher, or 8 to 11 percent greater than the HRS reference group. Older Early Boomers had participation rates of 4.7 to 6.2 percentage points higher, or 8 to 11 percent greater than the HRS reference group. The younger Mid-Boomers also were working more than the reference group, with 3.8 to 4.5 percentage point greater employment rates, or 6 to 7 percent versus the HRS reference cohort.

Second, when we compare differences in older women's self-reported expected chances of working at older ages, again we find evidence that more recent cohorts of older women anticipate working longer. For the baseline HRS cohort, 22.5 percent of the younger age group and 23.4 of the older age group intended to still work at age sixty-five. By contrast, both the Early and Middle Baby Boomer cohorts were significantly more likely to say they intended to work at age sixty-five. Early Boomers believed they had a 4 to 5 percentage points higher chance of working than the HRS cohort (on a base of about 26 percent), and the Middle Boomers were even more likely to be working for pay at age sixty-five compared with the HRS reference group. These patterns confirm that continued work and delayed retirement are becoming more prevalent for older women.

Third, when we explored the explanations for delayed retirement among older women, significant factors included education, marital disruption, health, and fewer children than prior cohorts. Yet household finances also appeared to be playing a key role, in that older women today have more debt than previously and they are more financially fragile than in the past. As an example, we showed that a standard deviation increase in the ratio of mortgage debt to home value was associated with a 3.4 to 5.5 percent rise in women's anticipated probability of working at age sixty-five. In large part, the impact can be attributed to having taken on larger residential mortgages due to the run-up in housing prices over time and lower down payments as well.

Our results using the NFCS are compatible with the HRS results, but the richer set of questions asked in this survey adds additional dimensions to the results. For instance, we found that women who were more financially literate were more likely to plan for retirement and less likely to have excessive debt or be more financially fragile. Having more children and unexpected large income shocks also played an important role. Overall, these findings speak to the important role of managing finances later in life, including debt.

Our work to date has been mainly descriptive rather than causal, but we are well aware that planning, saving, and retirement decisions are all made in a life cycle context. Accordingly, our future research will explore ways to identify how financial literacy, planning, and debt management can help drive decision making at older ages, which can be conducive to retirement security.

Appendix

Table 6A.1   **Descriptive statistics for HRS women**

Variables	Women ages 51–56 Mean	SD	Women ages 57–61 Mean	SD
Working for pay	0.71	0.45	0.61	0.49
Prob. working at 65 (%)	26.29	32.48	25.74	33.34
Have any debt (0/1)	0.45	0.50	0.40	0.49
Total debt (10k, $2015)	8.01	14.18	6.90	12.37
All primary res. loans/primary res. value > 0.5 (0/1)	0.26	0.44	0.21	0.41
Have less than $25,000 in savings (0/1)	0.24	0.43	0.20	0.40
Age	53.16	1.61	58.82	1.41
White	0.80	0.40	0.82	0.39
Hispanic	0.09	0.29	0.08	0.28
Education, < HS	0.15	0.36	0.18	0.38
Education, HS	0.32	0.47	0.32	0.47
Education, some college	0.26	0.44	0.25	0.43
Education, college +	0.27	0.44	0.25	0.43
Fair/poor health self-reported	0.23	0.42	0.25	0.43
Marital disruption	0.28	0.45	0.31	0.46
Number of children	2.65	1.77	2.82	1.92
Own home	0.79	0.41	0.81	0.40
All primary res. loans/primary res. value	0.30	0.54	0.25	0.62
Other debt/liquid assets	2.12	41.57	0.77	8.12
HRS	0.23	0.42	0.29	0.46
WB	0.21	0.41	0.32	0.47
EBB	0.25	0.43	0.39	0.49
MBB	0.31	0.46	0.00	0.00

Note: Question about the probability of working at age sixty-five asked only of those working at survey date. Total debt includes the value of mortgages and other loans on the household's primary residence, other mortgages, and other debt (including credit card debt, medical debt, etc.). All dollar values in $2015. Savings is defined as total net worth or total assets minus total debt. Marital disruption is defined as divorced/separated or widowed, all primary res. loans/primary res. value is defined as the value of all primary residence loans divided by the value of the primary residence, and other debt/liquid assets is defined as the ratio of other debt to liquid assets (excluding the home). The fifty-one to fifty-six age cohorts of women were surveyed in 1992 (the HRS baseline group, born 1936–1941), the 1998 War Babies (WB) group (born 1942–1947), the 2004 Early Baby Boomers (EBB) cohort (born 1948–1953), and the 2010 Middle Baby Boomer (MBB) group (born 1954–1959). The three fifty-seven to sixty-one age cohorts of women were surveyed in 1992 for the baseline HRS cohort, in 2004 for the WB, and in 2010 for the EBB.

Table 6A.2   **Descriptive statistics for variables from the National Financial Capability Study (NFCS)**

Variables	Mean	Median	Min.	Max.	SD
A. Women ages 51–56 (N = 1,844)					
Age	53.54	54	51	56	1.72
Married	.61	1	0	1	.49
Single	.12	0	0	1	.32
Separated or divorced	.22	0	0	1	.41
Widow	.05	0	0	1	.22
White	.70	1	0	1	.46
Black	.13	0	0	1	.34
Hispanic	.11	0	0	1	.31
Asian	.03	0	0	1	.18
Other	.02	0	0	1	.15
Education < high school	.07	0	0	1	.26
High school	.38	0	0	1	.48
Some college	.32	0	0	1	.46
College +	.23	0	0	1	.42
N dependent children	.58	0	0	4	.92
Income < $15K	.13	0	0	1	.34
Income $15–25K	.14	0	0	1	.34
Income $25–35K	.10	0	0	1	.30
Income $35–50K	.15	0	0	1	.36
Income $50–75K	.17	0	0	1	.37
Income $75–100K	.12	0	0	1	.32
Income $100–150K	.12	0	0	1	.32
Income > $150K	.07	0	0	1	.25
Working	.51	1	0	1	.50
Financial literacy (N correct answers)	2.74	3	0	5	1.41
Income shock	.33	0	0	1	.47
Retirement planning	.39	0	0	1	.49
Having too much debt	.43	0	0	1	.49
Financial fragility	.43	0	0	1	.49
B. Women ages 57–61 (N = 1,332)					
Age	58.99	59	57	61	1.42
Married	.57	1	0	1	.49
Single	.13	0	0	1	.34
Separated or divorced	.22	0	0	1	.41
Widow	.08	0	0	1	.27
White	.69	1	0	1	.46
Black	.18	0	0	1	.38
Hispanic	.08	0	0	1	.27
Asian	.03	0	0	1	.19
Other	.02	0	0	1	.14
Education < high school	.06	0	0	1	.24
High school	.37	0	0	1	.48

(*continued*)

Table 6A.2   (continued)

Variables	Mean	Median	Min.	Max.	SD
Some college	.31	0	0	1	.46
College or more	.25	0	0	1	.43
N dependent children	.34	0	0	4	.75
Income < $15K	.11	0	0	1	.31
Income $15–25K	.13	0	0	1	.33
Income $25–35K	.16	0	0	1	.36
Income $35–50K	.15	0	0	1	.36
Income $50–75K	.18	0	0	1	.38
Income $75–100K	.09	0	0	1	.29
Income $100–150K	.10	0	0	1	.30
Income > $150K	.09	0	0	1	.28
Working	.44	0	0	1	.50
Financial literacy (N correct answers)	2.79	3	0	5	1.40
Income shock	.30	0	0	1	.46
Retirement planning	.45	0	0	1	.50
Having too much debt	.39	0	0	1	.49
Financial fragility	.39	0	0	1	.49

Note: The sample includes all age-eligible women ages fifty-one to fifty-six and fifty-seven to sixty-one in the 2012 NFCS. Financial literacy refers to the number of correct answers to five financial literacy questions. Income shock refers to a dummy variable for those who experience a large drop in income in the previous twelve months that they did not expect. Financial planning is coded as 1 for those who tried to figure out how much they need to save for retirement. Having too much debt refers to respondents who chose values 5, 6, or 7 (on a scale from 1 to 7) when asked to evaluate if they have too much debt. Financial fragility is coded as 1 for those who probably or certainly could not come up with $2,000 within the next month. All statistics are weighted using survey weights.

References

AARP. 2013. *In the Red: Older Americans and Credit Card Debt.* AARP Public Policy Institute Report. www.aarp.org.

Agarwal, S., J. Driscoll, X. Gabaix, and D. Laibson. 2009. "The Age of Reason: Financial Decisions over the Life-Cycle with Implications for Regulation." *Brookings Papers on Economic Activity* 2:51–117.

Attanasio, O., H. Low, and V. Sánchez-Marcos. 2008. "Explaining Changes in Female Labor Supply in a Life-Cycle Model." *American Economic Review* 98 (4): 1517–52.

Banerjee, S. 2014. "The Gap between Expected and Actual Retirement: Evidence from Longitudinal Data." *EBRI Notes* 35 (11), Employee Benefit Research Institute, November. Available at SSRN: https://ssrn.com/abstract=2530165.

Begley, J., and S. Chan. 2015. "The Effect of Housing Wealth Shocks on Work and Retirement Decisions." NYU Wagner Research Paper no. 2634284, New York University.

Blakely, S., J. VanDerhei, and C. Copeland. 2016. "Retirement Confidence Stable, but Preparations Still Lag." *News* from EBRI, Employee Benefit Research Institute. https://www.ebri.org/pdf/PR1157.RCS-16.22Mar16.pdf.

Bricker J., L. Dettling, A. Henriques, J. W. Hsu, K. B. Moore, J. Sabelhaus, J. Thompson, and R. A. Windle. 2014. "Changes in US Family Finances from 2010 to 2013: Evidence from the Survey of Consumer Finances." *Federal Reserve Bulletin* 100 (4), September. http://www.federalreserve.gov/pubs/bulletin/2014/pdf.

Brown, M., D. Lee, J. Scally, K. Strair, and W. van der Klaauw. 2016. "The Graying of American Debt." *Liberty Street Economics*, Federal Reserve Bank of New York. http://libertystreeteconomics.newyorkfed.org/2016/02/the-graying-of-american-debt.html.

Bucks, B., A. Kennickell, T. Mach, and K. Moore. 2009. "Changes in US Family Finances from 2004 to 2007: Evidence from the Survey of Consumer Finances." *Federal Reserve Bulletin* 95:A1–55.

Butrica, B., and N. Karamcheva. 2013. "Does Household Debt Influence the Labor Supply and Benefit Claiming Decisions of Older Americans?" Working Paper, Urban Institute.

CFPB. 2014. "Snapshot of Older Consumers and Mortgage Debt." Consumer Financial Protection Bureau. http://files.consumerfinance.gov/f/201405_cfpb_snapshot_older-consumers-mortgage-debt.pdf.

Cheng, P., Z. Lin, and Y. Liu. 2011. "Do Women Pay More for Mortgages?" *Journal of Real Estate Finance and Economics* 43 (4): 423–44.

Cho, H. 2012. "Seniors Grow Old under Debt." *The Baltimore Sun/New America Media.* http://newamericamedia.org/2012/05/seniors-grow-old-under-debt.php.

Clark, P. 2015. "Return of the Single Female Homebuyer." *Bloomberg.* http://www.bloomberg.com/news/articles/2015-12-28/return-of-the-single-female-homebuyer.

Copeland, C. 2013. "Debt of the Elderly and Near Elderly, 1992–2010." *EBRI Notes* 36 (1), Employee Benefit Research Institute, January. https://www.ebri.org/pdf/notespdf/EBRI_Notes.Jan15.Debt.pdf.

Derousseau, R. 2016. "3 Ways to Reduce Debt as You near Retirement." *U.S. News*, March 25. http://money.usnews.com/investing/articles/2016-03-25/3-ways-to-reduce-debt-as-you-near-retirement.

Drew, R. B. 2006. "Buying for Themselves: An Analysis of Unmarried Female Home Buyers." Report, Joint Center for Housing Studies, Harvard University.

http://www.jchs.harvard.edu/research/publications/buying-themselves-analysis
-unmarried-female-home-buyers.

Farnham, M., and P. Sevak. 2016. "Housing Wealth and Retirement Timing."
CESifo Economic Studies 62 (1): 26–46.

Financial Industry Regulatory Authority (FINRA). 2006. *Investor Literacy and
Fraud Susceptibility Survey Executive Summary.* http://www.finra.org/Investors
/ProtectYourself/AvoidInvestmentFraud/.

———. 2007. *Senior Fraud Risk Survey.* http://www.finra.org/Investors
/ProtectYourself/AvoidInvestmentFraud/.

Fortin, N. 1995. "Allocation Inflexibilities, Female Labor Supply and Housing Assets
Accumulation: Are Women Working to Pay the Mortgage?" *Journal of Labor
Economics* 13:524–57.

Goldin, C. 2006. "The 'Quiet Revolution' That Transformed Women's Employment,
Education, and Family." *American Economic Review, Papers and Proceedings* (Ely
Lecture) 96:1–21.

———. 2014. "A Grand Gender Convergence: Its Last Chapter." *American Economic Review* 104 (4): 1091–119.

Institute for Financial Literacy. 2011. "2010 Annual Consumer Bankruptcy Demo-
graphics Report: A Five Year Perspective of the American Debtor." http://ssrn
.com/abstract=1925006.

Leland, J. 2008. "Baltimore Finds Subprime Crisis Snags Women." *New York Times*,
Jan. 15. http://www.nytimes.com/2008/01/15/us/15mortgage.html.

Lu, T., O. S. Mitchell, S. Utkus, and J. Young. 2017. "Borrowing from the Future:
401(k) Loans and Loan Defaults." *National Tax Journal* 70 (1): 77–110.

Lusardi, A. 1999. "Information, Expectations, and Savings for Retirement." In
Behavioral Dimensions of Retirement Economics, edited by Henry Aaron, 81–
115. Washington, DC: Brookings Institution Press and Russell Sage Foundation.

———. 2011. "Americans' Financial Capability." NBER Working Paper no. 17103,
Cambridge, MA.

Lusardi, A., and J. Beeler. 2007. "Saving between Cohorts: The Role of Planning." In
Redefining Retirement: How Will Boomers Fare? edited by B. Madrian, O. Mitchell, and B. Soldo, 271–95. Oxford: Oxford University Press.

Lusardi, A., and C. de Bassa Scheresberg. 2013. "Financial Literacy and High-Cost
Borrowing in the United States." NBER Working Paper no. 18969, Cambridge,
MA.

———. 2014. "Financial Capability near Retirement: A Profile of Pre-Retirees."
Report, Filene Research Institute, October. http://gflec.org/wp-content/uploads
/2015/01/a738b9_78b587a2660346d2af2271dd6cb3ad26.pdf?x87657.

Lusardi, A., and O. S. Mitchell. 2007a. "Baby Boomer Retirement Security: The
Role of Planning, Financial Literacy and Housing Wealth." *Journal of Monetary
Economics* 54:205–24.

———. 2007b. "Financial Literacy and Retirement Preparedness: Evidence and
Implications for Financial Education." *Business Economics* 35–44, January. http://
www.dartmouth.edu/~alusardi/Papers/Financial_Literacy.pdf.

———. 2008. "Planning and Financial Literacy: How Do Women Fare?" *American
Economic Review Papers and Proceedings* 98 (2): 413–17.

———. 2011a. "Financial Literacy and Planning: Implications for Retirement Well-
being." In *Financial Literacy: Implications for Retirement Security and the Financial Marketplace*, edited by O. S. Mitchell and A. Lusardi, 17–39. Oxford: Oxford
University Press.

———. 2011b. "Financial Literacy and Retirement Planning in the United States."
Journal of Pension Economics and Finance 10:509–25.

————. 2013. "Debt and Debt Management among Older Adults." Paper presented at the 15th Annual Joint Conference of the Retirement Research Consortium, Washington, DC, Aug. 1–2.

————. 2014. "The Economic Importance of Financial Literacy: Theory and Evidence." *Journal of Economic Literature* 52 (1): 5–44.

Lusardi, A., O. S. Mitchell, and N. Oggero. 2016. "Debt and Financial Vulnerability on the Verge of Retirement." GFLEC Working Paper no. 2016-5, Global Financial Literacy Excellence Center, George Washington University. December.

Lusardi, A., and P. Tufano. 2015. "Debt Literacy, Financial Experiences, and Overindebtedness." *Journal of Pension Economics and Finance* 14 (4): 329–65.

Michaud, P.-C., and S. Rohwedder. 2015. "Forecasting Labor Force Participation and Economic Resources of the Early Baby Boomers." MRRC Working Paper, Michigan Retirement Research Center, University of Michigan.

Pham, S. 2011. "Retirements Swallowed by Debt." *New York Times*, Jan. 26. newoldage.blogs.nytimes.com/2011/01/26/retirements-swallowed-by-debt/.

Pottow, J. 2012. "The Rise in Elder Bankruptcy Filings and Failure of US Bankruptcy Law." *Elder Law Journal* 19:220–57.

Rosnick, D., and D. Baker. 2014. "The Wealth of Households: An Analysis of the 2013 Survey of Consumer Finances." CEPR Paper, Center for Economic and Policy Research. November. http://cepr.net/documents/wealth-scf-2014-10.pdf.

Securian Financial Group. 2013. *Retirement Time Bomb: Mortgage Debt.* Securian Investments. www.securiannews.com/sites/securian.newshq.businesswire.com/files/research/file/RetDebtSummary-Apr2013-F78685-1_pod.pdf.

United States Government Accountability Office. 2015. "Most Households Approaching Retirement Have Low Savings." Washington, DC: USGAO.

US Congress Joint Economic Committee. 2008. "Women and their Families are Being Squeezed." http://www.jec.senate.gov/public/_cache/files/dd3a9c6d -c0b6-4f82-853d-55f6c72743f5/sqeezedwomanupdate-91608.pdf.

Utkus, S., and J. Young. 2011. "Financial Literacy and 401(k) Loans." In *Financial Literacy: Implications for Retirement Security and the Financial Marketplace*, edited by O. S. Mitchell and A. Lusardi, 59–75. Oxford: Oxford University Press.

7

Teaching, Teachers' Pensions, and Retirement across Recent Cohorts of College-Graduate Women

Maria D. Fitzpatrick

7.1 Introduction

Labor force participation rates of college-educated women ages sixty to sixty-four increased by 20 percent (10 percentage points) between 2000 and 2010. One potential explanation for this change stems from the fact that a lower proportion of the college-educated women in the more recent cohorts were ever teachers. The propensity of women to obtain a college degree increased by a factor of 5 between the 1925 and 1950 birth cohorts (from 5 to 25 percentage points). Since the number of female teachers remained relatively constant during the period, the fraction of college-educated women who were teachers fell precipitously.

This occupational shift among college-educated women could drive the recent increases in labor force participation for any number of reasons. For example, if teaching is more stressful than the other occupations that college-educated women are now more likely to be employed in, then the more recent cohorts of college-educated women will retire at older ages than previous cohorts. Alternatively, if teachers are more likely than other college-educated women to be secondary earners, they may retire earlier

Maria D. Fitzpatrick is an associate professor in the Department of Policy and Management at Cornell University and a research associate of the National Bureau of Economic Research.

Thanks to Claudia Goldin and Larry Katz for the invitation to explore these issues in collaboration with the other preconference participants and for their comments. Thanks, too, to Melinda Sandler Morrill and the other conference participants for their helpful comments. Research support was provided by the Sloan Foundation. I am also grateful to Corbin Miller for excellent research assistance and help with the public-use and RAND-created versions of the Health and Retirement Study and to Mohan Ramanujan for help with the restricted-use version of the Health and Retirement Study. For acknowledgments, sources of research support, and disclosure of the author's material financial relationships, if any, please see http://www.nber.org/chapters/c13804.ack.

either because they are not the primary earner or in order to time retirement with an older spouse.

In this chapter, I examine a third potential difference between teachers and workers in other occupations: pension eligibility (and wealth). Public school teachers are almost universally covered by defined-benefit pensions and, generally, defined-benefit pensions allow workers to retire at earlier ages than Social Security. Therefore, as the fraction of college-educated women without access to these defined-benefit pensions increased, the labor supply of older college-educated women increased. I provide evidence supporting the hypothesis in part by showing that older college-educated women who ever worked as teachers do not experience increases in labor force participation as large as their counterparts who never taught.

7.2   The Changing Nature of College-Educated Women's Occupations

At various moments during the last hundred years, women made enormous strides in their educational attainment. In figure 7.1, I use data from Goldin and Katz (2008), updated by Goldin and Katz to include data up to 2012, to plot college graduation rates (by age thirty) of women by birth

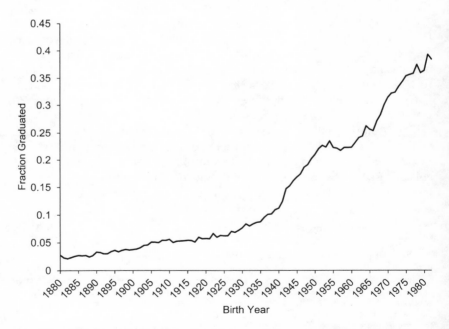

Fig. 7.1   College graduation rates (by thirty years) for women: Cohorts born from 1880 to 1982

Source: Goldin and Katz (2008), with updates from Goldin and Katz for 1976 to 1982 birth cohorts using CPS MORG, 2006–2012, and evaluated at age thirty for each birth cohort.

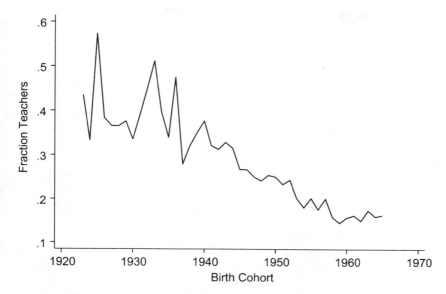

Fig. 7.2   Fraction of employed college-educated women who are teachers, by birth cohort

Source: Based on the author's calculations using the Current Population Survey, 1975 to 2000.
Note: Sample includes employed college-educated women ages forty-six to fifty.

cohort. Focusing on the cohorts most relevant for this study, in the 1925 cohort the female graduation rate starts around 5 percent and begins to climb. By the 1940 cohort, female graduation rates had more than doubled and by the 1950 cohort they doubled again, reaching nearly 25 percent.

As more women graduated from college, they also began to be employed in a more diverse set of occupations. In figure 7.2, I plot the fraction of employed college-educated women in the Current Population Survey (CPS) between the ages of forty-six and fifty who report being a teacher, by birth cohort.[1] The fraction of teachers decreases from around 40 percent for the cohorts born before 1940 to 30 percent for those born in 1950 and decreases further still to just 15 percent for the cohorts born after 1959. The shift in occupational choice may have implications for the labor supply of older women because, as described next, teachers, who are mostly public employees, have access to pensions that are different than those in other sectors.

1. The Current Population Survey only collects information about occupation and industry of those who report being employed. The fraction of college-educated women who are employed between the ages of forty-six and fifty across the cohorts born between 1920 and 1965 varies little. Restricting to women ages forty-six to fifty allows me to create a time series for cohorts as far back as 1920. The fraction of college-educated women who are employed and report being teachers by cohort is similar when measured at earlier ages.

7.3   Pensions

7.3.1   A Brief History of Teacher Pensions

Although the first statewide systems of teacher pensions in the United States were introduced in the last quarter of the nineteenth century, very few were in place before 1910 (Clark, Craig, and Wilson 2003). At that time, Social Security did not exist and teaching was an occupation largely reserved for unmarried women. Those who remained in teaching for many years were those who had never married and therefore could not rely on a spouse's income for retirement support.[2] As such, teacher pension systems were seen as a mechanism to provide assistance to women who might not otherwise have late-in-life support. During the early part of the twentieth century the use of pensions expanded until, by the late 1920s, teachers in twenty-eight states were covered by pensions.[3] By 2013, public school teachers in all states participated in publicly funded pension plans.

Pensions generally take one of two forms: defined benefit or defined contribution. In a traditional defined-benefit pension plan, upon retirement the employee receives a set benefit for life. The benefit size is determined by age, time spent with the employer and earnings history while employed, and is usually adjusted to account for inflation. In 2013, teachers in forty-four states participated in either a traditional (thirty-nine states) or hybrid (five states) defined-benefit pension system. In a defined-contribution pension plan, employer and employee contributions are made throughout the employee's tenure. The firm and the employees choose among investment options for the contributions. In 2013, only one state, Alaska, offered teachers only a defined-contribution plan.[4] In the remaining five states, public school teachers had a choice of participating in a defined-benefit plan, defined-contribution plan, or some combination.

Therefore, an overwhelming majority of public school teachers in the United States participate in some form of defined-benefit pension program. It is important to note that the current widespread use of defined-benefit pensions is unique to employers in the public sector. In 2006, 65 percent of older workers in the public sector participated in some form of defined-benefit plan, while only 39 percent of private-sector workers did (Gustman, Steinmeier, and Tabatabai 2010). Moreover, while only 22 percent of private-

2. Many districts had marriage bars that banned married women from working. For more information, see Goldin (1991a, 1991b, 2006).
3. In contrast to the pension systems available to most policemen and firefighters at the time, which were operated by municipalities, most teachers participated in statewide pension plans.
4. Even Alaska's defined-contribution plan is sufficiently new that teachers in the cohorts relevant for this study participate in the preexisting defined-benefit plan.

sector workers participate only in a defined-benefit plan, the same is true of 57 percent of public-sector workers.[5]

Although relatively few people in the private sector have access to a defined-benefit pension, nearly all private-sector workers are covered by Social Security, which is itself a type of defined-benefit pension. Teachers in many states also participate in Social Security, although that was not always the case. Starting in 1954, the Social Security Act was amended to allow state and local government employees who were members of a public retirement system to participate in the Social Security program. Since then, public employees have been able to gain membership in Social Security by majority vote of the employees. Such votes have been passed in thirty-five states and all teachers in these states participate in Social Security. In another three states, teachers in some districts participate in Social Security. Estimates suggest that between 61 and 73 percent of teachers currently participate in Social Security (Doherty, Jacobs, and Madden 2012).

7.3.2   The Structure of Teacher Pensions

Why might the type of pension plan influence labor supply at older ages? A notable characteristic of defined-benefit pension plans is defined rules governing eligibility for benefit collection and benefit size. In addition to plan rules being clearly delineated, the rules are often structured such that the monetary gain for the employee of continued employment past a certain point is negative (Stock and Wise 1990).[6] These rules often lead to large discrete changes in the present discounted value of income to employees of retiring at a particular age or year of tenure. This feature is in stark contrast to defined-contribution pensions where an employee can begin collecting benefits at almost any time and the present value of the pension wealth increases steadily with contributions (and oscillates only with market fluctuations).[7] Because there are no large eligibility-rule-induced discrete changes in the present value of defined-contribution pension accounts at

---

5. The shift toward defined-contribution plans in the private sector began in the 1980s. Potential causes include the introduction of 401(k) defined-contribution plans, a shift in private-sector employment away from heavily unionized industries, and the increased funding requirements for private-sector pension plans.

6. Specifically, continued employment with the employer offering the defined-benefit pension begins to have negative returns. Workers may find it beneficial to pursue employment with other employers, particularly if they are also eligible for Social Security and expect to live awhile (Maestas, chapter 2, this volume). Later, I explore whether there have been changes in the patterns of employment among college-educated women after they begin collecting pension benefits.

7. In 401(k) plans there is a 10 percent increase in present value of pension wealth when a worker hits age fifty-five and retires, at which point she avoids the early withdrawal penalty. If the worker retires before fifty-five or converts the 401(k) into an IRA, she must wait until age 59.5 to avoid the early withdrawal penalty.

specific ages or levels of experience, there are no clear incentives to retire at a particular age or level of experience.

However, even employees in the United States without defined-benefit pensions from their employer still participate in Social Security. The earliest age of retirement in Social Security is sixty-two and the full retirement age ranges from sixty-five to sixty-seven depending on the individual's year of birth. As with any defined-benefit pension system, Social Security eligibility ages are influential in the decision making of older Americans. About 40 percent of Social Security recipients begin collecting benefits at age sixty-two and another 10 percent begin collection at the full retirement age.[8] At issue is how these incentives to retire at certain ages in Social Security compare with those in the defined-benefit pensions provided to public school teachers.

Rules regarding eligibility for benefit collection in defined-benefit pension plans for teachers are based on age, years of service within the public school retirement system, or some combination thereof. For example, in California, teachers who have vested in the system can retire at age fifty-five. Teachers in the New York State pension system may retire with thirty-five years of service regardless of their age.[9] Still many other states use the combination of age and years of service. For example, in the Texas Teachers' Retirement System, eligibility is determined by the rule of 80: any combination of age and years of service totaling at least eighty makes someone eligible to begin collecting retirement benefits as long as the employee is at least age sixty.[10]

As illustrated in the examples of these three states, traditionally, eligibility rules in public-sector, defined-benefit pensions have been structured such that employees can retire much earlier than they would be eligible in the Social Security system. In figure 7.3, I present information on the earliest age at which a continuously employed teacher who started working at age twenty-two becomes eligible for an unreduced retirement benefit, known as the normal retirement benefit. The figure shows that the age of retirement eligibility for career teachers ranges from forty-seven to sixty-seven. The bulk of states (thirty-five) have retirement eligibility ages between fifty-two and sixty. Recall that the first age at which Americans are eligible for normal benefit collection in Social Security is sixty-five. In comparison, only three state systems have pension eligibility rules for career teachers that would preclude them from collecting their full pension benefits by age sixty-five.

What makes the comparison more remarkable is that the information in

8. Fitzpatrick and Moore (2016).

9. Tier I members (those that started before 1973) of the New York State Teachers' Retirement System can begin collecting benefits with thirty-five years of service at any age. They can also collect benefits at age fifty-five with at least five years of service. The rules have changed over time and teachers entering New York State public schools since 2010 are eligible to receive benefits at age fifty-five with ten years of service. (https://www.nystrs.org/Benefits/Service -Retirement. Accessed August 12, 2015.)

10. If she entered the Texas Teacher Retirement System for the first time after 2014, the member must have at least eighty years of combined age and experience and be at least sixty-two.

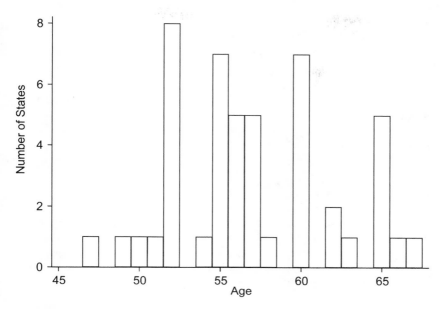

Fig. 7.3   Number of states with each normal retirement age for state teacher pensions systems

Source: Dougherty, Jacobs, and Madden (2012).

Notes: Includes the forty-nine states with defined-benefit pension systems for teachers in 2011. The normal retirement age is defined as the earliest retirement age at which someone who starts teaching at age twenty-two can retire and receive an unreduced retirement benefit.

figure 7.3 is about teachers' eligibility for a normal retirement benefit. Teachers in many state pension systems can retire even earlier if they are willing to accept a reduction in their annual benefit.[11] The size of the reduction is based on how early the worker claims benefits, known as an early retirement option or early retirement benefit. Almost all state pensions systems (forty-six) have an early retirement option for teachers. The option is similar to the early retirement option in Social Security, where benefit collection can start at age sixty-two with a reduction in the size of the benefit. I do not know of any source that has carefully cataloged the early retirement ages in teacher pension systems. However, since only eleven states have full retirement ages that are higher than the early retirement age in Social Security, it is safe to

---

11. For example, if a teacher in Texas satisfies the rule of 80 requirement, but is not yet sixty years of age, she can retire, but her benefit will be reduced by 5 percent for each year she is younger than age sixty. In other words, the Texas teacher who started teaching at age twenty-two and worked continuously is eligible for a normal retirement benefit at age sixty. She can retire at age fifty-one (with twenty-nine years of service) with a benefit that is just 55 percent of what her normal benefit would have been, at fifty-two with a benefit 60 percent as large, and so on.

say that the vast majority of teachers can collect early retirement benefits at a younger age than Social Security participants.

In addition to eligibility rules that allow earlier retirement in teaching than other occupations, there is another dimension of defined-benefit pensions that encourages retirement at relatively young ages. In many states there is a maximum allowed benefit. For example, in Illinois, the maximum benefit payable to a retiree is 75 percent of her final average salary, which is similar in size to the maximum benefit in other states. The annual benefit amount in a defined-benefit plan is generally determined by years of service and some measure of final average salary. To be specific, the annual annuity, B, is defined by the formula:

$$B = F \times \text{Years of Service} \times \text{Final Average Salary},$$

where F is known as the benefit factor. Benefit factors are generally around 2 percent or more per year of service. Given these benefit factors, career teachers often reach the maximum benefit point within thirty to thirty-five years of service, or in their midfifties to early sixties. After reaching the maximum benefit point, the return to continued work decreases precipitously because benefits no longer accrue at 2 percent per year.

The combination of these eligibility and benefit rules set up changes in accrued pension wealth that lead to clear incentives to retire at certain points. The present value of benefits increases sharply when a worker becomes eligible for early retirement, making early retirement eligibility a salient moment for teacher retirement. Pension wealth then continues increasing at a relatively fast rate (as compared to earlier in one's career) until the teacher hits the normal retirement age. At that point, the present value of pension wealth may still increase with time on the job, but it will do so at a slower rate than it did between early and normal retirement eligibility. Eventually, when the employee hits the point where she will receive the maximum benefit, her pension wealth accrual with an additional year of employment actually begins *decreasing*. This odd change occurs because, despite the increase in the salary used to calculate benefits, by continuing employment she forgoes some of the benefit payments entitled to her if she retired.

The large effect of these rules on teacher retirement behavior has been well documented in the literature. For example, Harris and Adams (2007) calculated that nationally, in 2005, 54 percent of the teachers first reaching early retirement eligibility took that option. Another three-quarters of teachers who reach normal retirement age began collecting benefits at that point. Therefore, nearly 90 percent of career teachers have retired by the normal retirement age in teaching, which, as I described, is at an earlier age in most states than the early retirement age in Social Security. Other researchers show that pension eligibility leads to similar increases in retirement using state administrative data (Brown 2013; Koedel, Ni, and Podgursky 2014; Mahler 2014). For example, in Missouri, the median retirement age is fifty-seven (Koedel, Ni, and Podgursky 2014).

Finally, in addition to pensions, there is one other notable piece of retirement-related compensation available for former public school teachers (and other public-sector workers) that is not as widely available for workers in the private sector: retiree health insurance. As of 2009, every state offered some form of retiree health insurance to its government employees, including teachers (Clark and Morrill 2010). These state-sponsored retiree health insurance programs provide subsidized health insurance to teachers collecting benefits from the state pension system. Therefore, these employees have access to health insurance that is not contingent on employment at younger ages than most people can receive it from the federal government (generally at age sixty-five, through Medicare). Research has shown that the offer of retiree health insurance leads public school teachers to retire earlier than they would have otherwise (Fitzpatrick 2014).

7.4   Evidence from the Health and Retirement Study

7.4.1   Employment, Retirement, and Benefit Collection

The existing literature clearly illustrates that teachers leave their main jobs as public school teachers when they reach retirement eligibility. While informative, this fact does not provide a rich understanding of the labor supply of female teachers and how it compares with other college-educated women. This is, in part, because teachers can continue to work even after collecting retirement benefits from their pension system. Most existing research on teacher retirement uses administrative data from teacher pension systems. Although such data offer large sample sizes, they do not include information on labor supply outside of a particular teachers' retirement system. Continued work unobserved in administrative data could include teaching for another school system and employment in another occupation or sector entirely.

I turn to the Health and Retirement Study ([HRS]; see appendix for more information) to create a more comprehensive picture of the older-age labor supply of college-educated women who spent time as teachers as compared to other college-educated women who did not. For this study, I limit the sample to women who report having obtained at least a bachelor's degree. I include information on women born between 1931 and 1950 whom I can observe at almost all ages between sixty and sixty-four. Because of sample size issues, I present information for the following groups of cohorts: 1931 to 1935, 1936 to 1940, 1941 to 1945, and 1946 to 1950. The most recent wave of the HRS was conducted in 2014, so age sixty to sixty-four outcomes for the last cohort group (the 1946 to 1950 cohorts) are incomplete. In discussing comparisons below, I detail where this data limitation may be important for interpretation.

The HRS respondents are asked a series of questions about their occupations at different points in time. These questions vary across waves of the survey. The most consistent way to identify teachers across waves of the survey is to categorize anyone who responds to any of the occupation

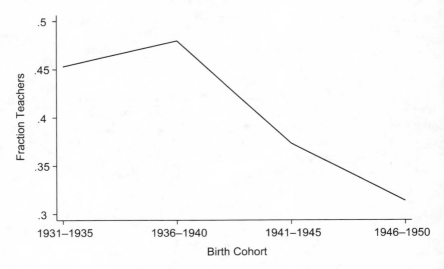

Fig. 7.4   Fraction of college-educated women ages sixty to sixty-four in the Health and Retirement Study reporting having ever been employed as a teacher, by birth cohort

Source: Based on the author's calculations using the Health and Retirement Study.

Notes: Respondents were asked the type of work done at each job about which they were surveyed (current, last, and previous). A woman is classified as a teacher if the occupation recorded was teaching for any of these jobs. The sample includes all college-educated women between the ages of sixty and sixty-four.

questions as a teacher (one could say "ever a teacher"). More precisely, I compare outcomes for college-educated women who were teachers at any point in their lives to other college-educated women who were never teachers. Note that this includes both public and private school teachers; I use this definition because many teachers who spent time as private school teachers were also once public school teachers. Because there are relatively few private school teachers, I cannot examine them separately and the results are unchanged if I omit them.

There are important differences in training and professionalization between teaching and many other occupations, even those in which other college-educated women are employed. Therefore, in some of what follows, I also present comparisons between college-educated women who were teachers and other college-educated women classified to have been in the same general occupation category, managerial and professional specialization occupations, who were not ever teachers.

Just as in the CPS, the HRS data show evidence of a shift in the occupations of college-educated women (figure 7.4).[12] More than 45 percent of

12. The same pattern is seen when using single-year cohorts and moving averages of three-year cohorts (see figure 1.6 of Goldin and Katz, chapter 1, this volume).

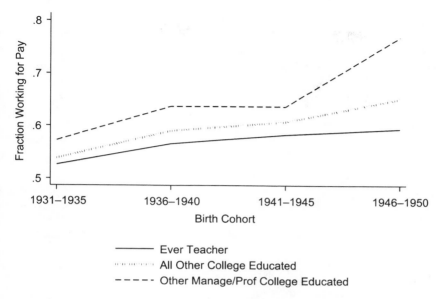

Fig. 7.5   Employment of college-educated women ages sixty to sixty-four, by occupation and birth cohort

Source: Based on the author's calculation using the Health and Retirement Study.

Notes: Respondents were asked the type of work done at each job about which they were surveyed (current, last, and previous). A woman is classified as a teacher if the occupation recorded was teaching for any of these jobs. Women were classified into the managerial and professional specialty occupations using similar methodology. The sample includes all college-educated women between the ages of sixty and sixty-four.

college-educated women born between 1931 and 1940 were employed as teachers at some point in their work lives, but just 31 percent of those born between 1946 to 1950 report ever being employed as teachers.[13] During this twenty-year span of birth cohorts, there was a 30 percent decline in the fraction of college-educated women who spent time employed as teachers.

Goldin and Katz (chapter 1, this volume) showed that college-educated women in the 1931 to 1951 cohorts who spent time employed as teachers were about 5 percentage points, on average, less likely to be in the labor force at ages fifty-nine to sixty-three. Information in figure 7.5 confirms this pattern using employment rates between the ages of sixty and sixty-four of college-educated women born between 1931 and 1950. However, the information in the figure shows that, not only are college-educated women who spent time as teachers less likely to be employed across all of these cohorts, there has been a widening of the older-age employment gap between those

---

13. The HRS asks information about occupation and pensions for the jobs about which it collects information. This includes jobs held at the time of each survey, the last job held, as well as up to three previous jobs if they were held for at least five years.

who spent time as teachers and other college-educated women. This is because college-educated women who were teachers at some point in their careers do not experience the same increase in labor force participation at older ages that other college-educated women who were never teachers do, particularly women in the category of managerial and professional specialization occupations who were never teachers (figure 7.5).[14] Employment of those who were teachers increased from 53 to 59 percent for the 1931–1935 to the 1946–1950 cohorts, respectively, an increase of 6 percentage points. This is only slightly more than half the increase in employment of college-educated women who were never teachers in these cohorts, which was 11 percentage points. The employment rate of other college-educated women in managerial and professional specialty occupations who were never teachers increased by nearly 20 percentage points across these cohorts. Therefore, the increase in employment of those who were once teachers was only 30 percent as large as the increase for other college-educated women in these similarly professionalized occupations who were never teachers. Clearly, the difference in occupational choices between these cohorts is related to the longer work lives of more recent cohorts of college-educated women.

Notably, although teachers were about as likely to be working between the ages of sixty and sixty-four as other college-educated women in the early cohorts, this was no longer the case for women born between 1946 and 1950 (figure 7.5). Instead, women who spent some time as teachers in the more recent cohorts were about 10 percent (6 percentage points) less likely to be employed at ages sixty to sixty-four than the rest of their college-educated peers who were never teachers. The difference in employment rates is even starker when compared to other women in managerial and professional specialization occupations who were never teachers. More than three-quarters (77 percent) of college-educated women born between 1946 and 1950 who worked in the broader set of managerial and professional specialization occupations but were never teachers were employed at ages sixty to sixty-four. In other words, college-educated women in occupations similar to teaching have a 30 percent (18 percentage points) higher employment rate than teachers.

Relatedly, there has been an 11 percentage point (30 percent) decline in the fraction of women in professional service occupations who did not teach that report being retired. At the same time, the fraction of college-educated women who spent time as teachers who say they are retired has increased by about 2 percentage points (figure 7.6). The recent relative decline in

14. The censoring of data in 2014 means the women in the 1946 to 1950 cohorts are on average younger than those in the earlier cohorts. This factor likely makes the employment rates for these cohorts slightly higher than they should be. Fully 90 percent of career teachers retire when they reach pension-eligibility milestones, which occur in one's late fifties and early sixties. There is no similar decline in employment of women when they reach Social Security eligibility. Therefore, the censoring of the data is likely leading me to underestimate the differences in employment growth across teachers and other college-educated women.

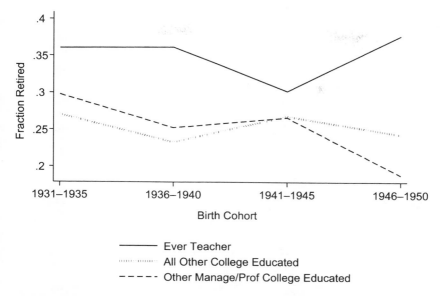

Fig. 7.6   **Retirement status of college-educated women ages sixty to sixty-four, by occupation and birth cohort**

Source: Based on the author's calculation using the Health and Retirement Study.

Notes: Respondents were asked the type of work done at each job about which they were surveyed (current, last, and previous). A woman is classified as a teacher if the occupation recorded was teaching for any of these jobs. Women were classified into the managerial and professional specialty occupations using similar methodology. The sample includes all college-educated women between the ages of sixty and sixty-four.

retirement and increase in employment of college-educated women who were never teachers is likely driven in part by the decreased likelihood that these women had access to pension benefits in their early sixties. As I now detail, the retirement and employment patterns are reflected in the relative decreased likelihood of collecting pension benefits among those who were never teachers.

As can be seen in panel A of figure 7.7, the fraction of those who spent time as teachers and who are collecting pension benefits between ages sixty and sixty-four hovered around 40 percent for those born between 1931 and 1945. The fraction collecting Social Security benefits also remained steady across these cohorts (panel B, around 23 percent). However, the pension and Social Security benefit collection of other college-educated women who were never teachers across the same cohorts both fell slightly (by about 5 percentage points each).[15]

For both the college-educated women who were once teachers and those

15. In part, this may be due to the slowdown in the growth of Social Security benefits discussed in Gelber, Isen, and Song (chapter 8, this volume).

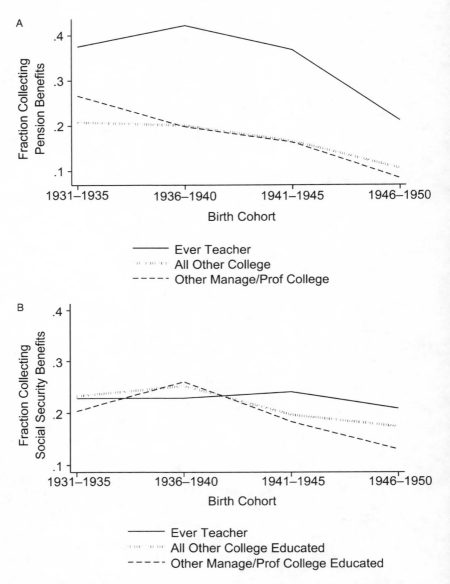

Fig. 7.7 Fraction of college-educated women collecting employer pensions and Social Security benefits by occupation, age, and birth cohort. (A) Pension benefits, ages sixty to sixty-four. (B) Social Security benefits, ages sixty to sixty-four. (C) Pension benefits, ages fifty-five to fifty-nine.

Source: Based on the author's calculation using the Health and Retirement Study.

Notes: Respondents were asked the type of work done at each job about which they were surveyed (current, last, and previous). A woman is classified as a teacher if the occupation recorded was teaching for any of these jobs. Women were classified into the managerial and professional specialty occupations using similar methodology. The samples include all college-educated women between the ages of fifty-five and sixty-four, as indicated in each panel. Pension and Social Security benefit collection is determined by whether a respondent reports any income from an employer-provided pension or Social Security, respectively.

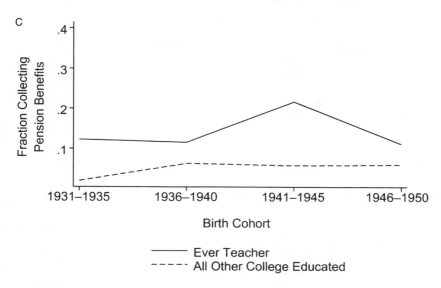

Fig. 7.7   (cont.)

who were never teachers, there is a relatively sharp decline in pension benefit collection among the 1946 to 1950 cohorts. This decrease is a distinct break from the previous pattern, particularly for those who were once teachers. Likely, the censoring of the data for these cohorts drives the drop. Only two of these cohorts (1946 and 1947) are observed at all of the ages from sixty to sixty-four. The other cohorts are only observed at the youngest ages in the sixty to sixty-four range, meaning the set of workers observed in the HRS in these cohorts is younger, on average, than the set of workers observed from other cohorts. Since defined-benefit pension collection, particularly among teachers, occurs in the late fifties and early sixties, the censoring causes the pension-benefit collection rates among people who spent time as teachers to be lower than if we were able to observe these cohorts at all ages from sixty to sixty-four.

To determine whether the censoring is likely to be driving the drop in pension benefits, in panel C of figure 7.7, I present pension-benefit collection for the same cohorts, but at ages fifty-five to fifty-nine. By observing people at earlier ages, I avoid the problem of censoring. Other than an uptick in pension-benefit collection for the 1941 to 1945 cohorts, the benefit collection between ages fifty-five and fifty-nine of college-educated women who were once teachers is steady across these cohorts.[16] Therefore, the pension

16. Why is there an uptick among the 1941 to 1945 cohorts? Those cohorts reached their late fifties in the late 1990s, which was a period of increased pension generosity and pension buyouts that enabled teachers to retire earlier than they would have otherwise. We can also

collection between ages fifty-five to fifty-nine of college-educated women who spent time as teachers and were born in the 1946 to 1950 cohorts is similar to that of earlier cohorts of college-educated women who spent time as teachers. This exercise provides evidence that the censoring of the data for the 1946 to 1950 cohorts when in their sixties drives the lower pension receipt among women who spent time as teachers seen in panel A of figure 7.7. If we extrapolate from their behavior at earlier ages, we would expect their fully realized pension receipt between ages sixty and sixty-four to be near 40 percent and similar to that of earlier cohorts of college-educated women who spent time as teachers.

7.4.2   Concurrent Employment and Pension Collection

To this point, I have shown that college-educated women who spent time as teachers have different patterns of labor supply and retirement at older ages than their similarly educated and professionalized counterparts. Namely, while the patterns of employment and retirement did not change much for the women who spent time as teachers that were born between 1931 and 1950, other older college-educated women in these cohorts who were never teachers saw increases in the propensity to be employed and decreases in the likelihood of being retired.

Retirement and employment are not binary; people may continue to work even once they consider themselves retired or begin collecting pension benefits (Maestas 2010). This may be particularly true for teachers who begin collecting benefits from a state pension system, but are not precluded from working for other employers. Of interest is whether the patterns of increased labor supply at older ages are driven by increased labor supply among those who are not collecting retirement benefits or if they are driven by increases in labor supply among those who have begun collecting benefits, but desire to keep working. Since teachers can begin benefit collection at such early ages, relative to other occupations, the distinction may be of particular relevance for understanding the labor supply of older workers who have spent time in teaching.

In figure 7.8, I examine whether there were shifts in concurrent employment and pension benefit collection among sixty- to sixty-four-year-old college-educated women born between 1931 and 1950 who spent time as teachers and those who did not. In panel A, the lines plot the rates of employment for women who were collecting pension or Social Security benefits in their early sixties. There is little change across cohorts in the rate of employment for these "retired" older women if they did not spend time in teaching. Among college-educated women who spent time in teaching and are collecting retirement benefits between ages sixty and sixty-four, there is

---

see the influence of the buyouts and other benefit generosity changes of the late 1990s in the slight increase in retirement of teachers ages sixty to sixty-four from the 1936 to 1940 cohorts.

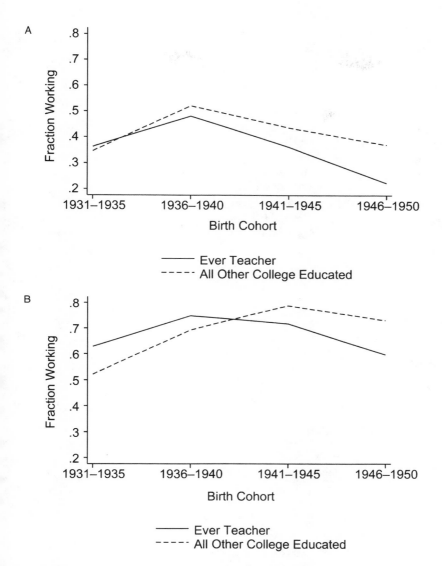

Fig. 7.8 Fraction of college-educated women working between ages sixty and sixty-four by occupation, birth cohort, and whether collecting pension benefits. (A) Collecting retirement benefits. (B) Not collecting retirement benefits.

Source: Based on the author's calculation using the Health and Retirement Study.

Notes: Respondents were asked the type of work done at each job about which they were surveyed (current, last, and previous). A woman is classified as a teacher if the occupation recorded was teaching for any of these jobs. Women were classified into the managerial and professional specialty occupations using similar methodology. The sample includes all college-educated women between the ages of sixty and sixty-four. Pension and Social Security benefit collection is determined by whether a respondent reports any income from an employer-provided pension or Social Security, respectively.

a large decrease in the likelihood of employment. In panel B, we see that the increases in labor supply of older college-educated women are driven by increases in the propensity of working and not collecting retirement benefits.

7.4.3   Teachers or Public-Sector Workers?

Teachers are not the only employees with employer-provided, defined-benefit pension that incentivize early retirement. The most obvious group of other employees with defined-benefit pensions are other public-sector workers. The labor supply of college-educated women ages sixty to sixty-four who worked in the public sector increased by 5 percentage points across the cohorts born between 1931 to 1935 and 1946 to 1950 (figure 7.9). As such, the labor supply of government workers more closely mirrors that of teachers, rather than that of other college-educated workers who were not teachers. The comparison makes sense since both groups have disproportionate access to defined-benefit pensions relative to college-educated women in other occupations, though it could be the case that teachers and

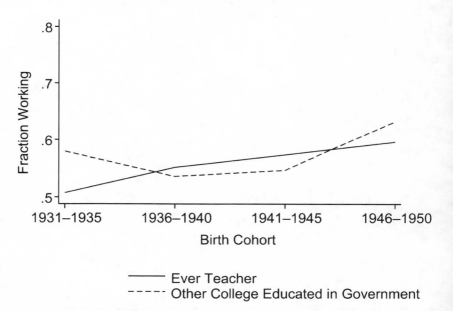

Fig. 7.9   Fraction of college-educated women ages sixty to sixty-four employed, by occupation and birth cohort

Source: Based on the author's calculation using the Health and Retirement Study.

Notes: Respondents were asked the type of work done at each job about which they were surveyed (current, last, and previous). A woman is classified as a teacher if the occupation recorded was teaching for any of these jobs. Women were classified into other government-related occupations using similar methodology. The sample includes all college-educated women between the ages of sixty and sixty-four who spent some time employed in government.

other government workers have other things in common (e.g., preferences) that drive their similarity and the differences between their labor supply and that of other college-educated women.

7.5 Conclusion

To summarize, teachers have different patterns of retirement and labor supply at older ages than their similarly educated and professionalized counterparts. Namely, recent cohorts of teachers are less likely to be employed and more likely to be retired between the ages of sixty and sixty-four than recent cohorts of similarly educated and professionalized women. A likely reason for these differences is that teachers in these recent cohorts have access to traditional defined-benefit pensions, while women who were never teachers do not. As shown, these defined-benefit pensions allow for, and even incentivize, retirement at earlier ages than Social Security. Support for this hypothesis stems from similar patterns of employment between ages sixty and sixty-four among teachers and other government workers, who also have access to defined-benefit pensions.

The difference in pension access across occupations is also likely a primary driver of changes in the patterns of labor supply among older college-educated women in recent decades. Specifically, while the patterns of older teachers' employment and retirement did not change much for the cohorts between 1931 and 1950, other older college-educated women who were never teachers saw significant increases in the propensity to be employed and decreases in the likelihood of being retired.

The employment changes for more recent cohorts correspond to the patterns of change in pension use in the private sector. Namely, there was a large decrease in the use of defined-benefit pensions in the private sector over the course of recent decades. At the same time, there was a large decline in the propensity of college-educated women to work as teachers, meaning more and more college-educated women were employed in the private sector where they had less access to defined-benefit pensions. The combination of these two shifts seems to have played a significant role in the recent increase in labor supply of older college-educated women.

As mentioned in the beginning of the chapter, the decline in the fraction of college-educated women who were teachers was driven by an enormous increase in educational attainment of women. Of interest is understanding the relative role of these two shifts—the increase in the fraction of women who were college educated and the decrease in the fraction of college-educated women who were teachers—in determining the increased labor supply of older women. In the appendix, I outline a simple two-period model of older-age female labor supply. Using data reported in this chapter, the model suggests that the decrease in the fraction of college-educated women who were teachers had an impact on the recent labor supply of older women that was less than one-tenth as large as the increase in the fraction of women who were college educated.

That said, evidence in this chapter suggests that there is some scope for the occupational shifts among recent cohorts of women to have played a role in the recent increases in the labor supply of older women. In the context of the model, it is useful to consider how the labor supply of older women would have changed if there had been an increase in the education of women without the corresponding decrease in the fraction of college-educated women who were ever teachers. In this counterfactual, the increase in female labor supply between ages sixty and sixty-four would have been just one-fifth as large as in the setting where the fraction of college-educated women who were ever teachers decreased. In other words, the combination of increased educational attainment and changing occupational choice both played a role in the increases in the labor supply of older women.

Appendix
Two-Period Model of Female Labor Supply

Consider a two-period model of female labor supply for a given cohort. The fraction of women with a college degree in the cohort is α; the fraction of these college-educated women who are teachers is t. Therefore, fraction αt of the cohort are teachers and $\alpha(1 - t)$ are college educated, but not teachers. The share of the cohort that is not college educated is $(1 - \alpha)$.

In period one, all women work. In the second period, some women work and others retire. The fraction of teachers who work in the second period is λ. The fraction of college-educated women who are not teachers and who work in the second period is β. The fraction of the less educated women who work in the second period is γ. Therefore, the fraction of women working in the second period is

$$E_2 = \lambda \alpha t + \beta \alpha (1 - t) + \gamma (1 - \alpha).$$

The change in the fraction working in the second period that results from a change in the fraction who are college educated is

$$\frac{dE_2}{d\alpha} = t(1 - \beta) + \beta - \gamma.$$

The change in the fraction working in the second period that results from a change in the fraction who are teachers is

$$\frac{dE_2}{dt} = \alpha(\lambda - \beta).$$

Table 7A.1   **Parameters of model from early and late cohorts**

	1931–1935	1946–1950
α	0.1	0.3
t	0.45	0.3
λ	0.53	0.59
β	0.55	0.65
γ	0.33	0.47
$\dfrac{dE_2}{d\alpha}$	0.229	0.198
$\dfrac{dE_2}{dt}$	−0.002	−0.018
$\dfrac{dE_2}{d\alpha}$, holding t fixed at 0.45		0.018

Using data from the HRS on the proportion of each group working at older ages (λ, β, γ), the proportion of college educated (α), and the proportion of college educated who are teachers (t), I can estimate the relative importance of changes in α and t. Using information on these parameters from the earliest cohorts, the effect of a change in the fraction of college-educated women who are teachers on employment in the second period is 1 percent as large (in absolute value) as the effect of a change in the fraction of women who are college educated. Using information on the parameters from the more recent cohorts, the former is one-tenth as large as the latter.

References

Brown, Kristine M. 2013. "The Link between Pensions and Retirement Timing: Lessons from California Teachers." *Journal of Public Economics* 98:1–14.

Clark, Robert, Lee Craig, and Jack Wilson. 2003. *History of Public Sector Pensions in the United States*. Philadelphia: University of Pennsylvania Press.

Clark, Robert, and Melinda Morrill. 2010. *Retiree Health Plans in the Public Sector*. Northampton, MA: Edward Elgar Publishing.

Doherty, Kathryn M., Sandi Jacobs, and Trisha M. Madden. 2012. "No One Benefits: How Teacher Pension Systems are Failing BOTH Teachers and Taxpayers." NCTQ Report, National Center for Teacher Quality. http://www.nctq.org /dmsStage/No_One_Benefits_Teacher_Pension_Systems_NCTQ_Report.

Fitzpatrick, Maria D. 2014. "Retiree Health Insurance for Public School Employees: Does It Affect Retirement?" *Journal of Health Economics* 38:88–98.

Fitzpatrick, Maria D., and Timothy Moore. 2016. "The Mortality Effects of Retirement: Evidence from Social Security Eligibility at Age 62." CRR Working Paper no. 2016-7, Center for Retirement Research at Boston College. http://crr.bc.edu

/working-papers/the-mortality-effects-of-retirement-evidence-from-social-secu
rity-eligibility-at-age-62/.
Goldin, Claudia. 1991a. "Marriage Bars: Discrimination against Married Women
Workers from the 1920s to the 1950s." In *Favorites of Fortune: Technology, Growth,
and Economic Development since the Industrial Revolution*, edited by Patrice Higon-
net, David S. Landes, and Henry Rosovsky, 511–36. Cambridge, MA: Harvard
University Press.
————. 1991b. "The Role of World War II in the Rise of Women's Employment."
American Economic Review 81 (4): 741–56.
————. 2006. "The Quiet Revolution That Transformed Women's Employment,
Education, and Family." *American Economic Review, Papers and Proceedings* 96
(2): 1–21.
Goldin, Claudia, and Lawrence F. Katz. 2008. *The Race between Education and
Technology*. Cambridge, MA: Belknap Press.
Gustman, Alan L., Thomas L. Steinmeier, and Nahid Tabatabai. 2010. *Pensions
in the Health and Retirement Study*. Cambridge, MA: Harvard University Press.
Harris, Douglas, and Scott Adams. 2007. "Understanding the Level and Causes of
Teacher Turnover." *Economics of Education Review* 26 (3): 325–37.
Koedel, Cory, Shawn Ni, and Michael Podgursky. 2014. "Who Benefits from Pension
Enhancements?" *Education Finance and Policy* 9 (2): 165–92.
Maestas, Nicole. 2010. "Back to Work: Expectations and Realizations of Work after
Retirement." *Journal of Human Resources* 45 (3): 718–48.
Mahler, L. P. 2014. "Three Essays on Teacher Labor Markets." PhD diss., University
of Virginia.
Stock, James H., and David A. Wise. 1990. "Pensions, the Option Value of Work,
and Retirement." *Econometrica* 58 (5): 1151–80.

The Role of Social Security Benefits in the Initial Increase of Older Women's Employment
Evidence from the Social Security Notch

Alexander Gelber, Adam Isen, and Jae Song

8.1 Introduction

One of the most intriguing phenomena in the US labor market over the past three decades is the striking rise of older women's employment. Current Population Survey (CPS) data in figure 8.1 show that the employment-to-population ratio of women sixty-five and older has more than doubled in less than thirty years, rising from 7.0 percent in 1985 to 14.2 percent in 2013. The large increase is notable in part because it represents a reversal relative to the secular decline in older women's employment rate from 1950 to 1985, from 9.4 percent in 1950 to 7.0 percent in 1985.

To understand the recent trends better, we probe the initial roots of this turnaround in the mid-1980s. Many factors could have contributed to the turnaround, such as compositional changes across birth cohorts including increases in education and prior employment across successively later cohorts of women (Goldin and Katz, chapter 1, this volume), changes in

Alexander Gelber is an assistant professor at the Goldman School of Public Policy at the University of California, Berkeley, and a faculty research fellow of the National Bureau of Economic Research. Adam Isen is an economist in the Office of Tax Analysis at the US Department of the Treasury. Jae Song is an economist in the Division of Economic Research at the Social Security Administration.

We thank Claudia Goldin, Larry Katz, Erzo Luttmer, and other participants in the Women Working Longer working group for helpful comments. We are grateful to Patricia Jonas and Gerald Ray at the Social Security Administration for their help and support. This chapter does not necessarily reflect the views of the Social Security Administration or the US Treasury. We thank the UC Berkeley IRLE, CGIF, CEDA, and Burch Center, NIH (2P30AG012839), and the Wharton Pension Research Council and Trio grant for support. We are grateful to Nicole Danna, Gita DeVaney, Jonathan Holmes, and Harsha Mallajosyula for outstanding research assistance. All errors are our own. For acknowledgments, sources of research support, and disclosure of the authors' material financial relationships, if any, please see http://www.nber.org/chapters/c13802.ack.

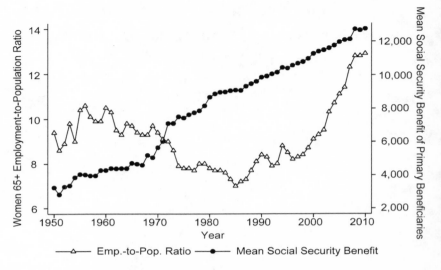

Fig. 8.1   Mean OASI benefits and employment-to-population ratio of older women

Notes: The figure shows the employment-to-population ratio for women sixty-five and older, as well as the mean OASI benefit, by year from 1950 to 2012. The data on the employment-to-population ratio among those sixty-five and older come from the Bureau of Labor Statistics. The data on mean OASI benefit of primary beneficiaries come from Social Security Administration (2013a).

private-pension arrangements like the increase in the 1980s of defined-contribution pensions relative to defined-benefit pensions (see Fitzpatrick, chapter 7, this volume, on defined-benefit pensions among teachers, as well as Munnell, Cahill, and Jivan [2003]), increases in debt (Lusardi and Mitchell, chapter 6, this volume), changes in marriage and divorce (Olivetti and Rotz, chapter 4, this volume), improvements in health, or other factors.[1]

We propose and explore a new partial explanation for the turnaround: Social Security. Social Security Old-Age and Survivors Insurance (OASI) is the single largest US federal program, with $706.8 billion in expenditures in 2014, or roughly 20 percent of federal government spending (Social Security Administration [SSA] 2015). OASI could be an important determinant of older Americans' work decisions, as it is a major source of their income, providing the majority of income for 65 percent of older beneficiaries (SSA 2015). Largely due to the 1977 Social Security Act amendments, OASI benefits and replacement rates grew far less rapidly beginning in the mid-1980s than prior to this time (Clingman, Burkhalter, and Chaplain 2014; Social Security Administration [SSA] 2013a). These changes should push toward older women's employment rates growing more rapidly starting in the mid-1980s, consistent with the evidence in figure 8.1.

---

1. Blau and Goodstein (2010), Gustman and Steinmeier (2009), and Schirle (2008) explore trends among men.

This observation about Social Security generosity serves as a motivation for investigating the microdata to assess the extent to which changes in Social Security played a role, relative to other factors, in explaining the turnaround observed in the time-series data. In particular, we investigate the effects of the Security "Notch" created by the 1977 Social Security Act amendments on the employment decisions of older women. Because of the policy change, individuals born on or after Jan. 2, 1917, faced very different OASI benefits than those born earlier. We exploit this change through a regression discontinuity design (RDD). We find that for women born after this date relative to those born earlier, on average, our measure of mean lifetime discounted real OASI benefits was discontinuously $2,094 lower.[2] The variation we investigate represents the largest discontinuous change in OASI benefits in its history to our knowledge.

Our main finding is that we estimate large effects of OASI on women's employment rate. Around January 2, 1917, we find a statistically significant discontinuous increase in older women's employment rates. We use this relationship to estimate that an increase in lifetime discounted OASI benefits of $10,000 causes a decrease in the percent of years with positive earnings from ages sixty-one to ninety-five of 1.24 percentage points. From ages sixty-two to seventy-five, when beneficiaries experience contemporaneous benefit cuts and have not reached older ages with very low participation rates, this effect is 2.36 percentage points.

We use these results to calculate how much of the turnaround in the mid-1980s in the growth of older women's employment rate can be accounted for by the reduction in the growth rate of OASI benefits. Under our RDD estimates, in a baseline specification we calculate that the reduction in the growth rate over time of OASI benefits around 1985 can account for around 28 percent of the contemporaneous increase in the growth rate of the employment rate of those over sixty-five, relative to the counterfactual that benefit growth continued at the same rate in real dollars per year. For the sixty-five- to sixty-nine-year-old population, an even larger turnaround in the employment rate is observed in the mid-1980s (figure 8.2). We calculate that the decrease in the growth over time of OASI benefits around 1985 can account for around 34 percent of the contemporaneous increase in the growth of the employment rate of sixty-five- to sixty-nine-year-olds.

Our chapter examines only women, whereas the earlier work that innovated the use of the Notch to study economic outcomes, Krueger and Pischke (1992), examines only men.[3] The research complements Gelber,

---

2. All dollar amounts are in real $2012. By "lifetime" we refer to benefits from 1978 to 2012. "Age" in a calendar year refers to the highest age an individual attained during this year.

3. Other literature has examined the effects of the Notch on other outcomes, including older Americans' living arrangements (Engelhardt, Gruber, and Perry 2005), mortality (Snyder and Evans 2006), prescription drug use (Moran and Simon 2006), weight (Cawley, Moran, and Simon 2010), long-term care services (Goda, Golberstein, and Grabowski 2011), and mental health (Golberstein 2015).

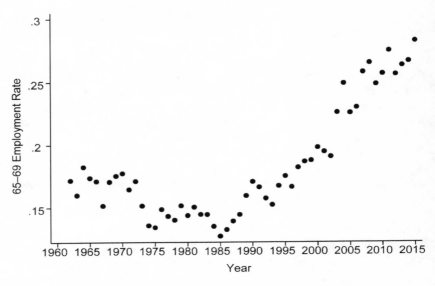

Fig. 8.2   Women's employment-to-population ratio by calendar year, ages sixty-five to sixty-nine

Notes: The figure shows the employment-to-population ratio for women ages sixty-five to sixty-nine by year from 1962 to 2015. The data on the employment-to-population ratio come from the Current Population Survey.

Isen, and Song (2016), who investigate the effects of the Notch in the full population of men and women combined (with only a limited separate analysis of women). More broadly, our chapter is related to other work on the effects of pensions for older individuals and other retirement income on employment decisions (e.g., Behagel and Blau [2012]; Coile and Gruber [2004, 2007]; Costa [1995]; Fetter and Lockwood [2016]; Manoli and Weber, forthcoming; Mastrobuoni [2009]; see Feldstein and Liebman [2002] for a review of earlier literature, and Gruber and Wise [1999] for a broad discussion of relevant evidence).

We proceed as follows: section 8.2 describes the policy change we study. Section 8.3 discusses the data. Section 8.4 estimates the causal effect of the Notch policy on older women's participation, as well as the effect of benefit levels on women's participation. Section 8.5 discusses implications for understanding the time series of older women's participation decisions. Section 8.6 concludes. Throughout much of the chapter, particularly in sections 8.2, 8.3, and part of 8.4, we draw on the description of the policy environment, data, and empirical specification from Gelber, Isen, and Song (2016).[4]

---

4. In some cases the description is nearly identical, which is natural because the policy environment, data, and some of our specifications overlap. Relative to that work, the current

8.2 Policy Environment

Eligible individuals can claim their OASI benefit through their own earnings history beginning at age sixty-two, the early entitlement age (EEA). In the cohorts we study, individuals can claim their full OASI benefit when they reach the normal retirement age (NRA) at sixty-five.

The 1977 amendments changed the way OASI benefits were determined by earnings histories. The primary insurance amount (PIA) forms the basis for the monthly OASI benefit. Prior to 1977, the PIA was a function of the average monthly wage (AMW). The AMW was calculated as an average of a claimant's nominal earnings over their highest-earning years. The 1972 Social Security Act amendments indexed the AMW-to-PIA replacement rate to the CPI. Inflation thereby increased benefits through two routes: AMW was calculated using nominal wages so inflation raised the AMW, and inflation mechanically increased the replacement rate due to the indexation. Since inflation was high in the mid- and late 1970s, this "double indexation" as it was called, led to benefits that increased very quickly, and policymakers saw this as financially unsustainable (GAO 1988).

Double indexation ended with the 1977 amendments. For those born in 1922 and later, PIA has been a function of average indexed monthly earnings (AIME). Like AMW, AIME is calculated as a function of past earnings. However, for calculating AIME, earnings prior to age sixty-two are inflated by the growth in national earnings.

The policy change led to much lower Social Security benefits for those receiving benefits under the AIME formula. To smooth the transition to the AIME formula, policymakers developing the 1977 amendments created a special formula for those born between 1917 and 1921 (inclusive), called the "transitional guarantee." Claimants born between 1917 and 1921 received the maximum of benefits calculated in one of the following ways: (a) under the new formula based on the AIME; or (b) under the old AMW formula with one change relevant for the 1917 cohort: earnings after age sixty-one are not used in calculating average earnings: $AMW = \Sigma_{t \in T \text{ and } t<62} w_t / N$.[5] The second method was called the "transitional guarantee."

Social Security rules in a given birth cohort apply to individuals born January 2 or later in that cohort. For example, the rules affecting what we

---

chapter focuses on women's employment decisions and the implications of these results for understanding the time series of women's employment rate. In the two cases in which results overlap between the two papers, we cite Gelber, Isen, and Song (2016) as the primary source of these estimates.

5. The 1972 Social Security Act amendments indexed the replacement rate within each bracket to the CPI, but the transitional guarantee formula also specified that after December 1978, no such inflation adjustments are made to benefits until the calendar year in which an individual reaches age sixty-two and following years. However, since those in the 1917 cohort reached age sixty-two in 1979 (that is just after December 1978), this provision did not discontinuously affect those in the 1916 and 1917 cohorts. However, this provision did lead to small discontinuities in average benefits at cohort boundaries from 1917/1918 to 1921/1922.

call the "1916 cohort" apply to individuals born January 2, 1916, through January 1, 1917 (inclusive). We use the term "cohort boundary" to refer to the boundary between the cohorts defined in this manner.

In the 1916 cohort, everyone was covered by the AMW formula, whereas in the 1917 birth cohort, a larger fraction was covered by the transitional guarantee than by the AIME formula (McKay and Schobel 1981).[6] As a result, those born on January 2, 1917, or after faced a substantially different OASI benefit structure than those born January 1, 1917, or earlier.

The policy change could create both income and substitution effects on participation. Because earnings after age sixty-one were not taken into account in calculating the AMW for those covered under the transitional guarantee, and because the OASI rules guarantee that earnings after age sixty-one can only cause an increase—but cannot cause a decrease—in an individual's PIA, the AMW of someone in the 1916 cohort whose earnings after age sixty-one were in their highest-earning years would be higher than the AMW of an individual with the same earnings history in the 1917 cohort. The average benefits for those in the 1917 cohort relative to those in the 1916 cohort were in consequence substantially lower. Under the typical presumption that leisure is a normal good, the income effect of this decrease in benefits should have led to an increase in average participation at the cohort boundary.[7] These cuts in benefits were widely publicized, including in a famous "Dear Abby" column on the discrepancies in benefits for similar individuals (GAO 1988).

There was also a change in substitution incentives at the cohort boundary. Because earnings after age sixty-one were not taken into account in calculating the AMW under the transitional guarantee, the net marginal returns to additional earnings after age sixty-one fell at the boundary. In other words, additional earnings after age sixty-one often raised (and never lowered) AMW and therefore OASI benefits in the 1916 cohort, but had no effect on OASI benefits for those receiving the transitional guarantee in the 1917 cohorts. The returns to extra earnings in the 1916 cohort were very large, as average marginal replacement rates were very large, in part because the 1972 amendments caused them to grow quickly. An increase in earnings in a given year led to a modest change in future OASI benefits received in each year; discounted over the course of the years an average individual collected OASI benefits, however, this typically cumulated to a large net incentive to earn more in any given year. By contrast, in the 1917 cohort, earning an extra dollar had at most a small average effect on lifetime Social Security benefits. For individuals subject to the actuarial adjustment or delayed retirement credit (DRC) (as they interact with the earnings test), a change in earnings

6. A very small percentage was covered by other methods, the 1977 Old Start Method or the Regular Minimum (McKay and Schobel 1981).

7. When we say that a variable (e.g., benefits) increased (decreased) at the cohort boundary, we mean that the variable increased (decreased) when moving from the end of the 1916 cohort to the beginning of the 1917 cohort.

in a given year could affect lifetime OASI benefits under the transitional guarantee, but on average such an effect is small in our data. Indeed, we calculate that the net lifetime return to additional pretax, pretransfer earnings in 1979 fell by 12 percent at the cohort boundary for women. The elasticity of participation with respect to the substitution incentive should be positive, so this substitution incentive should have led to lower participation in the 1917 cohort than the 1916 cohort (all else equal).

Thus, the net effect of the Notch on participation at the cohort boundary is ambiguous. Ceteris paribus the income effect should cause a rise in participation at the boundary, whereas ceteris paribus the substitution effect should cause a fall in participation at the boundary.

The 1977 amendments were signed into law on December 20, 1977. The legislative history shows that the discontinuity between benefits in the 1916 and 1917 cohorts could not have been anticipated with confidence until 1977 (GAO 1988). Because of this history, we assume that the policy discontinuity from the 1977 amendments would not yet have had a discontinuous effect on participation around the boundary in 1976 and earlier years; we treat 1978 and later as years when the policy discontinuity could have had an effect on participation, and we exclude 1977 from most of our analysis as expectations in this year are unclear.[8]

8.3   Data

We obtained administrative data on the full US female population from the Social Security Master Earnings File and Master Beneficiary Record for birth cohorts 1916 through 1923. The data have information on exact date of birth, OASI benefits paid in the last year an individual received benefits, exact date of death, month and year of initially claiming OASI, gender, race, and annual earnings in each year separately from 1951 to 2012. All of these data come from W-2 forms, mandatory information returns filed with the Internal Revenue Service (IRS) by employers for each employee for whom the firm withholds taxes and/or to whom remuneration exceeds a modest threshold. Thus, we have data on earnings regardless of whether an employee files taxes. Using information on Social Security rules from Social Security Annual Supplements—for example, benefit schedules of PIA as a function of AIME or AMW, cost-of-living adjustments, special minimum benefits, spousal benefit rules, the actuarial adjustment, the DRC, the earnings test

---

8. Because the transitional guarantee formula specified that after December 1978 no inflation adjustments were to be made to benefits until the calendar year in which an individual reaches age sixty-two, the 1977 amendments also created small discontinuities in benefits at the 1917/1918, 1918/1919, 1919/1920, 1920/1921, and 1921/1922 cohort boundaries (GAO 1988). Because these benefit discontinuities are much smaller than the 1916/1917 discontinuity, we expect to have less statistical power in these contexts, and we primarily focus on the 1916/1917 boundary. Indeed, even when pooling results from the other boundaries, we estimate insignificant results.

(and its interaction with the actuarial adjustment and DRC), and so forth—we calculated an approximate measure of OASI benefits on the basis of earnings, claiming histories, and spousal benefit rules.[9]

Our data allow us to calculate a measure of pretax OASI benefits; this makes a negligible difference to the results relative to measuring after-tax benefits, because OASI benefits only became taxable in 1984, when the vast majority of individuals in the 1916/1917 cohorts had low enough income that their Social Security benefits were not taxable. By examining pretax benefits, we answer the policy-relevant question of how a given cut in benefits paid by SSA would affect participation.

Our measure of earnings excludes self-employment income, as this can often be subject to manipulation (Chetty, Friedman, and Saez 2013). We remove from the data those who received disability insurance (DI) or OASI benefits before our period of interest begins in 1977, or who died before 1977. We include all other individuals (including those who collect benefits as retired workers, auxiliary beneficiaries, or survivors). Starting in the calendar year after an individual dies, until the final year in the data set (2012), benefits and earnings appear in the data as zeroes.

When one spouse earns less than the other, under the OASI rules, the lower-earning spouse in total receives the maximum of either: (a) the benefit to which they are entitled on their own record, or (b) one-half the benefit due to the higher earner (either because they collect this amount as a "secondary" beneficiary, or because they are "dual entitled" and their own benefit plus their spousal benefit equals this amount). Wives typically earn less than their husbands in these cohorts, and 60 percent of women in our sample collected benefits as a secondary or dual beneficiary. Thus, for wives who are secondary or dual-entitled beneficiaries, their total OASI benefit is constant (all else equal) regardless of which side of the discontinuity their own date of birth (DOB) lies on, because their total benefit received depends only on their husband's DOB.[10] For the higher earner (specifically non-dual-entitled primary beneficiaries), OASI benefits are discontinuous at the cohort boundary in their own DOB. Thus, our estimated effects for married women are local to a population with particularly high lifetime earnings relative to their husbands.

Due to the nature of the data, we cannot consistently estimate a wife's response to a husband's OASI benefit. We only observe wives linked to their husbands when one spouse is collecting as a dual or secondary beneficiary. Whether one is a dual or secondary beneficiary is endogenous to the size of the husband's and wife's separate benefits.

For illustrative purposes, in those cases in which we discount, in the base-

---

9. We lack population data on earnings or quarters of coverage before 1951, necessitating imputation. Claiming as primary is endogenous to the spouse's benefits, so we impute average benefits for nonprimary women based on halving men's benefits.

10. This assumes that the OASI benefit based on a wife's own earnings history does not exceed one-half the benefit of the primary earner, when the wife is born both in 1916 and in 1917.

Table 8.1   **Summary statistics: Mean (standard deviation) of main variables**

Variable	Mean (SD)
Discounted earnings, 1978 to 2012	$53,131.83
	(2,372.61)
Percent of years with positive earnings, 1978 to 2012	9.70
	(0.33)
Discounted OASI benefits, 1978 to 2012	$85,144.80
	(1,548.97)
Number of individuals per day of birth	1,906.77
	(258.86)

Notes: The source is SSA administrative data from the Master Earnings File and Master Beneficiary Record on the universe of US data on women, with the other sample restrictions described in the text. The table shows means and standard deviations of the main variables in our sample. We report the means and standard deviations of the means of variables by DOB, rather than reporting the mean and standard deviation in the individual-level SSA data, since we use the DOB-mean-level variables in our primary regression analysis. The sample consists of those born within 100 days of January 2, 1917. The means and standard deviations shown above are based on 200 observations in each case. Starting in the calendar year after an individual dies, their earnings and benefits are set to zero prior to averaging by DOB. All earnings amounts are expressed in real 2012 dollars. The number of individuals per day refers to the number of individuals per day of birth who are alive in 1978. This corresponds to 381,354 individuals within 100 days of the cohort boundary, or 13,347,390 individual-year observations from 1978 to 2012 (inclusive).

line benefits are discounted at a 3 percent real interest rate (the average real ten-year Treasury rate over 1978 to 2012, rounded to the nearest percent). We discount to 1977 terms and then express discounted benefits in real 2012 dollars.

Table 8.1 shows summary statistics. We use data from 384,354 individuals born within 100 days of the cohort boundary from 1978 to 2012, corresponding to 13,347,390 individual-year observations. After averaging by DOB, we have 200 observations on each of our main outcomes. Mean discounted earnings from 1978 to 2012 are $53,132; 9.7 percent of the sample has positive earnings in any given year from 1978 to 2012. Mean discounted benefits from 1978 to 2012 are $85,144.80. Each DOB on average has 1,907 observations; this is smaller than counts for the full US female population due to our sample restrictions.

8.4   Effects of Notch on Participation

As a first empirical step, we document the causal effects of the Notch policy. Next, we use these results to estimate an income effect of OASI on older women's participation.

8.4.1   Basic Empirical Strategy for Documenting Effect of Notch

To estimate the effect of the Notch policy, we use an RDD as in Gelber, Isen, and Song (2016), exploiting the discontinuous relationship between

DOB and OASI benefits at the cohort boundary, relative to the assumed smooth relationship between DOB and average participation that would exist in the absence of the discontinuous change in OASI benefits (see Imbens and Lemieux [2008] and Lee and Lemieux [2010] for surveys of RDD methods). Thus, our evidence will effectively document whether we see a sharp change in participation at the cohort boundary.

Specifically, we estimate this regression:

(1) $$E_j = \beta_1 D_j + \beta_2 \text{DOB}_j + \beta_3 (D \times \text{DOB})_j + \varepsilon_j.$$

Here j indexes DOB; E represents an outcome of interest (primarily the percent of years with positive earnings, which we call "participation"); D is a dummy for DOBs on or after January 2, 1917; DOB is a linear trend in day of birth; and ($D \times \text{DOB}$) is an interaction between D and DOB. Allowing for different slopes on either side of the boundary makes little difference to our results, relative to constraining the slope to be equal on both sides. The main coefficient of interest is β_1, representing the change in the mean level of participation at the cohort boundary. We interpret this as the average treatment effect of the Notch policy, estimated among those at the boundary. We use robust standard errors throughout the chapter.

Of course, many other factors could have affected participation in our sample, such as private pension amounts, health (including the effects of the pandemic flu of 1918), and macroeconomic factors. The RDD identification assumption is that such factors would have affected participation smoothly in date of birth, as opposed to the sharp change in benefits experienced by those in the 1917 cohort relative to those in the 1916 cohort. Similarly, the 1978 and 1986 amendments to the Age Discrimination in Employment Act (ADEA) extended the ages at which age discrimination in employment was prohibited, which could have increased older Americans' work (Burkhauser and Quinn 1983). However, neither of these changes to the ADEA has a discontinuous effect on older Americans' work incentives around the 1916/1917 cohort boundary and therefore should not confound our identification strategy. It is important to use our fine-grained data by DOB, as more aggregate data could be confounded by other factors that led to smooth trends in outcomes over the course of the calendar year (Buckles and Hungerman 2013).

We use data aggregated to the day-of-birth level—rather than at the individual level—to estimate standard errors that are likely to be "conservative" (Angrist and Pischke 2008), given the possibility of positively correlated shocks to individuals at the DOB level. We weight the regression by the number of nonmissing observations on each day of birth.

We use the procedure of Calonico, Cattaneo, and Titiunik (2014; hereafter CCT) to select the bandwidth. For our main outcome—the percent of years from 1978 to 2012 with positive earnings—CCT selects a bandwidth of sixty-two days. To hold the sample constant across specifications, in our main results we use this bandwidth throughout.

We call (1) a "linear" specification because we control for a linear function of DOB on both sides of the boundary. This specification without additional controls minimizes the Akaike Information Criterion (AIC) and Bayes Information Criterion (BIC).

We were able to obtain one additional predetermined variable in the SSA data, race. In some specifications we additionally control for the means of a dummy for being nonwhite by DOB.

We interpret the discontinuity in earnings at the cohort boundary as reflecting movements in an earnings supply curve (in the case of income effects) or movements along an earnings supply curve (in the case of substitution effects)—not changes in demand by firms, since such changes should have been materially similar on either side of the boundary as should any general equilibrium effects of the policy change more broadly. We interpret our measured effects as reflecting responses net of any adjustment frictions such as lack of awareness. Even without being explicitly aware of a policy discontinuity at the cohort boundary, we could observe a response because beneficiaries are reacting, for example, to the amount of OASI payments they are receiving, or to their total income, both of which could be more salient.

It will also be useful to compare the discontinuity β_1 in an outcome at the cohort boundary to the discontinuity in discounted real OASI benefits. We define mean lifetime discounted OASI benefits B_{jPDV} as as $B_{jPDV} \equiv \Sigma_{i \in I} \Sigma_{t=t_0}^{T} B_{ijt}/n$, where $t_0 = 1978$ and $T = 2012$ in our empirical application, the subscript j indicates that we have taken the mean on DOB j across all individuals i, and I reflects the full set of individuals in the sample. We can then run a regression of B_{jPDV} on the covariates:

$$(2) \qquad B_{jPDV} = \gamma_1 D_j + \gamma_2 \mathrm{DOB}_j + \gamma_3 (D \times \mathrm{DOB})_j + v_j.$$

8.4.2 Validating the Regression Discontinuity Design

Our figures show the means of outcome variables averaged by ten-day bins of DOB around the cohort boundary. We show seven bins on either side of the boundary to display at a minimum the variation within the CCT bandwidth of sixty-two days of the boundary.

Figure 8.3 shows that the number of observations appears continuous at the boundary (following McCrary 2008). Table 8.2 confirms that there is no significant discontinuity. Table 8.2 and figure 8.4 show that the proportion male (in the combined male and female population) and the proportion white are also smooth through the boundary.

Figure 8.5 verifies that discounted OASI benefits from 1978 to 2012 ("lifetime benefits") decrease discontinuously and quite substantially when crossing the cohort boundary. Table 8.3, row A, shows that in the baseline specification, lifetime benefits fall discontinuously by $2,094.

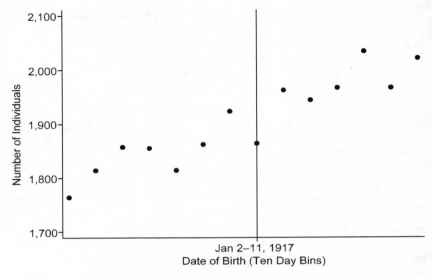

Jan 2–11, 1917
Date of Birth (Ten Day Bins)

Fig. 8.3 Number of observations by DOB bin

Notes: The figure shows the mean number of observations per DOB in ten-day bins around the boundary separating the 1916 birth cohort from the 1917 birth cohort (i.e., January 2, 1917). The data are a 100 percent sample of women from the Social Security Administration Master Earnings File and Master Beneficiary Record, with the sample restrictions described in the text.

Table 8.2   **Testing smoothness of predetermined variables**

Specification	(1) Percent white	(2) Percent male	(3) Number of observations
Coefficient (SE) on Jan. 2, 1917	0.34	−0.17	−47.55
Dummy (linear)	(0.61)	(0.28)	(81.45)

Notes: The table demonstrates the smoothness of predetermined variables around the 1916/1917 cohort boundary. The table shows the results of OLS regressions corresponding to model (1) in the text, where the dependent variable is shown in the column heading. We show a specification in which the control for the running variable (i.e., DOB) is a linear function (allowing for a change in slope at January 2, 1917). We use robust standard errors in table 8.2 and throughout the other tables. We show the results for the bandwidth of sixty-two, chosen using the CCT procedure when the outcome is our primary outcome (percent of years with positive earnings from 1978 to 2012), to hold the sample constant across regressions. Thus, all regressions have 124 observations. Percent male by DOB is calculated from the combined male and female population. None of the estimated coefficients is significant at a standard significance level. (See other notes to table 8.1.)

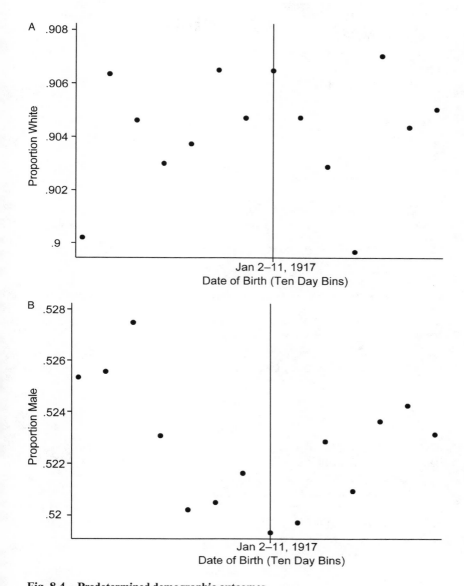

Fig. 8.4   Predetermined demographic outcomes
Notes: See notes to figure 8.3. In panel (B) the dependent variable is the fraction male in the full population of both men and women.

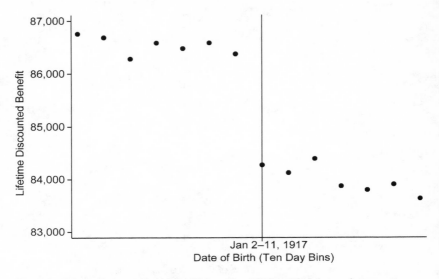

Fig. 8.5   Mean discounted real OASI benefits, 1978 to 2012 (ages sixty-one to ninety-five)

Notes: The figure shows individuals' mean discounted OASI benefits from 1978 to 2012, in ten-day bins around the discontinuity separating the 1916 birth cohort from the 1917 birth cohort. We discount to 1977 terms and then express all dollar amounts in real 2012 dollars. For illustrative purposes we use a 3 percent real discount rate. The 1917 birth cohort reaches ages sixty-one to ninety-five during the calendar years 1978 to 2012, respectively. (See other notes to figure 8.3.)

8.4.3   Discontinuities in Participation Rates at the Cohort Boundary

Our main outcome of interest for understanding the impacts of OASI benefits on women's employment patterns is the "participation rate," defined as the percent of individual-calendar year observations from 1978 to 2012 with positive earnings by DOB. Figure 8.6 shows a main result: at the cohort boundary, we observe a sharp increase in the participation rate from 1978 to 2012. Table 8.3 shows that in the baseline the participation rate increases by 0.26 percentage points at the boundary ($p < 0.05$). For ages sixty-five and over, which we will use to analyze the changes in older women's employment over the twentieth century, we find an increase of 0.25 percentage points at the boundary ($p < 0.01$). Beneficiaries first begin to experience contemporaneous cuts in benefits at age sixty-two, and mean participation rates reach very low levels after age seventy-five; from ages sixty-two to seventy-five, we find a larger increase at the boundary of 0.47 percentage points.

To illustrate how the effects vary across ages, in figure 8.7 we show the coefficient and confidence interval on β_1 from model (1) when the dependent variable is the percent of years from 1978 to 2012 with positive earnings by DOB in each three-year time period t, and we run the regression separately

Table 8.3　　　　　　**Effect of Notch on benefits and participation**

Outcome	(1) Linear	(2) Linear
(A) Discounted benefits 1978 to 2012	−2,093.66	−2,122.61
	(268.14)***	(272.26)***
(B) Percent years with positive earnings 1978 to 2012	0.26	0.26
	(0.12)**	(0.12)**
(C) Log odds of fraction years with positive earnings 1978 to 2012	0.030	0.030
	(0.014)**	(0.014)**
(D) Percent years with positive earnings 1982 to 2012	0.25	0.25
	(0.089)***	(0.091)***
(E) Percent years with positive earnings 1979 to 1992	0.47	0.48
	(0.22)**	(0.23)**
Controls?	N	Y

Notes: The table shows the results of OLS regressions corresponding to the RDD model (2) (row A) or model (1) (rows B and C) described in the text estimating the effect of the Notch on outcomes, in which each outcome is regressed on a dummy for being covered by the Notch policy (i.e., being born on or after January 2, 1917), as well as a linear spline in DOB with a knot at the cohort boundary. The "controls" columns show the regressions with additional controls for percent white and percent male by DOB. In all cases, the specification that minimizes the Akaike Information Criterion (AIC) and Bayes Information Criterion (BIC) is the linear specification without controls. (See other notes to table 8.2.)
***Significant at the 1 percent level.
**Significant at the 5 percent level.
*Significant at the 10 percent level.

for each t. The figure shows that the Notch has an insignificant effect on participation shortly after the policy went into effect, in 1978–1980. The effects of the Notch on participation are largest in the 1980s and early 1990s when individuals are sixty-four to seventy-five years old. The effects decline to insignificant in 1993 and after, corresponding to ages seventy-six and older for the 1917 cohort, when individuals typically have low participation rates (in all cohorts).

We can run a number of placebo tests that help establish that the discontinuity in participation was due to the causal effect of the Notch. First, figure 8.7 shows that the discontinuity in participation does not appear in our sample before the policy change could have been anticipated.

Second, in table 8.4 we show that no systematic discontinuity in participation occurs at thresholds between other birth cohorts that were not subject to a discontinuous change in Social Security benefits. If some individuals retire exactly on their birthday, a discontinuity in our measure of participation would be observed if people then receive positive earnings in an extra calendar year. However, the placebo tests in table 8.4 help rule out this scenario. We were able to obtain W-2 wage earnings data from IRS on the full US population from 1999 to 2013 on all cohort boundaries from 1923/1924 to 1936/1937. Among these boundaries, seven—1923/1924, 1925/1926, 1927/1928, 1929/1930, 1931/1932, 1933/1934, and 1935/1936—

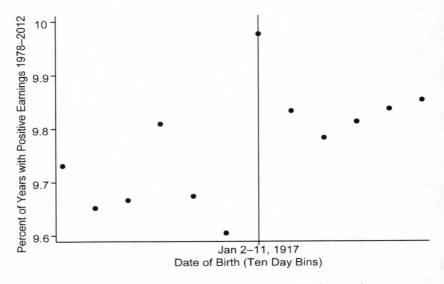

Fig. 8.6 Percent of years with positive earnings, 1978 to 2012 (ages sixty-one to ninety-five)

Notes: The figure shows results when the outcome of interest is the percent of years from 1978 to 2012 in which individuals have positive yearly earnings. (See other notes to figure 8.3.)

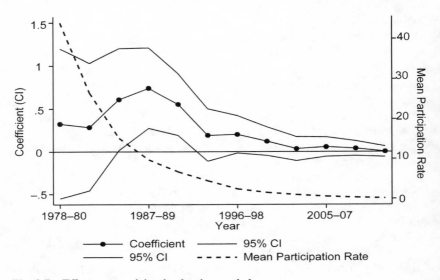

Fig. 8.7 Effects on participation by time period

Notes: The figure shows the discontinuity at the boundary in mean participation by three-year periods. It illustrates that the effects of the Notch on participation are largest in the 1980s and early 1990s when individuals are sixty-four to seventy-five years old, and decline to insignificant at later ages. Specifically, the y-axis (circles, left-hand scale) shows the point estimate of β_1 and its associated confidence interval from model (1) when we run it separately in each three-year time period t and the dependent variable is the mean percent of years with positive earnings (left axis). For context, we also show the mean participation rate in each three-year period (dotted line, right-hand scale). The x-axis shows the time period in question.

Table 8.4	Discontinuity in earnings and participation at placebo boundaries and the 1916/1917 boundary	
Age range (cohort boundary)	(1) SSA data, % of years with earnings > 0, 1916/17 boundary	(2) IRS data, % of years with earnings > 0, 1999–2013
(A) 75 to 89	0.20	0.081
(1923/1924)	(0.095)**	(0.062)
(B) 73 to 87	0.29	0.13
(1925/1926)	(0.11)**	(0.079)*
(C) 71 to 85	0.29	0.041
(1927/1928)	(0.11)***	(0.13)
(D) 69 to 83	0.38	−0.14
(1929/1930)	(0.13)***	(0.16)
(E) 67 to 81	0.42	−0.35
(1931/1932)	(0.15)***	(0.20)*
(F) 65 to 79	0.45	0.16
(1933/1934)	(0.17)**	(0.24)
(G) 63 to 77	0.46	−0.43
(1935/1936)	(0.20)**	(0.30)

Notes: The table shows using a 100 percent population sample from SSA and IRS data that a strong discontinuity in earnings only regularly shows up around the 1916/1917 boundary, not around placebo boundaries that do not have OASI policy discontinuities. In particular, we were able to obtain a 100 percent sample of IRS W-2 wage earnings data from 1999 to 2013 on all fourteen cohort boundaries from 1923/1924 to 1936/1937. Among these boundaries, seven—1923/1924, 1925/1926, 1927/1928, 1929/1930, 1931/1932, 1933/1934, and 1935/1936— have no associated discontinuity in the delayed retirement credit or another OASI policy, so we investigate these boundaries as placebos. These cohorts are observed in the IRS data over a subset of the ages that we observe the 1916/1917 cohorts when using in the SSA data: in the IRS data we observe ages seventy-six to ninety for the 1923 cohort, ages seventy-five to eighty-nine for the 1924 cohort, and so forth. To make an apples-to-apples comparison between the IRS data and the SSA data, we investigate the discontinuity in discounted real earnings in the SSA data over the same ages. Table 8.4 shows that over each of these sets of ages, we find highly significant discontinuities in discounted earnings and participation at the 1916/1917 boundary in the SSA data, but at the 5 percent level we do not find significant discontinuities in the IRS data. For a given cohort boundary, the age range reported refers to the highest age attained in a given calendar year of data for the *younger* cohort around the boundary; for example, "ages seventy-five to eighty-nine" refers to the fact that around the 1923/1924 boundary, those born in 1924 attained ages seventy-five to eighty-nine in 1999 to 2013, respectively. It makes sense that the standard errors are larger on the estimates for cohorts in the IRS data than those in the SSA data for 1916/1917 over the comparable set of ages; the means and standard deviations of earnings are larger in the IRS data due to the secular trend of increasing participation and earnings among older Americans across cohorts from 1917 to 1937 (see Gelber, Isen, and Song 2016). (See other notes to table 8.3.)

***Significant at the 1 percent level.

**Significant at the 5 percent level.

*Significant at the 10 percent level.

have no discontinuity in the DRC or another policy. Because the IRS data cover 1999 to 2013, these cohorts are observed in the IRS data over a subset of the ages we observe for the 1916/1917 boundary in the SSA data: in the IRS data we observe ages seventy-six to ninety for the 1923 cohort, ages seventy-five to eighty-nine for the 1924 cohort, and so forth. To make an apples-to-apples comparison between the IRS data and the SSA data, we investigate the discontinuity in discounted real earnings in the SSA data over the same ages, using the same sample restrictions as the SSA data. For comparability we also cap IRS W-2 earnings at the maximum taxable income level in each year.

Table 8.4 shows highly significant discontinuities in discounted earnings and participation at the 1916/1917 boundary in the SSA data over the same sets of ages we observe in the IRS data, but at the 5 percent significance level we do not find significant discontinuities in the IRS data around any of the seven boundaries.[11] When pooling all seven boundaries in the IRS data and defining a dummy for being born after January 1 around any of the boundaries, the coefficient on this dummy in the resulting pooled regression is insignificant ($p = 0.51$).[12] Moreover, the discontinuities in the SSA data for the 1916/1917 boundary in these age ranges are jointly significantly different from those in the IRS data at the 1 percent level and always show larger point estimates.[13]

Furthermore, we have tried limiting the sample to those born January 1, 1917, or up to sixty-two days prior and test whether those born January 1, 1917, show significantly different participation relative to a smooth linear trend over previous birthdays. Those born on this date faced the incentives of the 1916 birth cohort, but if they retired on their birthday, we should find that they have significantly higher participation. In fact, those born on this date have insignificantly *lower* participation than those born on previous days, suggesting that this factor does not drive the results, and we rule out more than a small positive change in participation on this date. The effect of the Notch on a dummy for earnings above a small positive threshold, such as $1,000, shows similar results to table 8.3.

8.4.4   Estimating an Income Effect

The fact that participation increases at the boundary means that the income effect must dominate the substitution effect in our context. Because, ceteris paribus, the substitution effect should unambiguously push participa-

---

11. Two of the coefficients are significant at the 10 percent level, but they are of opposite signs (one is positive while the other is negative).

12. In these regressions we cluster the standard error by DOB relative to the cohort boundary, though the results are also insignificant if we do not cluster.

13. It does not make sense to investigate the 1916/1917 boundary in the IRS data, since in the SSA data the effect on earnings and participation at this boundary turns insignificant by the 1999 to 2013 period covered by the IRS data (figure 8.7).

tion to fall at the boundary beginning in 1979, we can estimate a lower bound on the income effect by running a two-stage least squares (2SLS) regression in which we use the notch dummy to instrument for benefits. These estimates will be a lower bound as long as the substitution effect is (weakly) positive, a core presumption of standard theory. By a "lower bound" on the income effect, we refer to a lower bound on the *absolute value* of the income effect (which is itself negative when leisure is a normal good).

Under these assumptions, we can estimate a lower bound on the income effect of OASI benefits on participation through a 2SLS model in which equation (2) is the first stage, and the second stage is

(3) $\qquad E_j = \alpha_1 B_j + \alpha_2 DOB_j + \alpha_3 (D \times DOB)_j + \eta_j.$

We interpret α_1 as a lower bound on the local average treatment effect of discounted OASI benefits on participation, where this is local to those at the boundary.

Table 8.5 shows the 2SLS estimates. In the baseline specification in column (1), we find that a \$10,000 increase in lifetime discounted benefits causes a decrease of 1.24 percentage points in the mean yearly participation probability from 1978 to 2012 (recapitulating the estimates in Gelber, Isen, and Song [2016]). Evaluating elasticities at the means of the relevant variables, these estimates imply an elasticity of the participation rate with respect to lifetime-discounted benefits of -1.36. From ages sixty-two to seventy-five, a \$10,000 increase in lifetime-discounted benefits causes the

Table 8.5   Lower-bound income effect of discounted lifetime benefits on participation

	(1) Percent of years with pos. earnings 1978 to 2012	(2) Percent of years with pos. earnings 1978 to 2012	(3) Percent of years with pos. earnings 1979 to 1992	(4) Percent of years with pos. earnings 1979 to 1992
	−1.24	−1.23	2.36	2.54
	(0.59)***	(0.58)***	(0.78)***	(0.84)***
Controls?	N	Y	N	Y

Notes: The table shows the results of two-stage least squares regressions corresponding to regressions (2) and (3) in the text, estimating the effect of discounted lifetime OASI benefits on the percent of years with positive earnings from a linear probability model. The excluded instrument is the dummy for being in the 1917 cohort. The dependent variable is the percent of years with positive earnings from 1978 to 2012. For ease of interpretation, for the participation specification, the coefficient and standard error have been multiplied by 1,000,000 so that the quoted coefficients reflect the percentage point effect on participation of a \$10,000 increase in discounted lifetime OASI benefits (which, for reference, is 4.77 times larger than the actual discontinuity in discounted OASI benefits). We use the baseline linear specification of the running variable. As discussed in the main text, we interpret the results as estimates of lower bounds on the income effect in the context of a life cycle model. (See other notes to table 8.3.)

***Significant at the 1 percent level.

**Significant at the 5 percent level.

*Significant at the 10 percent level.

Table 8.6   Heterogeneity analysis

	(1) Below-median pre-1977 earnings	(2) Above-median pre-1977 earnings
Coefficient	−0.27 (0.60)	−2.38 (0.89)***

Notes: The table shows the results of two-stage least squares regressions corresponding to regressions (2) and (3) in the text, estimating the effect of discounted lifetime OASI benefits on the percent of years with positive earnings from 1978 to 2012. The dependent variable is the percent of years with positive earnings from 1978 to 2012 in the group shown in the column heading. Columns (1) and (2) show the results for those with mean real earnings in years prior to 1977 that are below and above the median, respectively. We use the baseline linear specification of the running variable. The results are similar when calculating separate optimal bandwidths for each group.
***Significant at the 1 percent level.
**Significant at the 5 percent level.
*Significant at the 10 percent level.

yearly participation probability to decrease by 2.36 percentage points. As we show and discuss in greater detail in Gelber, Isen, and Song (2016), when we investigate the income effect on earnings among women, we find that a one-dollar increase in OASI benefits leads to a decrease in discounted real earnings from 1978 to 2012 of eighty-nine cents (standard error forty-three cents), using a discount rate of 3 percent.

Different groups could show different-sized effects. Table 8.6 estimates the effects among those with average earnings prior to 1977 (from 1951 to 1976) that are below as opposed to above the median for the full population. The point estimate is larger in the above-median prior earnings group than in the below-median group, and the estimate is insignificant in the low prior earnings group. Relative to the above-median group, the below-median group is much more likely to receive one-half of a husband's benefit and therefore has a much smaller first-stage regression, so it is not surprising to estimate insignificant effects in the below-median group. Indeed, the graph of participation by DOB for the high lifetime income group shows a much clearer visual discontinuity in mean participation from 1978 to 2012 (figure 8.8). Given the larger first stage in this sample, as robustness checks it also makes sense to show that in this above-median sample: (a) in a wider range of DOBs, the discontinuity at the cohort boundary is unusual given the variation elsewhere in the range of DOBs (appendix figure 8A.1); and (b) when we use three-day bins of DOB, there is naturally more noise in each bin, but there still appears to be a clear shift upward in the level of the dependent variable—that is not a continuation of the trend on either side of the cohort boundary—from below to above the boundary (appendix figure 8A.2).

In most parameterizations of this life cycle model, the effect on the annual

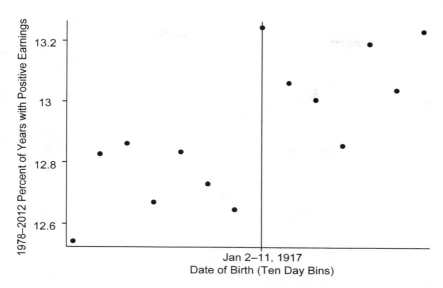

Fig. 8.8   Percent of years with positive earnings, 1978 to 2012 (ages sixty-one to ninety-five), above-median average prior earnings

Notes: The figure shows results when the outcome of interest is the percent of years from 1978 to 2012 in which individuals have positive yearly earnings among the group with above-median earnings prior to 1977. (See other notes to figure 8.3.)

participation rate should be larger when an unanticipated cut in benefits occurs closer to retirement rather than earlier in life (Imbens, Rubin, and Sacerdote 2001; Mastrobuoni 2009). The intuition is that when a change in benefits is anticipated further in advance, in most parameterizations the consumer can react by changing consumption over a longer period rather than changing earnings as much. When an unanticipated change in benefits occurs close to retirement, the individual has less time to alter consumption, and therefore adjusts participation more. In this light, our results would be most similar to evaluating the effects of unanticipated cuts in benefits that occur close to retirement age. Our estimates are most pertinent to contexts with an unanticipated change in OASI benefits experienced close to retirement age, relevant to policymakers interested in the effects of such changes along the transition path to a new steady-state OASI system.

In Gelber, Isen, and Song (2016) we find no evidence for a substitution effect of the policy change, by examining closely comparable years with sharply different substitution effects due to the policy change. Moreover, we estimate that the upper bound on the substitution elasticity is at most small. Thus, the lower bound on the income effect we estimate here can be considered tantamount to a point estimate of the income effect.

Gelber, Isen, and Song (2016) also show that the point estimates of the income effect on participation among women are around twice as large as those for men—consistent with the typical finding that women's labor supply is more elastic than men's, perhaps due to women's weaker historical attachment to the labor force. At the same time, the estimates are less statistically significant among women than among men: among men, the estimates are significant at the 1 percent level, but they are significant only at 5 percent among women. (The estimates are insignificantly different across the genders.) The finding of larger but less significant estimates among women may occur because the first-stage change in women's average benefits is smaller than men's—in part because many women's total benefits do not depend on their own DOB—thus driving a weaker and less statistically robust discontinuity in earnings in the reduced-form regression (1). The estimates among men and women combined are likewise more significant and robust, and a bit less than half as large, than among women alone.

8.5   Implications for the Time Series

8.5.1   Basic Calculations

Using these results, we can perform a simple calculation of the fraction of the change in the growth rate of the employment rate in the mid-1980s that can be accounted for with the reduction in the growth rate of OASI benefit levels. The timing of the turnaround in the mid-1980s matches well with the years when we find the biggest effects on participation—1981 to 1989. The mid-1980s occur several years after when the Notch legislation occurred (1977), but the 1917 cohort reached age sixty-five and thus became included in the older group shown in figures 8.1 and 8.2 only in 1982.

In a life cycle model, only unanticipated changes in benefits should have mattered to employment decisions through the income effect. Since the growth in benefits due to double indexation was in fact unanticipated, as were the cutbacks in the 1977 amendments, this is applicable in our setting.

From 1973 to 1984 the employment-to-population ratio among those age sixty-five and older decreased by 0.059 percentage points per year on average, whereas it rose by 0.22 percentage points per year on average from 1985 to 2010. Meanwhile, from 1973 to 1984 women's mean real annual OASI benefit rose by $191.35 per year on average, but due largely to the 1977 amendments it rose less quickly on average from 1985 to 2010, by only $148.02 per year (Social Security Administration 2013a). Discounted over the average of twenty years over which women collect OASI benefits after claiming in our data, this implies moving from an increase in discounted lifetime benefits from $2,932.21 per year (where $2,932.21 is the presented discounted value of annual payments of $191.35 for twenty years, using a 3 percent discount rate) to $2,268.23 per year (the presented discounted value of annual payments of $148.02 for twenty years). We estimate an effect of the Notch on the annual female participation rate from 1982 to 2012 of

0.25 percentage points, and in table 8.3 we find a discontinuity in lifetime-discounted benefits from the Notch of −$2,093.66.

To calculate the fraction of the post-1985 employment rate turnaround that can be accounted for with the slowdown in OASI benefit growth, we use these estimates as follows. First, we take the Notch-based estimates of how a dollar more in lifetime OASI benefits affects the employment rate, which is 0.25 divided by $2,093.66. Second, we multiply this by the change in the growth rate of lifetime benefits over the two periods, $2,932.21 per year minus $2,268.23 per year, to obtain the implied change in the growth of participation in annual percentage point terms. Third, we divide this by the actual annualized change in the participation growth rate in percentage points, 0.22 minus −0.059, or 0.28. Thus, we find that the slowdown in the growth rate of OASI benefits can account for 28 percent of the actual change in the participation growth rate around 1985 (0.25 × [2,932.21 − 2,268.23]/ (2,093.66 × [0.22 − (−0.059)]) = 28 percent). For the sixty-five- to sixty-nine-year-old group that was most directly affected immediately by the reform, we use analogous methods to calculate that the slowdown in the growth rate of OASI benefits can account for 34 percent of the actual change in the participation rate growth rate around 1985. Thus, overall, we find that the slowdown in growth of OASI benefits can account for quite a substantial fraction of the turnaround in older women's employment rates.

These statistics on employment rates are from the Current Population Survey, not our SSA data.[14] Nonetheless, our calculation illustrates that changes in the OASI benefit growth rate can account for a substantial fraction of the increase in the growth rate of older women's participation. Although the point estimates are notable, it is important to note that the confidence intervals on the estimates are large enough that we cannot rule out that the true fraction is small (9 percent at the bottom end of the 95 percent confidence interval) or nearly half (48 percent at the top end of the 95 percent confidence interval).

We ignore substitution elasticities in this calculation since our results in Gelber, Isen, and Song (2016) suggest they were not important. In other contexts—for example, with more salient substitution incentives—substitution elasticities could be larger. Since the OASI replacement rate also grew less quickly after the mid-1980s than before, incorporating the effects of substitution incentives would, if anything, strengthen our conclusion that the reduction in the OASI benefit growth rate can account for an important part of the increase in the growth rate of the employment-to-population ratio.

---

14. Our data are only for the cohorts near the Notch cohorts, so we are unable to calculate the fraction with positive earnings in earlier years in our data.

8.5.2   Extrapolating Local Estimates

A number of other issues could arise in determining the implications of our estimates for the time series of the employment rate. Like other empirical work that estimates local effects, our results apply locally to individuals born in 1916 and 1917 in the period after the Notch legislation whose benefits were affected by the Notch legislation. Importantly, we extrapolate our RDD estimate to the full population, but we do not have direct evidence on whether our local estimate generalizes to the full population. Indeed, it is worth noting that in the structural retirement models estimated in Coile and Gruber (2004, 2007), the effects of Social Security wealth on female employment appear smaller than those we have estimated.[15] One important issue is that because the Social Security benefits of women who have relatively low lifetime income in relation to their spouses are unaffected by the policy variation, our RDD estimate applies only to the combined population of single women and married women with relatively high lifetime income in relation to their spouses, but our extrapolation implicitly assumes that our results generalize. Our extrapolation also implicitly assumes that our results generalize beyond just those around the 1916/1917 birth cohort cutoff.

Several further assumptions are necessary to extrapolate our estimates. If spousal leisure is complementary (substitutable), this would suggest that the change in the OASI benefit growth rate could account for a larger (smaller) fraction of the change in the growth rate of the employment rate. Generally, our estimates also do not capture general equilibrium impacts of the OASI benefit changes. We also ignore the possibility that changes in OASI policy affected realized benefits through the channel of effects on earnings (though any effect on earnings would only occur for a few years before the mid-1980s, so such effects on benefits are likely to be small). Overall, we view our calculations of the implied effect of OASI on older Americans' participation rate as merely illustrative of the order of magnitude of the implications of the slowdown in the growth rate of OASI benefits, which appears to be quite substantial.

8.5.3   Evaluating Other Counterfactuals

It is worth considering the counterfactual we are assuming in our estimates of the fraction of the increase in the growth rate of older female labor force participation around 1985 that can be accounted for by the reduction in the growth rate of OASI benefits. Our counterfactual effectively assumes that the fast benefit growth under double indexation in the 1970s and early

---

15. The estimates of Mastrobuoni (2009) show substantial effects of the increase in the normal retirement age on women's employment decisions. However, the increase in the normal retirement age both decreased Social Security wealth and also could have changed the focal retirement age (Behagel and Blau 2012), and thus is not directly comparable to our setting.

1980s would have continued from 1985 to 2010. A key takeaway from this exercise is that this benefit growth would have otherwise caused women's employment rate to grow significantly less quickly. Phrased differently, much of the downward trend in women's employment rate prior to the mid-1980s was due to the sharp upward trend in OASI benefits, and was greatly lessened by the slower OASI benefit growth beginning in the mid-1980s. Thus, this counterfactual illustrates the role that fast OASI benefit growth played in explaining the downward trend in women's employment rate prior to 1985.

Of course, the fast benefit growth under double indexation was unsustainable absent significant tax increases, which indeed was the rationale for the cuts in OASI in the 1977 amendments. Figure 8.1 does show that comparable benefit growth occurred for much of the rest of the period from 1950 to 1980, most of which was financed through repeated payroll tax increases (Social Security 2013b). It is not unreasonable to believe that further sustained benefit growth could have occurred, though perhaps that was significantly less likely amid the fast benefit growth driven by the high inflation of the late 1970s.

Of course, other counterfactuals are possible, as we show in table 8.7. In the baseline, we choose the periods 1973 to 1984 and 1985 to 2010 because benefits and older women's employment rate usually changed in relatively smooth ways over each of these periods. However, it is possible to choose other historical time periods over which to make this comparison, and other choices usually yield comparable conclusions. If we consider the full time period shown in figure 8.1, 1950 to 2010, we can separate this into the period from 1950 to 1985 when OASI benefits grew faster on average and women's employment trended down overall, and the period from 1985 to 2010 when benefits grew more slowly on average and women's employment trended up. In this case, performing an analogous calculation to the one above shows that using the slowdown in the growth rate of OASI benefits we can account for 25 percent of the turnaround in the women's employment rate (0.25 ×

Table 8.7	Evaluating fraction of turnaround explained under other counterfactuals		
	(1) Baseline	(2) 1950–2010	(3) Percentage increases in benefits
Fraction of turnaround explained	28.42%	25.33%	77.38%

Notes: The table shows the percentage of the turnaround in the older women's employment rate around 1985 that can be accounted for given the slowdown in OASI benefit growth rate around 1985, under different assumptions described in the column headings. Column (1) shows the baseline, in which we compare the growth of the absolute level of benefits and older women's employment in 1973–1984 and 1985–2010. Column (2) shows the analogous calculations, but expands the earlier time period to 1950–1984. Column (3) shows the calculations when we assume that benefits continued to grow from 1985 to 2010 at the same yearly percentage rate as they grew from 1973–1984. See the main text for details of these calculations.

[2,891.91 − 2,268.23]/(2,093.66 × [0.22 + 0.074]) = 25 percent) as shown in column (2) of table 8.7. This calculation involves extrapolating the estimates further back in time, when the setting may not have been as comparable. It is notable that the explained fraction of the turnaround, 25 percent, is similar to our calculation of 28 percent in the baseline. In other words, since the mid-1980s turnaround we investigate, older women's employment rates have largely continued to increase at a rapid rate until the time of this writing, with certain pauses but also a clear and striking upward trend (figure 8.1 and Goldin and Katz, chapter 1, this volume). Our calculations suggest that the slower growth rate of OASI benefits could potentially help account not only for the turnaround in the older women's employment rate in the mid-1980s, but also the continued growth today. However, this involves extrapolation of the estimates to a wider time period.

As another possible counterfactual, if OASI benefits had grown at the same rate in percentage terms as from 1973 to 1984, this would have implied still higher growth in the absolute level of OASI benefits from 1985 to 2010, since the baseline level of benefits grew over time. This would make the slowdown in benefits appear still starker, and therefore imply that we could account for still more of the turnaround in older women's employment rate relative to this counterfactual. We show this in column (3) of table 8.7. In percentage terms, mean benefits grew by an average of 2.22 percent per year over our baseline period from 1973 to 1984. If benefits had instead continued their growth rate of 2.22 percent over 1985 to 2010, then benefits would have been $15,767.51 in 2010, implying annual benefit growth in absolute terms of $266.43 per year, or growth in discounted lifetime benefits of $4,082.72 per year. As a result, the implied change in the participation growth rate, from the world in which discounted benefits rise at $4,082.72 per year to the reality where they rose $2,268.23 per year, is 0.25 × (4,082.72 − 2,268.23)/2,093.66 = 0.22 percentage points per year. Dividing by the true change in the participation growth rate, 0.28 percentage points per year, we can account for 77 percent of the turnaround in the employment growth rate relative to this counterfactual. However, this counterfactual implicitly makes the assumption that the increases in benefits were sustainable in yearly percentage terms, which implies still faster benefit growth than the baseline and therefore is still less realistic for the reasons described above.

A final possible counterfactual is that benefit levels would have stayed at their 1985 level. This is unrealistic, primarily because OASI benefits grow in real terms through the fact they are based on earnings (in the AIME and AMW formulae), which have on average grown in real terms over time. As mean OASI benefits grew in absolute terms after the mid-1980s, it must be the case that other, unrelated factors led to the increase in the absolute level of employment in this period. The change in benefit growth can provide a partial explanation for the change in slope, though clearly other factors have played important independent roles in determining older Americans' employment rates. It is possible, for example, that factors such as greater average educational attainment and prior labor market experience led to significant increases in older women's employment rates beginning around the same time, but that growth in OASI benefits led these increases to be slower than they otherwise would have been—and that the even faster OASI benefit growth prior to 1985 helped contribute to the downward slope in older women's employment rates over this period.[16]

8.6   Conclusion

We propose that a reduction in the growth rate of OASI benefits may have played a role in the increase in older women's employment rates that began in the mid-1980s. To shed light on this using microdata, we study the effects of the Social Security Notch. The point estimate shows that a $10,000 increase in discounted lifetime OASI benefits causes a decrease in the yearly participation rate of 1.24 percentage points from ages sixty-one to 95. If these results apply more broadly, we calculate that the reduction in the growth rate of Social Security benefits can account for over one-quarter of the turnaround in the trend in older women's employment rates in the mid-1980s, relative to the counterfactual that benefit growth continued at the same rate in real terms. Thus, Social Security may be an important factor, among others, in explaining this turnaround.

OASI also experienced other changes in substitution incentives around this period, including through a slowdown in the growth rate of the replacement rate. For example, the OASI earnings test gradually became less stringent over this period, leading to stronger employment incentives that could have also played a role in increasing the employment rate. In investigating the role that OASI may have played in explaining recent trends in older workers' employment, it would be valuable to complement this work by investigating further the potential role of substitution effects of OASI in explaining recent trends in older Americans' employment rates.

16. If the level of OASI benefits relative to prior income or wealth matters for the magnitude of the income effect—as we might expect, for example, if individuals display "habit formation" in their consumption and grow accustomed to their prior income—then the growth of prior income over time could help explain why employment grew after 1985 despite the contemporaneous rise in benefits.

Appendix

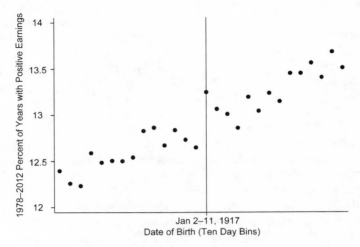

Fig. 8A.1   Percent of years with positive earnings, 1978 to 2012 (ages sixty-one to ninety-five), above-median average prior earnings, wider DOB range

Notes: The figure shows results when the outcome of interest is the percent of years from 1978 to 2012 in which individuals have positive yearly earnings, among the group with above-median earnings prior to 1977, in a wider range of ten-day bins of DOB. (See other notes to figure 8.3.)

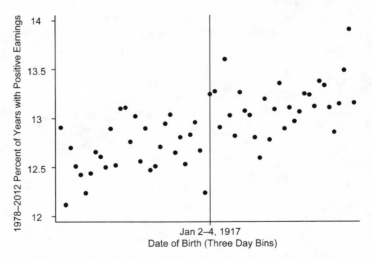

Fig. 8A.2   Percent of years with positive earnings, 1978 to 2012 (ages sixty-one to ninety-five), above-median average prior earnings, three-day bins of DOB

Notes: The figure shows results when the outcome of interest is the percent of years from 1978 to 2012 in which individuals have positive yearly earnings, among the group with above-median earnings prior to 1977, in a wider range of ten-day bins of DOB. (See other notes to figure 8.3.)

References

Angrist, Joshua, and Jörn-Steffen Pischke. 2008. *Mostly Harmless Econometrics: An Empiricist's Companion.* Princeton, NJ: Princeton University Press.

Behagel, Luc, and David Blau. 2012. "Framing Social Security Reform: Behavioral Responses to Changes in the Full Retirement Age." *American Economic Journal: Economic Policy* 4 (4): 41–67.

Blau, David M., and Ryan Goodstein. 2010. "Can Social Security Explain Trends in Labor Force Participation of Older Men in the United States?" *Journal of Human Resources* 45 (2): 328–63.

Buckles, Kasey, and Daniel M. Hungerman. 2013. "Season of Birth and Later Outcomes: Old Questions, New Answers." *Review of Economics and Statistics* 95 (3): 711–24.

Burkhauser, Richard V., and Joseph F. Quinn. 1983. "Is Mandatory Retirement Overrated? Evidence from the 1970s." *Journal of Human Resources* 18 (3): 337–58.

Calonico, Sebastian, Matthias Cattaneo, and Rocio Titiunik. 2014. "Robust Nonparametric Confidence Intervals for Regression-Discontinuity Designs." *Econometrica* 82 (6): 2295–326.

Cawley, John, John Moran, and Kosali Simon. 2010. "The Impact of Income on the Weight of Elderly Americans." *Health Economics* 19 (8): 979–93.

Chetty, Raj, John Friedman, and Emmanuel Saez. 2013. "Using Differences in Knowledge across Neighborhoods to Uncover the Impacts of the EITC on Earnings." *American Economic Review* 103 (7): 2683–721.

Clingman, Michael, Kyle Burkhalter, and Chris Chaplain. 2014. "Replacement Rates for Hypothetical Retired Workers." Social Security Administration Actuarial Note 2014 (9).

Coile, Courtney C., and Jonathan Gruber. 2004. "The Effect of Social Security on Retirement in the United States." In *Social Security Programs and Retirement around the World: Micro Estimation,* edited by Jonathan Gruber and David Wise, 691–729. Chicago: University of Chicago Press.

———. 2007. "Future Social Security Entitlements and the Retirement Decision." *Review of Economics and Statistics* 89 (2): 234–46.

Costa, Dora L. 1995. "Pensions and Retirement: Evidence from Union Army Veterans." *Quarterly Journal of Economics* 110 (2): 297–319.

Engelhardt, Gary V., Jonathan Gruber, and Cynthia D. Perry. 2005. "Social Security and Elderly Living Arrangements: Evidence from the Social Security Notch." *Journal of Human Resources* 40 (2): 354–72.

Feldstein, Martin, and Jeffrey Liebman. 2002. "Social Security." In *Handbook of Public Economics,* vol. 4, edited by Alan Auerbach and Martin Feldstein, 2245–324. Amsterdam: Elsevier.

Fetter, Daniel, and Lee Lockwood. 2016. "Government Old-Age Support and Labor Supply: Evidence from the Old Age Assistance Program." Working Paper, Wellesley College. http://www.wellesley.edu/sites/default/files/assets/departments/economics/files/fetter_lockwood_oaa_ls.pdf.

Gelber, Alexander, Adam Isen, and Jae Song. 2016. "The Effect of Pension Income on Elderly Earnings: Evidence from Social Security and Full Population Data." Working Paper, University of California, Berkeley. https://gspp.berkeley.edu/assets/uploads/research/pdf/gelberisensong051716.pdf.

Goda, Gopi Shah, Ezra Golberstein, and David Grabowski. 2011. "Income and the Utilization of Long-Term Care Services: Evidence from the Social Security Benefit Notch." *Journal of Health Economics* 30 (4): 719–29.

Golberstein, Ezra. 2015. "The Effects of Income on Mental Health: Evidence from the Social Security Notch." *Journal of Mental Health Policy and Economics* 18 (1): 27–37.

Government Accountability Office (GAO). 1988. "Social Security: The Notch Issue." Washington, DC, Government Printing Office.

Gruber, Jonathan, and David Wise. 1999. "Introduction." In *Social Security Programs and Retirement around the World*, edited by Jonathan Gruber and David Wise, 1–35. Chicago: University of Chicago Press.

Gustman, Alan, and Thomas Steinmeier. 2009. "How Changes in Social Security Affect Recent Retirement Trends." *Research on Aging* 31 (2): 261–90.

Imbens, Guido, and Thomas Lemieux. 2008. "Regression Discontinuity Designs: A Guide to Practice." *Journal of Econometrics* 142 (2): 615–35.

Imbens, Guido, Donald B. Rubin, and Bruce I. Sacerdote. 2001. "Estimating the Effect of Unearned Income on Labor Earnings, Savings, and Consumption: Evidence from a Survey of Lottery Players." *American Economic Review* 91 (4): 778–94.

Krueger, Alan B., and Jörn-Steffen Pischke. 1992. "The Effect of Social Security on Labor Supply: A Cohort Analysis of the Notch Generation." *Journal of Labor Economics* 10 (4): 412–37.

Lee, David S., and Thomas Lemieux. 2010. "Regression Discontinuity Designs in Economics." *Journal of Economic Literature* 48 (2): 281–355.

Manoli, Dayanand, and Andrea Weber. Forthcoming. "Nonparametric Evidence on the Effects of Financial Incentives on Retirement Decisions." *American Economic Journal: Economic Policy*.

Mastrobuoni, Giovanni. 2009. "Labor Supply Effects of the Recent Social Security Benefit Cuts: Empirical Estimates Using Cohort Discontinuities." *Journal of Public Economics* 93 (11–12): 1224–33.

McCrary, Justin. 2008. "Manipulation of the Running Variable in the Regression Discontinuity Design: A Density Test." *Journal of Economic Literature* 142 (2): 698–714.

McKay, Steven F., and Bruce D. Schobel. 1981. "Effects of the Various Social Security Benefit Computation Procedures." Actuarial Study no. 86, Social Security Administration Office of the Actuary.

Moran, John, and Kosali Simon. 2006. "Income and the Use of Prescription Drugs by the Elderly: Evidence from the Notch Cohorts." *Journal of Human Resources* 41 (2): 411–32.

Munnell, Alicia, Kevin Cahill, and Natalia Jivan. 2003. "How Has the Shift to 401(k) s Affected the Retirement Age?" Issue Brief no. 13, Boston College Center for Retirement Research.

Schirle, Tammy. 2008. "Why Have the Labor Force Participation Rates of Older Men Increased Since the Mid-1990s?" *Journal of Labor Economics* 26 (4): 549–94.

Snyder, Stephen E., and William N. Evans. 2006. "The Effect of Income on Mortality: Evidence from the Social Security Notch." *Review of Economics and Statistics* 88 (3): 482–95.

Social Security Administration. 2013a. *Annual Statistical Supplement*. Washington, DC: Government Printing Office.

———. 2013b. *Social Security Handbook*. Washington, DC: Government Printing Office.

———. 2015. *Social Security 2015 Trustees Report*. Washington, DC: Government Printing Office.

The Hidden Resources of Women Working Longer
Evidence from Linked Survey-Administrative Data

C. Adam Bee and Joshua Mitchell

9.1 Introduction

We begin with a puzzle. Why has the dramatic rise in female life cycle labor force participation not been accompanied by an increase in retirement income for women at older ages?

The basis for this puzzle is the Current Population Survey Annual Social and Economic Supplement (CPS-ASEC), the source of the nation's official income and poverty statistics. We use it to plot in figure 9.1 the rate of retirement income receipt for women age sixty-five to sixty-nine and age seventy to seventy-four between 1987 and 2012.[1] As we will discuss in more detail, our measure of retirement income also includes survivor and disability income but excludes all payments from Social Security and veterans benefits. (The sample in figure 9.1 is further restricted to women who also report receiving Social Security income to focus attention on women who are very likely to be retired.) For both women age sixty-five to sixty-nine and age

C. Adam Bee is an economist at the US Census Bureau. Joshua Mitchell is a senior economist at the US Census Bureau.

The views expressed herein are those of the authors and do not necessarily reflect the views of the US Census Bureau or NBER. We would like to thank Courtney Coile, Claudia Goldin, Larry Katz, and the other Women Working Longer conference participants for providing feedback and guidance. We would also like to thank Jon Rothbaum and Trudi Renwick at Census for their support. For the Survey of Income and Program Participation (SIPP) Gold Standard File, we thank Gary Benedetto and Lori Reeder at Census for their assistance and patience. All results have been formally reviewed to ensure that no confidential Census Bureau data have been disclosed. For acknowledgments, sources of research support, and disclosure of the authors' material financial relationships, if any, please see http://www.nber.org/chapters/c13803.ack.

1. For survey years prior to the 1988, our CPS-ASEC files do not allow us to define retirement income in a way that is fully consistent with the 1987 to 2012 reference-year period. In 2014, the CPS-ASEC underwent a major redesign that altered the questions relating to retirement income. See Semega and Welniak (2015) and Mitchell and Renwick (2015) for more details.

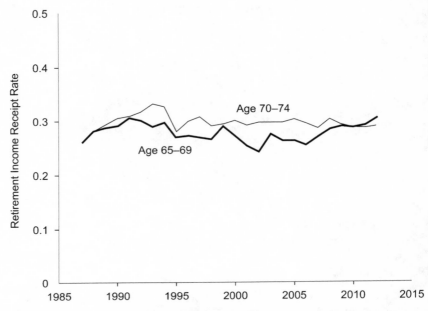

Fig. 9.1   **Trends in retirement income receipt for women who report receiving Social Security**

Source: The 1988–2013 CPS-ASEC surveys.

Notes: Sample is all women ages sixty-five to sixty-nine and seventy to seventy-four who report receiving Social Security income in the reference year. "Retirement income receipt" is the fraction of women with positive retirement, survivor, or disability income in the reference year, excluding Social Security income and VA benefits.

seventy to seventy-four, it is remarkable how little retirement income receipt has apparently changed in twenty-five years. The rate of receipt fluctuates within a band of about 7 percentage points, and it never exceeds 34 percent.

The lack of any measurable trend comes in spite of many changes during working years that one might think would alter the trajectory of retirement income, particularly for women. More recent cohorts of women are attached to the labor force for longer periods of time (Goldin and Mitchell, forthcoming), are more likely to have careers rather than just jobs (Goldin 2006), are more likely to graduate from college (Goldin, Katz, and Kuziemko 2006), and are paid at higher rates relative to men (DeNavas-Walt and Proctor 2015). So why would they not be more likely to have a pension, a 401(k), or an individual retirement account (IRA)?

We use linked survey-administrative data to argue that surveys such as the CPS-ASEC are increasingly failing to capture much of the retirement income received by women, and this omission has significant implications for understanding their material well-being in retirement. We do not mean to suggest that underreporting is unique to women. In related work (Bee and

Mitchell, in progress), we provide an in-depth analysis of underreporting and its causes. That work shows that underreporting is also prevalent among men and therefore has consequences for measuring the incomes of the entire population age sixty-five and over. In fact, retirement income underreporting results in a substantial understatement of median household income and an overstatement of the official poverty rate among the aged. However, in keeping with the theme of this volume, we choose to focus exclusively on women born from the early 1920s to the late 1940s and draw out implications of their increasing labor force attachment across successive birth cohorts.

Our main contribution is to highlight that to the extent underreporting is a growing problem, household surveys will fail to reflect the full consequences of women working longer and understate the economic progress of women at older ages. We show that underreporting not only biases trends in income across cohorts, but also distorts the relationship between career work experience and retirement income within a given cohort. Last, we show that for recently retired women, accurate measures of retirement income are crucial for understanding the transition to retirement. In contrast to previous work, we find very little evidence of total household income falling for most women as they and their spouses (if present) withdraw from the labor market and begin to receive Social Security.[2] Our finding poses a challenge to the literature on the "retirement consumption puzzle," which seeks to explain household consumption behavior under the assumption that incomes are falling predictably at retirement.

We should note that concerns about measuring retirement income in the CPS-ASEC are not new (Czajka and Denmead 2012). Conceptually, the CPS-ASEC aims to capture money income, or a stream of regular payments. This accounting fits naturally with traditional defined-benefit pension plans, which typically provide annuity income, but it is more challenging to reconcile with defined-contribution (DC) retirement plans, where withdrawals are often done on an as-needed basis. Partly in response to the changing retirement landscape, the CPS-ASEC underwent a major redesign in 2014. That design change was intended to provide more accurate information on income from defined-contribution plans (Mitchell and Renwick 2015; Semega and Welniak 2015). For our purposes we will consider both annuities and retirement account withdrawals as income, but note that many of the cohorts of women examined in this chapter are likely to have only defined-benefit income.

We begin in section 9.2 by briefly reviewing the relevant literature. We next describe the construction of our newly linked survey-administrative data set in section 9.3. In section 9.4, we document trends in work, Social Security, and retirement income for successive cohorts of women born

---

2. Using panel tax data, Brady et al. (in progress) also find little evidence of an income drop at retirement.

between the early 1920s and the late 1940s. In section 9.5, we compare CPS self-reports with administrative records to demonstrate growing retirement income underreporting rates across birth cohorts and the consequences for measuring women's total incomes. In section 9.6, we explore the relationship between years of work experience and bias in retirement income measurement for women born in the late 1940s. In section 9.7, we examine incomes for women and their spouses (if present) as they transition to retirement. Section 9.8 concludes.

9.2   Prior Work

The literature on measuring income and well-being in surveys is vast and we do not attempt an exhaustive review here. Studies most related to our chapter reassess the well-being of the aged in retirement. Cutler and Katz (1991), Hurd and Rohwedder (2006), and Meyer and Sullivan (2010, 2012) compare consumption- and income-based measures of poverty and find evidence of considerably more economic progress for the aged when using consumption measures. The life cycle model motivates a focus on consumption because consumption is more closely connected to long-run economic status. Consumption may also be preferable if certain types of income are difficult for survey respondents to report. We contribute to the above studies by uncovering substantial underreporting of retirement income for women using administrative records. Our findings thereby help reconcile the differences found between survey-based measures of consumption and income for the aged.

Beyond measuring income and consumption at points in time, our findings also relate to longitudinal studies that examine changes in well-being over time, especially as households transition into retirement. A number of prominent studies such as Banks, Blundell, and Tanner (1998) and Bernheim, Skinner, and Weinberg (2001) have noted that consumption appears to fall sharply at retirement. Because the standard life cycle model predicts that forward-looking households should be able to smooth consumption in response to anticipated declines in income, this apparent empirical violation gives rise to the "retirement consumption puzzle" and is taken as evidence that households are myopic and inadequately prepared for retirement. More recent studies have questioned this initial conclusion.

Hurst (2008) surveys the recent literature and finds that it is mainly work and food expenditures that decline, while recreational spending and donations to charity actually increase. Moreover, the decline in food expenditures is offset by an increase in home production and an increase in shopping for grocery bargains such that actual food consumption does not fall (Aguiar and Hurst 2005, 2007). Although we do not measure consumption directly, our findings challenge the premise that income falls for most households in retirement. Our administrative record measure of retirement income plays an important role in obtaining this result. Even though the composition of consumption may change at retirement, we show that it is not possible to test the life cycle model against alternatives when annual incomes remain steady, at least for a cohort of recently retired women.

Last, our use of administrative records to validate survey responses contributes to the large literature on survey measurement error. With the exception of our work in Bee (2013) and Bee and Mitchell (in progress), few studies have been able to validate retirement income directly. Studies reviewed in Munnell and Chen (2014) compare survey aggregates to outside sources such as the National Income and Product Accounts or SOI tax tables (which exclude nonfilers) and conclude that the CPS-ASEC is missing substantial amounts of retirement income, usually with an emphasis on income from defined-contribution accounts. But without the ability to link survey and administrative data, the distributional implications of underreported retirement income remain strongly disputed. For the cohorts of women examined, we show that correcting for underreporting does, in fact, have broad distributional consequences.

Other studies do address survey measurement error with respect to pensions and retirement accounts but focus on current workers, comparing survey responses to employer-provided plan descriptions (Gustman, Steinmeier, and Tabatabai 2010; Mitchell 1988). These studies reveal that workers in general do not understand key features of pension plans such as early retirement options and the distinction between defined-benefit and defined-contribution systems. Workers also have trouble reporting participation in defined-contribution plans and the amount of their contributions (Dushi and Honig 2015; Dushi and Iams 2010). A lack of financial literacy may hinder the gathering of accurate information on retirement preparation (Lusardi and Mitchell [2014] and chapter 6, this volume). It may also provide clues as to why underreporting of incomes in retirement appears to be a significant problem.

9.3   Data and Methods

We construct a novel data set that links survey data with several administrative record sources. For most of our analysis, the underlying samples are drawn from the Survey of Income and Program Participation (SIPP). The SIPP is a series of nationally representative samples of households interviewed over a multiyear period. We use the first waves of the 1984, 1990, 1996, 2001, 2004, and 2008 SIPP panels. We use a harmonized version of the SIPP known as the Gold Standard File.[3] Because we are only using a single wave from each panel, we are treating the SIPP data as a series of cross

---

3. Data from the SIPP Gold Standard File are confidential. All results have been formally reviewed to ensure that no confidential Census Bureau data have been disclosed.

sections, drawing mainly demographic and household-relationship information from the SIPP. The longitudinal dimension of our analysis comes exclusively from the administrative records with the advantage that we can follow our SIPP samples forward and backward in time without attrition.

We do not use income data directly from the SIPP because SIPP income data are collected for a four-month reference period that does not correspond to calendar-year information available in several of our administrative record sources. Instead, we compare annual income from the linked administrative records to standalone data from the CPS-ASEC.

As mentioned above, the CPS-ASEC is the source of the nation's official income and poverty statistics. Between February and April of each year, the CPS-ASEC surveys a nationally representative sample of approximately 75,000 households and ascertains income types and annual amounts for the previous calendar year. We are particularly interested in the extent to which retirement income is underreported in the CPS-ASEC and how that may bias our assessment of women's well-being at older ages. The CPS-ASEC asks the following question for each member of the household related to retirement income:

> Other than Social Security or VA benefits, did . . . receive any pension or retirement income?

If the response is affirmative, then follow-up questions elicit the amount and source of income. There are two analogous sets of questions about survivor income and disability income outside of Social Security and VA benefits. We aggregate responses to all three questions in our definition of retirement income.

We choose to use the linked SIPP data rather than the linked CPS-ASEC for most of our analysis because the linked SIPP data are available further back in time and allow us to examine earlier cohorts of women. Furthermore, the SIPP data tend to have higher linkage rates.[4] But when we examine the most recent birth cohort of women in their older ages in section 9.6, we need to use the linked 2013 CPS-ASEC rather than the SIPP.

Our administrative records allow us to examine five types of income that are particularly important at older ages: earnings (both wages and self-employment), Social Security benefits, Supplemental Security Income (SSI), interest and dividends, and retirement income. Data on earnings, Social Security benefits, and SSI are obtained from the Social Security Administra-

---

4. The SIPP and CPS-ASEC data are assigned a Personal Identification Key (PIK), which is a confidentiality-protected version of a Social Security number. The PIK allows the survey data to be linked to the administrative records. (See Wagner and Layne [2014] for more details.) Linkage rates vary across each survey, but are generally in the high 80 percent range. In order to account for any differences between the PIK subsample and the overall sample, we run for each survey a logit model using demographic information to predict the assignment of a PIK and calculate an estimated propensity score. We then multiply the survey weight by the inverse of the estimated propensity score.

tion (SSA). Data on taxable and tax-exempt interest and dividends come from IRS Form 1040 records. Not everyone files a 1040 in a given year, but we can assume that those with more than minimal amounts of capital income would be required to file.

Last, retirement income data come from two sources and are available regardless of whether or not an individual filed a tax return in a given year. We have discovered data from Form W-2P "Statement for Recipients of Annuities, Pensions, Retired Pay, or IRA Payments," in SSA administrative records for years 1978 to 1990. These records contain periodic payments and withdrawals but exclude rollovers and other total distributions that are best thought of as moving money from one retirement account to another. After 1990, Form W-2P was merged with IRS Form 1099-R, "Distributions From Pensions, Annuities, Retirement or Profit-Sharing Plans, IRAs, Insurance Contracts, etc." We have obtained from IRS the 1099-R information returns from 1995 onward. Our version of the 1099-R extracts also excludes direct rollovers and other transactions we would not wish to consider as increasing the resources available to women in retirement. In short, we have reliable and reasonably consistent retirement income data spanning 1978 to 1990 and 1995 onward. These data allow us to examine long-run trends in underreporting of retirement income in the CPS-ASEC.

From each linked survey, we draw a five-year birth cohort group of women such that they are in their sixties when interviewed. Across all linked surveys, we cover women born from the early 1920s to the late 1940s. The women in our sample are either the householder or spouse of the householder. Last, for tracking incomes over time, we often require that women survive until age seventy to maintain a balanced panel. All income amounts are adjusted for inflation using the Consumer Price Index Research Series Using Current Methods (CPI-U-RS) and are expressed in 2012 dollars.

Summary statistics for each of the six birth cohorts groups are shown in table 9.1 along with approximate sample sizes. Across cohorts, college graduation rates have more than doubled while the share of women who are currently married has declined slightly.

9.4   Cohort-Age Patterns

9.4.1   Employment

We first describe patterns of work at older ages for women born between 1921 and 1948. Throughout our analysis, employment is defined as having annual administrative earnings (both W-2 wages and self-employment) of at least the year's prevailing hourly federal minimum wage times ten hours per week times fifty-two weeks per year, as in Goldin and Katz (chapter 1, this volume). Figure 9.2 plots employment rates for five-year birth cohort groups between ages fifty-five and seventy. Because our earnings records

Table 9.1   **Summary statistics**

SIPP panel	Birth cohort group	Approximate N	College graduate	Married
1984	1921–1925	900	0.12	0.72
1990	1926–1930	900	0.11	0.70
1996	1932–1936	1,200	0.15	0.74
2001	1937–1941	700	0.20	0.68
2004	1940–1944	1,800	0.24	0.68
2008	1944–1948	2,400	0.27	0.68

Sources: The SIPP Gold Standard File linked to Social Security Administration and IRS administrative records.
Notes: Sample is all women who are either the SIPP householder or spouse of the householder, ages sixty to sixty-four at time of SIPP interview, and survive until age seventy. College completion and marital status are measured at time of SIPP interview. Sample is restricted to those with a Personal Identification Key (PIK) that allows linking to the administrative records. The SIPP sample weights are adjusted to account for selection into having a PIK. For each SIPP panel we estimate a logit model for the presence of a PIK as a function of SIPP demographic characteristics and predict the estimated propensity score. We then take the SIPP sample weight and multiply it by the inverse of the estimated propensity score. Resulting weights are used in analysis.

extend from 1978 until 2012, we are unable to observe the earliest and the latest cohorts at extreme ages. Nevertheless, a clear pattern emerges.

Consistent with the theme of this volume, women are working longer—the entire employment path for a more recent cohort is generally above the employment path of previous cohorts. Among women born between 1921 and 1925 (the earliest cohort), only 46 percent worked at age fifty-seven. In contrast, for women born between 1944 and 1948 (the most recent cohort) the employment rate at age fifty-seven was 61 percent. The same pattern holds when women are in their sixties. At age sixty-four, 24 percent of women born between 1921 and 1925 were working compared with 39 percent for women born between 1944 and 1948. These employment patterns provide supporting evidence for the hypothesis that more recent cohorts of women are attached to the workforce longer and therefore are more likely to be eligible for a pension, and in recent years, are more likely to be able to make contributions to an employer-sponsored DC plan or to an IRA.

We explore how changing demographic characteristics of women affect cohort employment patterns in table 9.2. We run linear probability models for work on a full set of age fixed effects covering the age ranges where we have a balanced panel across cohorts. We examine the cohort group coefficients (the 1921 to 1925 cohort is the omitted group) and compare their magnitudes to a second specification where we control for five categories of educational attainment—high school dropout (omitted), high school graduate, some college, college graduate, and advanced degree—and five categories of marital status—never married (omitted), married, widowed,

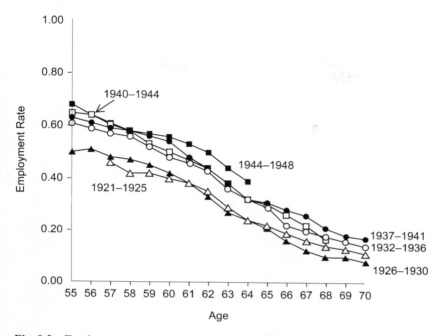

Fig. 9.2   Employment rates for women by age and cohort

Source: The SIPP Gold Standard File linked to Social Security Administration and IRS administrative records.

Notes: Sample is all women who are either the SIPP householder or spouse of the householder, are ages sixty to sixty-four at time of SIPP interview, and survive until age seventy. Women are considered as working in a given year if their total earnings from wages and self-employment in the administrative records are at least equal to the prevailing hourly federal minimum wage in that year times ten hours per week times fifty-two weeks per year.

Sample is restricted to those with a Personal Identification Key (PIK), which allows linking to the administrative records. The SIPP sample weights are adjusted to account for selection into having a PIK. For each SIPP panel we estimate a logit model for the presence of a PIK as a function of SIPP demographic characteristics and predict the estimated propensity score. We then take the SIPP sample weight and multiply it by the inverse of the estimated propensity score. Resulting weights are used in analysis.

divorced, and separated. Not surprisingly, higher levels of educational attainment are strongly associated with labor force attachment. Married, widowed, and separated women are about 13 to 16 percentage points less likely to work than never-married women, all else equal. The coefficients on the later cohorts are somewhat muted after controlling for education and marital status, indicating that some of the trend toward working longer reflects greater educational attainment and reduced marriage, but there are still important cohort effects for women born in the 1930s and 1940s.[5]

5. Note this is an earlier set of birth cohorts than those in the HRS examined by Goldin and Katz (chapter 1, this volume).

Table 9.2   Employment and income receipt regressions

Independent variable	Employed (ages 57–64)		Receives Social Security early (ages 62–64)		Receives retirement income (ages 59–64)	
	(1)	(2)	(3)	(4)	(5)	(6)
Cohort (1921–1925 omitted)						
1926–1930	0.009	0.009	0.052**	0.049**		
	(0.021)	(0.021)	(0.022)	(0.021)		
1932–1936	0.093***	0.072***	0.031	0.049***		
	(0.019)	(0.019)	(0.019)	(0.019)		
1937–1941	0.117***	0.072***	0.023	0.060***	0.120***	0.092***
	(0.022)	(0.022)	(0.022)	(0.022)	(0.018)	(0.018)
1940–1944	0.104***	0.042**	0.000	0.049**	0.146***	0.105***
	(0.020)	(0.021)	(0.021)	(0.021)	(0.019)	(0.018)
1944–1948	0.150***	0.079***	-0.101***	0.039*	0.148***	0.105***
	(0.020)	(0.020)	(0.020)	(0.021)	(0.017)	(0.017)
Marital status (never married omitted)						
Married		-0.161***		0.160***		-0.101***
		(0.034)		(0.038)		(0.036)
Widowed		-0.129***		0.262***		0.083**
		(0.037)		(0.041)		(0.042)
Divorced		0.006		0.079*		-0.038
		(0.038)		(0.042)		(0.040)
Separated		-0.156**		0.082		-0.110
		(0.064)		(0.081)		(0.109)
Educational attainment (less than HS grad. omitted)						
HS grad.		0.140***		-0.017		0.088***
		(0.016)		(0.017)		(0.018)

	(1)	(2)	(3)	(4)	(5)	(6)
Some college		0.181***		−0.081***		0.122***
		(0.018)		(0.019)		(0.018)
College grad.		0.192***		−0.182***		0.167***
		(0.024)		(0.025)		(0.025)
Advanced degree		0.302***		−0.263***		0.258***
		(0.026)		(0.028)		(0.027)
Age fixed effects	Yes	Yes	Yes	Yes	Yes	Yes
N	45,656	45,656	17,121	17,121	22,362	22,362
R-squared	0.040	0.078	0.055	0.095	0.041	0.078

Source: The SIPP Gold Standard File linked to Social Security Administration and IRS administrative records.

Notes: Sample is all women who are either the SIPP householder or spouse of the householder, ages sixty to sixty-four at time of SIPP interview, and survive until age seventy. College completion and marital status are measured at time of SIPP interview. In columns (1) and (2) outcome variable is equal to 1 for women who had annual administrative record earnings (combined wages and self-employment) of at least the prevailing federal hourly minimum wage times ten hours per week times fifty-two weeks per year. In columns (3) and (4) outcome variable is equal to 1 for women who had positive annual administrative record income from OASDI. In columns (5) and (6) outcome variable is 1 for women who had positive annual administrative record retirement income from either Form W-2P for years 1978 to 1990 or Form 1099-R for years 1995 to 2012. Sample is restricted to those with a Personal Identification Key (PIK) that allows linking to the administrative records. The SIPP sample weights are adjusted to account for selection into having a PIK. For each SIPP panel we estimate a logit model for the presence of a PIK as a function of SIPP demographic characteristics and predict the estimated propensity score. We then take the SIPP sample weight and multiply it by the inverse of the estimated propensity score. Resulting weights are used in analysis. Standard errors in parenthesis are clustered at the individual level.

***Significant at the 1 percent level.

**Significant at the 5 percent level.

*Significant at the 10 percent level.

9.4.2   Social Security Receipt

Figure 9.3 describes the age pattern of Social Security income receipt across cohorts. Social Security receipt is defined as having any positive amount of annual OASDI benefits in the administrative records. At preretirement ages, more recent cohorts are actually somewhat more likely to receive Social Security than are earlier cohorts. This difference reflects the

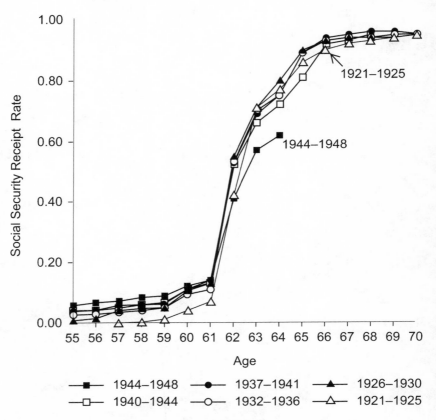

Fig. 9.3   Social Security receipt rates for women by age and cohort

Source: The SIPP Gold Standard File linked to Social Security Administration and IRS administrative records.

Notes: Sample is all women who are either the SIPP householder or spouse of the householder, ages sixty to sixty-four at time of SIPP interview, and survive until age seventy. Social Security receipt in a given year is defined as having positive annual OASDI benefits in the administrative records for that year. Sample is restricted to those with a Personal Identification Key (PIK), which allows linking to the administrative records. The SIPP sample weights are adjusted to account for selection into having a PIK. For each SIPP panel we estimate a logit model for the presence of a PIK as a function of SIPP demographic characteristics and predict the estimated propensity score. We then take the SIPP sample weight and multiply it by the inverse of the estimated propensity score. Resulting weights are used in analysis.

fact that more recent cohorts of women are more likely to be eligible for Social Security Disability Insurance (SSDI) due to their longer earnings histories and also because the medical examination process has become more relaxed (Autor and Duggan 2006). Starting at age sixty-two, and for those below what is known at the "full retirement age," reduced Social Security retirement benefits are available.[6] The most recent cohorts of women are less likely to claim Social Security retirement benefits before full retirement age. For example, at age sixty-four, 77 percent of women born between 1921 and 1925 received Social Security benefits but only 62 percent of women born between 1944 and 1948 did. Thus, women are working longer and also claiming Social Security later.

Columns (3) and (4) of table 9.2 explore regression results for Social Security receipt during early retirement years—ages sixty-two to sixty-four. Higher-educated women are less likely to claim Social Security early. Not surprisingly, widows are 26 percentage points more likely to be receiving Social Security benefits than never-married women, all else equal. The cohort effects start declining for women born in the 1930s and turn sharply negative for the 1944 to 1948 birth cohorts. Adding controls for education and marital status produces cohort effects that are more strongly positive, with a smaller drop for the 1944 to 1948 birth cohorts.

9.4.3 Retirement Income Receipt

Estimates of retirement income receipt from SSA and IRS administrative records are shown in figure 9.4. Recall that annual amounts of pension and annuity income as well as periodic withdrawals from employer-sponsored DC accounts and IRAs are included in the definition of retirement income. Transactions that move money from one retirement account to another, such as rollovers and conversions, are excluded. Also important is that we observe receipt of retirement income but not the reason for receipt. Some women may be receiving survivor income that reflects their deceased spouses' earnings histories rather than their own, although that is less likely at younger ages. Note that data age gaps in figure 9.4 reflect the time period between 1991 and 1994 during which we do not have retirement income data for all members of a cohort group. Nevertheless, the combined series provides novel evidence of an important component of women's total retirement resources spanning over three decades.

Rates of retirement income receipt rise substantially with age, for example, from 23 percent to 52 percent for the 1937 to 1941 cohort between ages sixty and seventy. Rates also rise across cohorts. At age sixty, the 1921

---

6. The full retirement age is sixty-five for individuals born before 1938. After 1938, the full retirement age is gradually increased until it reaches sixty-seven for those born after 1959. (See https://www.ssa.gov/planners/retire/retirechart.html.)

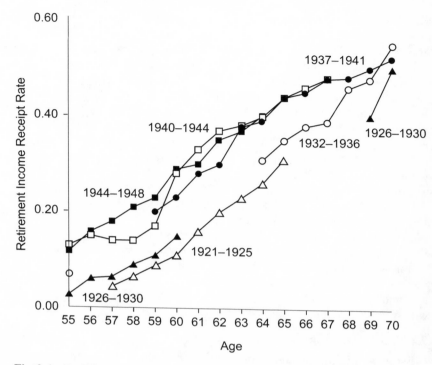

Fig. 9.4   Retirement income receipt rates for women by age and cohort

Source: The SIPP Gold Standard File linked to Social Security Administration and IRS administrative records.

Notes: Sample is all women who are either the SIPP householder or spouse of the householder, ages sixty to sixty-four at time of SIPP interview, and survive until age seventy. Retirement income receipt in a given year is defined as having positive annual retirement income in the W-2P records for years 1978–1990 and in the 1099-R records for years 1995–2012. Retirement income includes pension/annuity income (excluding Social Security) as well as periodic withdrawals from defined-contribution accounts. Gaps in series refer to years 1991–1994 where administrative records are not available. Sample is restricted to those with a Personal Identification Key (PIK), which allows linking to the administrative records. The SIPP sample weights are adjusted to account for selection into having a PIK. For each SIPP panel we estimate a logit model for the presence of a PIK as a function of SIPP demographic characteristics and predict the estimated propensity score. We then take the SIPP sample weight and multiply it by the inverse of the estimated propensity score. Resulting weights are used in analysis.

to 1925 cohort had a rate of receipt of 11 percent while the 1944 to 1948 cohort had a rate of receipt of 29 percent.

These results provide preliminary evidence that is in stark contrast to the CPS-ASEC numbers shown in figure 9.1. While retirement income receipt at advanced ages never exceeds 34 percent in the CPS-ASEC (even conditioning on those receiving Social Security), the administrative data indicate that no cohort observable at age seventy has a rate of receipt lower than 50 percent. We will provide more direct evidence of underreporting in section 9.5.

Regression results confirm that educational attainment strongly predicts retirement income receipt. Widowed women are also more likely than other groups to have retirement income, which would likely include survivor pension income. For recent observable cohorts, the rates of receipt between ages fifty-nine and sixty-four remain about 11 percentage points higher relative to the 1921 to 1925 birth cohorts, after controlling for educational attainment and marital status.

9.5   Cross-Cohort Patterns in Underreporting

We now turn to survey underreporting across calendar years and its implication for measuring the incomes of women across cohorts. Our analysis draws on a series of cross sections based on linked SIPP-administrative data. We compare these administrative measures of income to the stand-alone CPS-ASEC measures. Table 9.3 illustrates the extent of underreporting in 1984, 1989, 1995, 2000, 2003, and 2007. We select women from each survey when they are ages sixty-five to sixty-nine. The first rows compare Social Security receipt and median benefit amounts in the linked data and the CPS-ASEC. Across all years, there is a very close correspondence of both receipt and benefit amounts. The discrepancy in receipt is not more than 3 percentage points in any year. Median benefits conditional on receipt are never different by more than 3 percent. The CPS-ASEC appears to capture Social Security income quite well.

Retirement income receipt shows a very different pattern. Starting in 1984, receipt rates are close and actually higher in the CPS-ASEC with 29 percent of women in the CPS-ASEC reporting retirement income and 23 percent actually having retirement income in the linked sample. Moving to later surveys (and therefore more recent cohorts), the linked sample receipt rates grow rapidly and then reach a plateau, while the CPS-ASEC rates remain essentially flat for the entire time period. By 2007, the CPS-ASEC shows a receipt rate of 26 percent while the linked sample has a receipt rate over 45 percent. In contrast to receipt rates, survey and administrative measures of (conditional) median amounts continue to track each other reasonably well, except for a large discrepancy in 2003 that diminishes in 2007.

Overall, retirement income underreporting appears to occur mostly at the extensive rather than intensive margin. It is also worth noting that due to its rapid growth, the median amount of retirement income in recent years is now quite close to the median amount of Social Security income—the difference is that Social Security receipt remains much more widespread despite retirement income's growing importance.

The bottom half of table 9.3 summarizes the implications for women's total household income. The CPS-ASEC total income as well as income from five sources (earnings, Social Security, SSI, interest and dividends, and retirement income) are reported. We show income based on these five sources alone because this is directly comparable to the income available

Table 9.3   Income receipt and percentiles by cohorts of women ages sixty-five to sixty-nine

	Cohort 1	Cohort 2	Cohort 3	Cohort 4	Cohort 5	Cohort 6
Income year	1984	1989	1995	2000	2003	2007
Birth year	1916–1920	1921–1925	1927–1931	1932–1936	1935–1939	1939–1943
Social Security receipt						
CPS	0.906	0.882	0.880	0.874	0.863	0.800
SIPP-linked	0.886	0.877	0.876	0.889	0.890	0.831
Median Social Security amount, cond. > 0						
CPS ($)	8,246	7,589	8,920	9,262	9,827	10,438
SIPP-linked ($)	8,361	7,727	8,787	8,980	9,742	10,452
Retirement income receipt						
CPS	0.288	0.289	0.268	0.271	0.272	0.260
SIPP-linked	0.233	0.323	0.399	0.404	0.435	0.454
Median retirement income amount, cond. > 0						
CPS ($)	5,200	7,429	7,305	8,630	8,668	10,426
SIPP-linked ($)	4,934	6,801	6,951	8,628	11,132	11,893
Household income						
25th percentile						
(1) CPS all sources ($)	18,368	20,458	20,810	22,837	21,893	23,138
(2) CPS five sources ($)	—	19,400	19,933	21,913	21,210	22,485
(3) SIPP-linked admin. ($)	—	22,436	23,235	28,825	26,063	33,714
Percent diff. (3)/(2)		16	17	32	23	50
50th percentile						
(1) CPS all sources ($)	33,029	36,050	35,520	40,470	39,453	43,205
(2) CPS five sources ($)	—	34,780	34,238	39,025	38,310	41,977
(3) SIPP-linked admin. ($)	—	38,689	41,864	50,774	46,755	60,939
Percent diff. (3)/(2)		11	22	30	22	45

75th percentile					
(1) CPS all sources ($)	55,963	61,774	59,896	68,091	69,011	77,702
(2) CPS five sources ($)	—	59,696	58,007	65,982	67,367	74,691
(3) SIPP-linked admin. ($)	—	62,374	67,065	79,914	76,049	95,083
Percent diff. (3)/(2)		4	16	21	13	27

Sources: The SIPP Gold Standard File linked to Social Security Administration and IRS administrative records and CPS ASEC.

Notes: Sample is all women who are either the householder or spouse of the householder, ages sixty-five to sixty-nine at time of interview in either the SIPP or the CPS-ASEC. Social Security receipt is fraction of women with positive annual OASDI benefits either in the administrative records or in the CPS-ASEC. Retirement income receipt is fraction of women with positive annual administrative record retirement income from either Form W-2P for years 1978 to 1990 or Form 1099-R for years 1995 to 2012 or positive amounts of retirement, survivor, or disability income outside of Social Security and VA benefits in the CPS-ASEC. The SIPP sample is restricted to those with a Personal Identification Key (PIK) that allows linking to the administrative records. The SIPP sample weights are adjusted to account for selection into having a PIK. For each SIPP panel we estimate a logit model for the presence of a PIK as a function of SIPP demographic characteristics and predict the estimated propensity score. We then take the SIPP sample weight and multiply it by the inverse of the estimated propensity score. Resulting weights along with CPS-ASEC sample weights are used in analysis. "CPS all sources" refers to total income in the CPS-ASEC while "CPS five sources" includes only earnings, Social Security, SSI, interest and dividends, and retirement income, which are the same types of income available in the linked SIPP-admin. data. Amounts are inflation adjusted using the CPI-U-RS and expressed in 2012 dollars. Total income amounts are unavailable for 1984. The CPS-ASEC retirement income for 1984 includes an estimate of survivor and disability income for that year, which raises the rate by 7 percentage points.

in our administrative records. At the 25th, 50th, and 75th percentiles there is a growing dissimilarity between survey and administrative measures of income that parallels the rise in retirement income underreporting.[7] For example, the median household income is 11 percent higher in the linked data than in the CPS-ASEC in 1989 ($3,900), but is 45 percent higher in 2007 ($19,000). Note that these are household incomes, so they reflect the effects of underreporting of all household members.

The administrative measures of income seriously change our understanding of the economic progress of women at older ages across cohorts. Across the 1921 to 1925 and 1939 to 1943 cohorts, the CPS-ASEC shows an increase in median household income of 21 percent, but the linked data reveal the increase was actually 58 percent. The evenness of economic progress has also been understated. The CPS-ASEC shows a monotonic relationship in income growth across the 25th, 50th, and 75th percentiles of 16 percent, 21 percent, and 25 percent, respectively, but the corresponding numbers in the linked data are 50 percent, 58 percent, and 52 percent.

9.6   Work Experience and Underreporting

If retirement income underreporting has understated economic progress across cohorts, it may also affect our understanding of the relationship between work experience and well-being within a cohort. Table 9.4 uses administrative records linked to the 2013 CPS-ASEC to estimate the relationship between middle to late career work experience and income at older ages for the most recent cohort, those born between 1944 and 1948. We have already established that this cohort is working longer, claiming Social Security later, and is more likely to receive retirement income than previous cohorts. But there is also significant within-cohort variation.

Using administrative record earnings histories, we calculate whether each woman earned enough in a given year for us to deem that she was employed. We then total the years of employment across the twenty-year period between ages forty and fifty-nine. Next we group women into four experience categories based on the total number of years worked (zero to five, six to ten, eleven to fifteen, and sixteen to twenty years). We show the results for the full sample of women as well as separately by current marital status. Overall, 58 percent of women in the 1944 to 1948 cohort worked at least sixteen out of twenty years with a fairly even split across the other categories. The distribution of work experience does not vary much by marital status.

We next examine survey and administrative record measures of retirement

---

7. We are unable to provide administrative estimates of total income for the 1984 sample at this time, but our preliminary analysis suggests the survey and administrative estimates are quite close in that year.

Table 9.4   Income of retirement-age women by years of work experience between ages forty and fifty-nine (2012)

Work experience between ages 40–59	Distribution of sample (%)	Own retirement income receipt		Median own income			Median household income		
		CPS	Admin.	CPS ($)	Admin. ($)	Percent difference	CPS ($)	Admin. ($)	Percent difference
All women									
Work 0–5 years	17	0.108	0.154	9,974	8,692	–13	31,220	39,120	25
Work 6–10 years	11	0.163	0.272	12,056	12,132	1	46,406	52,977	14
Work 11–15 years	15	0.250	0.426	16,182	18,863	17	41,867	52,693	26
Work 16–20 years	58	0.377	0.598	26,020	31,686	22	53,875	64,715	20
N = 3,361									
Married women									
Work 0–5 years	17	0.055	0.101	9,195	7,684	–16	44,339	50,138	13
Work 6–10 years	12	0.125	0.228	11,541	11,717	2	60,674	64,551	6
Work 11–15 years	14	0.186	0.353	13,632	15,331	12	58,597	71,146	21
Work 16–20 years	56	0.338	0.572	21,895	28,916	32	68,995	82,609	20
N = 2,032									
Not married women (includes cohabitators)									
Work 0–5 years	15	0.204	0.250	11,802	10,231	–13	15,361	15,211	–1
Work 6–10 years	9	0.247	0.371	13,890	14,227	2	18,508	22,119	20
Work 11–15 years	16	0.343	0.530	19,255	23,075	20	24,051	30,812	28
Work 16–20 years	60	0.435	0.637	30,465	34,781	14	36,314	41,629	15
N = 1,329									

Source: The CPS-ASEC linked to administrative records.

Notes: Sample consists of women ages sixty-five to sixty-nine in the 2013 CPS-ASEC who are either the householder or the spouse of the householder. Years of work experience between ages forty to fifty-nine are calculated as the number of years where annual earnings (wages and self-employment combined) in the administrative records exceed the prevailing hourly federal minimum wage times ten hours per week times fifty-two weeks per year. Marital status is determined as of the CPS-ASEC interview date. The CPS columns refer to amounts reported on the 2013 ASEC survey, while admin. columns refer to amounts after substituting values from administrative records. Admin. sample is restricted to CPS respondents with a Personal Identification Key (PIK) that allows linking to the administrative records. The CPS-ASEC sample weights are adjusted to account for selection into having a PIK. For each year of the CPS-ASEC we estimate a logit model for the presence of a PIK as a function of CPS-ASEC demographic characteristics and predict the estimated propensity score. We then take the CPS-ASEC sample weight and multiply it by the inverse of the estimated propensity score. Resulting weights along with CPS-ASEC sample weights are used in analysis.

income receipt across the experience distribution. The linked CPS-ASEC does show that women whose earnings records indicate they spent more years in the labor force are more likely to report receiving retirement income when sixty-five to sixty-nine years old, with receipt rates rising from 11 percent to 38 percent. But extensive-margin underreporting is present for all four work-experience groups, and the discrepancy is largest in absolute terms for women who work longer, with actual rates ranging from 15 percent to 60 percent. Similar patterns are observed when the sample is restricted to married women, indicating that underreported income is not simply received on account of a deceased spouse.

The next columns of table 9.4 illustrate the effects of underreporting for women's *own* incomes, across the work-experience distribution. Compared with the administrative records, the CPS-ASEC actually shows a somewhat higher median own income for the lowest experience group and only a slightly lower income for the second experience group. For the higher experience groups, which also have the highest extensive-margin underreporting, the administrative record incomes are a substantial 17 and 22 percent above the survey incomes. Qualitatively similar results are found for both currently and not currently married women.

One implication of these findings is that if future cohorts of women acquire additional years of work experience, household surveys may miss a larger fraction of their own incomes at older ages. However, the relationship between women's work experience and *household* income is less straightforward, as there is considerable evidence of income underreporting across most work experience groups. The relationship is complicated by the fact that underreporting is also present for other household members who live with women of all experience levels.[8]

Despite the weaker relationship found between women's work experience and household income underreporting, there are still household income anomalies in the CPS-ASEC that the administrative records help to clarify. For example, for married women, survey income does not rise monotonically with women's work experience. Women who work six to ten years have a median household income of $60,700, while women who work eleven to fifteen years have a median household income of $58,600. Using the administrative records, median incomes are instead ascending for the two groups—$64,600 and $71,100.

9.7   The Retirement Transition

We have so far explored how underreporting affects women's total incomes at a point in time. We can also exploit the panel nature of the administrative

---

8. As noted in the introduction, Bee and Mitchell (in process) find high rates of underreporting for both women and men. This explains why *household* income underreporting can be substantial, even among women with few years of labor market experience.

records to track the same women's incomes over time. We focus on a period covering the transition to retirement and examine to what extent women are able to maintain their preretirement living standards.

We draw a sample of women from the 2008 SIPP panel. We use only the most recent SIPP panel because we require data on all types of income for many consecutive years. Like our previous analyses, our sample consists of women who are either the householder or spouse of the householder, who either themselves or their husbands (if present) first claimed Social Security between 2003 and 2007, and who were age sixty to seventy when claiming. We further restrict to those claiming nondisability benefits. Our nine-year panel window runs from three years prior to first claiming benefits until five years after claiming. We also require women to survive to the end of the panel window but place no mortality restrictions on the husband, if present. One limitation of our analysis is that we only can observe women's living arrangements at the time of the SIPP interview. Therefore, for this exercise we choose to track the total incomes of either the married couple or the not-married women, fixing the marital status at the time of the SIPP interview. However, we do observe mortality of husbands in the administrative records and we equivalence-adjust total incomes in each year to reflect whether our unit of analysis has one or two people.[9] A second limitation of our analysis is that we can follow women only for five years after claiming because our administrative records are available only through 2012. We could therefore miss important income changes that take place later on in retirement.

Figure 9.5, panel A, plots the mean of the 45th to 55th percentile of equivalence-adjusted overall income in each year for the full sample of women. As shown, the mean of the 45th to 55th percentile is a very close approximation to the median and has the added advantage that it can be decomposed into income-source subcomponents (also plotted). These subcomponents are Social Security income, earnings, interest and dividends, and retirement income. By construction, Social Security income is zero in the years prior to claiming and then rises sharply after claiming. Five years after claiming, average equivalence-adjusted Social Security benefits, for those in the middle of the total income distribution, are a little under $19,000. Not surprisingly, income from earnings declines as women and their husbands transition to retirement. Earnings fall from $38,000 to $35,000 in the years before claiming and then accelerate their decline until they are just under $10,000 five years after claiming. Interest and dividends are a comparatively small amount of income for most households in all years with a value of just $2,400 five years after claiming. Average amounts of retirement income, on the other hand, are substantial. Three years prior to claiming they average close to $11,000, and rise after claiming to nearly $18,000. Thus, average

---

9. We use the same equivalence scale that is used for the Supplemental Poverty Measure. In practice, this simply means dividing our couples' incomes by 1.41. (See Short 2015.)

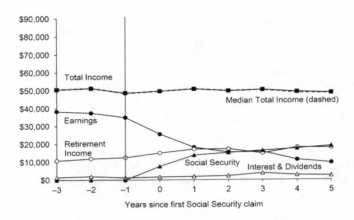

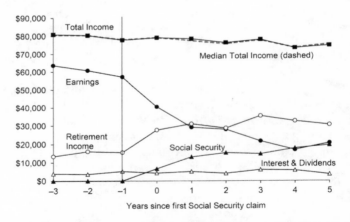

Fig. 9.5   Mean of the 45th–55th percentile of total income and its subcomponents

Source: The SIPP Gold Standard File linked to Social Security Administration and IRS administrative records.

Notes: Panel A: All women. Sample is all women from 2008 SIPP panel who are householder or spouse of householder, either first claimed or their spouse (if present) first claimed Social Security benefits between 2003 and 2007, did not claim disability benefits, and survived for full nine-year window. Panel B: College-graduate women. Sample is college-graduate women from the 2008 SIPP panel who are householder or spouse of householder, either first claimed or their spouse (if present) first claimed Social Security benefits between 2003 and 2007, did not claim disability benefits, and survived for full nine-year window. Panel C: Non-college-graduate women. Sample is non-college-graduate women from the 2008 SIPP panel who are householder or spouse of householder, either first claimed or their spouse (if present) first claimed Social Security benefits between 2003 and 2007, did not claim disability benefits, and survived for full nine-year window. Panel D: Married women. Sample is married women from

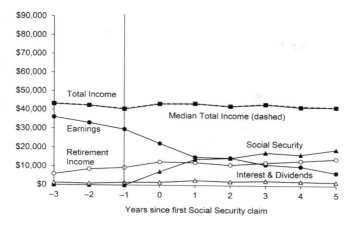

C. Non-College Graduate Women

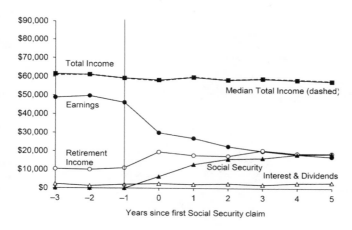

D. Married Women

Fig. 9.5 **(cont.)**

the 2008 SIPP panel who are householder or spouse of householder, either first claimed or their spouse (if present) first claimed Social Security benefits between 2003 and 2007, did not claim disability benefits, and survived for full nine-year window. Panel E: Not-married women. Sample is women from the 2008 SIPP panel who are not currently married and are the householder, either first claimed or their spouse (if present) first claimed Social Security benefits between 2003 and 2007, did not claim disability benefits, and survived for full nine-year window. Total income is the sum for the women and her spouse (if present) of administrative record amounts of earnings, Social Security, interest and dividends, and retirement income. Income amounts are equivalence-adjusted by dividing by 1.41 for married couples. (See Short [2015] for more details.) Marital status is determined as of SIPP interview date but is adjusted if administrative records indicate death of husband. Incomes are inflation-adjusted using the CPI-U-RS deflator and are expressed in 2012 dollars. Mean of the 45th–55th percentiles in each year is calculated as well as the median for total income. Mean amounts of

E. Not-Married Women

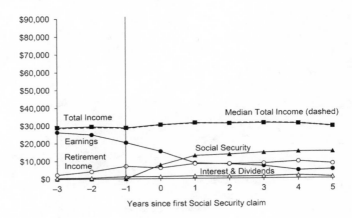

Fig. 9.5   (cont.)
each subcomponent of total income are also displayed for those with total incomes in the
45th–55th percentile range. Sample is restricted to those with a Personal Identification Key
(PIK), which allows linking to the administrative records. The SIPP sample weights are adjusted to account for selection into having a PIK. For each SIPP panel we estimate a logit
model for the presence of a PIK as a function of SIPP demographic characteristics and predict
the estimated propensity score. We then take the SIPP sample weight and multiply it by the
inverse of the estimated propensity score. Resulting weights are used in analysis.

retirement income and Social Security amounts are quite comparable for
those in the middle of the overall income distribution.

When we examine income from all sources combined, we find that median
incomes are surprisingly flat across the full nine-year window, with an approximate value of $48,600 both one year before claiming and five years
after claiming. In other words, there is little evidence of a drop in median
income at retirement and up to five years after retirement. This is in sharp
contrast to several previous studies reviewed earlier that suggest substantial
drops in income (and consumption) at retirement. Indeed, the premise of
the retirement consumption puzzle is that incomes are falling predictably at
retirement and that rational, forward-looking households should be able to
smooth consumption in response. Although we cannot measure consumption changes directly, our finding of steady incomes surrounding retirement
challenges this premise. Crucial to this result is an accurate measure of retirement income from the administrative records.

We also plot event studies separately for college-graduate and non-
college-graduate women and for currently married and not currently married women as shown in figures 9.5, panels B, C, D, and E. While the levels
of income are quite different across demographic subgroups, the same story
holds—total incomes do not fall very much, if at all, in retirement. The big-

gest drop is for college-educated women where the level of overall income starts higher at around $77,800 one year before claiming and falls to $74,500 five years after claiming. Even this modest drop takes several years to materialize—we never observe a sharp fall in incomes. For women without a college degree, incomes, if anything, rise slightly over the same period from $40,500 to $41,700. For married women, incomes decline modestly from $59,200 to $57,500 and for not-married women, incomes rise slightly from $28,800 to $29,400.

Beyond total incomes, it is interesting to examine the relative importance of retirement and Social Security income across demographic groups. Five years after claiming, retirement and Social Security income are roughly equally important for middle-income women in the full sample. That is, they account for 37 percent and 39 percent of total income, respectively, for women in the middle of the total income distribution. For college-graduate women, retirement income accounts for 41 percent of the total compared to 26 percent for Social Security. For non-college-graduate women, Social Security is the more dominant income source at 46 percent of the total, although retirement income still makes up an important 34 percent. For married women, the two income sources are equally important at 32 percent, but for not-married women, Social Security makes up 51 percent of the total, compared with 28 percent for retirement income.

Our findings on women's transition to retirement and the relative importance of retirement income require two caveats. First, our sample consists of those claiming OASI benefits. This removes from the sample those who experience permanent health shocks that would qualify them for SSDI, but who would also likely have declines in their overall incomes. It also ignores the group that has too little earnings to qualify for any Social Security and is instead receiving SSI. Meyer and Mok (2013) show that consumption does, in fact, decline after workers become disabled. However, from the perspective of validating the life cycle model, we would expect consumption to decline exactly for those who do experience negative permanent income shocks. Thus, the life cycle model cannot easily be tested against alternatives in this setting.

Second, although we have provided strong evidence that women's incomes do not fall during the first five years after retirement, this does not necessarily imply that women and their families have saved adequately for retirement. It is still possible that they could "run out of money" in future years should they live longer than expected, incur higher out-of-pocket medical expenses than expected, and have their retirement income exhausted. Relatedly, this analysis examines women (and their husbands) who retired in the middle of the first decade of the twenty-first century, a time where retirees still had considerable retirement income from defined-benefit plans. Our results may not extrapolate to future cohorts, who will only have access to defined-contribution accounts. Will they save adequately for retirement during working years and then manage to budget their savings during retirement, given that annuitization rates in defined-contribution accounts remain low (Hurd and Panis 2006)?

9.8   Conclusion

We have shown that as women increased employment across cohorts born from the early 1920s to the late 1940s, they also received greater amounts of retirement income at older ages. The CPS-ASEC, however, fails to reflect the growing importance of retirement income and thus understates the economic progress of women in retirement. The CPS-ASEC has recently been redesigned to improve measures of income received from several sources, including retirement accounts. It remains an open question whether the redesign will better capture retirement incomes of future cohorts of women as they continue to work longer.

We have also shown that recently retired (nondisabled) women do not experience noticeable declines in total income at retirement. The finding is in sharp contrast to others in the literature on the retirement consumption puzzle. Our results cast doubt on the ability to convincingly test the life cycle model in this setting. They also imply that total income replacement rates are quite high, at least five years into retirement. Most employee retirement plans are currently completing a transition from defined-benefit to defined-contribution-based systems. We began with a puzzle that we believe we have solved. We end with the question: Will future cohorts of women continue to maintain their preretirement standards of living as we have shown past cohorts have done?

References

Aguiar, Mark, and Erik Hurst. 2005. "Consumption versus Expenditure." *Journal of Political Economy* 113 (5): 919–48.

———. 2007. "Life-Cycle Prices and Production." *American Economic Review* 97 (5): 1533–59.

Autor, David H., and Mark G. Duggan. 2006. "The Growth in the Social Security Disability Rolls: A Fiscal Crisis Unfolding." *Journal of Economic Perspectives* 20 (3): 71–96.

Banks, James, Richard Blundell, and Sarah Tanner. 1998. "Is There a Retirement-Savings Puzzle?" *American Economic Review* 88 (4): 769–88.

Bee, C. Adam. 2013. "An Evaluation of Retirement Income in the CPS ASEC Using Form 1099-R Microdata." Working Paper, US Census Bureau. http://www.census.gov/content/dam/Census/library/working-papers/2013/demo/Bee-PAA-paper.pdf.

Bee, C. Adam, and Joshua Mitchell. In progress. "Do Older Americans Have More Income than We Think?"

Bernheim, B. Douglas, Jonathan Skinner, and Steven Weinberg. 2001. "What Accounts for the Variation in Retirement Wealth among US Households?" *American Economic Review* 91 (4): 832–57.

Brady, Peter J., Steven Bass, Jessica Holland, and Kevin Pierce. In progress. "Using Panel Tax Data to Examine the Transition to Retirement."

Cutler, David M., and Lawrence F. Katz. 1991. "Macroeconomic Performance and the Disadvantaged." *Brookings Papers on Economic Activity* 1991 (2): 1–74.

Czajka, John L., and Gabrielle Denmead. 2012. "Getting More from Survey Income Measures: Empirically Based Recommendations for Improving Accuracy and Efficiency." Paper presented at 2012 Federal Committee on Statistical Methodology Research Conference, Washington, DC, Jan. 10–12. https://fcsm.sites.usa.gov/files/2014/05/Czajka_2012FCSM_III-D.pdf.

DeNavas-Walt, Carmen, and Bernadette D. Proctor. 2015. "Income and Poverty in the United States: 2014." Current Population Report no. P60-252, US Census Bureau. https://www.census.gov/content/dam/Census/library/publications/2015/demo/p60-252.pdf.

Dushi, Irena, and Marjorie Honig. 2015. "How Much Do Respondents in the Health and Retirement Study Know about Their Contributions to Tax-Deferred Contribution Plans? A Cross-Cohort Comparison." *Journal of Pension Economics and Finance* 14 (3): 203–39.

Dushi, Irena, and Howard M. Iams. 2010. "The Impact of Response Error on Participation Rates and Contributions to Defined Contribution Pension Plans." *Social Security Bulletin* 70 (1): 45–60.

Goldin, Claudia. 2006. "The Quiet Revolution that Transformed Women's Employment, Education, and Family." *American Economic Review* 96 (2): 1–21.

Goldin, Claudia, Lawrence F. Katz, and Ilyana Kuziemko. 2006. "The Homecoming of American College Women: The Reversal of the College Gender Gap." *Journal of Economic Perspectives* 20 (4): 133–56.

Goldin, Claudia, and Joshua Mitchell. Forthcoming. "The New Lifecycle of Women's Employment: Disappearing Humps, Sagging Middles, Expanding Tops." *Journal of Economic Perspectives*.

Gustman, Alan L., Thomas L. Steinmeier, and Nahid Tabatabai. 2010. *Pensions in the Health and Retirement Study*. Cambridge, MA: Harvard University Press.

Hurd, Michael, and Constantijn Panis. 2006. "The Choice to Cash Out Pension Rights at Job Change or Retirement." *Journal of Public Economics* 90 (12): 2213–27.

Hurd, Michael, and Susann Rohwedder. 2006. "Economic Well-Being at Older Ages: Income- and Consumption-Based Poverty Measures in the HRS." Working Paper no. WR-410, RAND. November. https://www.rand.org/content/dam/rand/pubs/working_papers/2007/RAND_WR410.pdf.

Hurst, Erik. 2008. "Understanding Consumption in Retirement: Recent Developments." In *Recalibrating Retirement Spending and Saving*, edited by J. Ameriks and O. Mitchell. Oxford: Oxford University Press.

Lusardi, Annamaria, and Olivia S. Mitchell. 2014. "The Economic Importance of Financial Literacy: Theory and Evidence." *Journal of Economic Literature* 52 (1): 5–44.

Meyer, Bruce, and Wallace K. C. Mok. 2013. "Disability, Earnings, Income, and Consumption." NBER Working Paper no. 18869, Cambridge, MA.

Meyer, Bruce, and James X. Sullivan. 2010. "Consumption and Income of the Poor Elderly Since 1960." Working Paper, September. http://www3.nd.edu/~jsulliv4/Elderly_Poverty3.4.pdf.

———. 2012. "Winning the War: Poverty from the Great Society to the Great Recession." *Brookings Papers on Economic Activity* 2012 (2): 133–200.

Mitchell, Joshua, and Trudi Renwick. 2015. "A Comparison of Official Poverty Estimates in the Redesigned Current Population Survey Annual Social and Economic Supplement." SEHSD Working Paper no. 2014-35, Social, Economic and Housing Statistics Division of the US Census Bureau. January. https://www.census.gov/content/dam/Census/library/working-papers/2014/demo/SEHSD-WP2014-35.pdf.

Mitchell, Olivia. 1988. "Worker Knowledge of Pension Provisions." *Journal of Labor Economics* 6 (1): 21–39.

Munnell, Alicia, and Anqi Chen. 2014. "Do Census Data Understate Retirement Income?" CRR Working Paper no. 14-19, Center for Retirement Research. December. http://crr.bc.edu/wp-content/uploads/2014/12/IB_14-19-508.pdf.

Semega, Jessica L., and Edward Welniak Jr. 2015. "The Effects of Changes to the Current Population Survey Annual Social and Economic Supplement on Estimates of Income." Paper presented at the 2015 Allied Social Science Association Meetings, Boston, MA, Jan. 3–5. https://www.census.gov/content/dam/Census/library/working-papers/2015/DEMO/ASSA-Income-CPSASEC-Red.pdf.

Short, Kathleen. 2015. "The Supplemental Poverty Measure: 2014." Current Population Survey Report no. P60-254, US Census Bureau.

Wagner, Deborah, and Mary Layne. 2014. "The Person Identification Validation System (PVS): Applying the Center for Administrative Records Research and Applications' (CARRA) Record Linkage Software." CARRA Working Paper Series no. 2014-01. https://www.census.gov/srd/carra/CARRA_PVS_Record_Linkage.pdf.

Appendix: The Health and Retirement Study (HRS)

The Health and Retirement Study (known as the HRS and as the University of Michigan Health and Retirement Study) is a widely used data set. (More information can be found at http://hrsonline.isr.umich.edu/.) This brief appendix will discuss certain details of general importance to the chapters in the volume that use the HRS. These include the chapters by Goldin and Katz, Maestas, Lahey, Fahle and McGarry, Lusardi and Mitchell, and Fitzpatrick (listed in order of presentation in the volume).

The HRS has been supported by the National Institute on Aging and the Social Security Administration. The study was begun in 1992 with a random sample of households in which at least one member was born between 1931 and 1941 and thus between fifty-one and sixty-one years old.

The initial sample is known as the HRS cohort, and also as the "Intermezzo" cohort. In households containing a married or partnered couple, the "spouse" and "respondent" categories were randomly assigned. Spouses were not given positive sample weights until 1998, if born from 1931 to 1941. If they were born from 1942 to 1947, they are not given positive sample weights until the "War Baby" (WB) cohort was added. The War Baby (WB) cohort was born 1942 to 1947. The "Early Baby Boomer" (EBB) cohort, born 1948 to 1953, was added in 2004. The Mid-Boomer (MBB) cohort, 1954 to 1959, was added in 2010. The WB, EBB, and MBB cohorts were between fifty-one and fifty-six years old. Figure VA.1 provides a concise visual summary of the various HRS cohorts and waves.

The cohorts mentioned have all been surveyed every two years. Additional cohorts born before 1931 are also part of the HRS, but the HRS, WB, and EBB are the primary cohorts used by the authors in this volume. At the time of this writing, the HRS data are available to 2012.

Some of the authors in this volume have also used the restricted-access

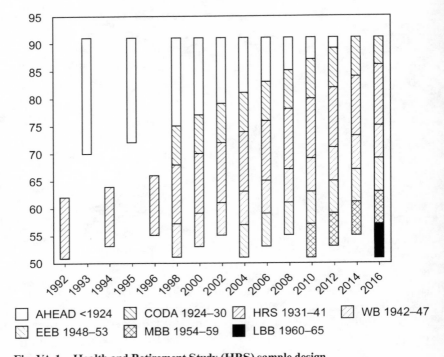

Fig. VA.1   Health and Retirement Study (HRS) sample design
Source: http://hrsonline.isr.umich.edu/index.php?p=sdesign&_ga=1.72094355.1277731491.1
414899467. *Note:* The years 2014 and 2016 were not available at the time of writing.

versions of the HRS. These restricted-access versions contain additional information, such as annual income from Social Security Administration records and W-2 forms. Some authors have also used versions that have detailed information on occupation and industry.

Most authors have used the RAND HRS Data Files, which are a harmonized compilation of much, but not all, of the HRS data. The RAND version allows the use of the (public access) HRS files without having to access the separate waves for each of the various cohorts. Many of the authors have also used the RAND HRS Family Data Files, which do the same for information on family members of HRS respondents.

Contributors

C. Adam Bee
US Census Bureau
4600 Silver Hill Road
Washington, DC 20233

Sean Fahle
Department of Economics
State University of New York at
    Buffalo
Buffalo, NY 14260-1520

Maria D. Fitzpatrick
Department of Policy and
    Management
Cornell University
Ithaca, NY 14853

Alexander Gelber
Goldman School of Public Policy
University of California, Berkeley
2607 Hearst Avenue
Berkeley, CA 94720

Claudia Goldin
Department of Economics
Harvard University
Cambridge, MA 02138

Adam Isen
Office of Tax Analysis
US Department of the Treasury
1500 Pennsylvania Avenue, NW
Washington, DC 20220

Lawrence F. Katz
Department of Economics
Harvard University
Cambridge, MA 02138

Joanna N. Lahey
The Bush School
Texas A&M University
Mailstop 4220
College Station, TX 77843

Annamaria Lusardi
The George Washington University
School of Business
2201 G Street, NW
Washington, DC 20052

Nicole Maestas
Department of Health Care Policy
Harvard Medical School
180 Longwood Avenue
Boston, MA 02115

Kathleen McGarry
Department of Economics
University of California, Los Angeles
Los Angeles, CA 90095-1477

Joshua Mitchell
US Census Bureau
4600 Silver Hill Road
Washington, DC 20233

Olivia S. Mitchell
University of Pennsylvania
The Wharton School
3620 Locust Walk
Philadelphia, PA 19104-6302

Claudia Olivetti
Department of Economics
Boston College
Maloney Hall
Chestnut Hill, MA 02467

Dana Rotz
Mathematica Policy Research
955 Massachusetts Avenue, Suite 801
Cambridge, MA 02139

Jae Song
Social Security Administration
Office of Disability Adjudication and
    Review
5107 Leesburg Pike, Suite 1400
Falls Church, VA 22041

Author Index

Subject Index

Note: Page numbers followed by "f" or "t" refer to figures or tables, respectively.

education (*continued*)
66t, 77t, 113–16, 119, 120–25t, 130–40,
146–50t, 153t; family care and, 168,
169t, 172t, 173, 175t, 176–77, 179t, 194,
205–7t, 211t; graduation and, 4, 12–13,
32, 34, 218–19, 275; Health and Retirement Study (HRS) and, 47t, 50–51t,
225–35; hidden resources and, 270,
275–77, 278–79t, 281, 283, 290f, 293;
high school, 88 (*see also* high school
education); marital status and, 44, 115,
120–21t, 122, 124–25t, 131t, 132–38,
140, 146–47t, 153t; older women and,
186, 190–94, 198–200t, 201n16, 201n17,
202, 204, 207t, 209, 210–11t, 239,
265; participation rates and, 14–17,
19, 21–32, 24–27t, 35–36t, 37, 43–44,
47–51t, 217–18, 239–40; pensions and,
221n6; returns to employment and, 5;
teachers and, 217 (*see also* teachers);
two-period model of female labor
supply and, 236–37; younger women
and, 44
Employment Cost Index, 106
employment decisions: age-earnings profiles
and, 64–73; baby boomer cohorts and,
57–81; birth cohorts and, 55n1, 58, 74,
76n15, 114–15, 119, 132; black women
and, 59t, 66t, 77t; children and, 55,
74, 114, 127, 132, 144, 186, 190–94,
198–200t, 204–9, 210–12t; college
and, 58–60, 65, 66t, 77t; divorce and,
56, 68n10, 74, 76n14, 78n16; earnings
and, 56–60, 64–81, 114, 123; education
and, 66t, 77t, 113–16, 119–22, 120–25t,
130–40, 146–50t, 153t; employment
by age cohort and, 60–63; full-time
employment and, 60–63; Health and
Retirement Study (HRS) and, 57–58,
59n5, 61f, 62–74, 75f, 76n13, 76n15,
77t, 79, 80t; health issues and, 56–58,
59t, 65, 67t, 68f, 70t, 71–73f, 75f, 77t,
79–80t; Hispanic women and, 59t, 66t,
77t, 120–22t, 124–25t, 131t, 133–34t,
136–38t, 148–50t, 153t; insurance and,
56, 76n13; labor supply and, 56n2,
56n3, 58–63, 68, 72–73, 81, 114; life
cycle and, 114–15, 117, 127–28, 139;
marital status and, 58–63; men and,
55–76, 80–82; Old-Age and Survivors
Insurance (OASI) and, 240; opportunity cost and, 57, 81; participation rates
and, 55–56; part-time employment

and, 59–62, 64; pensions and, 56, 64n8;
potential gains and, 5, 57, 74, 80–81;
regression analysis and, 64, 67t, 70t, 76,
77t, 79, 119–26, 129, 131t, 132, 133–38t,
153t; retirement and, 55–57 (*see also*
retirement); return to work and, 57,
63–81; savings and, 114, 139; separated
women and, 68n10, 76n14, 120–21t,
122, 124–25t, 146t, 148–50t; SIPP and,
115–30, 131–47t, 153t, 269n, 274–75,
276t, 277f, 279t, 280f, 282f, 283,
284–85t, 289, 290–92f; Social Security
and, 6–7, 11n1, 56–57, 64, 74–81, 115,
123–26, 130, 135–36, 139, 147t, 240–41;
wages and, 59t, 60, 68–72; War Babies
cohort and, 58, 59t, 61f, 63t, 65f, 67t,
68f, 70t, 71–73f, 75f, 77t, 79–80t, 186n2,
190–92; widows and, 56, 74, 78–79, 119,
120–25t, 140, 146t, 148–50t; younger
women and, 55–58

family care, 5; activities of daily living
(ADLs) and, 159; aging population
and, 6, 157, 159, 177, 297; baby boomer
cohorts and, 161; birth cohorts and,
163, 168n13, 171, 173, 177; black
women and, 170n16; caregiver burden
and, 158–61, 164, 168, 176; caregiver
status and, 168, 169–70t; children and,
158, 161n5, 165, 168n14, 169t, 172t,
173–74, 175t, 179t; cohort variables
and, 179–80t; data for, 161–63; descriptive analysis of, 163–71; determinants
of caregiving and, 171–74; divorce and,
157–58; earnings and, 160, 163, 168–71,
179t; education and, 168, 169t, 172t,
173, 175t, 176–77, 179t, 194, 205–7t,
211t; full-time employment and, 168;
Health and Retirement Study (HRS)
and, 158–59, 161–67, 168n12, 177, 179–
80t; health issues and, 157–61, 172t,
173–77; Hispanic women and, 168–73,
175t, 179t; insurance and, 160; labor
market attachment and, 158, 165, 171,
173–74, 178; labor supply and, 160,
168, 176; long-term, 157–59, 160n2,
176; marital status and, 171, 176n20;
Medicare and, 56, 157, 225; men and,
157–58, 161, 163n7; opportunity cost
and, 158, 165, 170, 176n19; parental,
158–78, 179–80t; participation rates
and, 157–58, 165n10, 170n16, 177; pensions and, 158, 160; regression analysis